RE-THINKING SEXUALITIES
IN AFRICA

D1567133

Edited by
Signe Arnfred

Indexing terms

Women
Gender relations
Sexuality
Culture
Botswana
Ghana
Kenya
Mali
Namibia
Senegal
South Africa
Tanzania

Language checking: Elaine Almén
Cover photo: Seydou Keïta, Mali, © Fondation Seydou Keïta
© all other photos: the photographers and the Sokkelund African Collection
© the authors and Nordiska Afrikainstitutet, 2004

ISBN 91-7106-513-X
Second edition 2005
Printed in Sweden by Almqvist & Wiksell Tryckeri AB, Uppsala 2005

Contents

Photo: Abderramane Sakalay, 1958

1. Re-Thinking Sexualities in Africa: Introduction

Signe Arnfred

The time has come for re-thinking sexualities in Africa: The thinking beyond the conceptual structure of colonial and even post-colonial European imaginations, which have oscillated between notions of the exotic, the noble and the depraved savage, consistently however constructing Africans and African sexuality as something 'other'. This 'other' thing is constructed to be not only different from European/Western sexualities and self, but also functions to co-construct that which is European/Western as modern, rational and civilized.

In a context of empirical studies as in this volume, re-thinking necessitates a double move of de-construction and re-construction, developing an analysis whereby, through critique of previous conceptualisations, attempts are made to approach materials in new ways, coming up with fresh or alternative lines of thinking. The chapters in the first section—*Under Western Eyes*—are various versions of this type of exercise; they are all polemical against established, mainstream lines of thinking regarding gender and sexuality in Africa, and they all show in their different ways how alternative approaches produce different images —and concomitantly different realities. In one of the chapters (Jungar and Oinas) such mainstream lines of thinking, applied particularly in contexts of HIV/ AIDS investigations and with an undertone of 'Africa is lost anyway' are dubbed 'dark continent discourse'. I find this a very fitting expression, which I shall apply in the following discussion.

In the second section—*Problems of Pleasure and Desire*—the concerns are different, in some sense building upon the first section, taking the issues one step further. Here the focus is on investigation of areas, which have often been rendered invisible by mainstream thinking. The areas here under investigation are male and female lust and desire. A regards female sexual desire in particular, it has rarely been an object of analysis. If it has, it has generally been in a context of or with undertones of moral condemnation. Rarely has it been written about from the points of view of the women. In this section issues of male and female sexual lust and desire are analyzed and discussed by African male and female social scientists, based on analysis of empirical material, and with the benefit of experiences of the authors themselves.

In the third section the focus is on *Female Agency*. From different professional inroads—literature and social anthropology—current socio-economic changes in African societies are investigated, particularly as impacting on gender power relations, and different suggestions in terms of patterns of interpretation of current trends are presented. Uniting these chapters is an analytical concern with investigating ways in which gendered effects of current changes on the continent are acted upon by men and women, co-producing future developments. In spite of overwhelming obstacles, such as widespread poverty and soaring HIV/AIDS infection rates, examples are given of women's agency in ways which sometimes reproduce and at other times challenge patriarchal structures.

With this introduction, by discussing theoretical issues of importance for each of these sections, I hope to provide a broader context in which to read and appreciate the individual contributions. Almost all of the chapters were first presented at the conference/workshop: "Contexts of Gender in Africa"organized in Uppsala in February 2002 by the Nordic Africa Institute's *Sexuality, Gender and Society in Africa* research programme.

Under Western Eyes

The title for this section is taken from Chandra Talpade Mohanty's soon twenty years old but still current critique of Western feminist lines of thinking regarding women in Africa.[1] In her paper Mohanty pinpoints the mechanisms of Western thinking as 'othering' Third World women: "It is only insofar as 'Woman/Women' and 'the East' [or 'Africa'] are defined as Others, or as peripheral, that (Western) Man/Humanism can represent him/itself as the center. It is not the center that determines the periphery, but the periphery that, in its boundedness, determines the center. … Universal images of 'the Third World woman' (the veiled woman, chaste virgin etc.)—images constructed from adding 'the Third World difference' to 'sexual difference'—are predicated upon (and hence obviously bringing into sharper focus) assumptions about Western women as secular, liberated, and having control over their own lives" (Mohanty 1991:74). Mohanty shows how in this process of 'othering', which is rooted in and based upon dichotomies, the self is created by means of the other.

Dangerous dichotomies

As frequently shown and discussed by philosophers and social scientists over the last 20–30 years, much Western thinking from Enlightenment onwards has been constructed in terms of dichotomies and hierarchized binaries, where one is not only separate/different but also above/better than the other. Such figures of thought are part and parcel of the 'dark continent discourse'.

The importance of not only exposing dichotomies, but also dissolving them — effectively making them evaporate in order to create a space for radically different lines of thinking—is negatively demonstrated in a number of recent speeches by

---

1.   The paper in question was first published in 1986, and again in 1988. An updated and modified version was published in Mohanty et al. (eds) 1991, from which I quote. In a recent paper: *"Under Western Eyes" Revisited* (2002) Mohanty discusses current intellectual and political challenges for feminist scholarship and organizing. Her critique in the 1986 paper remains, however, valid.

South African president Thabo Mbeki.[1] Negatively, because Mbeki only exposes dichotomies, proceeding to turn them upside down, but he does not *dissolve* them. By failing to dissolve the dichotomies, Mbeki inadvertently supports and maintains these lines of thinking. In the speeches in question, Thabo Mbeki goes out against the 'dark continent discourse': "It used to be that the superiority of those who are white and the inferiority of those who are black, was enforced, presented and justified as the natural order of things. Equally we can and must say that the superiority of those who are male and the inferiority of those who are female, was enforced, presented and justified as the natural order of things. As has been said, as long as the lions do not have their own historians, so long will the hunters emerge as heroic, mighty and right" (Mbeki 2001a). The quote is from a speech given at the opening of the NGO forum at the World Conference against Racism in Durban, August 2001. Mbeki goes on to talk about economic inequalities on a global scale, as created by globalization, and the extent to which these inequalities coincide with race:

> Put starkly, where this process of globalization has had negative consequences, its worst victims within countries and universally have been those who are not white. For these countless black people, this has not only meant that the development gap has grown even wider, it has also meant the further entrenchment of the structural dis-empowerment of billions of people, making it even more difficult for them to break out of the trap of poverty and underdevelopment (Mbeki 2001a).

Mbeki locates racism in colonial history, talking about "the legacy of slavery, colonialism and racism", but he is also acutely aware of *colonial continuities* in present day globalization, and of the continued existence of this colonial discourse.

So far so good. The problem, however, of just identifying such dichotomies (white/black; man/woman; rich/poor) and turning them upside down (cf. the history of the lions) but otherwise remaining within their circumscriptions, becomes apparent in a following speech, in October 2001, at the University of Fort Hare (for a long time the only Black university in South Africa**).** This speech is also about racism, or rather about strategies against racism, where Mbeki is juxtaposing strategies working solely for economic improvements with strategies which are also aiming at changing people's minds. Mbeki approvingly quotes ZK Matthews (whose memorial lecture he is giving): "It is in the *minds* of Africans that revolutions which are rocking the foundations of African societies are taking place" (emphasis added).

Again, the problem is not what Mbeki says (e.g. that changed minds are important) but the way he constructs his argument. Taking as a point of departure the colonial continuities regarding the 'dark continent discourse' and pointing to the fact that even in African universities racist instructions has taken place, he says:

> There are those among us who ... have studied in schools of theology where the bible is interpreted by those who have justified segregation; law schools where they are told that they belong

---

1. Two papers presented at the Sex & Secrecy Conference in Johannesburg, 22–25 June 2003. Neville Hoad (2003) and Heike Becker (2003) alerted me to these particular Mbeki speeches.

to the most criminal element in the country; medical schools where they are likewise convinced of their inferiority by being reminded of their role as germ carriers; schools where they learn a history that pictures black people as human beings of the lower order, unable to subject passion to reason (Mbeki 2001b).

But then, in the following passage, he turns South African organisations and individuals fighting against HIV/AIDS into epigones and followers of a 'dark continent discourse', thus transforming them in dichotomous ways into 'the enemy' along with apartheid spokespersons—which is obviously absurd:

> Thus it comes about that some who call themselves our leaders ... take to the streets carrying their placards, to demand that because we are germ carriers, and human beings of a lower order that cannot subject its passions to reason, we must perforce adopt strange opinions, to save a depraved and diseased people from perishing from self-inflicted disease. ... Convinced that we are but natural-born, promiscuous carriers of germs, unique in the world, they proclaim that our continent is doomed to an inevitable mortal end because of our unconquerable devotion to sin and lust (Mbeki 2001b).

Mbeki may be right regarding a certain international HIV/AIDS discourse— along the lines of the argument in the influential 1989 paper by Caldwell et al. (cf. Arnfred's chapter) or as expressed in the medical discourses regarding male circumcision as a cure for AIDS, as analyzed by Jungar and Oinas. But sadly, his one-eyed analysis prevents him from seeing the work of the numerous HIV/AIDS prevention organizations in South Africa, and the ways in which these organizations (as also reported by Jungar and Oinas) while struggling against HIV/AIDS, in the very process are redefining the issues, thus effectively and in practice *dissolving* the 'dark continent discourse'. Unfortunately Thabo Mbeki, by just squarely confronting this discourse without dissolving it, becomes himself a co-producer and carrier of the very discourse, which he perceives himself as being up against.

Also the Sarah Bartmann speech in August 2002—a speech given on the South African women's day on the occasion of the burial on the banks of the Gamboos River of the remains of Sarah Bartmann[1]—provides examples of Mbeki's turning the dichotomies upside-down: "This young woman was treated as if she was something monstrous. But where in this affair is the monstrosity? ... It was not the lonely African woman in Europe, alienated from her identity and her motherland that was the barbarian, but those who treated her with barbaric brutality" (Mbeki 2002). In this speech, by quoting at length and in detail Georges Couvier's dissection report from 1815 (which is very racist indeed), Mbeki re-created a racist imagery which—according to contemporary reports from the event[2]—was previously unknown to large parts of the audience.

The flip side of Mbeki's rage against 'dark continent discourses' is the re-valorization of Africa-based traditions and customary knowledge, which is part of what the president's high-profile project of African Renaissance is all about (cf. Mbeki 1999). One such custom, the re-vitalization of which is enjoying the support of certain African Renaissance proponents (cf. Leclerc-Madlala 2001) is vir-

---

1. For further analysis of the Sarah Bartmann case, cf. Arnfred's chapter.
2. Neville Hoad's presentation at the Sex & Secrecy Conference in Johannesburg, June 2003.

ginity testing. Virginity testing is said to be an ancient Zulu custom,[1] applied by older women to their junior female kin as a pre-marriage control. To be sure, the impetus for a revitalization has apparently come from below, from older Zulu women themselves, and also seems to be supported by the young women who (presumably voluntarily) are subjecting themselves to the test. In this new, modern edition, virginity-testing is conceived as a measure to curb and control the spread of HIV/AIDS. Not surprisingly some 'modern' feminist bodies like the Commission for Gender Equality (CGE) are squarely against the practice, invoking gender-and-development type arguments of bodily integrity, rights to privacy and gender equality (cf. Leclerc-Madlala 2001, 2003, CGE 2000).

However, both sides may be off the point. Those who use the African Renaissance project to revalorize traditions are off because in supporting 'African customs' such as virginity testing they show themselves unable (or unwilling?) to see that the context of the struggle has changed. In the present situation 'virginity testing' appears to place an absurd and unjustifiable burden of responsibility for controlling the spread of HIV/AIDS upon the shoulders of very young women; the custom totally leaves out the responsibility of men and poses no challenge to masculinities; it leaves patriarchy undisturbed. The simple and dangerous dichotomies are still at work: Mbeki and other people who favour going back to tradition seem unable to perceive the shifts, modifications, and subtle changes in emphasis to which any 'custom' anywhere is subjected. On the other hand, the CGE may be off because its argumentation tends to be too general and universalist; it does not sufficiently take the predicament of the old and younger women living in the midst of the HIV/AIDS pandemic into consideration (cf. CGE 2000).

The overall argument in this section is that Mbeki's lines of thinking do not bring us very far in these indeed complicated situations of which daily life in Africa, in South Africa, no less than elsewhere in the world, is composed. Of course Thabo Mbeki has got a point—but this point must be dealt with in different ways, which is what this volume aims to do. The 'dark continent discourse' is by no means dead and gone. On the contrary, it goes on multiplying, sometimes changing focus, but basically repeating itself; colonial continuities are still with us, reproducing dichotomies.

Colonial continuities: GAD discourse[2]

One of the areas where, surprisingly, colonial continuities are still alive and kicking is in gender-and-development discourse. In gender-and-development (GAD) discourse 'world wide patriarchy' and 'universal female subordination' look like primordial facts of nature (cf. Becker, this volume). This in spite of thinking and ev-

---

1. Investigating issues of gender and sexuality in Mozambique in the early 1980s, I found similar customs in Manica/Sofala in patrilineal central Mozambique.
2. In regard to gender-and-development (GAD) *discourse* I am referring not only to a particular line of thinking and talking, a certain vocabulary etc, but also to the institutions in which these lines of thinking are produced and the practices with which they are connected.

idence, in feminist theory and elsewhere, regarding 'patriarchy' itself being many different things,[1] and in spite of the work of prominent African feminists like Ifi Amadiume and Oyèrónké Oyewùmí, who—based on their own empirical work in Nigeria—show that talking of 'female subordination' is far too simple and off the mark. Amadiume and Oyewùmí explicitly critizise Western gender dichotomies and oppositional gender discourse (cf. also Kolawole, this volume). They point to different ways of conceiving 'gender': of gender as much more dependent on social contexts and specific relations, and much less depending on bodies. According to Oyewùmí, 'universal female subordination' is a generally misleading conceptualization (Oyewùmí 1997:xii ff).

Nevertheless, the GAD discourse has taken over a number of assumptions from the colonial/missionary images and imaginations of 'African culture', with ideas of excessive patriarchy and African women as overworked and downtrodden beasts of burden, as ideological corner stones (Becker 2003). African women are constructed as victims, thus legitimizing concerted Western efforts to come to their rescue. Colonial governments and Christian missions—who (as discussed below) effectively undermined whatever power positions African woman might have occupied in pre-colonial, pre-mission days—perceived themselves as gallant saviours of African women from endless African male oppression. Increasingly, in GAD discourse, the *victimization* of African women is questioned and criticised, but the overall framework of 'othering' remains intact.

The GAD images are very powerful, structuring the minds of not only donors, but also Africans, including African gender researchers, who as often as not work part-time as consultants, in contexts where this conceptual framework of 'universal female subordination' and 'primordial patriarchy' is taken for granted. These images filter down into the minds of rank and file African women. Through 'gender training'—a widespread donor-financed NGO activity everywhere in Africa—workshop participants are being trained to use (and to some extent to see their own lives in terms of) this gender-and-development vocabulary, without adequately taking socio-cultural contexts into account (cf. Kolawole's chapter, this volume). According to my own fieldwork in matrilineal northern Mozambique, gender power dynamics work very differently in matrilineal as compared to patrilineal areas, and much more in favour of women. In spite of this, however, even here women, who participate in donor-sponsored NGO activities, learn to see themselves as oppressed under patriarchal power; they do not learn to see, appreciate and further develop the specific gender dynamics of this particular society. In Kolawole's words (this volume): "The conceptualization of gender in Africa is male-biased and Western oriented." As an alternative, Kolawole suggests that Af-

---

1. As outlined e.g. by Judith Butler: "The very notion of patriarchy has threatened to become a universalizing concept that overrides or reduces distinct articulations of gender asymmetry in different cultural contexts. As feminism has sought to become integrally related to struggles against racialist and colonialist oppression, it has become increasingly important to resist the colonizing epistemological strategy that would subordinate different configurations of domination under the rubric of a transcultural notion of patriarchy" (Butler 1993:46).

rican women should use their existing, often uncharted power base and build on that instead of following the Western lead of 'trying to be like men'.

In GAD lines of thinking, 'tradition' and 'African culture' are detrimental to women, being posed in opposition to gender equity and modernity. Even if this construction of tradition/modernity as a binary pair has been debunked incessantly by critical social scientists at least since Ranger and Hobsbawn's influential arguments regarding 'tradition' as invented by 'modernity' (Hobsbawn and Ranger 1983), this conceptual pair is still going strong, breeding new categories, such as HTP: *harmful traditional practices* (cf. Becker's chapter). HTP is a most unfortunate expression, a) because it tends to classify everything 'traditional' as harmful, and b) by labelling them 'harmful' it also implicitly enforces a specific morality, an unspoken norm, compared to which this or that is considered 'harmful'. Parallel to the famous 'repugnancy clause' regarding customary law in colonial days, where the implicit morality was that of the colonial master, the implicit morality here is the morality of 'modernity', i.e. of the West.

Prominent among practices classified as traditional and harmful are female initiation rituals, whatever these may entail. Significantly Becker reports that "when researchers from the University of Namibia were commissioned to study (male and female) initiation in the mid-1990s, word quickly made the rounds that they were researching female genital mutilation (FGM)"—even if female initiation in Namibia contains no kind of genital cutting. The reactions of the Namibian colleagues should come as no surprise, however; since 1997 the officially accepted name for any kind of modification of the female genitalia—often linked to initiation rituals—is *female genital mutilation*, FGM. In a joint statement issued in April 1997 by WHO, UNICEF and UNFPA the following definition is given: "Female genital mutilation comprises all procedures involving part or total removal off the external female genitalia or other injury to female genital organs whether for cultural or other non-therapeutic reasons" (WHO 1998:5). So there we are: international authorities have spoken. Forget about details or local conditions and contexts, or that in some places—as for example in northern Mozambique—a repeated exercise, gradually producing an elongation of the small lips of the vagina (*labiae minorae*) is reported, by women and men alike, to greatly enhance physical pleasure in the sexual encounter (Arnfred 1988, 1990, 2003). Everything, which happens to be different from the way in which we in the West treat our genitals, is classified as mutilation. This is basically what the concept of HTP is all about: if is different, not 'natural'—it is defined as harmful.

Actual female genital mutilation, where some sort of cutting does take place, is of course a different matter. A discussion is still relevant, however, regarding the basis on which to wage what kind of struggle against such practices. Dellenborg (this volume) interestingly reports from her investigations in southern Senegal, that contrary to what most people would have expected a) female genital cutting among the Jola is a very new custom, almost modern, hardly fifty years old, b) the defenders of the custom are not the men—most young men are actually against it—but the older women, c) in Jola contexts female circumcision is a strategy for women's empowerment! Previously, before the Jola adopted Islam and female circumcision from their Mandinka neighbours, it was only through marriage/motherhood that women could achieve ritual status. But now, with a new form of female secret society connected to Islam and to female circumcision, women are no longer dependent on their relations to men for ritual distinction. Dellenborg points to the fact of the increase in Western interest in and critique of female genital mutilation coinciding with the growth of the Western women's movement in the 1970s, with its focus on sexuality and especially on clitoral orgasms. One may thus speculate, as Dellenborg does, if it is the Western women's movement's focus on the clitoris, which creates FGM as a paramount problem, more than the situation of African women as such?

In interesting and apparently contradictory ways the Western feminist concern with FGM is re-working a colonial/missionary trope: in the type of AIDS discourse, to which Thabo Mbeki is referring, African men and women are driven by uncontrollable passions and unconquerable devotion to sin and lust, and as becomes evident in Caldwell's arguments (Caldwell et al. 1989) it is the lasciviousness of women, which is the decisive factor. In Caldwell's vision of the world, female chastity is a precondition for civilization (cf. Arnfred's chapter). The feminist protest, as far as FGM is concerned, takes as its point of departure a very different valorization of female sexuality: in the FGM campaigns it is not too much sexuality, which is the problem, but rather too little. The issue, which has been able to rouse such concern among Western feminists, is that African women through FGM are being deprived of their possibilities for sexual fulfilment. This does appear as a contradiction—but on a deeper level maybe it is not after all. The similarities between the two positions are apparent: a) in both cases othering processes are at work: whether lascivious or deprived, African women are perceived as 'others'; and b) in both cases the focus is—once again—on the sexuality of African women .

Legacies of Christianity

Obviously the Christian influence on the ways in which sexuality in Africa has been/is seen is decisive. Furthermore, as has been the case for something like a century now, in many parts of Africa, Christianity is no longer just determining the ways in which gender relations are perceived from the outside; Christianity is also influencing the ways people see themselves, their past and present. As reported from Namibia by Becker, gender identities that were promulgated by the missionaries in the first half of the 20th century are presented in postcolonial discourse as 'traditional'. Interviewing men and women in rural Owamboland, Becker was told that 'in our tradition we are very Christian'. According to her "Christianity has largely succeeded in restructuring people's conceptual universe in important respects, including the social, cultural and political representations of everyday life."

This is yet another indication that 'traditions' change all the time. So what is the point in trying to disentangle, to say which parts of 'tradition' are traditional, which parts Christian, which parts not? The major reason for such endeavour in the context of this volume, is to broaden the vision, to keep alert a notion of possible alternatives, and to maintain a perpetual awareness regarding what otherwise might very easily pass as implicit assumptions. The fact that virtually all African 'traditions' and 'customs' have been conceptualized by men and women (mostly men) with Western/Christian educational backgrounds, have made some aspects less visible than others. Three aspects of Christian assumptions regarding sexuality show how such implicit assumptions have led to misinterpretations on the part of Western observers (missionaries, anthropologists, colonial administrators) if not to outright failures to see certain parts of the societies in question.

First the assumption of heterosexuality. *Heteronormativity* being taken for granted has made any kind of same-sex relations invisible. As noted by Blackwood and Wieringa: "For many ethnographers, travellers and colonial authorities the possibility of married women engaging in non-heterosexual practices was unthinkable" (1999:41). And to their respondents, same-sex relations between women were not classified as 'sex' since no penis was involved: "No penis, no sex". As Blackwood and Wieringa correctly point out a major reason for the invisibility of same-sex practices was more likely due to the limitations of the observers than to the conditions of women's lives (Blackwood and Wieringa 1999:41). Ways of understanding and not understanding same-sex relations will be further discussed below, in the section on *Pleasure and Desire*.

As for the second aspect of Christian assumptions regarding gender and sexuality, note the case of the German missionary quoted in Becker's chapter. It is 1913 and the Reverend August Wulfhorst angrily corrects a young colleague who does not see that local women, in their lascivious sexual conduct, and being as *sinful as men*, are not and cannot be subordinate. The social group in question is matrilineal, and the Reverend sensibly makes a connection between this fact and the (in his eyes) disrespectful, improper behaviour of the women. What is important here, however, is that with this statement the Reverend implies a connection between organized and reasonable social structures and *male/female double standards*. In his eyes the problem in Owamboland is not that women are oppressed, but rather that they are subject to too little male control. The very same line of thinking in fact, as Caldwell's regarding female chastity as emblem of civilization (cf. above). In this line of thinking male control of female sexuality—in practice often equal to male/female double standards—is a pivotal issue, a *sine qua non* for social development.

The third aspect has to do with sexuality in Christian contexts being conceived as an issue of morality and sin (primordial sin, nothing less), obscuring insight in the importance in many (most?) African pre-colonial societies (and to some extent even today) of a division between sexuality and fertility—or between *sex for pleasure* and *sex for procreation*. In Western contexts, with Western lines of thinking—which, as correctly pointed out by Oyewùmí, are firmly rooted in biology, body-reasoning or *bio-logic* as she calls it (Oyewùmí 1997:5, ix)—sex-as-linked-to-procreation is perceived as the 'natural' state of affairs, only brought under human control through modern contraceptives (so-called family planning). The assumption regarding people in Africa (or in the Third World in general) being more 'primitive' than the West, would be that they are also more 'natural', with sex as a matter of course being linked to procreation. This however is not the case. There are many indications of clear distinctions between sex for pleasure and sex for procreation. There are also indications that marriage in Africa in pre-colonial days dealt with control of fertility, more than with control of sexuality as such. "This separation of fertility and sexuality is crucial to any analysis of Southern Africa's pre-capitalist societies," Jeff Guy says (1987:32)—a statement which can be generalized, I presume, to larger parts of the continent. There is also plenty of evidence that in pre-colonial, pre-Christian times, "non-reproductive sexual relations took place comparatively freely between unmarried adults" (Guy 1987:32. Cf. also: Guy 1990; Hunter 2002; Delius and Glaser 2002; Becker, this volume).

What mattered in kinship contexts was control of sex for procreation. Sex in itself was much less severely controlled, as long as it did not result in pregnancies. Historical sources from Kwa-Zulu Natal describe how *ukusoma*—non-penetrative thigh-sex—made it possible for young men and women to engage in sex before marriage without fearing for the consequences in terms of pregnancies (Hunter 2002:106, CGE 2000:24). In matrilineal northern Mozambique pre-puberty/pre-marriage sexual relations were distinctly encouraged, in order that the women should be properly educated for adulthood. The marker of adulthood was the initiation ritual, immediately after which young women were expected to marry. The *efundula*-ceremony reported by Becker from matrilineal Owamboland had a similar function of marking the transformation from free playful sexuality to a different stage where women (and men) must take responsibility for procreation. In Owamboland, according to Becker (building on among others Reverend Wulfhorst's observations) prior to the advent of Christianity, young women had enjoyed largely unrestrained sexual freedom. Many had sexual relations with men "as if they were married" and many young women had fiancés who visited them at their leisure with the knowledge and approval of their parents. The society being matrilineal, marriage was not a big deal—the offspring would stay with the mother's family anyway—and men were largely brought into the context as procreators. Parallel to marriage ceremonies in patrilineal contexts, it was here the female initiation rituals, *efundula*, which marked the transformation from young girls to adult women.

Playful sexuality might continue however, even after adulthood/marriage, in extra-marital relations, provided that they were conducted with proper *discretion*, and provided that no pregnancies resulted. In Zimbabwe, in the mid-1990s, I was told about a rule demanding that a man, who has been away for a while and who unexpectedly returns to his homestead, must whistle when approaching his house in order to alert his wife to his coming —thus making sure he will not catch her in an embarrassing situation. In colonial Zululand according to Hunter (2003) married women's secret lovers were called *isidikiselo*, the top of the pot; these complemented the woman's husband, her *ibhodwe*, the main pot (Hunter 2003:15). There is a lot of difference, between calling a secret lover 'the top of the pot'—signifying something extra, something nice, a pleasure and luxury—or stigmatising a married woman with a lover as a 'loose' woman. Nevertheless, in the period with which Hunter is concerned (the 1920s and 1930s) a married woman with one or more lovers also ran the risk of being positioned as *isifebe*—a loose woman.

With Christianity and colonization, Christian lines of thinking and Christian norms for social conduct grew increasingly dominant in those (vast) parts of Africa where Christian missions gained an effective foothold. Rules regarding sexuality and fertility coalesced into a single moral code, and norms for male and female sexual behaviour developed along different lines: for a man to have multiple sexual relations with women to whom he was not married became associated in positive ways to masculinity and manhood, *isoka* in Zulu contexts, whereas women were increasingly not allowed to have multiple sexual partners (Hunter 2003:6). Gradually a Christian moral regime is created: sexual pleasure for women is defined out of existence, female chastity and passionlessness (Cott 1978) becoming the model and the norm. Sex for women is legitimized only as a means of procreation; pleasure is seen as very close to sin—the idea of sexuality as 'primordial sin' being a cornerstone in Christianity. In practice however the curse of 'primordial sin' works differently for men compared to women. For men an idea of sexuality for pleasure, and multiple sexual partners continues to exist—it becomes understood, and even naturalized, as a part of male nature: 'men just are like that'—whereas for women sex as such is perceived as linked to procreation. *Male/female double standards* thus become the order of the day, along with the idea of female sexual purity (chastity), and female sexuality under male control.

Sex for procreation and male/female fertility remain an important issue, especially in kinship contexts. But not only that, development planners have also taken an interest in fertility control ('family planning') generally based on a kind of neo-Malthusian understanding of excessive population growth as a major cause of poverty. Adomako Ampofo (this volume) shows how KAP surveys (KAP = Knowledge, Attitudes, Practices) setting out to measure women's so-called 'unmet need' for contraceptives, miss the mark by not taking local contexts and gender power relations between husband and wife into consideration. Like the previously discussed 'development discourse' concepts, such as HTP and FGM, the concept of 'unmet need' is based on implicit and invisibly normative assumptions, in this case the 'need for modern contraception'. "Whose need?" Adomako Ampofo asks, pointing to the fact that any identification of an 'unmet need' also means a ready market for contraceptives.

Problems of Pleasure and Desire

Increasingly, as shown above, sexuality for pleasure—for men and for women—is acknowledged as a social fact, and investigated as such by sociologists, anthropologists and historians. A direct focus, however, on pleasure and desire opens a wide field of investigations, the contributions in this volume showing a range of possible approaches.

Race and sexuality

Frantz Fanon and Simone de Beauvoir belong to the same historical age and the same intellectual environment. Some of their questions were parallel, as were some of their answers. De Beauvoir posed the question: 'What is a woman?' Frantz Fanon: 'What is a black man?' De Beauvoir's statement: "One is not born, but rather becomes, a woman" (1949/1997:295) could have been echoed by Fanon. According to Ratele, (himself a psychologist) who takes important inspiration from Fanon, black people got their colour when white colonialists conquered and defined them:

> There are no black men before the introduction of whiteness in this country [i.e. South Africa] or anywhere else on the continent. In the early seventeenth century black men were other things: AmaZulu, AmaXosa, AmaNdebele, AmaSwazi, Basotho, Batswana, Khoi and San, and so on. Before that they were other things. They were bound together by explicitly cultural bonds (which themselves are fluid) rather than yet to be defined by blackness (Ratele 1998:38).

Blackness, according to Ratele, is constructed by discourse, and a very particular discourse, closely connected to the violent realities of colonialism. People in Africa became black when they were conquered and defined by European people, who in the same move defined themselves as white. In this process black people got not only their colour, but also, following Fanon, their sexuality: "For the majority of white men the Negro represents the sexual instinct (in its raw state)" (Fanon 1952/1986:177). 'Blackness' in itself, and 'blackness as sexual' is the double outcome of the very processes of othering, discussed above: in defining the other you define yourself. The dynamics of othering have been succinctly analyzed by Judith Butler (1990), as combined processes of disavowal and projection: in order to maintain his precious rationality, and in order to maintain the illusion—in accordance with Cartesian mind/body divisions—that he, the man, represents pure mind, European/Western man "disavows [his] socially marked embodiment, and further, projects that disavowed and disparaged embodiment on to the female sphere, effectively renaming the body as female" (Butler 1990:16). The same move of disavowal/projection of body, feeling, sexuality is extended from women to Third World/colonized populations, as shown by Mohanty (1984/1991; cf. above).

In Enlightenment thought, rationality is constructed as opposite to passion, emotion, sexuality (a pattern which also surfaces in Mbeki's speeches): civilized, rational man must master his feelings, passion must be subordinated to reason. Fanon himself subscribes to the same line of thought:

> Every intellectual gain requires a loss in sexual potential. The civilized white man retains an irrational longing for unusual eras of sexual license, of orgiastic scenes, of unpunished rapes, of unrepressed incest. [...] Projecting his own desires onto the Negro, the white man behaves 'as if' the Negro really had them (Fanon 1952/1986:165).

Whatever the processes involved, 'the black man' like 'the black woman' is defined as quintessentially sexual, albeit in different ways. While black (colonized) women are tantalizing objects for white men's sexual dreams and fantasies, sexualized, large-penis bestowed black men are differently positioned in the white imaginations—as threats and rivals, objects of fear[1] and loathing. Fanon, not unlike Mbeki, rehearses the myths: "as for the Negroes, they have tremendous sexual powers. What do you expect, with all the freedom they have in their jungles! They copulate at all times and in all places. They are really genital. They have so many children that they cannot even count them. Be careful, or they will flood us with little mulattos. Things are indeed going to hell ... Our women are at the mercy of the Negroes" (Fanon 1952/1986:157). As Fanon acknowledges with a sigh: "The sexual potency of the Negro is hallucinating" (Fanon 1952/1986:157).

Thus, "if one wants to understand the racial situation psychologically, not from a universal viewpoint, but as it is experienced by individual consciousnesses, considerable importance must be given to sexual phenomena" (Fanon 1952/1986:160). Ratele (this volume) goes on from here; based on analysis of essays written by male students at the University of Western Cape, he wants to say something about South Africa today. Taking a point of departure in Fanon's rhetorical question: 'Is the sexual superiority of the Negro real?' he follows the gist of Fanon's own answer: "Everyone *knows* that it is not. But that is not what matters. The prelogical thought of the phobic[2] has decided that such is the case" (Fanon 1952/1986:159). Ratele is dealing with myths as they materialize and multiply in the minds of their onetime objects—not unlike the Christian morality which, as shown by Becker, turns into 'African tradition'. "Kinky politics", Ratele says "follows the fetish of, and re-fetishes ~~race~~. There can be no racism without this constant re-fetishisation. ... Kinky politics is personal and institutionalised practices, politics, programmes and cultures that naturalise, objectify and stabilise difference". As a protest against the constructions of 'race', Ratele writes the word with a strikethrough. This strikethrough is an expression of the "insubordinate vigilance against simple categories" and the "enduring revolt against naturalizations", which for Ratele are necessary precautions under present conditions. "Against the backdrop of continuing 'nature' discourses, pushing for varied and more sophisticated positions ... retains urgency" he says.

The object of Ratele's investigation is present-day South African politics and the ways in which "in spite of good intentions transformation debates and resultant politics, institutions and programmes have tended to reproduce certain old, as well as creating novel cultural, social, economic and political divisions."—

---

1. Fanon as a psychiatrist talks of 'phobia' rather than of 'fear'—"the Negro is phobogenic" (Fanon 1952/1986: 154).
2. Cf. the previous footnote.

Thabo Mbeki's speeches (above) are a case in point. This politics further tends to keep *desire* out of the politics of 'race', as well as that of sex and gender. Nevertheless, particularly as not acknowledged, this politically incorrect desire goes on working as an active force in the continued re-producing and re-fetishisation of 'race'.

Pleasure and desire

Even if sexuality and (white, male) sexual desire have been active factors in establishing the very notion of Africa and Africans, sexual pleasure and desire have rarely been objects of study for scholars studying Africa—female sexual pleasure and desire even less. Seen in this light, Diallo's chapter provides novel information regarding measures taken in Mali for enhancement of sexual pleasure in married life. Sexual enjoyment—for men as well as for women—is explicitly condoned by the Koran (Mernissi 1975; Naamane-Guessous 1997). The co-existence in Mali of institutions for enhancement of sexual bliss in married couples, with institutions for various forms of female genital cutting, points to the fact that, in spite of the cutting, in Muslim contexts (unlike in Christianity) sexual enjoyment for women is not defined out of existence. Sexual enjoyment should, however, take place only in marriage, i.e. under male control. Where control of women in Christian cultures tends to be implicit, working through the ways in which women are defined and looked upon by society, control of women in Muslim cultures tends to be more direct and physical—and thus also more tangible and visible. Fatema Mernissi writes about this difference as reflected on one hand in Western imaginations of an Oriental harem, filled with passive, voluptuous, sexually accessible women, and on the other hand the Muslim imagination that women have wings, and that femininity is an uncontrollable power. "Femininity is the emotional locus of all kinds of disruptive forces, in both the real world and in fantasy," Mernissi says (2001:24), pointing at the same time to the apparent *absence* of femininity as a threat in the Western imagination of passive accessible women. The importance of marriage, in Christian as well as in Muslim contexts, points to the shared axioms of heteronormativity, and also of male/female double standards, pillars of patriarchy, as discussed above. Acknowledgement of same-sex relations (cf. Machera's chapter) pulls the carpet from under such axioms, implicitly endangering patriarchal power. This presumably is a major reason for present-day African patriarchs going out so massively against it.

Same-sex relations

Amazingly, until recently, same-sex relations have been understood as (largely) non-existent in Africa, the official (and widespread) opinion being that same-sex is decadence, imposed on Africa from the outside. Zimbabwe's president Robert Mugabe made that very clear in his (in)famous speech at the opening of the Zimbabwe International Book Fair in 1995: "I find it extremely outrageous and repugnant to my human conscience," he said, "that such immoral and repulsive organizations, like those of homosexuals, who offend both against the law of nature and the morals of religious beliefs espoused by our society, should have any advocates in our midst and even elsewhere in the world" (quoted in Dunton and Palmberg 1996:9). Kenyan president Danial Arap Moi was of the same opinion, claiming that "words like lesbianism and homosexuality do not exist in African languages" (*Mail & Guardian*, Sept 1995, quoted in Dunton and Palmberg 1996:24).

Incidentally Moi may have a point, but the point is different from what he thinks: same-sex practices did and do exist in Africa, in remarkable quantity and diversity (Murray and Roscoe 1998:267), but not necessarily as *identities*. Murray and Roscoe have done an admirable job of collecting data material from old anthropological pieces and writings by travellers, as far back as 1732, supplemented with new research. The evidence is overwhelming. The bulk of documented same-sex behaviour takes place either at particular times during a lifetime, or concurrently with heterosexual behaviour. This points to a remarkably different social code, compared to social codes espoused by Christianity and Islam: "This social code does not require that an individual suppresses same-sex desires or behaviour, but that she or he never allows such desires to overshadow or supplant procreation" (Murray and Roscoe 1998:273). Compare again the distinction between 'sex for pleasure' and 'sex for procreation': as long as it does not interfere with procreation, there is a certain scope for sexual enjoyment.

Kurt Falk, a German traveller/anthropologist writing in the 1920s from Namibia and Angola, reports on woman/woman relations:

> One might guess that the tribades [as he calls these women] were old women, no longer visited by men, or women without husbands, but almost the opposite is the case: only the newly married, younger wifes, who could not complain over the lack of heterosexual intercourse, practice same-sex intercourse with each other almost insatiably (Falk 1925–26, in Murray and Roscoe 1998:193).

There is also evidence of 'thigh-sex' between men and boys, and between young men and women before marriage. Similar data are provided by Dunbar Moodie writing about all-male life in the gold mines of the Rand: before going to the mines the young men would be herdboys, and in the bush they would be visited by girls, and thigh-sex would be practiced; thigh-sex was also the reported form of older men's sex with younger men in the mines (Moodie 2001). The young 'lovers' also perform domestic duties, for which they are remunerated by the older men. Thus "men became 'wives' on the mines in order to become husbands and therefore full 'men' more rapidly at home" (Moodie 2001:305).

Also regarding female same-sex relations evidence abounds. Kendall (1999) reports from Lesotho how close and intimate relationships between married women, locally called *mpho*-relationships, were not conceived as 'sexual' since no penis was involved (once again, "no penis, no sex"). Husbands, according to Kendall, would often know about the *mpho*-relationship, the wife's female lover sometimes having a status as a family friend. Woman-woman and woman-man relationships were conceived as differently constructed and thus not mutually threatening. Gloria Wekker (quoted in Machera's chapter) reports very similar

structures among Creole women of African descent in Suriname, where such relationships are called *mati*. In Suriname, 'mati-work' is part of working-class culture, as opposed to the middle-class, where according to dominant values women
must be 'feminine' and dependent on men; as seen from middle-class positions
'mati-work' is perceived as 'rowdy, unseemly behaviour' (Wekker 1997:338). According to Wekker, categories of 'identity' in this context are misplaced and misleading: "Conceiving of same-gender sexual behaviour embodied in the mati-
work in terms of 'identity' inscribes and reproduces Western thought categories
with their legacy of dichotomy, hierarchy and permanency, thus distorting a phenomenon that is emically experienced in quite different terms" (Wekker
1999:133).

Wekker talks about *multiplicitous sexualities* (cf. Machera's chapter), and basing
her arguments on Afro-Surinamese working class language and patterns of behaviour, she insists on the futility of thinking about these matters in terms of 'sexual identity', following a Western line of thinking, seeing 'the subject' as 'unitary,
authentic, bounded, static and trans-situational' (1999:125). According to her, it
is much more to the point to acknowledge the co-existence of a variety of different aspects within the same individual, conceptualizing self and sexuality as multiplicitous, dynamic and malleable (Wekker 1997:335).

'Dividuality'

This last point about multiplicitous sexualities and critique of the conception of
the subject as a bounded, trans-situational unit, corresponds neatly with Helle-
Valle's critique of the mainstream notion of a person as a unitary, bounded individual. Instead he introduces the term 'dividual', in order to "lead our attention
to that fact that human beings, irrespective of ideas about 'indivisibility' have different perspectives, and in a sense are different persons depending on the communicative contexts they are parts of" (Helle-Valle, this volume). 'Dividuality'
thus depends on social context. Everybody, in Africa as elsewhere, belong to multiple social contexts, in and out of which they move routinely. Different social
contexts of relevance for studies of sexuality are *sex in contexts of marriage*, and *extra-
marital sex*. During fieldwork in Botswana Helle-Valle noticed widespread practices of extra-marital sexual relationships, locally termed *bobolete*. These relationships
belonged to social contexts, which were locally defined and recognized as distinc-
tively different from the marital setting, and different rules would apply to sex in
these different settings, a social norm regarding discretion being important in
contexts of extra-marital sex. Keeping in mind the distinction introduced above
between 'sex for pleasure' and 'sex for procreation', this distinction between 'extra-marital' sex and 'sex in contexts of marriage', may be seen as a qualification:
there is a partial, not total overlap between the two. In principle sex for procreation should always take place in contexts of marriage, but sometimes sex for
pleasure may take place in contexts of marriage as well (cf. Diallo's chapter).

Female Agency

Female agency is nothing new in Africa. On the contrary, as forcefully pointed out by Kolawole (this volume), not only are notions of 'universal female subordination' misplaced in Africa, but there is also a long tradition of women's struggles against colonial domination, and resisting traditional rulers' oppression. However, with social and economic transformation, female agency takes on new forms. A rather novel phenomenon is that of women choosing not to marry.

Women choosing not to marry: Motherhood vs wifehood

In traditional patrilineal societies, marriage is the link between procreation and kinship. It is through marriage that children born of mothers are brought into fathers' lineages. Until recently in many African societies marriage has been a precondition for adulthood. Compare here the discussions in Becker's chapter of *efundula*, the initiation ritual which is seen as a synonym for marriage, as well as the discussion of same-sex relations, where it was found that social codes in many African societies have been permissive regarding same-sex relations or desires, as long as these did not overshadow or supplant marriage and procreation. Whatever sexual relations men and women practised or preferred, they would always also be married.

This pattern is now changing, a change in which women are the agents. Helle-Valle shows from Botswana, and Haram from Tanzania, how women increasingly have been able to take the initiative and to negotiate extra-marital sexual relationships on terms, which are at least partially set by themselves. Young women in Botswana may decide not to marry, or to postpone marriage plans, in order to remain for a longer time in the more independent (but also risky) position of an extra-marital girlfriend, or an informal second wife. The socio-economic basis for this strategy is a norm of informal sexual relationships involving a transfer of economically significant gifts from the man to the women. Unlike norms in Christian/Western contexts, where "romantic love and/or personal pleasure [...] are the 'proper' motives for engaging in sex, while strategic, materially oriented uses of sexuality are strictly tabooed" (Helle-Valle, this volume), sexual mores in Botswana and other parts of Africa include as a matter of course notions of reciprocity and acknowledgement of sex by gifts of money (cf. also Helle-Valle 1999, Helle-Valle and Talle 2000)

Similarly, modern women in semi-urban northern Tanzania are increasingly choosing not to marry, thus opting out of kinship based traditional control and circumscription. Yet, "in their pursuit for self-fulfilment and economic independence, they become dependent on another type of attachment to men" (Haram, this volume). In spite of 'modern' romantic ideals of partnership and intimacy, and in spite of the women's own dreams of one day meeting 'the right one', they tend to choose well-settled, generous, married men, so-called 'sugar daddies', rather than young and penniless ones, referring to their male partners as their 'project', 'business' or 'donor'. In this way the women manage to "maintain some degree of social independence and avoid the severe control often exercised by a true husband."

Marriage is an option and a choice for these economically active women, who may prefer to navigate between various 'donors' rather than to risk the subordination to one particular husband. Whether also motherhood is seen as an option is less clear; but there are few reports of women opting out of motherhood. Haram discusses the general preference of 'motherhood' to 'wifehood' in terms of Jane Guyer's useful and illustrative conceptualization: *polyandrous motherhood* (Guyer 1994). This term captures the particular life situation of unmarried mothers, who may often have children by various men, and it also points to the primacy of motherhood over marriage. Polyandrous motherhood, if cleverly managed, may be beneficial for women; childbearing is highly valued among both men and women, and the success of single mothers' lives depends to a large extent on the ways in which they manage their reproductive capacity (cf. Haram's chapter).

Motherhood as pivotal in African cultures and in women's lives is a theme which has been developed by African feminists like Ifi Amadiume and Oyèrónké Oyewùmí, cf. Amadiume's discussion of 'the motherhood paradigm' (Amadiume 1997) and Oyewùmí's analysis of the wife/mother distinction (Oyewùmí 2000). This distinction further adds to the critique of Western gender/feminist theoretical conceptualizations (including GAD discourse). The importance of the wife/mother distinction, Oyewùmí says, is that 'female subordination' is embedded in the position as 'wife', whereas the position as 'mother' is a position of power in African contexts, "motherhood [being] the preferred and cherished self-identity of many African women" (Oyewùmí 2000:1096). Kolawole echoes this point of view (Kolawole 1997).

In Oyewùmí's analysis, Western feminist theory runs off the track, because the 'woman' in Western feminist theory is conceived as a 'wife'—i.e. subordinated to a man/a husband; this wifely subordination being embedded in the Western conception of 'woman' (Oyewùmí 2000:1094). In Africa, Oyewùmí says, the subordination of the 'wife' (in patrilineal settings) has to do with her position as an *outsider to the lineage*; it has nothing to do with her gender; in matrilineal settings the subordinated outsiders will be the young in-married husbands (cf. Peters 1997, Geffray 1990, Arnfred 2001). Oyewùmí gives as an example the distinction between the Yoruba terms *oko* and *iyawo* , which are usually translated as 'husband' and 'wife', but which in actual fact is not a distinction of gender; it is a distinction between those who are birth members of a family/a lineage and those who enter by marriage (Oyewùmí 2002:4). In patrilineal systems, however—as commonly in the West—the subordinated outsider, the *iyawo*, will be a woman.

For this reason, in Oyewùmí's understanding, where subordination is embedded is in the positioning as a *wife*, not in being a *woman* as such. When Western women also see subordination in *motherhood*, this is because motherhood in Western patriarchal systems is linked unilaterally to wifehood, cf the concept of 'illegitimate children' if the mother is not a wife. The young women of Botswana and Tanzania (and elsewhere in Africa) in choosing not to marry make use of this distinction between wifehood and motherhood, opting out of wifehood (= subordination), while maintaining the position as mothers. Cherryl Walker reports from Durban regarding how :

> [T]eenage mothers ... did not view their pregnancies as shameful disasters but, rather, as an affirmation of their womanhood. ... An extremely high value is placed on children for and in themselves ... so high that marriage is, in some contexts, quite irrelevant to the bearing of children (Walker 1995:431).

These findings make Walker conclude that:

> [I]ncreasingly during the twentieth century motherhood and marriage have been uncoupled for and by African women. ... There is a large literature documenting and commenting upon the rise of female-headed households in the course of the twentieth century. There is also evidence that the stigma of single motherhood has continued to decline, to the point where many women look upon it as a preferable option to marriage. ... Growing numbers of young women are increasingly sceptical of marriage but are not relinquishing their desire to have children. ... Fertility—the capacity to bear children and assume the social identity of motherhood—continues to be very highly valued by women and to inform their choices around motherhood (Walker 1995:431).

AIDS as a feminist issue

One drawback, of course, of 'polyandrous motherhood' is the mounting risks of AIDS. Women's sexual transactions and attempts at strategic allocation of their reproductive power are performed in contexts of high level risks and uncertainties, as vividly illustrated in Haram's chapter; risks which are exacerbated by the scaringly rapid spread of HIV/AIDS. The epidemic furthermore is used as a tool in ongoing gender struggles, women being pointed out as the major carriers of the virus, and thus as the contaminators. Most current HIV/AIDS prevention efforts are based on gender stereotypes rooted in the West, i.e. on mainstream notions of male domination and female subordination. Silbersmith (this volume) shows the shortcomings of such campaigns, with the situation of African *men* taken into consideration. The shortcomings are equally evident seen from the position of African women. With changing socio-economic conditions, traditional African masculinities—based in pre-colonial days on male positions as warriors and cattle herders and later, with increasing money economies from the mid-20th century onwards, on male roles as breadwinners—have been undermined. Nowadays, with increasing unemployment and many men incapable of fulfilling 'traditional' social roles and expectations, "male identity and self-esteem become increasingly linked to sexuality and sexual manifestations" (Silbersmith, this volume). Because of this, AIDS prevention campaigns focused on the ABC of Abstinence, Be faithful and Condom use, are not very likely to be successful; men, who see their masculinity as based on sexual conquests, in line with the Zulu *isoka* ideal (cf. Hunter 2003) are unlikely to listen to such messages. As for the women, campaigns which do not challenge prevailing gender stereotypes are of little use. Nevertheless, as argued in the chapter by Jungar and Oinas, certain types of HIV/AIDS prevention research support and maintain prevailing gender stereotypes and power relations. This is the case for example regarding the medical media pet project, which is the focus of their critical analysis: male circumcision as AIDS prevention. Jungar and Oinas show a) that the scientific evidence backing the connection between male circumcision and HIV/AIDS prevention is shaky, to say the least, and b) that, in fact, if taken seriously this 'prevention strategy' would have very negative consequences for women: "If circumcision were seen as a way of prevention, it would probably decrease women's possibility to negotiate safe sex. ... The real risk for women is that medical 'knowledge' of the protective effects of male circumcision may lead to neglect of other prevention measures." The male circumcision debate, Jungar and Oinas conclude, seems more involved in reproducing imagery on 'African sexuality' than in envisioning actual change.

Seen from women's points of view—as also pointed out by Jungar and Oinas—HIV/AIDS research and feminist theory share conceptual interests, regarding challenging gender stereotypes and identification and change of gender power relations. There is a correlation between high rates of HIV/AIDS infection and women's lack of *bedroom power*: "If more women have the power to 'say no' to unwanted and unsafe sex, the HIV infection rate would dramatically decline in Africa" (Machera, this volume). Thus the HIV/AIDS pandemic may be seen as an opportunity to focus discussions on sexuality in the context of gender power relations. According to a report from a colloquium in Durban in 2002 HIV/AIDS may be regarded "as an opportunity to work with young people on the basis of their self-knowledge, and towards achieving a range of goals—from better health to better relationships and more confident adulthood. ... Prevention of the spread of HIV can only be achieved through greater de facto gender equality" (Burns 2002:6–7). Along these lines HIV/AIDS may be conceived as a key feminist issue (cf. Jungar and Oinas, this volume).

Female militancy or 'culture of silence'?

Historical evidence exists regarding African women's militant action against colonial oppression and patriarchal power (cf. Kolawole, this volume) as well as against sexual insults from men. Based on data from Cameroon in the 1950s, Shirley Ardener (1975) has described how women collectively would confront a male offender, singing abusive songs accompanied by obscene gestures. Machera supports this kind of evidence with data from her native Kenya, where "a form of curse employed by women involved deliberate exhibition of their private parts towards the person being cursed." Similar stories are told by Susanna Yene Awasom from contemporary Cameroon, where in the early 1990s a group of postmenopausal women were fighting government troops by raising their dresses high in the air, and holding out their old women's breasts towards the soldiers as if to fire bullets from them:

> These octogenarian women were believed to possess potent mystical powers because of their sex and age. As women who had brought life, it was believed that they could use these very reproductive organs to curse and terminate lives (Awasom 2002:5).

The contrast between on one hand these kinds of stories from various parts of Africa, of female genitals seen as sources of power, fear and awe, and on the other hand present-day conceptions of female genital organs as invisible and unmentionable (cf. Machera's chapter) is striking. A speculation regarding the importance of missionary interventions in this context does not seem far-fetched. Likewise Christianity might be an active factor in the so-called 'culture of silence' regarding African women in general and African women's sexuality in particular (cf. Arnfred's and Kolawole's chapters).

Kolawole sets out to contest and divert this notion of 'culture of silence', in this endeavour drawing on a long list of African women writers and theorists. Convincingly she shows that African feminist (or womanist) thought has developed significantly through African (women) writers' works of fiction:

> Many African women literary writers and critics have emerged as gender theorists. ... It is remarkable that many of the theorists who are attempting to re-conceptualize gender in Africa do so through a double approach, in creative writing as well as in theoretical propositions (Kolawole, this volume).

This also points to a certain approach in investigations of gender power relations in Africa, Kolawole's own emphasis being on analysis of "myths, proverbs, anecdotes and folktales", the rationale being that these shape the mind-set of men and women. Thus the *interpretations* of myths and proverbs, folktales and customs are seen as arenas of gender struggle: patriarchal interpretations must be contested; feminist understandings of proverbs, customs, history do not emerge on their own: they must be constructed, maintained and fought for. The aim of this volume is to contribute to this struggle.

References

Amadiume, Ifi, 1997, *Reinventing Africa. Matriarchy, Religion and Culture*. London: Zed Books.

Ardener, Shirley, 1975, "Sexual Insult and Female Militancy", in S. Ardener (ed.), *Perceiving Women*. New York: John Wiley and Sons.

Arnfred, Signe, 1988, "Women in Mozambique: Gender Struggle and Gender Politics", *Review of African Political Economy* 41.

Arnfred, Signe, 1990, "Notes on Gender and Modernization. Examples from Mozambique", in A. W. Bentzon (ed.), *The Language of Development Studies*. Copenhagen: New Social Science Monographs.

Arnfred, Signe, 2001, "Ancestral Spirits, Land and Food: Gendered Power and Land Tenure in Ribáué, Nampula Province", in R. Waterhouse and C. Vijfhuizen (eds), *Strategic Women, Gainful Men. Gender, Land and Natural Resources in Different Rural Contexts in Mozambique*. Maputo, Mozambique: Universidade Eduardo Mondlane.

Arnfred, Signe, 2003, "Contested Construction of Female Sexualities: Meanings and Interpretations of Initiation Rituals". Paper presented at the *Sex & Secrecy Conference*, Johannesburg, 22–25 June 2003.

Awasom, Susanna Yene, 2002, "A Critical Survey of the Resuscitation, Activation and Adaptation of Traditional African Political Institutions to the Exigencies of Modern Politics in the 1990s: The Case of the Takumbeng Female Society in Cameroon". Paper presented at CODESRIA General Assembly, Kampala, 2002.

Beauvoir, Simone de, 1949/1997, *The Second Sex*. London: Vintage.

Becker, Heike, 2003, "Imagining tradition and modernity. Sexuality and gender in southern African academic and popular discourse". Paper presented at the Sex & Secrecy Conference in Johannesburg, 22–25 June 2003.

Blackwood, Evelyn and Saskia Wieringa (eds), 1999, *Female Desires: Transgender Practices across Cultures.* Columbia University Press.

Burns, Catherine, 2002, "A commentary on the colloquium Instituting Gender Equality in Schools: Working in an HIV/AIDS environment", *Agenda* 53, 2002.

Butler, Judith, 1990, *Gender Trouble.* London and New York: Routledge.

Butler, Judith, 1993, *Bodies That Matter.* London and New York: Routledge.

Caldwell, John et al., 1989, "The Social Context of AIDS in Sub-Saharan Africa", *Population and Development Review,* vol. 15, no 2.

Commission on Gender Equality (CGE), 2000, Report: "Consultative Conference on Virginity Testing, Richards Bay, 12–14 June 2000". www.cge.org.za (accessed in 2003).

Cott, Nancy, 1978, "Passionlessness: An Interpretation of Victorian Sexual Ideology 1790–1850", *Signs: Journal of Women in Culture and Society, vol. 4 (*winter).

Delius, Peter and Clive Glaser, 2002, "Sexual Socialization in South Africa: a Historical Perspective", *African Studies,* vol. 61, no. 1.

Delius, Peter and Clive Glaser, 2003, "The myth of polygamy: A history of extra-marital and multi-partnership sex in South Africa". Paper presented at the *Sex & Secrecy Conference,* Johannesburg, 22–25 June 2003.

Dunton, Chris and Mai Palmberg, 1996, *Human Rights and Homosexuality in Southern Africa.* Current African Issues No. 19. Uppsala: Nordiska Afrikainstitutet.

Falk, Kurt, 1925–1926, "Homosexuality among the Natives of South-West Africa", in Murray, Stephen O. and Will Roscoe (eds), 1998, *Boy-Wives and Female Husbands: Studies of African Homosexualities.* New York: St Martin's Press.

Fanon, Frantz, 1952/1986, *Black Skin, White Masks.* London: Pluto Press.

Geffray, Christian, 1990, *Ni père ni mère—critique de la parenté: le cas makhuwa.* Paris: Seuil.

Guy, Jeff, 1987, "Analysing Pre-Capitalist Societies in Southern Africa", *Journal of Southern African Studies,* vol. 14, no. 1.

Guy, Jeff, 1990, Gender oppression in southern Africa's pre-capitalist societies, in Walker, Cherryl (ed.), *Women and Gender in Southern Africa to 1945.* London: James Currey.

Guyer, Jane, 1994, "Lineal Identities and Lateral Networks: The Logic of Polyandrous Motherhood", in Bledsoe and Pison (eds), *Nuptiality in Sub-Saharan Africa. Contemporary Anthropological and Demographic Perspectives.* Oxford: Clarendon Press.

Helle-Valle, Jo, 1999, "Sexual mores, promiscuity and 'prostitution' in Botswana", *Ethnos,* vol. 64, no. 3.

Helle-Valle, Jo and Aud Talle, 2000, "Moral, marked og penger: Komparative refleksjoner over kvinner og sex i to afrikanske lokaliteter", *Norsk Antropologisk Tidsskrift,* vol. 11, no. 3.

Hoad, Neville, 2003, "Race, Desire and Voyeurism: Thabo Mbeki and Mark Behr on the libidinal economy of the South African nation, old and new". Paper presented at the *Sex & Secrecy Conference,* Johannesburg, 22–25 June 2003.

Hobsbawn, Eric and Terence Ranger (eds), 1983, *The Invention of Tradition,* Cambridge University Press.

Hunter, Marc, 2002, "The Materiality of Everyday Sex: Thinking beyond 'prostitution'", *African Studies,* vol. 61, no. 1.

Hunter, Marc, 2003, "Masculinities and multiple-partners in Kwa-Zulu Natal: The Making and Un-making of Isoka". Paper presented at the *Sex & Secrecy Conference,* Johannesburg, 22–25 June 2003.

Kendall, [Kathryn], 1999, "Women in Lesotho and the (Western) Construction of Homophobia," in E. Blackwood and S. Wieringa (eds), *Female Desires: Transgender Practices across Cultures.* Columbia University Press.

Kolawole, Mary, 1997, *Womanism and African Consciousness.* Trenton, New Jersey: Africa World Press.

Leclerc-Madlala, Suzanne, 2001, "Virginity Testing: Managing Sexuality in a Maturing HIV/AIDS Epidemic", *Medical Anthropology Quarterly*, vol. 15, no. 4.

Leclerc-Madlala, Suzanne, 2003, "Protecting Girlhood? Virginity revivals in the era of AIDS", *Agenda*, vol. 56.

Mbeki, Thabo, 1999, Speech at the Launch of the African Renaissance Institute, Pretoria, Oct. 11, 1999. www.anc.org.za/ancdocs/history/mbeki (accessed in 2003).

Mbeki, Thabo, 2001a, Speech at the Opening of the NGO Forum of the World Conference against Racism, Durban, 28 August 2001. www.anc.org.za/ancdocs/history/mbeki (accessed in 2003).

Mbeki, Thabo, 2001b, Address at the Inaugural ZK Matthews Memorial Lecture, University of Fort Hare, 12 October, 2001. www.anc.org.za/ancdocs/history/mbeki (accessed in 2003).

Mbeki, Thabo, 2002, Speech at the Funeral of Sarah Bartmann, 9 August 2002. www.anc.org.za/ancdocs/history/mbeki (accessed in 2003).

Mernissi, Fatema, 1975, *Beyond the Veil: Male-Female Dynamics in Muslim Society*. London: Al Saqi Books.

Mernissi, Fatema, 2001, *Scheherazade Goes West*. New York: Washington Square Press.

Mohanty, Chandra Talpade, 1986/1991, "Under Western Eyes: Feminist Scholarship and Colonial Discourses", in Mohanty et al. (eds), *Third World Women and the Politics of Feminism*. Indiana University Press.

Mohanty, Chandra Talpade, 2002, "'Under Western Eyes' Revisited: Feminist Solidarity through Anticapitalist Struggles", *Signs*, vol. 28, no. 2.

Moodie, T. Dunbar, 2001, "Black Migrant Mine Labourers and the Vicissitudes of Male Desire", in Morrell, Robert (ed.), *Changing Men in Southern Africa*. London: Zed Books.

Murray, Stephen O. and Will Roscoe, 1998, "Diversity and Identity: The Challenge of African Homosexualities", in Murray, Stephen O. and Will Roscoe (eds), 1998, *Boy-Wives and Female Husbands. Studies of African Homosexualities*. New York: St Martin's Press.

Murray, Stephen O. and Will Roscoe (eds), 1998, *Boy-Wives and Female Husband: Studies of African Homosexualities*. New York: St Martin's Press.

Naamane-Guessous, Soumaya, 1997, *Au-delà de toute pudeur: la sexualité féminine au Maroc*. Casablanca: Éditions Eddif.

Oyewùmí, Oyèrónké, 1997, *The Invention of Women: Making an African Sense of Western Gender Discourse*. Minneapolis and London: University of Minnesota Press.

Oyewùmí, Oyèrónké, 2000, "Family Bonds/Conceptual Binds: African Notes on Feminist Epistemologies", *Signs, vol.* 25, no. 4.

Oyewùmí, Oyèrónké, 2002, "Conceptualizing Gender: The Eurocentric Foundations of Feminist Concepts and the Challenge of African Epistemologies", *Jenda: A Journal of Culture and African Women Studies, vol.* 2, no. 1.

Peters, Pauline E., 1997, "Introduction", *Critique of Anthropology,* vol. 7, no. 2.

Ratele, Kopano, 1998, "Relating to Whiteness: Writing about the black man", *Psychology Bulletin,* vol 8 no 2, University of the Western Cape.

Walker, Cherryl, 1995, "Conceptualising Motherhood in Twentieth Century South Africa", *Journal of Southern African Studies*, vol 21, no 3.

Wekker, Gloria, 1999, "'What's Identity Got to Do with It?' Rethinking Identity in the Light of the *Mati* Work in Suriname", in Blackwood, Evelyn and Saskia Wieringa (eds), 1999, *Female Desires. Transgender Practices Across Cultures*. Columbia University Press.

Wekker, Gloria, 1997, "One Finger Does Not Drink Okra Soup: Afro-Surinamese Women and Critical Agency", in Alexander, Jacqui M and Chandra Talpade Mohanty (eds), *Feminist Genealogies, Colonial Legacies, Democratic Futures*. New York and London: Routledge.

World Health Organization (WHO), 1998, *Female Genital Mutilation: An Overview*. Geneva: World Health Organization Publications. http://www.int/dsa/cat98/fgmbook.htm (accessed in 2003).

Under Western Eyes

Photo: El Hadj Tidjan Shitou, 19?

1. *Efundula:* Women's Initiation, Gender and Sexual Identities in Colonial and Post-Colonial Northern Namibia

Heike Becker[1]

Introduction

In the early 1990s I, together with colleagues, carried out research into 'customary' marriage in Owambo, northern Namibia.[2] In the course of the research, we were told by a large number of local residents that getting married was primarily a matter of Christian rites. However, many also spoke freely about 'customary' aspects of marriage, such as the wedding gift, *oyonda*, and its part in establishing a valid marriage. Contrary to this, other aspects of what established a 'traditional' marriage were conspicuously absent from people's representations. This was curious. Missionaries, colonial officials and anthropologists who had worked in Owambo from the late 19th century through to the 1960s had emphasised the outstanding cultural significance of young women's combined initiation *cum* wedding group rites. Now, none of our informants made even the most cursory mention of it. This profound silence puzzled me. I wondered, what had happened to initiation. Did it still take place?

In 1995, I enquired of several friends and colleagues who had grown up in Owambo at different times from the 1940s through to the 1970s whether women's initiation was still practised. Some of these women and men had left Namibia for exile in the early 1970s; others had spent most of their life in their home area and had migrated to Windhoek only in the 1990s. None of them, however, felt competent to answer my question. While some suggested that the continuing practice of initiation was unlikely because "today we are all Christians", others thought that it might still be conducted, but that this happened only in very remote areas or across the border in Angola, in other words, in areas that northern Namibian residents commonly regard as 'the bush'.

---

1. This chapter has benefited substantially from comments on an earlier draft made by the participants of the conference "Contexts of Gender in Africa", 21–24 February 2002, Uppsala, Sweden; and during the University of Cape Town/University of the Western Cape Joint Anthropology Seminar, 28 February 2002.
2. This commissioned study was carried out under the auspices of a collection of local and international research and development Non-Governmental Organisations (cf. NDT & CASS 1994; Becker and Hinz 1995).

It came as a surprise, therefore, when in early 1996 the national television channel screened a half-hour programme on a recently held *efundula*.[1] The TV programme (Carstens 1996) recorded the preparation of the ceremony, the performance of dances, songs and specific ritual practices, as well as interviews with some initiates and the ritual leader, an elderly man. The next surprise came when I prepared for field research later in 1996. Some of the very people who had said earlier that they did not know whether the ceremonies were still held now informed me that in recent weeks they had heard announcements over the Namibian Broadcasting Company's (NBC) oshiWambo radio service that *omafundula* were to take place in different areas of Oukwanyama, the most populous of the Owambo districts that straddles the Namibian-Angolan border.

This was even more puzzling: initiation ceremonies undoubtedly took place regularly as public events. And yet, so many Owambo friends had pleaded ignorance when I had asked them about initiation. These apparent contradictions raised a set of questions concerning the shifting, multiple representations of culture, gender and sexuality in colonial and postcolonial Namibia. Revisiting the shifting and seemingly contradictory representations of women's initiation during the colonial and postcolonial eras provided an opportunity to rethink the gendered reconstruction and re-appropriation of such cultural spaces as are tied in with the evocation of sexuality. Furthermore, it allowed the questions to be asked of how local identities and identity politics have rested, and continue to rest, on shifting constructions of gender.[2]

Representing 'African sexuality'

Following Richard Werbner and Terence Ranger's argument that we need to look to the *longue durée* in the study of the dynamic complexity of postcolonial African societies (Werbner and Ranger 1996), I suggest that studies of the gendered constructions of culture and sexuality in postcolonial, and this includes postapartheid, southern Africa require an approach that acknowledges that the colonial society's dynamics continue to shape postcolonial society. Sexuality and gender are

1. *Efundula* (pl. *omafundula*) is currently used in Namibian discourse as the generic term for Owambo women's initiation. More precisely, it is known as *efundula* in Oukwanyama, *ohango* in Ondonga and Uukwambi, and *olufuko* in most parts of western Owambo.
2. The chapter draws on field research on various occasions from 1996 through to 1999, on archival research at the Vereinigte Evangelische Mission archives in Wuppertal, Germany and at the ELCIN (Evangelical Lutheran Church in Namibia) Leonard Auala archives in Oniipa in January and May 1999 respectively, and on the analysis of ethnographic and documentary film. The field research was assisted by Nangula Amoonga and Natangwe Shapange in 1996, by Piteimo Hainyanyula in 1997, Penoshinge Shililifa in 1998, and Monica Kalondo in 1999, to whom many thanks are due. The 1996 research was carried out jointly with Patricia Hayes. Nepeti Nicanor transcribed and translated the interviews recorded in 1996; transcriptions and translations of the later research were done by Piteimo Hainyanyula, Monica Kalondo, Sacky Shanghala and Penoshinge Shililifa. Research was supported by the Sonderforschungsbereich 389 'Kultur- und Landschaftswandel im ariden Afrika, Entwicklungsprozesse unter ökologischen Grenzbedingungen', University of Cologne in 1996, by the Swedish International Development Agency in 1997, the Department for Cooperation and Cultural Affairs of the French Embassy to Namibia in 1998, and the Ford Foundation in 1999.

prominent among a plurality of contested arenas where it would be inappropriate to assume a break between the colonial past and postcolonial present.

In a range of recent publications on 'black' and 'white' sexualities and colonialism, anthropologists and historians such as Ann Laura Stoler, Sander Gilman and Megan Vaughan have shown how colonial discourses constructed the colonised's sexualities as the opposite to the 'civilised' cultural identity of the colonisers (cf. Gilman 1985; Stoler 1997; Vaughan 1991). The notion of 'African sexuality' as unitary, coherent and different, served as a pivotal point in how Europeans viewed the indigenous 'Other'. As has been pointed out by this body of literature, African sexuality, and indeed Africans themselves, allegedly diseased, primitive, uncontrolled and excessive, came to represent the darkness and dangers of the continent.

However, there was not just one colonial discourse on African sexuality; instead, there were at least two variations on the theme as Megan Vaughan has pointed out (Vaughan 1991:129). For some, particularly the missions, African sexuality was, and had always been, 'primitive', uncontrolled and excessive, and as such it represented the darkness and dangers of the continent. For others, including colonial officials, precolonial African sexuality had been 'innocent', and the danger lay rather in the degeneration of this sexuality which was seen as having come about through social and economic changes caused by external forces.

In spite of their different angles, both perspectives concurred that African sexuality was essentially 'other', namely, that it belonged to the realm of nature. In both views Africans and their sexuality were savage; at issue was merely whether African sexuality was of the noble or the ignoble savage variety. Their protagonists agreed that it had to be contained. But how this should be done developed into a major controversy. To the missions, excessive African sexuality was to be restrained as a salient element of their 'civilising mission' project. For the colonial state, on the other hand, the containment of African sexuality emerged as a concern of gendering mobility and control. Scholars of gender and colonial state formation in southern Africa have argued that 'African women' emerged from the often obscured gendered and gendering process of colonial state formation as objects of rule in a specific way. Studies from South Africa and Namibia have shown how state policy and practices constructed 'women' by reproducing and reshaping meanings of gender and culture (cf. Manicom 1992; Hayes 1998b). Central to this colonial discourse and practice was the reconstructed realm of 'tradition', in which, as in the Owambo case, rituals to define and legitimise female sexuality and fertility assumed centrality. In the present chapter I am thus much concerned with how in Owambo internal tensions of the colonisers revolved around the discursive and practical conflicts about women's initiation.

Sander Gilman (1985:83) has famously argued that in 19th century literary discourse, "the black female [came] ... to serve as an icon for black sexuality in general". On the other hand, it appears that the colonial state's controlling engagement with male and female sexualities was uneven. In different times and spaces the focus was variously on either male or female 'natives' as the peril to white sexual and reproductive health.[1] I argue that divergent discourses on the gendered sexualities of the indigenous population were thus central to the most basic tension of empire, namely that the Otherness of colonized persons was neither inherent nor stable; their difference had to be continuously redefined and maintained. As Ann Stoler and Frederick Cooper have elaborated, the designation of 'nature' and 'culture' took a major part in this enterprise:

> Social boundaries that were at one point clear would not necessarily remain so. In pursuing a 'civilizing mission' designed to make colonized populations into disciplined agriculturalists or workers and obedient subjects of a bureaucratic state, colonial states opened up a discourse on the question of just how much 'civilizing' would promote their projects and what sorts of political consequences 'too much civilizing' would have in store (Stoler and Cooper 1997:7).

Stoler and Cooper (1997:7) have raised concerns that few anthropologists and historians of colonialism have analysed the repercussions of these shifting categories in the mundane spaces of everyday life. Work such as the Comaroffs' on colonialism and modernity on the South African frontier (Comaroff and Comaroff, 1991; 1992; 1997) has begun to point out the instability of the colonial encounter in social spaces, such as domesticity. How they are related to the colonial constructions of gender and sexual identities, and the improvising strategies of their postcolonial refashioning, still remains a challenge.

I have argued elsewhere for more attention to everyday life, and gender relations and sexuality within it, when examining processes of culture, power and hegemony, and indeed the refashioning of identities and cultural memory in the postcolonial situation (Becker 2001). In the postcolonial as in the colonial situation, the question presents itself as to which forms of gender and sexual identities are audible, as opposed to merely visible. In other words, which, and whose, voices can make themselves heard in the gendered and gendering cultural discourse? What are the gendered and gendering meanings of the silences around women's initiation? What are the gendered and gendering meanings around its ostensibly contradictory public presence, as exemplified in a prime time national TV programme?

These are some of the questions I engage when discussing the postcolonial situation where women's initiation is still controversial. The forms these contestations take differ from the colonial to the postcolonial periods, however. Variations of cultural memory, and contrasting meanings of *efundula* are being invoked in the realms of local and national postcolonial public culture by different people. The postcolonial variations present at once continuities and discontinuities of earlier discourses with respect to the trope of African ('traditional') sexuality and gendered local practices. The present cultural discourses are refashioned by the material conditions and cultural representations of postcolonial Namibian society, situated within an increasingly globalising world. I thus suggest that distinct

---

1.   Megan Vaughan (1991:21) argues that in British colonial medical discourse *male* African sexuality became a signifier for 'the African', although female sexuality became an object of concern and control at specific moments, in particular in the debate on sexually transmitted diseases. Marion Wallace (1998), and Lynette Jackson in a presentation at the 2001 African Studies Association meeting in Houston/Texas, have shown attempts at subjecting African women to compulsory examinations for STDs in colonial Namibia and Zimbabwe respectively.

representations of *efundula* have been invoked by different sections of the Owambo population in attempts to affirm claims to hegemonic defining power over local and national, gendered public culture.[1]

Numerous recent studies, such as Cooper and Stoler (1997), have shown that colonialism was not a stable model, but subject to multiple internal tensions. Images of gender and sexuality were no exception to this. However, thus far the consequences of the contested colonial sexual and gender imagery for the colonised has been given precious little attention. While the 'new' colonialism studies have shed important new light on the sexual and gender politics of imperial cultures in metropolitan Europe and the colonies, I suggest that we need to turn and take a fresh look at the forms the refashioning of gender and sexual identities took among the colonised. The studies of 'European' gender identities and forms of sexual control in the colonies and in the centres of empire have demonstrated that, in all its contested forms, the very representation of colonial power rested on prior constructions of gender power. How then did the contested imperial authority and colonial mission, based on such prior constructions, reshape local gender and sexual identities? What about the agency of colonial subjects: which constructions of gendered sexualities did Africans appropriate in specific situations, which did they appropriate piecemeal, and which did they, perhaps, reject outright?

The ethnography of *efundula*

Cross-cultural surveys indicate that 50 to 60 per cent of societies initiate girls, compared to 30 to 40 per cent that initiate boys (quoted in Geisler 1997:125). A certain connection between matriliny and women's initiation as cultural practice seems a possibility, as Audrey Richards (1982:160, 172, 185) noted, although the correlation is certainly not a direct one. There is insufficient basis for conclusive comparative studies, as anthropological studies of women's initiation are a rarity.[2]

The following overview of ethnographic information on Owambo women's initiation relies on a variety of published and unpublished sources from the colonial era, written by colonial administrators, missionaries and, in the later period (1940s to 1960s), the odd South African or American trained anthropologist. As a rule, these observers were partial adherents to the notion of the otherness of African sexuality. This is especially the case with the mission-based texts, but also

---

1. I understand public culture in this context broadly as cultural strategies aimed at pulling local, national and, potentially, transnational communities together.
2. Audrey Richards' dense text on a 1931 girl's initiation among the Bemba is still an outstanding example (Richards 1982). Victor Turner (1967; 1969) has partly drawn on Ndembu female initiation in his writings on ritual. More recent are Corinne Kratz's work on ritual efficacy in Okiek women's initiation in Kenya (1994), and Signe Arnfred's on Mozambique (1990).

applies to the written and visual ethnographic *oeuvre* of the native commissioner cum self-styled ethnographic authority C.H.L. ('Cocky') Hahn.[1]

The colonial era ethnographies are typified by their stasis in space and time. Most published sources only depict the eastern Owambo communities of Oukwanyama and Ondonga, in spite of their authors' claims that they had for their subject 'the Owambo' in general (e.g. Hahn 1928). There is not sufficient space here to deconstruct the representation of a uniform Owambo culture, although this has a definite bearing on current representations of initiation.[2] Contrary to the assumption of cultural uniformity in the colonial ethnography of Owambo, women's initiation rites were and are subject to enormous variation in detail and duration. There is thus a need to cautiously depict what happened in different places and at different times as alterations in ceremonial style and practice affect songs and costumes, ritual roles and ritual events, and, in effect, cultural meaning and understanding. None of this is reflected in the ethnographic representations that, therefore, need to be read with caution.

Owambo women's initiation was, first of all, a rite of social maturation. It publicly transformed the initiates, denominated 'brides' (*aafuko* in oshiNdonga, ovafuko in oshiKwanyama), into adults, completing them with the essential attributes of their new status. In the past these attributes included the attire and hairstyle of an adult woman. What is most important, after having passed through the ceremony a young woman could give birth legitimately, because she was regarded as a married woman (oshiNonga: *omukulukadhi*; oshiKwanyama: *omukadi*) even if she did not have a husband immediately thereafter. Ethnographic sources stress that a young woman who fell pregnant before she had undergone the initiation, and was thus regarded as a 'girl' (*omukadhona*), was burnt to death in most precolonial Owambo communities (Louw 1967:31, 42 on Ongandjera; Tuupainen 1970:47 on Ondonga; Loeb 1962:240 on Oukwanyama). The *efundula, ohango* or *olufuko* ceremonies were thus the cornerstones of legitimising female sexuality and reproduction.

It appears that, secondly, the rites were meant to enhance fertility (Williams 1991:110; Tuupainen 1970:50–51). This aspect was especially highlighted by the Powell-Cottons, as Gwyneth Davies has emphasised in her thesis based on the sisters' *oeuvre* (Davies 1987:102–103). Davies further argues that the *efundula* provided a context for teaching and instruction. The rites and stages of the initiation expressed a reiteration of social knowledge on appropriate gender roles. Through participating in the *efundula*, the initiates experienced the society's views towards such knowledge (Davies 1987:85–86).

---

1. Patricia Hayes has critically appraised Hahn's photography in general, and his visual narratives of initiation in particular (Hayes 1998a). An exception among the Owambo ethnography is the work by British sisters Diana and Antoinette Powell-Cotton, who observed and filmed a Kwanyama *efundula* in southern Angola in 1937. A recent analysis of their work commended that they had made a remarkable effort for their time, "a genuine and successful attempt at studying women as active members of society and not merely as passive observers or even sex objects" (Davies 1987, 7).

2. It should particularly be taken into account that there is a definite lack of relevant ethnographic accounts of western Owambo. Nothing has been written on initiation in the West that is not in either Oshiwambo or Finnish. I am grateful to Meredith McKittrick (1999) for alerting me to this point.

While most authors described the rites as initiation ceremonies, which precede the actual marriage (cf. Tuupainen 1970:53), the Kwanyama *efundula* has also been dubbed a 'group-marriage ceremony' (Loeb 1962:34). Nubility, if not the actual nuptials, is central to the meaning Owambo attach to it today, when commonly translating *efundula* as 'traditional wedding'. It is possible that the meaning of the ceremony encompassed the notion of marriage in Oukwanyama, where no elaborate marriage ceremonies took place after the *efundula*, and the young wife rather unceremoniously went to live with her husband soon after the ceremony (Tönjes 1911:143; Tuupainen 1970:57). Certain parts of the Kwanyama *efundula*, moreover, involved the initiate's future husband, who ritually 'proposed' during the ceremony, which has been described as 'symbolic engagement' (Bruwer 1959:119). On the other hand, the *ohango* in Ondonga was possibly not understood as 'marriage' proper, as the initiation was followed by specific individual marriage ceremonies conducted afterwards (Hahn 1928:32; Tuupainen 1970:56–57). It thus appears that the meanings attached to women's initiation may have varied over time and space.

Different forms of political and ritual power, and their gendered embodiment, require a closer examination. It appears that generally the kings decided the date of commencement of a cycle of initiation rites. The actual impact of the ruler remains unclear, however; Native Commissioner Hahn greatly stressed the role of the king (Hahn 1928:29); he may have overemphasised this for reasons of his own, however, as I discuss below (see: *Lining up bare-breasted maidens*). Missionaries usually accorded the kings a far less prominent part in the ceremony (cf. Tönjes 1911:135–36; Estermann 1976:70–72). The rites were directed by a ritual leader (*namunganga* in oshiNdonga, *omupitifi* in oshiKwanyama). Most of the older ethnographies depict the ritual leadership as a male prerogative. Hahn (1928:29) and Tuupainen (1970:46) noted that in Ondonga the ceremony involved one male and one female ritual leader; however, they described the male *namunganga* as the 'master of ceremonies', whereas the female's part was depicted as that of an assistant. For Oukwanyama, Tönjes (1911:139), Bruwer (1959:118) and Loeb (1962:246) all emphasised that *ovapitifi* were invariably old, circumcised men. Since male circumcision in Oukwanyama as with most other Owambo polities had ceased during the 19th century, *ovapitifi* were invited from those areas where male circumcision was still practised, and by the early twentieth century those were all in Angola. In contrast to the hegemonic depiction of exclusively male ritual leadership, Gwyneth Davies, drawing on the Powell-Cottons' 1930s research, noted that a woman might also direct an *efundula* if she was the daughter of a circumcised man (Davies 1987:109).

The ethnographic emphasis on male ritual leadership is indeed curious. Present-day informants in Oukwanyama have pressed home the point that the position of *omupitifi*, often combined with that of a healer (*onganga*) has been passed on 'for generations', as some stressed, from either a mother or a father to either a son or daughter. Gender appears to be largely irrelevant, if this is indeed the case. Instead, the selection of a ritual leader seems to have been based on certain ritual 'tests' that the member of the younger generation had to pass.[1] While the ethnographic silence about female ritual leaders may be partly due to the colonial omission and outright non-recognition of women, who were regarded as an anomaly in any positions of power, it may also be more in line with an overly hetero-sexualised presentation of these ceremonies, especially by the Christian missionaries, whose allegations include practices such as ritual masturbation and the 'doctoring' of millet beer with semen (cf. Tuupainen 1970:48).

Transitional periods of about six to eight weeks in Oukwanyama, or even three to four months in northwestern Owambo followed the rites in the first half of the 20th century. During this "period of social freedom" (Bruwer 1959:119) the initiates were known as *oihanangolo* ('white things', as they were smeared with white clay and ashes), or as *ovamati* (boys). This ritual stage encompassed gender inversion, where the young women temporarily moved into 'male' roles. They assumed the names of great warriors, and were regarded as being possessed by the spirits of their namesakes. Armed with knobkerries, and accompanied by prepubescent girls (*omufundifi*) they moved freely throughout the country. The *oihanangolo* were entitled to whatever food they found during their wanderings, and could mock at, and beat every man they encountered. According to oral sources, this included their (future) husbands, who received beatings as well, and were made to dance as 'women' before their brides.[2] Estermann, a Roman Catholic missionary who lived among the Kwanyama on the Angolan side of the colonial border for many years during the first half of the 20th century, recorded a proverbial expression that exemplifies the privileges enjoyed by the young women during that stage, '*omunu utoka kena osidila*'. This literally translated means, 'to a white person'—so called because of being powdered with white ashes—'nothing is prohibited' (Estermann 1976:72).

When we read against the grain of the colonial-era ethnographies, it emerges that the rites were marked by enormous fluidity in form and meaning, contrary to the cultural and temporal stasis suggested by most ethnographic texts. It remains particularly doubtful that the meanings officials and missionaries from the earlier colonial periods ascribed to the women's initiation truly reflected Owambo motives. In both cases, and also extending to the small number of professional anthropologists such as the conservative American Loeb and the South African *volkekundiges* of the later period, such as Bruwer and Louw, ethnographers drew their information generally from a minuscule selection of the local population, namely, older elite men, preferably with a background of authority. The views of women, and particularly those of young women, were certainly not sought.[3]

---

1. Interviews; Evaristus Amweelo, 12.12.1996, Ondjondjo; Fransina Kuutondokwa, 12.12.1996, Omusheshe; Peyavali Naliende, 14.12.1996, Omatunda; Haikali Hamunyela, 16.12.1996, Ongha; Ester Kashikuko kaNande, 17.12.1996, Onengali. In western Owambo, women seem to have been the main leaders of initiation (Meredith McKittrick, personal communication).
2. Interviews; Julia Mbida, 16.12.1996, Odibo; Ester Kashikuko kaNande, 17.12.1996, Onengali.
3. Only Diana and Antoinette Powell-Cotton were apparently more sensitive to androcentrism and sexism (cf. Davies 1987:6–7).

Between 'tribe' and church: Women's initiation and the tensions of colonialism

Efundula, ohango or *olufuko* became fiercely contested when women's mobility and sexuality evolved into major issues in the altercations between the male triad of missions, colonial administration and Owambo authority. A battle over patriarchal control of women marked the early decades of colonialism in Ovamboland[1]. In northern Namibia, as elsewhere in the colonial world, struggles over the redistribution of power between heterogeneous groups of colonisers and colonised men tended to take the shape of conflicts surrounding the control of women's labour, mobility, and sexuality (cf. Becker 1995:38–40). These contestations commonly found the colonial administration and male Owambo traditionalists and authorities in the same camp, while they were often at loggerheads with the Christian missions as the third player in the field of colonial sexual and gender politics.

Lining up bare-breasted maidens: Colonial representations of *efundula*

Megan Vaughan (1991:130) reminds us that in the colonial state's dominant discourse on African sexuality, women's sexuality was to be contained by means of social control and order, represented by African men in the name of 'tradition'. She argues that the containment of women's sexuality was regarded as one measure of the effectiveness of an indirect rule policy in shoring up existing systems of social control. In northern Namibia, the South African administration from its inception in 1915 sought to rule indirectly through the embodiments of African power: chiefs and headmen. Official recognition of indigenous rulers was combined with interventions where the administration deemed this fit. The colonial administration backed Owambo political authorities in their conflicts with the Christian missions that had been working in Owambo since 1870. Longtime Native Commissioner C.H.L. Hahn argued that in Ondonga the Lutheran Finnish Mission had "practically destroyed the authority of chiefs and headmen; so much so that little tribal discipline is left."[2]

In the contestations between the administration and its male traditionalist allies versus the missions, *efundula* representations procured a place centre-stage. The former argued that the initiation rites were cornerstones of healthy, 'tribal' traditions that should be preserved. This discourse bolstered the paradigm of indirect rule. It also fed well into Owambo traditionalists' efforts to tighten control over their subjects. Women were thus assigned the role of bearers of culture in the administration and their allies' efforts to guarantee a redefined 'traditional' order in the colonial society. While Owambo women were silenced in the structures of local power where at least certain elite women had made their voices heard prior to colonial rule, they acquired a new form of muted visibility.

1. I refer to the area as Owambo unless specified contexts require the colonial designation, Ovamboland.
2. NAN, NAO Vol 13 6/2/5, NC Ovamboland - Secretary SWA, 27.8.1935, cited in: Hayes 1992:303.

Native Commissioner C.H.L. Hahn's written and visual ethnographic narratives of initiation pertained crucially to the discursive reconstruction of a patriarchal and hierarchical Owambo 'tradition'. Hahn loved to attend and take pictures at the ceremonies. In the event, residents occasionally had to reschedule or repeat their *efundula* dances to coincide with his visits.[1] Hahn's photography underscores the representation of initiation as a massive event close to the core of indigenous power that already has a strong presence in his ethnographic writing (cf. Hahn 1928:29–31). The ostentatious glamour of his photographic *efundula* representations becomes even more obvious when we consider the striking contrast between his visual narratives and the film the Powell-Cottons made on an *efundula* which took place in the district of Owangwe in southern Angola in July 1937, (Powell-Cotton and Powell-Cotton 1937); that is, roughly about the same time Hahn took his pictures on the Namibian side of the border. The Powell-Cottons' filmic narrative of a ceremony that involved four young women presents a modest ritual in an intimate environment; it strongly contrasts with Hahn's images of large numbers of *ovafuko* participating in a dazzling, public event.

Hahn's glamourisation of the ceremonies was much in line with his representation of the rites as determined and authorised by 'native authorities' (cf. Hahn 1928:29–31). His rule in Ovamboland built on social control and order, represented by African men in the name of 'tradition'. Patricia Hayes has argued that Hahn's ethnographic photography seems to "effect an interruption, stabilisation and stasis" as it erased the signs of hybridity, such as Western clothing and other commodities, from the picture (Hayes 1998a:177).

Hahn's representations of initiation certainly originated in his endeavours to reinvent a precolonial, premodern African order in the construction of colonial modernity. But his constructions also implied sexual connotations. Lining up large numbers of people on public occasions such as an *efundula* may have suited his sense of power: Hahn certainly felt "flattered with the shows of tribute and deference, taking on a temporary African-ness" when in the habitus of an African ruler ceremoniously tasting food and drink, as Patricia Hayes (1998a:176, 179) has argued. It may be more explicit, though: work done in different contexts suggests the imagined heterosexualisation of spaces where huge numbers of 'other' women are being massed and moved (cf. Theweleit 1980). Male phantasies in colonial Ovamboland arguably extended between attempts at incarnating the imagined, unlimited power of precolonial, premodern African kings and an assumption of female sexuality which was ostensibly 'innocent', yet readily available to the desiring heterosexual male gaze. Beyond, and at once as part of his constructions of Ovamboland as archaic Africa, Hahn's ethnographic writing and photo-graphy embraced the notion of an innocent, uncontaminated African sexuality embodied in bare-breasted young women dancing rites to enhance their fertility.

---

1.   Interview with Haikali Hamunyela, 16.12.1996, Ongha.

Sexual mores of the dark continent: Mission discourse on sexuality, gender and initiation

The Christian missions, on the other hand, objected to the initiation of young women as 'savage' and indecent. To them the 'nakedness' of the traditionally clad Owambo embodied the darkness, disorder and danger, in other words, the 'savagery' of African sexuality and culture. Whereas the Anglicans adopted a rather practical stance, the Finnish mission banned the traditional attire altogether. The efforts to cover women's bodies were accompanied by attempts to strip them of their traditional decorations and ornaments, which the Protestant missionaries abhorred as the embodiment of sinful vanity.[1]

In the dominant missionary discourse the Owambo women's initiation was a perverse occasion for sexual licence. As to what took place during the ceremonies, the Rhenish missionary Karl Sckär expressed his disgust at their 'true piggish nature' (*reinste Schweinerei*)[2]. In the Catholic view, the ceremony comprised endless "excesses and indecencies" and represented the "triumph of darkest paganism" (Seiler 1940:1
0; my translation). Finnish missionaries proclaimed that no decent person could even speak of it, and Anglicans condemned the rites because of their 'phallic flavour' (correspondence cited by Hayes 1996:372). Missionaries suggested that the rites were highly-sexed as the beer given to the initiates was allegedly "doctored by penis of the witchdoctor", and that the rite involved illicit sexual intercourse (cf. Tuupainen 1970:48).

All Owambo missions, the Lutherans, i.e. the Finnish Mission Society and the Rhenish Mission, the Roman Catholic Church, and the Anglicans forbade their adherents to participate in initiation. The Rhenish missionaries' early battles against *efundula* reached a climax with a drawn-out conflict with the last Kwanyama King Mandume in 1912/1913. In December 1913, the Rhenish missionaries in Oukwanyama devoted their annual conference to a discussion of initiation. The missionaries conceded that a total ban of *efundula* could not be enforced at this point. Mandume had already accommodated the missionaries and their Christian followers with the suggestion that young Christian women should partake in the rite for a few hours to satisfy local expectations. The missionaries were certainly not happy with this but eventually grudgingly accepted the compromise. The full participation of mission adherents in *efundula* was to be avoided at all costs, however. It was recommended that in such a case a Christian should flee Oukwanyama in order to avoid taking part in *efundula*.[3] In later years, the missions increased the stakes: in the 1930s, defiance of the church ban on initiation became an offence punishable by excommunication (cf. Seiler 1940:10; Mallory 1971:33).

1. In a study of the Basler Mission's efforts directed at women, Prodolliet (1987, 71-75) has shown how the missionaries' efforts to 'clothe' the 'natives' targeted particularly women, since women were perceived as sensual and potentially sinful, which implied their alleged uncontrolled sexuality.
2. VEM, RMG 1.658a B/c II 85; Sckär, Karl an Inspektor der Rheinischen Mission; Namakunde, 30.12.1911.
3. VEM, RMG 2.629 C/k 5 Missionarskonferenzen im Ovamboland:Protokolle; Protokoll der Konferenz rhin. Missionare in Ukuanjama. Vom 6.-9. Dez. 1913. The next *efundula* which had been intended for 1915 was called off when a devastating famine ravaged Owambo that year.

For the most part, the missionaries posed as saviours of African women whom they imagined as downtrodden 'beasts of burden', trapped in the sinful darkness of the continent. However, the Christian discourse on gender and sexuality was far from unitary. From the early years of the Rhenish Lutherans' work in Oukwanyama their views on Owambo gender relations and women's sexuality were marked by discord. Generally the missionaries were appalled that marriages were unstable, and that especially women seemed to leave undesirable marriages without much inhibition. A 1909 report in the Rhenish Missionary Society's journal noted that out of ten older women, nine had had a sequence of husbands, ranging from three through to six. The missionaries were equally abhorred at the absence of punishment of adulterous wives (RMG 1909:89). While the Rhenish missionaries agreed that Kwanyama women's sexual mores were questionable, their views on women's status in the family and society were at variance. Albert Hochstrate, then in charge of the mission at Ondjiva, emphasised in a 1913 report to the mission headquarters in Barmen the need to 'uplift' Kwanyama women's status which he depicted as exceedingly low and disgraceful (*unwürdig*). The Presiding Missionary, August Wulfhorst, who over the years hardly ever commented on his juniors' reports, in this instance expressed his disagreement in an extended handwritten addendum. Wulfhorst remonstrated that, in no way were women subordinated to men and that in the family mothers in fact enjoyed more respect than fathers. This he linked to the matrilineal social organisation. He went further, however, putting much stress on Kwanyama women's improper sexual conduct: where women were as sinful as men—how, then, could they feel despised in the society?[1]

Unlike the majority of Owambo missionaries of all denominations, Wulfhorst was not convinced that the initiation involved illicit, 'indecent' sexual rites. He even conceded that it might be seen as an attempt to restrain young people's sexual activities due to the serious consequences of a pre-initiation pregnancy. The practice of burning transgressors had been abandoned by the time the missionaries entered Oukwanyama but young women who fell pregnant before their *efundula*, were still subject to enormous social pressures, comparable to those Meredith McKittrick (1999) has shown for the context of western Owambo.

Wulfhorst objected to the *efundula*, however, because initiation was a part of 'pagan' Kwanyama's wider sexual mores which left much to be desired in the puritan world view of the Wilhelmian German empire. Young women were not in a rush to undergo *efundula* and become a wife, as they enjoyed a largely unrestrained sexual freedom. Many had sexual relations with men 'as if they were married', Wulfhorst noted: many had a 'fiancé' who visited her at their leisure with the knowledge and approval of her parents. This was unacceptable for the mission, although he admitted that it was not easy for young Christians to resist temptations. Wulfhorst conceded that, in comparison to their 'pagan' relatives, the personal freedom of young Christian women was much curtailed as they were com-

---

1.   VEM, RMG 2.518 C/h 34 Quartalsbericht der Station Ondjiva vom 1. Januar–31. März 1913. Absender: Hochstrate.

pelled to sit chastely and virtuously at home, waiting for a suitable Christian bride-groom.[1]

Christianity, 'tradition', identity and gender

There is no doubt that the cultural discourse and practice of gender and sexuality in Owambo were shifting through the impact of Christianity. Earlier, the initiation was central to the definition of female identity. It legitimatised women's adult-hood, sexuality and fertility. A long process of preparation for womanhood which had begun during early girlhood, culminated in the transition during the initiation.[2] The missions set out to redefine femininity and masculinity, gender and sexuality. Notions about 'sin' and 'morality' occupied the centre-stage, especially in refashioning femininity. The introduction of European-style dress was a point in question. So were the puritan notions about 'virginity' that attached 'shame and sin' to any premarital sexual ventures whereas previously certain forms of pre-marital sexual relations had been an accepted part of young people's lives unless they resulted in pregnancy (Becker 1995:102–104). Christianity entailed a new set of ideas about 'legitimate' sexuality. It tied sexuality and motherhood down within the framework of a Christian, monogamous marriage whereas in earlier times in-itiation had provided the transition to full female adulthood, and had legitimised fertility and full heterosexual relations for young women and their male sexual partners.

It appears doubtful, however, that the Christian colonial modernity fully over-ruled older local forms. Patterns of continuity and discontinuity persisted, rather, which also found expression in the language adopted to describe 'new' institutions, such as when oshiKwanyama-speakers used the term *efundula* as the synonym for 'marriage', including a Christian wedding.[3] An attempt to approach the complexities of colonial Christian modernities and gender and sexual identities is admittedly bold where information on people's strategies to adjust to and adapt the changing discourses on sexuality and gender is sparse. Some young women and men continued to observe or participate in the ceremonies and thus defied church rulings. On the other hand, the refusal of young Owambo women to take part in initiation indicates resistance against earlier forms of social control, and at-tempts by young women to make use of opportunities that came with the new discourse. The promulgation of the 'Christian housewife' model and the puritan discourse certainly served to control women's labour and sexuality. Yet the missions also provided new opportunities for women. The discourse of 'Christian' marriage allowed women to opt out of unwanted polygynous marriages. It was through the missions, particularly the Finns, that Owambo women first got the

---

1. VEM, RMG 2.636 C/k 22; Vorträge und Aufsätze zur Ovambo-Mission von A. Wulfhorst 1910–1933.
2. The preparation for the *efundula* has been described in detail by Tönjes (1911:133–136) and Bruwer (1959:115–116).
3. Estermann (1976:70) wrote that from the early years of Christianisation among the Kwanyama of Southern Angola 'to marry in church' was frequently translated as *okufukala m'okapela* (to do the initiation rite in the chapel/church).

opportunity of obtaining training in professions such as nursing which allowed them to develop new perspectives within a changing society (Becker, 1995:105).

Altered gendered sexualities played themselves out in different ways in the Owambo communities. The growing attraction to Christianity as a cultural strategy to claim modernity did not necessarily mean that people abandoned older cultural forms altogether. The practice of initiation and other cultural institutions related to gender and sexuality, such as the *oudano* moonlight dances of the youth, continued throughout the colonial era.[1] Ian Fairweather (2001:218) has argued recently that the participation or non-participation in ceremonies such as *efundula* were significant ways of making statements about identities. This may be the case, to an extent at least. However, as has been discussed elsewhere, even members of the Christian elite in the Finnish mission's heartland in Ondonga appropriated heterogeneous strategies that enveloped Christian and older local cultural discourses on gender (Becker 2000b). It appears that cultural forms that had played a significant role in shaping and giving expression to gendered sexualities persevered, but were discursively increasingly shrouded in silence. The ostensibly contradictory discourse of the administration and Owambo authorities on the healthy, 'tribal' traditions picturing young women rarely presented a counterpoint: while it rendered young women's bodies visible, it silenced their desires and aspirations.

Discourses and practices of *efundula* in postcolonial Namibia

In the postcolonial society, representations of *efundula* continue to play a major part in the Owambo, and beyond in the national Namibian, cultural discourse. This final section of the chapter revisits the silences around women's initiation that I encountered in the mid-1990s. It then engages with the increasingly public presence of *efundula* over the past few years, as exemplified in a prime time national TV programme. How do these, seemingly contradictory, postcolonial strategies refashion gender and sexual identities? Do they do this, and if so, where do they continue to be shaped by the colonial dynamics discussed above? I conclude by considering how the reconfiguration of cultural strategies since Namibian national independence in 1990, has possibly impacted on shifting gender and sexual identities.

Before I focus on the multiple discourses on *efundula* in the postcolonial context, I need to draw attention to changes in ritual style and practice.[2] Many Owambo, especially those of the older generation, speak about *efundula* ceremonial history in ways that serve to demonstrate continuity. In the different context of Okiek women's initiation in Kenya, Corinne Kratz (1994:323) has found a similar discourse-based image of 'tradition' that affirms continuity. In contrast to the dis-

---

1. It appears that the 23 years of the liberation war (1966–1989) did more to discourage such events that involved all-night outdoor sessions. (Interview; Mirjam Kautwima, Shipola Kukenge, Mukwaluwala Hitombo, 18.5.1999, Ongha.)

2. The following discussion is mainly based on the 1996 research in Oukwanyama.

cursive assertion that ritual changes have been peripheral, some moves have in fact had profound repercussions for constructions of Owambo gender and sexuality.

In general, despite past and present variations in detail and duration, changes in ritual practices during the ceremony itself appear to be limited. *Efundula* ceremonies in Oukwanyama now last no more than three days. The days and stages are called *okambadjona* (the little jackal), *ombadye yakula* (the big jackal) and *omuuhalo* (the day of love). After numerous preparations the initiates are kept in a special hut inside the homestead where the ritual takes place, called the *ondjuo*, where they are fed by the ritual leader. On the morning of the second day, the young women are summoned out of the *ondjuo*, one by one. On leaving the hut they have to crawl through the *omupitifi's* legs. The ritual leader then presents each initiate with a drink of millet beer mixed with herbs. If she vomits upon taking this drink, it is regarded as proof that she is pregnant, and will thus be removed from taking part in the ceremony. The initiates are also required to step over the fork of a cleft stick (*olumana*), which is regarded as a second test for possible illicit pregnancy. Following this stage the *ovafuko* have to pass what has been described as further 'endurance tests', that is, continuous dancing. These more public parts of the ceremony involve other members of the community, particularly men and boys who come forward to play the long *efundula* drums (*eengoma*), which are only used for the specific purpose of the initiation.

Efundula establishes a valid marriage, even if there is no husband, which is, however, apparently an uncommon occurrence. 'Wedding' appears to be the dominant meaning present-day Owambo attach to the rites. Informants described the stage of the rites that involves the initiates' prospective spouses as significant. The husband-to-be sends a male messenger (*ongeleka*) to put a palm ribbon around the *omufuko's* arm. If she accepts him, she keeps this bracelet. If she rejects him, however, she tears it off.[1] Younger women who had been to initiation more recently told us that the palm ribbon may nowadays be replaced by a ring or a watch.[2]

A significant change with respect to gender concerns the former *oihanangolo* period, which has been reduced to a symbolic few hours during the *efundula*, when the *ovafuko* fake a period of social freedom by moving within the area near the homestead where the ceremony has taken place. After the ceremony the initiates immediately return to their homes, from where they may then leave to live with their husbands.

The *oihanangolo* stage was previously central to the ceremony when the initiates temporarily assumed 'male' gender attributes, which were complemented by the expected 'female' behaviour on the part of men, and particularly the *oshihanangolo's* future husband. The multi-layered meanings this involved are of particular interest for the analysis of the shifting gendered connotations linked to the ritual.

---

1. Interviews; Evaristus Amweelo, 12.12.1996, Ondjondjo; Fransina Kuutondokwa, 12.12.1996, Omusheshe; Peyavali Naliende, 14.12.1996, Omatunda; Haikali Hamunyela, 16.12.1996, Ongha.
2. Focus group discussion with women aged 20-29, 20.8.1998, Tsumeb.

Davies (1987:102) argues that the male-female reversal served as a visual and possibly psychological contrast between girlhood and adult (married) womanhood where the sanctioned period of liberty was complementary to the "serious and responsible" position of women in marriage. It then was first and foremost a stage of liminality, where the young women stripped off preliminal (girlhood) and postliminal (adult womanhood) attributes. The complementarity of male and female which earlier observers attributed to Kwanyama society (Davies 1987, based on the observations of the Powell-Cottons in 1937), may have been lost along with the possibility of gender inversion. That current forms of gender power have become naturalised as a primordial fact, seems another likely repercussion of the disappearance of gender inversion from Owambo cultural practice.

Preserving 'morality': *Efundula* in the time of AIDS

"In our tradition we are very Christian". This commonly-heard statement exemplifies the cultural identity of many Owambo in the postcolonial era. In Owambo, where the proportion of practising Christians is estimated at about 90 per cent, Christianity has largely succeeded in restructuring people's conceptual universe in important respects, including the social, cultural and political representations of everyday life. Discourse in Owambo has been framed in a 'Christian' language for decades. At a first glance not much appears to have changed from the colonial-missionary to the postcolonial, dominant discourse of moral identity, gender and sexuality in the time of AIDS.

Apparently, however, in some aspects the Christian churches, today all under Namibian leadership, have taken a more accommodating stance towards the initiation of young women. In 1996 we came across a Catholic school in Owambo where students who had recently taken part in *efundula* had presented their experience in a school play. We also met a female *omupitifi* who was at the same time an active member of the Anglican church. The Lutheran church may still be harder on young women who undergo initiation (see below), but even ELCIN (Evangelican Lutheran Church in Namibia) no longer proscribes the mere observation and celebration of the ceremony.

Yet, the air of secrecy surrounding initiation has continued to prevail. Despite the wide-spreaded presence of initiation, numerous Owambo-based informants expressed the conviction that the ceremonies no longer took place. On various occasions people have told us that *efundula* was still not allowed "by Christianity". This is no unfounded perception. In 1996, Kleopas Dumeni, the then Bishop of ELCIN, by far the largest Christian denomination in Owambo, told me in no uncertain terms that his church would never tolerate the participation in *efundula* because it legitimised sex outside marriage and, thus, was in fundamental contradiction of 'Christian values'.[1] For the most part, the churches reject redefinitions of the initiation ceremonies in the face of current social challenges, such as large-

---

1. Telephone interview; Bishop Kleopas Dumeni, 8.5.1996.

scale premarital pregnancies of young women ('teenage pregnancies') and AIDS. The social significance of *efundula* in regulating female sexuality and fertility, which, as informants in Owambo have suggested, need more attention in research and education, has certainly not been recognised by the Christian churches. Instead, the Lutheran church particularly persists in its policy that young women have to 'repent' for partaking in initiation ceremonies by confessing in front of the congregation. They also have to attend the church-run 'schools of repent', usually of three weeks duration, before they will be re-admitted to the community of believers.[1] Individual parish pastors, on occasion, express different personal views, but the prevailing moral discourse of all Christian denominations in Owambo continues to reject 'traditional', African sexual and ritual practices for their perceived immorality. The message to young people is, put simply, that they should 'behave', that is, abstain from any sexual activities until their church wedding.[2]

The dominant church discourse of gender and sexuality is strongly reminiscent of the mission's earlier prescriptions. Gendered identities that were promulgated by the missionaries in the first half of the 20th century are presented in the postcolonial discourse as 'traditional': a 'good woman' is depicted as being weak, shy, passive—in fact, she 'does not speak up'. Women, like children, 'are to be seen, not heard'. This notion of femininity is opposed by that of a hegemonic masculinity that emphasises strength and virility (Becker 1995:115). With the 'Christian' language and system of belief goes an idealised concept of a desexualised mother-woman. If women do not live by the standards of 'Christian' gendered morality, this is cause for considerable moral anxiety even among the youngest generation of church leaders. This point was driven home to me when, in 1999, I lectured at the Lutheran training seminary in Windhoek on 'AIDS and the church'. A number of male students articulated the perception that women and female sexuality were root causes of the AIDS pandemic in Namibia because of women's lax sexual mores. The women students in the class sat silent throughout.

On a more general level there is also a postcolonial, secular reincarnation of the Christian morality discourse on the excessive African sexuality, with a comparable summary rejection of local practices. This discourse has gained currency in Namibia among some local feminists as well as among international researchers, consultants, and development aid workers. At its core, it has indiscriminately redefined local practices pertaining to gender and sexuality as 'harmful traditional practices' (HTPs). Women's initiation has come to occupy a central place in this discourse, partly, it appears, drawing on the international campaigns against women's circumcision.[3] These campaigns are irrelevant in Namibia in the absence of any modifications on the initiates' bodies. Yet, when researchers from the Uni-

---

1. Telephone interview; Bishop Kleopas Dumeni, 8.5.1996.
2. Interview; Rev. Linekela Shidute, 13.8.1998, Tsumeb.
3. The politics of these campaigns have been questioned by anthropologists and African feminist scholar-activists on the grounds of their implicit racism and ethnocentrism (cf. Kratz 1994:341–347; Nnaemeka 2001).

versity of Namibia were commissioned to study (male and female) initiation in the mid-1990s, word quickly made the rounds that they were researching 'female genital mutilation'(FGM).

The local Namibian variant is framed by an international gender-and-development discourse and a concomitant school of thought in feminist Africanist research. With its stress on the perceived binary opposition of gender equity and 'African culture', it denounces 'tradition' in general, and women's initiation ceremonies in particular as generally detrimental to women (cf. Geisler 1997) while casting aside arguments that emphasise female bonding and the experience of liberty during women's rituals (cf. Davies 1987:104–105; Arnfred 1988:8–9). This school of thought looks curiously like a refashioned, academic version of the puritan missionary discourse. Because it proscribes anything 'traditional' as harmful to women, it similarly enforces a specific morality. It has been shown elsewhere that, for some years after 1990, the popular discourse of modernity as African women's saviour dominated the Namibian postcolony's public debates on gender (Becker 2000a, especially 171–173). I therefore suggest that, along with the churches, local and international feminist protagonists of modernisation have played a part in hiding practices such as women's initiation from public view, and in silencing alternative cultural strategies.

Preserving 'tradition': *Efundula* as cultural heritage

This last section draws on very recent developments in Owambo, and the wider postcolonial Namibian society, where beginning in the mid-1990s disputes over the values that pull the national and local community together have increasingly embraced notions of 'tradition' and 'heritage'. The production and prime-time screening of a documentary on *efundula* (Carstens 1996) exemplified this eruption of Owambo cultural practice into public presence in postcolonial Namibian society.

The new national public discourse mirrors shifting local strategies. The past half-dozen years or so have seen the emergence of a vocal discourse in northern Namibia about the 'loss of culture' that Owambo have supposedly experienced because of the activities of the missionaries. This discourse revolves around the role 'Christianity' had in suppressing 'culture' in the past, and the obligation of the modern-day Namibian churches to contribute to the present and future preservation of cultural heritage. Among the most vocal proponents of the new heritage discourse are several leading Owambo clerics who have been outspoken in their criticism of what they see as the missionary responsibility for the decline of culture and history in northern Namibia.[1]

---

1. Several leading ELCIN clergy have expressed their respective views in conversations with myself and other researchers. I refrain from naming those who have shared their thoughts with me for reasons of privacy, but still wish to express my gratitude. Ian Fairweather's insightful doctoral thesis on identity politics and the heritage industry in Owambo (2001), as well as our earlier conversations, have helped to clarify my thoughts on the role of *efundula* in identity formation.

The postcolonial Namibian state having come forth through the nationalist struggle against the South African colonial apartheid state was initially also wary of local practices because of the apartheid regime's use of cultural difference. As a commentator in the governmental weekly wrote, "In the past culture was mis-used and this has left the impression that talking about culture means talking about invaluable things aimed at separating people" (Denis Nandi in *New Era*, 27.1–2.2.1994; quoted in Fairweather 2001:137).

In the years that have passed since 1994, culture has become a much talked-about item in Namibian postcolonial discourse. Yet, the use of 'cultural' social practices in the organisation of everyday life has remained largely taboo. Nor have new representations of initiation and other practices relevant to gender and sex-uality been aiming at integrating local practices into strategies to cope with the so-cial stresses of the postcolonial era, such as teenage pregnancies, gender-based vi-olence or AIDS. Instead, the reclamation of culture has taken shape predomi-nantly as exhibit and performance. As Ian Fairweather (2001:4) has argued, cul-tural heritage has become a means by which the Namibian state seeks to engender national unity through the incorporation of distinct local cultures.

The regular regional and national cultural festivals organised by the Namibian state and local and regional cultural associations have become rallying points for showcasing culture. In Owambo, the *oudano* songs and dances, in earlier times thriving components of all-night opportunities for young men and women's courtship, are important items on the list of heritage performance; even local schools run regular *oudano* competitions. In contrast, they have seemingly lost their former social significance in the formation of gendered sexual identities and practice of partner choice.

The discourse of cultural heritage has been driven predominantly by urban-ised Owambo, and indeed often the most cosmopolitan members of the postco-lonial elite in attempts to reclaim and display their 'roots' in a concurrent demon-stration of their very cosmopolitan modernity. This indeed appeared to be the main social significance at the August 1998 urban reinvention of an *efundula* on the eve of the high-society church wedding that I witnessed when a daughter of a prominent SWAPO Women's Council politician married her British fiancé in the presence of half a dozen members of the Namibian cabinet, including the country's (non-Owambo) Prime Minister. The '*efundula*' held for the bride, a post-graduate student at a European university, lasted a couple of hours and lacked the ritual's defining activities except for the modern-day ritual garb, and the charac-teristic drumming and dancing. It was obviously regarded as a success, however. The elderly woman who had acted as the 'ritual organiser' at the event, when in-terviewed a couple of days afterwards, reported that two other members of the town's emerging elite had on the spot requested her to also organise *omafundula* for their soon-to-be married daughters.[1]

---

1. Interview; Martha Waalye, 18.8.1998,Tsumeb.

While there has been the odd suggestion about staging *omafundula* as a tourist attraction, (cf. Fairweather 2001:223) initiation ceremonies on the whole appear to have survived and enjoy a modest revival as *living* culture, not merely as heritage in performance. The 1996 TV programme showed pupils from a local primary school who attended the event in their school uniforms and took notes to 'learn about culture', and interviews with some initiates revealed that they perceived the ritual as meaningful in their sexual and reproductive lives. To these young rural Owambo women, initiation was obviously a defining cornerstone of their social and sexual identity.

Conclusion

The new public presence of *efundula* has shown that, despite the significant impact of Christianisation on Owambo culture and history, it would be wrong to assume that gender and sexual identities in present-day Owambo were solely determined by the dominant Christian discourse. This is so despite the apparently so overwhelming impact of Christianity. It has become clear rather that the Christian churches' longtime opposition has transformed the ritual significantly, without, however, questioning the social institution of women's initiation and its multiple meanings. The fact that there was, and to an extent still is, a pertinent silence among sections of Owambo society, may indicate that people accepted the prohibitive stance of the Christian churches discursively, without, however, relinquishing the practice. In postcolonial Namibia an increasingly vibrant discourse has emerged on initiation as part of the reconstructed Owambo heritage.

It appears that the new discursive prominence of *efundula* as a cultural practice has torn away the veil of colonial silence that prevailed during much of the colonial era and into the postcolonial era until a few years ago. The partial incorporation of cultural spaces that define gender and sexual identities, into the emerging heritage industry is not without its own problems, though; more so as it seems thus far that it has not been complemented by a wide interest in exploring the social implications of older cultural discourses on gender and sexualities. Some vocal Namibian feminist activists, however, have begun, in the process of reclaiming their 'roots', to question the hegemonic colonial assertions of a highly-patriarchal Owambo past. Despite the inherent limitations, the new visibility, and nascent audibility, of these cultural spaces does have significant repercussions. The concurrence of silence and, ostensibly contradictory, public presence relates to past tensions of colonialism as well as current multiple identities in the postcolonial Namibian society.

References

Arnfred, Signe, 1988, "Women in Mozambique: Gender Struggle and Gender Politics", *Review of African Political Economy*, no 41.

Arnfred, Signe, 1990, "Notes on Gender and Modernization. Examples from Mozambique", in Agnete Weis Bentzon (ed.), *The Language of Development Studies*. Copenhagen: New Social Science Monographs.

Becker, Heike, 1995, *Namibian Women's Movement 1980 to 1992. From Anti-colonial Struggle to Reconstruction*. Frankfurt: IKO Verlag für Interkulturelle Kommunikation.

Becker, Heike, 2000a, "A Concise History of Gender, 'Tradition' and the State in Namibia", in Christiaan Keulder (ed.), *State, Society and Democracy. A Reader in Namibian Politics*. Windhoek: Gamsberg Macmillan.

Becker, Heike, 2000b, "'Let me come to tell you'. Loide Shikongo maps out power. Gender identity and gendered subjectivities in colonial Ovamboland". Paper presented at the confernce *Public History—Forgotten History*, 22–25 August 2000, Windhoek, Namibia.

Becker, Heike, 2001, "Living the postcolonial empirical. New perspectives on doing anthropology in southern Africa". Paper presented at the American Anthropological Association's Annual Conference, 28.11–2.12.2001, Washington D.C., USA.

Becker, Heike, and Manfred O. Hinz, 1995, *Marriage and Customary Law in Namibia*. Namibia Papers. Working Documents, No. 30. Windhoek: CASS.

Bruwer, Johannes Petrus van Schalkwyk, 1959, "The Kuanyama of South West Africa. Stellenbosch" (unpublished).

Carstens, Gene, 1996, "Efundula. The traditional Ovambo wedding initiation". (video).

Comaroff, Jean and John Comaroff, 1991, *Of Revelation and Revolution. Christianity, Colonialism and Consciousness in South Africa*. Volume 1. Chicago and London: The University of Chicago Press.

Comaroff, John and Jean Comaroff, 1992, *Ethnography and the Historical Imagination*. Boulder, San Francisco and Oxford: Westview Press.

Comaroff, John L. and Jean Comaroff, 1997, *Of Revelation and Revolution. The Dialectics of Modernity on a South African Frontier*. Volume Two. Chicago and London: The University of Chicago Press.

Cooper, Frederick and Ann Laura Stoler (eds), 1997, *Tensions of Empire. Colonial Cultures in a Bourgeois World*. Berkeley, Los Angeles and London: University of California Press.

Davies, Gwyneth, 1987, "The Efundula: Fertility and Social Maturity among the Kwanyama of Southern Angola". Thesis submitted for the degree of M.A., University of Kent (unpublished).

Estermann, Carlos, 1976 (1957), *The Ethnography of Southwestern Angola*. New York: Africana Publishing Company.

Fairweather, Ian, 2001, "Identity Politics and the Heritage Industry in Post-Apartheid Northern Namibia". Thesis submitted for the degree of PhD, University of Manchester (unpublished).

Geisler, Gisela, 1997, "Women are Women or How to Please your Husband. Initiation ceremonies and the politics of 'tradition' in Southern Africa", *African Anthropology,* vol.4, no.1.

Gilman, Sander L., 1985, *Difference and Pathology. Stereotypes of Sexuality, Race, and Madness*. Ithaca and London: Cornell University Press.

Hahn, Carl Hugo Linsingen, 1928, "The Ovambo", in C.H.L. Hahn, H. Vedder and L. Fourie, *The native tribes of South West Africa*. Cape Town: Cape Times Limited.

Hayes, Patricia, 1992, "A History of the Ovambo of Namibia, c 1880–1935". Thesis submitted for the degree of PhD, University of Cambridge (unpublished).

Hayes, Patricia, 1996, "'Cocky' Hahn and the 'Black Venus': The Making of a Native Commissioner in South West Africa, 1915–46", *Gender & History*, vol.8, no. 3.

Hayes, Patricia, 1998a, "Northern exposures: The photography of C.H.L. Hahn, Native Commissioner of Ovamboland, 1915–1946", in Wolfram Hartmann, Jeremy Silvester and Patricia Hayes (eds), *The Colonising Camera. Photographs in the making of Namibian History*. Cape Town: UCT Press.

Hayes, Patricia 1998b, "The 'Famine of the Dams'. Gender, Labour & Politics in Colonial Ovamboland", in Patricia Hayes, Jeremy Silvester, Marion Wallace and Wolfram Hartmann (eds), *Namibia under South African Rule. Mobility & Containment, 1915–46*. Oxford: James Currey.

Kratz, Corinne A., 1994, *Affecting Performance. Meaning, Movement, and Experience in Okiek Women's Initiation*. Washington and London: Smithsonian Institution Press.

Loeb, Edwin M., 1962, *In Feudal Africa*. Bloomington: Mouton & Co.

Louw, Walter, 1967, "Die sosio-politieke stelsel van die Ngandjera van Ovamboland". Thesis submitted for the degree of M.A., University of Port Elizabeth (unpublished).

Mallory, Charles Shannon, 1971, "Some Aspects of the Mission Policy and Practice of the Church of the Province of South Africa in Ovamboland: 1924–1960". Thesis submitted for the degree of M.A., Rhodes University (unpublished).

Manicom, Linzi, 1992, "Ruling Relations: Rethinking State and Gender in South African History", *Journal of African History* 33.

McKittrick, Meredith, 1999, "Faithful Daughter, Murdering Mother: Transgression and Social Control in Colonial Namibia", *Journal of African History*, 40.

NDT and CASS, 1994, *Improving the Legal and Socio-Economic Situation of Women in Namibia. Uukwambi, Ombalantu and Uukwanyama Integrated Report*. Windhoek: NDT.

Nnaemeka, Obioma, 2001, "If Female Circumcision Did Not Exist, Western Feminism Would Invent It", in Susan Perry and Celeste Schenck (eds), *Eye to Eye. Women Practising Development Across Cultures*. London and New York: Zed Books.

Powell-Cotton, Antoinette and Diana Powell-Cotton, 1937, "Efundula. Marriage ceremonies, Kwanyama tribe (Ovambo group) Lower Kunene, Angola, 1937". (film)

Prodolliet, Simone, 1987, *Wider die Schamlosigkeit und das Elend der heidnischen Weiber. Die Basler Frauenmission und der Export des europäischen Frauenideals in die Kolonien*. Zürich: Limmat.

Richards, Audrey, 1982 (1956), *Chisungu. A girl's initiation ceremony among the Bemba of Zambia*. Introduction by Jean La Fontaine. London and New York: Routledge.

RMG, 1909, *Berichte der Rheinischen Missionsgesellschaft*. Barmen.

Seiler, Franz, 1940, *Ein Frauenschicksal in Ovamboland*. Hünfeld: Verlag der Oblaten. (Blüten und Früchte vom heimatlichen und auswärtigen Missionsfelde; dargeboten von den Oblaten der unbefleckten Jungfrau Nr. 17)

Stoler, Ann Laura, 1997, "Carnal Knowledge and Imperial Power. Gender, Race, and Morality in Colonial Asia", in Roger M. Lancaster and Micaela di Leonardo (eds), *The Gender/Sexuality Reader: Culture, History, Political Economy*. New York and London: Routledge.

Stoler, Ann Laura and Frederick Cooper, 1997, "Between Metropole and Colony. Rethinking a Research Agenda", in Frederick Cooper and Ann Laura Stoler (eds), *Tensions of Empire. Colonial Cultures in a Bourgeois World*. Berkely, Los Angeles and London: University of California Press.

Theweleit, Klaus, 1980, *Männerphantasien. 1. Frauen, Fluten, Körper, Geschichte*. Reinbek bei Hamburg: Rowohlt.

Tönjes, Herrman, 1911, *Ovamboland. Land, Leute, Mission. Mit besonderer Berücksichtigung seines größten Stammes Oukuanjama*. Berlin: Martin Warneck.

Turner, Victor, 1967, *The Forest of Symbols. Aspects of Ndembu Ritual*. Ithaca, N.Y.: Cornell University Press.

Turner, Victor, 1969, *The Ritual Process. Structure and Anti-Structure*. London: Routledge & Kegan Paul.

Tuupainen, Maija, 1970, *Marriage in a matrilineal African tribe: A social anthropological study of marriage in the Ondonga tribe in Ovamboland*. Helsinki: Academic Bookstore.

Vaughan, Megan, 1991, *Curing Their Ills. Colonial Power and African Illness*. Cambridge: Polity Press.

Wallace, Marion, 1998, "'A Person is Never Angry for Nothing'. Women, VD & Windhoek", in Patricia Hayes, Jeremy Silvester, Marion Wallace and Wolfram Hartmann (eds), *Namibia under South African Rule. Mobility & Containment, 1915–46*. Oxford: James Currey.

Werbner, Richard and Terence Ranger (eds), 1996, *Postcolonial Identities in Africa*. London: Zed Books.

Williams, Frieda-Nela, 1991, *Precolonial Communities of Southwestern Africa. A History of Owambo Kingdoms 1600–1920*. Windhoek: National Archives of Namibia.

Wulfhorst, August, n.d., *Beantwortung des Fragebogens über die Rechte der Eingeborenen in den deutschen Kolonien. Ovambogebiet (Stamm der Ovakuanjama) (Deutsch-Südwestafrika)*. p. l.

Photo: El Hadj Bassirou Sanni, 1982

2. 'African Sexuality'/Sexuality in Africa: Tales and Silences

Signe Arnfred

Introduction

This chapter is an intermediate outcome of an ongoing effort to think sexualities in contexts of gender in Africa. I have called it 'tales and silences' a) because in the field of 'African sexuality' there seems to be an abundance of re-circulated ideas and conceptions, which on closer scrutiny tell more about the minds of those who made them than they tell about Africa and Africans (cf. Abrahams 1997:37), and b) because there might be an inner connection between this type of tales and one type of silence:the general absence of 'sexuality' as an issue in African feminists' writings.

This then is the guiding question of the chapter: Why is it that discussions of sexuality are so noticeably absent in analytical works of African feminists?[1] The contrast in this respect to the Western women's movement and feminist studies is striking: here analysis and critique of discourses on female sexuality were key issues right from the start (cf. Simone de Beauvoir 1949, Kate Millet 1969, Germaine Greer 1970 among others). Amina Mama—one of the few African feminists who has touched on sexuality in her writings—suggests that the Western tales and the African silences may be interlinked, that it is "the historical legacy of racist fascination with Africans' allegedly profligate sexuality [that] has deterred researchers" (Mama 1996:39). There may be other reasons as well linked to the ways in which sexuality is and has been dealt with in daily and ritual life. As has been analyzed by Foucault, the, according to him, obsessive "putting into discourse of sex" (Foucault 1978:12) is a particular characteristic of post-Enlightenment Western society.

The chapter is divided into three parts. In the first part, I follow Amina Mama's lead, also urged by the ways in which issues of sexuality in Africa are conceptualized in contemporary (often donor-driven) investigations and debates, centring on illness and violence (HIV/AIDS, Female Genital Mutilation) and often *victimizing* as well as *blaming* women. Sexuality—and female sexuality in particular—seems to be linked to violence and/or death. Not much is said about pleasure and enjoyment, or desire—certainly not *female* desire. How come that sexuality in Africa is approached and contextualized in such ways? Looking into the issue took me back to the heyday of imperialism and evolutionary thinking in the

---

1. It was the absence of any references to sexuality in the analytical works of Ifi Amadiume and Oyèrònké Oyewùmí—authors whose work I admire and which I have used a lot—that first alerted me to this general absence. I later saw it confirmed by Amina Mama (1996).

19th and early 20th centuries, the times when hierarchies of 'race' were facts of science. This makes one speculate regarding what passes as 'science' today. It also means that you cannot just jump into talking and thinking about sex in Africa. The conceptual terrain is carved and cut in all sorts of often invisible ways; if unaware of this, your thinking might be following tracks whose course you do not even know. A thorough work of conceptual de-constructing is called for, the challenge of this part of the chapter being an inquiry regarding colonial lines of thinking on sex in Africa, which of course again were linked to structuring of sex in the imperial metropolis. Tracing some of these lines of thinking I look closer at two colonial 'tales'. One is a novel: *King Solomon's Mines*, first published in 1885, and the other the conception and staging in Europe of *Sarah Bartmann*, a Khoikhoi woman, in 1810–1815.

In the second part of the chapter I investigate a contemporary text considered an important scholarly contribution, a 1989 paper by demographer John Caldwell et al. discussing 'African AIDS'. The Caldwell paper, as I shall show, is based on some of the same conceptions as those active in the 19th century 'tales'. Midway in the second section I reverse the perspective, looking at the Caldwell paper, and particularly at the anthropological data on which it is based, from a feminist point of view—a vantage point which gives rise to a very different reading. The feminist reading is further supported by data from my own investigations and interviews in northern Mozambique.

Finally, in the third part of the chapter, I very tentatively look into other possible causes for the absence of discussions of 'sexuality' in African feminists' works, briefly discussing different types of silences. The aim of the entire chapter is to be a contribution to attempts to clear the way for lines of thinking about sexuality in Africa *not* determined by the tales of 'African sexuality'.

Colonial tales and 'dark continent discourse'

Both of the two old 'tales' I have selected for discussion have been analysed before for what they reveal regarding the complicated relationships of power and identity as entangled with male sexual anxieties and desires, all connected to the colonizing enterprise and to the ways in which it was conceived. The reason for taking them up again here is to point to the ways in which very similar lines of thinking in actual fact persist even today, impacting heavily on seemingly scientific discourses. Tales like these are at the root of what has aptly been termed the 'dark continent discourse' (Jungar and Oinas, this volume) and—as also shown in Jungar and Oinas' chapter—the 'dark continent discourse' is still alive and kicking, structuring ways of seeing and understanding even today. The two tales are (in reverse historical order) a) Rider Haggard's very popular and widely read novel *King Solomon's Mines*, never out of print since it was first published in 1885, and b) the story of *Sarah Bartmann*, a Khoikhoi woman who was taken to Europe in 1810. As opposed to the novel by Rider Haggard, the Sarah Bartmann story is based on a real event. But the way this event was produced, staged and perceived makes it as much of a tale as the novel.

Imperialist anxieties and sexual fears: The virgin lands

Rider Haggard's imperialist fiction was often staged in Africa where Haggard as a very young man, from 19 to 25 years of age, had been first a civil servant (as junior secretary to the Governor of Natal, South Africa) and later tried his hand at ostrich farming (Stiebel 2001:21 ff). Back in England Haggard "divided his energies between writing about African landscapes, the state of British farmlands and on agricultural matters generally" (Stiebel 2001:27), being a highly respected member of the landed gentry, a tireless participant in various government commissions, and eventually knighted for his services to the empire (Stiebel 2001:80). Unknown, of course, to the Victorian gentleman Haggard himself, the landscapes and the story of *King Solomon's Mines* provide prime views of imperialist male imagination, anxieties and fears. An obvious illustration of the pivotal role played by *sexuality* in this context is the treasure map from *King Solomon's mines*, written in blood by the dying explorer José Silvestre, and later guiding the male hero Alan Quatermain (Haggard's alter ego, cf. Stiebel 2001:46) and his comrades in their quest to find the hidden treasure, and to penetrate and conquer the land. The map itself underscores the sexual nature of the quest.[1] If the map is turned upside down it becomes evident that it represents the body of a woman: the woman has no head, but the breasts are two mountains, named on the map as 'Sheba's breasts', with the arms of the headless woman stretching out as mountain ranges to either side. The path our heroes must travel follows the passage between the breasts, continuing down to a triangular (three-peaked) mountain hiding the crucial place, the opening, the entrance into the interior, which is the passageway to the treasure itself. The penetration is a quest full of dangers and perils. Alan Quatermain and his comrades are on the verge of becoming absorbed and engulfed by the fearful forces which they have to confront. Now instead they succeed in crushing the keeper of the secret, Gagool, the old woman, the witch (as she is called) but also the 'mother, old mother' of the land, the one that holds all power of life and death (McClintock 1995:246). Here we meet African female regenerative power, of course in a grotesquely distorted version: Gagool is tremendously old and described as a 'wizened, monkey-like figure' more like an animal than a human being. In European cultural tradition there are standard ways of demonizing female power, perceived as threatening by men. Gagool, like so many women before her, is evil, she is a witch. According to Anne McClintock "colonial documents are eloquent on the unease with which white male administrators regarded the African *isanusis*, [diviners] who were dominantly female" (McClintock

---

1. According to Lindy Stiebel (2001) an early interpretation of this treasure map as a woman's body can be seen in one of the many film versions of the book, where the map is engraved on the body of a small nude female sculpture (Stiebel 2001:101).

1995:246). Thus in McClintock's reading the subtext regarding Gagool is "a narrative disciplining of female reproductive power" (McClintock 1995:246).

King Solomon's Mines, like others of Haggard's novels, is fiction written for boys and men. It is dedicated, on the front page "to all the big and little boys that read it". As a girl I read it in a Danish translation, and the fact that it is still in print testifies to its continued powers of fascination, even though more than a hundred years old. It is a story for men, about men; as Haggard (alias Quatermain) explicitly states: "I can safely say that there is not a petticoat in the whole history" (Haggard 1885/1994:3), meaning no (white) woman. It is a story about masculine courage and male initiation, as pointed out by Rebecca Stott: it is all about "adventure, tests of strength, morality and decency ... a man-centered discourse, clearly focused on the experience of the white male out on the imperial frontier. ... The quest motif becomes a quest for and initiation into manhood" (Stott 1989:71).

Similarly, on a deeper level, the story is about sexual exploration and penetration, and about sexual anxieties and fears. Also in non-fiction texts of the period, the lands to be conquered and penetrated are often called *virgin lands* —just lying there waiting passively to be conquered and penetrated[1]. The metaphor 'virgin lands' also points to the idealized image of the white woman: that she should be passive and passionless, gracefully and gratefully waiting for the moment when a man—her husband—would penetrate her, thus introducing her to the happiness of married life. The Victorian ideal of female 'passionlessness' fits this image: the woman as 'the Angel of the House' and the incarnation of high moral standards, has to be a-sexual. According to Nancy Cott this was a kind of trade-off established by the Church: "Evangelical Protestants constantly reiterated the theme that Christianity has raised women from slaves in status to moral and intellectual beings. The tacit condition for that elevation was the suppression of female sexuality" (Cott 1978:227). Writing about Victorian sexual ideology 1790–1850, Cott further states that "by elevating sexual control highest among human virtues the middle class moralists made *female chastity* the archetype for human morality" (Cott 1978:223). "Female passionlessness was a key-stone in men's construction of their own sexuality" (Cott 1978:235).

In the above quotations a cluster of Victorian/Evangelical Protestant (and by implication White Male) notions of femininity and sexuality are expressed. First the mind/body division, with mind as male and body as female, and male projection of dangerous and tempting sexuality onto women. Secondly the dichotomising of the conception of woman in Madonna/whore: woman-as-body is carrier of sexuality, but even women have a chance and opportunity for salvation, provided that—through efforts of chastity and self-control with passionlessness as a model—they succeed in turning into the Angel-woman pedestal. Sexuality as such is relegated to darker and lower spheres, in Haggard's world typically under-

---

1. The fact that they were inhabited did not really count in this context, since Africans were anyhow seen as living outside History. According to Hegel, Africa was 'no historical part of the world, with no movement or development to exhibit' (McClintock 1995:40).

ground caves and passages.[1] Thus this male-invented split in female sexuality is also presented in Haggard's novels: virgin lands contra gruesome caverns. The implicitly sexualized landscape is serene and pure—but also threatening.

In the lines of thinking at Haggard's time, metaphors of imperialism and sexuality were closely interwoven. The land was seen as a female body ('virgin land') and the female body was seen as a continent yet to be explored. Freud spoke of the female psychology as the 'dark continent' (mysteriously other, unmapped, to be explored). Science, along with imperialism, are conceived as quests for mapping and mastering this unknown Other. Jung confirms the parallels between imperialism and knowledge by talking about Freud's "passion for knowledge which was to lay open a dark continent to his gaze" (quoted in Stott 1989:85).

As the land so the people. The loaded symbolism of one spills over into the other. According to 'the great chain of being' established by evolutionary theory, white man was at the top and black man at the bottom, with various other races in between. Since women in general were perceived as lower, less civilized and more animal-like than men, black women were even further down than were black men. Evolutionary theory had given white man a prime position (of course) but *also* a savage inheritance by linking civilized whites to apes, *and* to uncivilized blacks in the hierarchy of stages in evolutionary development (Stott 1989:75). This relationship worked in two interconnected ways, partly as *projection* of repressed sexual desires to the black man/woman as Other, and partly as a *fear of barbarism* beneath the facade of civilization. The vision of 'barbarism' as opposed to 'civilization' had a lot to do with repression of 'primitive' sexual energies. In order for the white man—whose prototype is the colonizing male—to maintain civilization and control, disturbing sexual energies had to be kept in check. Thus these constant anxieties and fears "that for the white male explorers confrontation with barbarism in Africa might release primitive impulses in themselves" (Stott 1989:87).

As for *projection* of repressed male sexuality there were (at least) two types of 'Others' on whom such sexuality was projected: (white) women and black—i.e. non-white—women and men. Projection, as pointed out (in a different, yet similar context) by Judith Butler, often involves a double process of *disavowal* and *projection:*

> [The abstract, masculine epistemological] subject is abstract to the extent that it disavows its socially marked embodiment [including sexuality] and further, projects that disavowed and disparaged embodiment on to the feminine sphere, effectively renaming the body as female (Butler 1990:16).

In fact, as Butler makes clear, disavowal and projection are crucial parts of the very mechanism of constructing 'Others'. Also regarding the mechanisms of projection Sander Gilman writes: "The control of the woman's body becomes the projection of the male's own sense of lack of control over his own body. Thus the sexualized female is but a projection of his own anxiety about the 'primitive' na-

---

1. Stiebel points to the fact that Haggard and Freud are contemporaries (2001:49) noting several parallels in their lines of thinking.

ture of his own sexuality" (Gilman 1989:302). In Gilman's reasoning black women are targets for projection in a double capacity (as women and as black) thus becoming sexual beings par excellence; sexuality as such is savage, and implicitly black. As also expressed in Haggard's landscapes: beneath the peaceful and inviting virgin land—as surveyed by the explorers' imperial gaze—danger and terror are lurking: "The white body conceals the black body with its threatening and primitive sexuality ... beneath the veneer is a sexuality that corresponds to the myth of black female sexuality, primitive, sadistic, active and death-threatening" (Stott 1989:81). That is: the white woman conceals the black (sexual) woman. Aggressive, devastating black sexuality may break through at any moment: In so far as the white woman is sexual—she is black.

Imperialist anxieties and sexual fears: The Sarah Bartmann story

This leads on to the introduction of the second tale of sexuality as related to Africa: the story of *Sarah Bartmann*[1] —the Khoikhoi woman who was taken to Europe from Cape Town in 1810 and exhibited as the 'Hottentot Venus'. The factual course of events behind the mythical story, is a sad tale of a young woman who in 1810—a few years after the definitive British occupation of the Cape colony in 1806—was persuaded by an English army surgeon to accompany him to London. Here she was put on display in the Egyptian Hall in Picadilly Circus, where she appeared on a raised platform and was ordered to walk, sit or stand by a 'keeper' who threatened her when she disobeyed him (South African History Project 2002). Judging from an abundance of contemporary prints[2] she caused a sensation, but also consternation in abolitionist circles, resulting in a court case and efforts to set her free.[3] With no result, however, as she was later taken to France, where she not only became a popular attraction, but also an object for keen scientific attention, studied and investigated by a team of scientists headed by Georges Cuvier. She died in 1815 not yet 30 years old. Cuvier made sure to obtain her body for dissection, cutting out among other things her genitalia and conserving them for posterity in a glass jar. Cuvier also published a report on his findings in *Memoires du musée d'histoire naturelle* in 1817.[4] Allegedly Sarah Bartmann's genitalia in the glass jar, as well as her skeleton and a plaster cast of her body were on display in the Musée d'Homme in Paris until 1974, when they were removed to the store rooms of the museum.

Sarah Bartmann's story was re-launched in the 1980s—by Sander Gilman (1985a, b, 1989) and others—now in the context of critical studies of racism, sex-

---

1. According to Strother, contemporary documents often refer to Baartman as Saartje, which is a diminutive of Sarah. Such diminutives were, however, often used for slaves and blacks—similar to calling a grown up black man 'boy'. Strother therefore prefers to use the adult name Sarah, and I follow her example.
2. Sander Gilman (1989) shows no restraint in reproducing these demeaning pictures. Considerable more concern is shown by Yvette Abrahams (1997, 1998) and Z.S. Strother (1999).
3. Strother's paper carries as annexes a series of documents from the court case.
4. Title: Extraits d'observations faites sur le cadavre d'une femme connue à Paris et à Londres sous le nom de Venus Hottentote (Gilman 1989:359).

uality and the history of science. Since then Sarah Bartmann has become an icon of colonial, racist oppression. A movement in South Africa has claimed back her remains for proper burial in the land of her home, and on August 9, 2002, on the South African National Women's Day, Sarah Bartmann was buried on the banks of the Gamtoos River, in the place where she was born (South African History Project 2002).

Right from the start the Sarah Bartmann story has a double aspect: one is a story about what actually happened, and the other is the myth of African sexuality into which the Sarah Bartmann case was fed, and on which her popularity was based. Interestingly, as highlighted by Strother, she was launched by a double set of posters, one showing her as an ethnological type,[1] "a most correct and perfect specimen" (a contemporary newspaper quoted in Strother 1999:25) of the race of people inhabiting the new British colony in South Africa, and the other intended to advise the spectators regarding how to *interpret* what they saw (Strother 1999:27). In the first poster Bartman was shown dressed in a form-fitting dress, supposed to match her skin tone (Strother 1999:27) adorned with exotica in terms of beadwork and animal hides. The second poster refers more directly to already existing ideas of the wild and barbaric Hottentot race, with large buttocks and smoking a pipe. In this poster Sarah Bartmann is almost nude, but as also pointed out by Yvette Abrahams (1998:224) it is unlikely that she was ever exhibited naked: "The illustrations represent not Sarah Bartmann, the living woman, but the minds of those who made and viewed them" (Abrahams 1998:224).

There is some disagreement regarding the ways in which Sarah Bartmann fed into existing notions of black sexuality. Sander Gilman reads her directly as an icon of black sexuality, whereas according to Strother the issues are more complex. Obviously the exibition of Sarah Bartmann was sexualized, but in Strother's interpretation neither her large buttocks (*steatopygia* in Latin), nor her elongated vaginal lips, the so-called 'Hottentot apron' (*tablier* in French) were perceived as sexually attractive or erotically arousing at the time, quite the opposite. Strother's reading of the contemporary prints—as well as a 1814 Parisian vaudeville play: 'The Hottentot Venus' where the 'Venus' is disclosed as a monster—is that "however highly sexed, the Hottentot woman can never become an erotic threat" (Strother 1999:30). The fascination is mixed with abhorrence.

The element of abhorrence is underplayed in Sander Gilman's analysis. Most probably, as also hinted by Strother, Gilman's reading of the event draws on ideas which developed more fully in the course of the 19th century (Strother 1999:38). Gilman bases his reading of the Sarah Bartmann story on a contemporary essay in the widely cited *Dictionary of the Medical Sciences* from 1819, where the author summarizes his views on the sexual nature of the black female in terms of acceptable medical discourse: their "voluptuousness" is "developed to a degree of lascivity unknown in our climate, for their sexual organs are much more developed

---

1. Even if the exhibition of Sarah Bartmann entered into the line of 'freak shows' popular in England at the time, Sarah Bartmann was exhibited as a typical, as opposed to an extraordinary specimen (i.e. freaks like dwarfs, giants, porcupine men etc), cf. Strother 1999:24 .

than those of whites" (Gilman 1989:292). In this dictionary article the 'Hottentot' woman is seen as the epitome of lasciviousness, for which the author's "central proof is a discussion of the unique structure of the Hottentot female's sexual parts, the description of which he takes from the anatomical studies of his contemporary, Charles Cuvier" (Gilman 1989:292).

In his detailed analysis of the Sarah Bartmann case, Sander Gilman makes several points. First the—at the time very important—establishment of obvious details of physical *difference* between this Khoikhoi woman and 'civilized Europeans'. Apart from her skin colour, the 'difference' that is seen as particularly important is her large buttocks, the so-called *steatopygia*. In almost every image of Sarah Bartmann her buttocks are indeed excessive.[1] According to Gilman—and this is his second point—in nineteenth century imagination and fascination, the buttocks may be seen as a displacement for the genitalia. "Female sexuality" he says, "is tied to the image of the buttocks, and the quintessential buttocks are those of the Hottentot" (Gilman 1989:296). The really interesting part of Gilman's analysis, however, starts with his third point: that white Parisian prostitutes were depicted in painting and drawing—Gilman refers to works by Edouard Monet and Edgar Degas—with remarkably large buttocks.[2] This brings home his point (which has already been introduced in the discussion of *King Solomon's Mines*) that *in so far as the white woman is sexual—she is black*. A prostitute of course is an icon of a sexualized woman (cf. the Madonna/whore dichotomy) and thus a prostitute is imagined as similar to the black woman. The shared large buttocks are the proof. "The perception of the prostitute in the late nineteenth century has merged with the perception of the black. ... It is a commonplace that the primitive was associated with unbridled sexuality. This was either condemned ... or praised" (Gilman 1989:303). The praise—in a kind of Noble Savage line of thinking, attributed here to Diderot, and also voiced in early 19th century colonial discourse (cf. Megan Vaughan 1991, and Heike Becker, this volume)—seems however to have been less frequent than the condemnation.

Condemnation and fear of unbridled sexuality also make up an important ingredient in Gilman's fourth point: "Black females do not merely represent the sexualized female; they also represent the female as the source of corruption and disease" (Gilman 1989:303). Gilman now extends his analysis of excessive and fascinating, but also threatening (black) female sexuality with further images and imaginations of *sexuality as pathology*: sex is dangerous and may bring death. This was also introduced as a motif in *King Solomon's Mines* above, but Gilman (of course) refers to what was in the late 19th century the core producer of such imaginations: the spectre of syphilis. The fear of syphilis was very alive and a potent producer of mental images from the 19th century onwards, often with a female seductress as the source of the disease. "The 'taming' of syphilis and other related

1. As for another difference, regarding which people like Cuvier were particularly curious, the so-called *tablier* (elongated lips of the vagina), Bartmann managed to keep this a secret until after her death, when Couvier could finally get his will with her (Strother 1999:35).
2. This aspect of Gilman's analysis is discussed and developed by Susanne Thorbek (1998).

sexually transmitted diseases" Gilman writes, "with the introduction of antibiotics in the late 1940s left our culture with a series of images of the mortally infected and infecting patient suffering from a morally repugnant disease, but without a disease sufficiently powerful with which to associate these icons" (Gilman 1989:311). Well, this is no longer the case. The icons of syphilis are no longer homeless. They have been appropriately filled up and even extended with new related icons of HIV/AIDS.

The connections between (female) sexuality, sin and disease are also traced by Megan Vaughan in her analysis of a debate initiated in 1908 on what was supposed to be an epidemic of syphilis amongst the Baganda people in the Uganda Protectorate. In this debate "the medical missionaries stressed the essential and 'innate' sinfulness of traditional African society and the connection between this essential sinfulness and disease" (Vaughan 1991:135). Then, just as now in the case of AIDS, women were seen as the principal carriers of the disease, and female sexuality was seen as responsible for the syphilis problem (Vaughan 1991:133). The same old story about the dangers of excessive and unbridled female sexuality. Vaughan's analysis takes the discussion further, linking it back to the issues of female chastity and passionlessness:

> Female sexuality was everywhere a danger, it seemed, but the enlightened early-twentieth century male medic saw that female sexuality in 'civilized' countries had been successfully tamed. Only when female passions had been brought under control was it possible to grant women greater freedom without endangering the whole society (Vaughan 1991:133).

Thus *the very mark and emblem of civilization is female chastity,* and conversely, uncontrolled 'free' female sexuality is the root of evil, sin and disease.

The undying tale: 'African sexuality' revisited

That these lines of thinking have not expired during the three quarters of a century which have passed between the (supposed) epidemic of syphilis in Uganda in the first decades of the 19th century and the present pandemic of AIDS is evident in many a discussion of 'African sexuality'. When John Caldwell et al. launched the idea of 'African sexuality' in their much debated paper from 1989, it was more a re-vitalization of these age-old images fed by sexual anxieties and fears than an introduction of something new. It is all there: The unbridled black female sexuality, excessive, threatening and contagious, carrying a deadly disease.

Caldwell et al.'s basic line of argument is well known: they contrast a so-called 'Eurasian model' of sexuality, where female chastity is the central moral norm (cf. female chastity as emblem of civilization) with what they call 'African sexuality' characterized by 'permissiveness', indicating that having sex is as simple and straightforward as eating or drinking (Caldwell et al. 1989:195). Marriage bonds are loose (i.e. there is little control of women) and there is no moral ban on exchange of sex for money. For a hundred years Christian missionaries tried to change all of this, according to Caldwell et al. however without much success. Thus so-called 'sexual networking' is rampant, and this is what must be studied, and changed, if HIV/AIDS is to be curtailed. Caldwell et al. are well aware that the 'Eurasian' obsession with 'female sexual purity' and abhorrence of "sexuality that had contrived, and especially commercial, components" (Caldwell et al. 1989:192) have influenced Western ways of seeing, to the extent that "even now Western social analysts find it difficult to see Africa from any other viewpoint" (Caldwell et al. 1989:193). Nevertheless, Caldwell et al. themselves are doing exactly that: looking at sexuality in Africa from Western points of view, inadvertently biased by the whole load of cultural bagage, which determines what they see and don't see, as well as the ways they describe their findings. Valid points of critique have been raised by several authors, among others Beth Maina Ahlberg (1994) and Suzette Heald (1995), both pointing to weak points in the argumentation put forward by Caldwell et al. None of them, however, cut the matter to the bone. Ahlberg takes issue with the Caldwell et al.'s dismission of Christian influence (which goes more or less like this: 'the missionaries struggled to impose female chastity, but alas in vain') and argues that what they call 'permissiveness' is a *result* of Christian preaching, not something which has survived from age-old African customs in spite of missionary presence.[1] "Conversion to Christianity was measured by the extent to which the Africans abandoned their customs" (Ahlberg 1994:229). This meant that all the rules and restrictions guarding pre-Christian sexual life—including various forms of 'safe (i.e. non-penetrative) sex' were broken down. "With no public discourse or socially imparted and maintained sexual discipline, and with changed beliefs ... coupled with the individualization characteristic of Christian morality, socially sanctioned non-penetrative sexual activity was replaced in time by full sexual intercourse" (Ahlberg 1994:231).

Heald's critique is partly overlapping, but also different. Like Ahlberg, Heald is adamant that 'no Christian morals' does not mean no morals at all, and as a contrast she wants to portray "African societies as preoccupied with sexual morality" (Heald 1995:491)—but a morality which, of course, is different from the 'Eurasian' one. Building on knowledge from her own fieldwork among the Gisu in Kenya, Heald stresses what she sees as the 'profound ambiguity' of the sexual act: it is life-giving, but also dangerous (Heald 1995:501). Sex is not just like 'eating and drinking' as Caldwell et al. have it (although also eating and drinking may be serious business at times). Engaging in sex is to engage with strong, even sacred powers, and rules and restrictions are accordingly manifold. Mandatory sexual intercourse takes place for instance after the death of a spouse, when the impurity linked with death still hangs on to the surviving spouse.

> Intercourse is used by the living spouse to remove pollution and transfer its contagion. This is a dangerous act, and widows and widowers are required to walk far from their house to find an unwitting partner ... In the context of death, coitus is thus presented as a positive counter, neutralizing its pollution. (Heald 1995:499.)

---

1. The line of argument taken by Ahlberg is parallel to one of the sides in the Uganda-syphilis debate, according to Vaughan (1991): That the vulnerability of the Baganda to the disease had been created by the disintegration of their traditional social and political systems brought about primarily by the introduction of Christianity (Vaughan 1991:133).

To Caldwell et al. presumably a custom like this would be just another case of 'extra-marital relations', and thus 'permissiveness'. "What the Caldwell's model really fails to do" Heald says, "is to grasp the essential sacredness of sex in Africa" (Heald 1995:497).

So far so good: Ahlberg's points that Christianity altered sexual mores and previous restrictions; Heald's points that sexuality is seen as powerful, sacred and dangerous. What intrigues me about the Caldwell paper however is the way that it may be read 'against the grain'. Even if I find the paper abominable, and even if I agree with both of the critics, I still want to give it a second reading, from a feminist point of view. The authors think persistently from an all-male perspective. As also demonstrated by the critics, their viewpoint is—in spite of certain attempts to pretend something else—part and parcel of the Christian 'Eurasian' perspective. This also implies a firm male point of view: Men are subjects, women objects. But what if this perspective is subverted? What happens if the author's impressive array of anthropological data (more than 200 works in the reference list) are read from a feminist perspective? If 'sexuality' is seen not as risk and danger, and 'chastity' not as inherent virtue—what then will emerge from their data?

'African sexuality' against the grain: A feminist reading

Boiled down to essentials the problem regarding 'African sexuality' from the point of view of Caldwell et al. is that necessary (male) control and regulation of female sexuality is lacking, and that 'female chastity' (emblem of civilization) is not held in sufficient regard. From a feminist point of view readings and evaluations will obviously differ: Less male control and regulation of female sexuality seem to indicate more female self-determination, and the central position of 'female chastity' is highly questionable, of course. The interesting thing is that the author's do provide sufficient data to make a reading against the grain possible. In the section of their paper titled 'Aspects of society influencing sexuality' (Caldwell et al. 1989:199 ff) they focus on four phenomena, which contribute to the 'permissiveness' or 'sexual networking'—the pivotal issue in their description of 'African sexuality'. These four phenomena are the following:

— lineage is more important than marriage,
— polygyny emphasizes the mother-children unit,
— separation of the world of women from the world of men,
— sexual transactions.

In the context of Caldweill et al., these characteristics of (some) African societies all contribute to the sad state of affairs with voluptuous sexual networking all over the place and little understanding of the grand importance of female chastity. I shall take a look at them one by one.

Lineage is more important than marriage

As far as my anthropological knowledge goes[1] the lineage/marriage balance differs from one society to the next, and in matrilineal/matrilocal societies (like the
northern Mozambican Makhuwa) the lineage group to which you belong by birth
is more important that the one to which you are connected by marriage. This goes
for men as well as for women, and as I have seen the system work, it gives the
women several advantages, compared to the situations I met when previously I
worked in patrilineal southern Mozambique (Arnfred 1990). As a young woman
you stay put with your family, while the young man, who is going to be your husband, comes in as a stranger and is looked upon as such. It is only if he manages
to convince his parents-in-law of his qualities in terms of procreation as well as in
agricultural work that the marriage will prevail. Divorce is easy, and it often happens at the woman's request. The husband then is the one that will have to leave,
while the wife stays on in the house with the children, her daily life taken care of
by lineage mates. Such a wife is much better off than in the patrilineal South of
Mozambique, where the abandoned wife has to remain as a stranger in the husband's family, even if he himself stays away, maybe taking another wife in the city.
In Makhuwa society, even if the men (the big uncles) here as elsewhere are the
masters in public contexts, women play significant roles, also in lineage matters.
The male lineage head must have a woman of the lineage (his sister, cousin or
niece) at his side for important decisions. In certain ceremonies this woman will
take the lead (Arnfred 2001). According to my own experience Karen Sacks'
point that women are better off as sisters than as wives (Karen Sacks 1979) holds
true. Thus from a feminist point of view the Caldwell generalization sounds quite
acceptable: If lineages are more important than marriages—all the better for
women's social positions.

Polygyny emphasises the mother-children unit

Caldwell et al. should be credited for looking at polygyny like this—instead of the
usual approach which pities the co-wives for competing with one another for the
husband's favours. In polygyny, according to Caldwell et al. and the sources to
which they refer, "the economic unit is the woman and her children—and in contemporary society she is sufficiently economically independent that the dissolution of a marriage is not a financial disaster" (Caldwell et al. 1989:202). I have my
doubts regarding the second half of the statement, and the authors do not offer
any documentation; the economic situation of the divorced wife will depend a lot
on the circumstances, and in patrilineal/patrilocal societies dissolution of a polygynous marriage may well be tough on the woman. Nevertheless, the observation
regarding the daily life which is centred on the mother-children unit fits my experience, and it also fits into the lines of Ifi Amadiume's thinking, which places a

---

1. By training I am a sociologist, not an anthropologist; I have conducted 'anthropologocal' fieldwork, however, in
   northern Mozambique.

specific emphasis on the mother/child matri-centric unit (Amadiume 1987) even in patrilineal societies. Another feature of polygynous households (in a patrilineal environment) is the collaboration of co-wives. Especially in a place like southern Mozambique, where many men are away for long periods as labour migrants, it will be the women left on the land—two or three co-wives together, or mother-in-law/daughter(s)-in-law—who run the show. This leads directly on to the author's next characteristic: separation of the world of women from the world of men.

Separation of the world of women from the world of men

In this section, Caldwell et al. refer to the 'dual sex system' "characterized by separate women's traditional political organizations, and even by queens of women" (Caldwell et al. 1989:203)—a point generally highlighted particularly by feminist authors (e.g. Okonjo 1976; Amadiume 1987, 1997). I find it very important to be aware of this possibility, in some African societies, of separate hierarchies for men and women as a contrast to Western political (and economic) systems, where women must fit themselves into a male mould if they want to rise to power. As an observation of daily life, I also see the separation of the world of women from the world of men as a quite fitting description, in Mozambique maybe even more in the patrilineal South than in the matrilineal North, partly because many men in the South are labour migrants, whereas in the North they tend to be peasants. But on the whole, in the countryside, women often spend time with women and men with men, in work, leisure and at central ritual occasions. For Caldwell et al. all of this is intended as evidence for lack of male control of women (in marriage) and thus for the disastrous lack of female chastity. Separation of the world of women from the world of men also means: women out of control (by men). This is actually what they write: "Such separation [of the male/female spheres] renders extramarital sexual relations easier for both men and women" (Caldwell et al. 1989:203). They seem to have censored themselves on this point, writing 'for both men and women'. It is evident, however, that it is the *women's* extramarital relations that are the issue of concern. That men are promiscuous is nothing new, and even a fact of 'Eurasian' civilization. What makes 'African sexuality' *African* (in the Caldwell interpretation) is that *women* are promiscuous as well!

Sexual transactions

The final point about sexual transactions, is the central and decisive one, the point where African women go beyond the pale, mixing sex and money. The moral dividing line between sex and money cuts deep in the Christian 'Eurasian' culture in which the Caldwells are embedded, and whose lines of thinking they are unable to escape. Maurice Bloch has—based on his fieldwork among the Merina of Madagascar—provided some good insights regarding such lines of thinking:

> In Europe the linking of monetary exchange and sexual or familial exchange is seen as either typically immoral or as a source of humour and dissonance. By contrast, in Madagascar the need to keep the two areas separate is not present. The right thing for a man to do is to give his lover a present of money or goods after sexual intercourse. This applies not only to pre-marital or extra-marital sex, but also to marital relations, though on a less regular basis. ... It is thus clear that if the Merina attitude to money strikes us ... as needing elucidation *it is because the symbolism of money is powerful, not in Merina culture, but in European culture*" (Bloch 1989:166–167, emphasis added.)

Obviously, self-reflection of this calibre is no characteristic of the writing of Caldwell et al. On the contrary their text is permeated by implicit evaluations of a kind not totally unlike the imperialist discourse analyzed in the start of this paper, as also pointed out by Heald: "Ultimately their [Caldwell et al.'s] view of African sexuality turns out to be little different from the received version; if the Caldwells use the term 'sexual networking' the message nevertheless is that *they* are permissive, if not promiscuous" (Heald 1995:490). *They* are the Africans on the whole, but particularly the African women, as demonstrated above with reference to some aspects of African societies, allowing for women's greater freedom of movement, greater autonomy, greater power—individually and as a group—than where the Caldwells come from.

Read with feminist eyes this is the bottom line of the Caldwell paper: *that women in Africa have greater freedom, autonomy and power than women are accorded in the Christian edition of 'Eurasian' culture,* with female sexuality under male control and female chastity as the emblem of civilization. This in fact is quite an interesting outcome, especially compared with other tales of the deplorable state of patriarchal power and female oppression in Africa. The tales of female oppression in Africa were keenly supported by the Church, which—as pointed out by Nancy Cott—offered education and general elevation to women, demanding female chastity in return: "The evangelical view, by concentrating on women's spiritual nature, simultaneously elevated women as moral and intellectual beings and disarmed them of their sexual power" (Cott 1978:227; Becker, this volume). An interesting observation in this context is offered by Nici Nelson, based on her fieldwork among beer-brewing women in Mathare Valley in Nairobi:

> Christian philosophy has always made a separation between body and spirit: things of the body (sexuality?) are valued less than things of the spirit. ... [The] fear of women's unbridled sexuality has continued through the Christian era and permeated the work of philosophers and psychologists until the twentieth century. ... In Africa this division of the flesh and the spirit into immoral and moral does not seem to exist (Nelson 1987:235).

As also pointed out by Saskia Wieringa the very idea that sexuality should be placed in the realm of *morality* and not in the realm of lineage identity and obligations, was introduced by Christianity: "Illegitimate sexual practices were thus no longer seen as illicit (violating lineage rules), but as sinful (breach of spiritual purity)" (Wieringa 2001:9).

It is because all these layers of connotations and hierarchized dichotomies—spirit/body, Madonna/whore, chastity/promiscuousness—are part and parcel of the concept of 'woman' in a Western context that an African feminist like Oyèrónké Oyewùmí simply refuses to use the concept 'woman'. She writes:

I came to realize that the fundamental category 'woman'—which is foundational in Western gender discourses—simply did not exist in Yorùbáland prior to its sustained contact with the West. ... The concept 'woman' as it is used and as it is invoked in the scholarship, is derived from Western experience and history, a history rooted in philosophical discourses about the distinctions among body, mind, and soul and in ideas about biological determinism" (Oyewùmí 1997:ix, xiii).

The load of implicit meanings is too heavy, and even worse: it distorts the view. Different concepts and different lines of thinking are badly needed.

Cultures of silence?

Investigating sexuality in Africa beyond the load of Christian, colonial, patriarchal connotations is no easy matter. Particularly so because the keen obsession with 'sexuality' which accompanied the colonial intervention did not seem to be matched by a similar focus on sexuality from the African side. What was important in African systems of kinship and marriage was *fertility*, not sexuality as such. Compounding the issue is a certain uncertainty regarding what actually counts/ counted as 'sexual'. Kathryn Kendall (1999) reports from work in Lesotho that women she interviewed who engaged in what seen with Western eyes would be same-sex practices did not see this behaviour as sexual at all. To them sexuality had to do with penetration. From their point of view "you cannot have sex unless somebody has a *koai* (penis)." Thus: No *koai*, no sex. "No *koai*, no sex means that women's ways of expressing love, lust, passion, or joy in each other are neither immoral nor suspect," Kendall notes (1999:167)[1]. Similarly, Wieringa reports from the work of German anthropologist Karsch-Haack (1911) about a German judge Autenrieth, who "in 1907 asked a Wassiba man whether there existed any 'unnatural vices' in his ethnic group. The answer was that such practices did not exist. This has to be understood that same-sex practices or other practices considered 'unnatural' in the contemporary European context were not outlawed in this group, or even considered unnatural, whereas Autenrieth concluded that they did not exist at all" (Wieringa 2001:11). Same-sex practices in African contexts seems to have been quite effectively silenced, even to the extent that heads of state nowadays claim these to be Western imports. A rapidly increasing body of research shows this not to be the case (cf. Murray and Roscoe 1998, Kendall 1999, Aarmo 1999, Moodie 2001, among others).

A notion regarding a 'Culture of Silence' seems to have currency in certain African contexts, indicating a "socially accepted behavioural constraint" dictating "women's reserve, modesty and discretion in sexual relations" (Osakue and Martin-Hilber 1998:193. Cf. also Kolawole, this volume). On a closer look, however, the usefulness of this notion is doubtful; it tends to merge all sorts of different silences together into one. What seems to be important, in an initial phase, is rather to identify *different types* of silences.

---

1.   These practices, as also stressed by Kendall, coexisted with the women being engaged in 'normal' heterosexual marriages. Women-to-women relationships were a supplement, not an alternative to marriage.

In this vein, one type of silence has to do with the fact that some important ways of structuring sexuality takes place through proceedings that are often *performative* rather than discursive. Commenting on Audrey Richard's puzzled confusion when attending the Bemba *chisungo* ritual of female initiation in the 1930s, Henrietta Moore points out that:

> [T]he fact that symbols are concretizised in the body in forms which have no direct linguistic referent accounts perhaps for Audrey Richard's puzzlement about what the girls were learning and for her assertion that some of the meanings were obscure. The ambiguity of meaning associated with embodied experience is something which can only be incompletely copied in language (Moore 1999:13).

Moore also says that "[i]t is a mistake to underestimate the importance and power of embodied knowledge which does not require precise linguistic referents" (Moore 1999:12).

Beyond and connected to these areas of non-discursive social relationships there is also the issue of *discretion*. It is my impression from my work in northern Mozambique that what actually goes on in terms of extra-marital sexual relations, is one thing, but to talk about it is another. *Discretion* is important (cf. also Helle-Valle, this volume). As long as you do not talk about a certain extra-marital affair, nobody has to take action against it. For instance as recorded by Catholic priest Valente de Matos, who worked in northern Mozambique in the 1950s and 1960s, regarding Makhuwa female initiation rites: "The women have to give the impression in talk and gesture of being shy and modest women, especially when confronted with other men, so that nobody, and least of all their own husband, should consider them women of bad reputation. Afterwards, in a low voice and taking advantage of some distraction on the part of the men present, the *conselheira* [old woman master of the ritual] will add that, provided that they take the proper precautions, they may arrange a secret lover" (Matos 1968). The rules for decent wifely behaviour include rules for a decent love affair. Officially women's monogamy is important, and extra-marital affairs do not exist as long as they are not spoken about. In my own work I met the importance of discretion in very explicitly, when during a session of young boys' initiation rituals it was pointed out to them that "in case you see your mother in the bush making love to another man, you must not tell your father about it. You run the risk that he'll kill your mother, in which case her death will be your fault." The transgression in this case seems to be the discursive act rather than the sexual one: the one to blame is not the mother and not her lover, but the son who brought word to the father.

Against this background it is difficult to see from where to take the clues for the construction of a language in which to talk about sexuality. In South Africa there has been, for the last few years, a push for opening up a debate on female and male sexualities, a debate which is not developed on the terrain of mainstream AIDS/'African sexuality' discourse, but which is struggling to find a voice reflecting *female sexual agency,* while at the same time resisting hegemonic male power (cf. *Agenda* no. 28, 1996). This is an uphill struggle. Of course the missionaries have not worked in vain; in South Africa too the Madonna/whore discourse is active. Local studies have found that "women are viewed and view themselves as 'slags', 'sluts' or 'loose' if they are sexually active and take multiple partners, while men are congratulated for such behaviour. Such language also reproduces female sexuality as receptive, as a vessel to receive male sexuality [seeing women] as either pure (and asexual) or impure (and sexual)" (Shefer 2001:8; see also Machera, this volume). Generally, according to Tamara Shefer, "sexuality gets framed as a male domain, in which men control and set the terms, and to which women must be inducted and guided" (Shefer 2001:10). This is the well known theme of the male actor and the waiting virgin. But as Shefer also insistently points out: "there is a need for the development of discourses which challenge the negative construction of girls'/women's sexuality and sexual desires, and put forward a positive acknowledgment of women as sexual agents" (Shefer 2001:14).

The aim of this chapter has been to help in making the development of such discourses possible, through the auxiliary tasks of de-stabilizing existing notions, venturing feminist readings and mapping silences, thus trying to clear a space, as it were, for alternative discourses.

References

Aarmo, Margrethe, 1999, "How Homosexuality Became 'Un-African': The Case of Zimbabwe", in E. Blackwood and S. Wieringa (eds), *Female Desires*. Columbia University Press.

Abrahams, Yvette, 1997, The great long national insult: 'Science', sexuality and the Khoisan in the 18th and early 19th century", *Agenda* no. 32, 1997.

Abrahams, Yvette, 1998, "Images of Sarah Bartmann" in Ruth R. Pierson and Nupur Chaaudhuri (eds), *Nation, Empire, Colony*. Indiana University Press.

Arnfred, Signe, 1990, "Notes on Gender and Modernization. Examples from Mozambique", in A. W. Bentzon (ed.), *The Language of Development Studies*. Copenhagen: New Social Science Monographs.

Arnfred, Signe, 2001, "Ancestral Spirits, Land and Food: Gendered Power and Land Tenure in Ribáué, Nampula Province", in R. Waterhouse and C. Vijfhuizen (eds), *Strategic Women, Gainful Men. Gender, Land and Natural Resources in Different Rural Contexts in Mozambique*. Maputo, Mozambique: Universidade Eduardo Mondlane.

Agenda, 1996, "Women's Sexuality—Let's talk about it...", *Agenda* no. 28, 1996.

Ahlberg, Beth Maina, 1994, "Is there a distinct African Sexuality? A critical response to Caldwell", *Africa*, vol 64, no 2.

Amadiume, Ifi, 1987, *Male Daughters, Female Husbands*. Zed Books.

Amadiume, Ifi 1997, *Reinventing Africa. Matriarchy, Religion and Culture*. Zed Books.

de Beauvoir, Simone, 1949/1972, *The Second Sex*. Penguin Books.

Blackwood, Evelyn and Saskia Wieringa (eds), *Female Desires*. Columbia University Press.

Bloch, Maurice, 1989, "The Symbolism of Money in Imerina", in Maurice Bloch and Jonathan Perry (eds), *Money and the Morality of Exchange*. Cambridge University Press.

Butler, Judith, 1990/1999. *Gender Trouble*. London and New York: Routledge.

Caldwell, John, Caldwell Pat and Pat Quiggin, 1989, "The Social Context of AIDS in sub-Saharan Africa", *Population and Development Review* 15, no 2.

Cott, Nancy, 1978, "Passionlessness: An Interpretation of Victorian Sexual Ideology, 1790–1850", *Signs* 4, no. 2 (Winter 1978).

Foucault, Michel, 1976/1978, *The History of Sexuality*. Penguin Books.

Gilman, Sander, 1985a, "Black Bodies, White Bodies: Towards an Iconography of Female Sexuality in Late Nineteenth Century Art, Medicine and Literature", *Critical Inquiry* 12, no. 1.

Gilman, Sander, 1985b, *Difference and Pathology. Stereotypes of Sexuality, Race and Madness.* Cornell University Press.

Gilman, Sander, 1989, *Sexuality. An Illustrated History.* New York: John Wiley and Sons.

Greer, Germaine, 1970, *The Female Eunuch.* Paladin.

Haggard, Rider, 1885/1994, *King Solomon's Mines.* Penguin.

Heald, Suzette,1995, "The Power of Sex: Some reflections on the Caldwells' 'African Sexuality' thesis," *Africa* 65, no. 4.

Kendall, [Kathryn], 1999, "Women in Lesotho and the (Western) Construction of Homophobia," in E. Blackwood and S. Wieringa (eds), *Female Desires: Transgender Practices Across Cultures.* Columbia Universitry Press.

Mama, Amina, 1996, *Women's Studies and Studies of Women in Africa during the 1990s.* Working Paper Series 5/96. Codesria, Dakar.

Matos, Alexandre Valente de, 1968, "Cerimónias da iniciação das raparigas, Mutuali e Malema, Província de Nampula". Mimeo. Departamento de Antropologia e Arquelogia, Universidade Eduardo Mondlane, Maputo, Mozambique.

McClintock, Anne, 1995, *Imperial Leather. Race, Gender and Sexuality in the Colonial Context.* London and New York: Routledge.

Millett, Kate, 1969, *Sexual Politics.* London: Granada Publishing.

Millett, Kate, 1970, *Seksualpolitik.* Gyldendal. (Danish translation)

Moodie, T. Dunbar, 2001, "Black Migrant Mine Labourers and the Vicissitudes of Male Desire", in R.Morrell (ed.), *Changing Men in Southern Africa.* University of Natal Press and Zed Books.

Moore, Henrietta, 1999, "Introduction", in H.Moore, T.Sanders and B.Kaare (eds), *Those Who Play with Fire.* The Athlone Press.

Morrell, Robert, 2001, *Changing Men in Southern Africa.* University of Natal Press and Zed Books.

Murray, Stephen and Will Roscoe (eds), 1998, *Boy-Wives and Female Husbands.* St. Martin's Press.

Nelson, Nici, 1987, "'Selling Her Kiosk': Kikuyu notions of sexuality and sex for sale in Mathare Valley, Kenya", in Pat Caplan (ed.), *The Cultural Construction of Sexuality.* London and New York: Routledge.

Okonjo, Kamene, 1976, "The Dual-Sex Political System in Operation: Igbo Women and Community Politics in Midwestern Nigeria", in Nancy Hafkin and Edna Bay (eds), *Women in Africa. Studies in Social and Economic Change.* Stanford University Press.

Osakue, Grace and Adriane Martin-Hilber, 1998, "Women's Sexuality and Fertility in Nigeria. Breaking the Culture of Silence", in Rosalind Petchesky and Karen Judd (eds), *Negotiating Reproductive Rights.* Zed Books.

Oyewùmí, Oyèrònké, 1997, *The Invention of Women: Making an African Sense of Western Gender Discourse.* Minneapolis: University of Minnesota Press.

Sacks, Karen, 1979, *Sisters and Wives. The Past and Future of Sexual Equality.* Greenwood Press.

Shefer, Tamara, 2001, *Reflections on contemporary local research on heterosex among young people in South Africa.* University of Western Cape.

South African History Project (SAHP), 2002, *Celebrating Women* (newspaper), 9 August 2002.

Stiebel, Lindy, 2001, *Imagining Africa. Landscape in Rider Haggard's African Romances.* Greenwood Press.

Stott, Rebecca, 1989, "The Dark Continent: Africa as Female Body in Haggard's Adventure Fiction", *Feminist Review* no. 32.

Strother, Z. S., 1999, "Displays of the Body Hottentot", in Bernth Lindfors (ed.), *Africans on Stage,* Indiana University Press.

Thorbek, Susanne, 1998, "Human Rights and Bodies: Sex, Race and Sexuality", in Henrik Secher Marcussen and Signe Arnfred (eds), *Concepts and Metaphors: Ideologies, Narratives and Myths in Development Discourse,* IDS Occasional Paper no. 19. Roskilde University.

Vaughan, Megan, 1991, *Curing Their Ills.* Polity Press.

Wieringa, Saskia, 2001, *Gender, Tradition, Sexual Diversity and Aids in Postcolonial Southern Africa.* ISS Working Paper Series no. 343.

Photo: Abderramane Sakaly, 1958

3. A Reflection on the Cultural Meanings of Female Circumcision

Experiences from Fieldwork in Casamance, Southern Senegal

Liselott Dellenborg[1]

> *The men don't know how to come to a decision. They used to say that a girl must be circumcised in order to approach the mosque, to be able to pray. But now they say circumcision is archaic and that uncircumcised women are more pleasurable, more 'tasty'. Men are only thinking of* màsumam *('taste')! It's the only reason that they are against excision and, really, that is nothing!*—a Jola female circumciser

Introduction

One especially vivid memory from my fieldwork is how the women I interviewed got tired of my questions concerning circumcision. "It is done so that the girl can pray and be initiated. That's all! Surely, it hurts, but then it heals up and is forgotten", the women constantly repeated, unable to understand why on earth I was so interested in this simple act of cutting. In the end, I became truly embarrassed, as I could not help asking myself the same question: Why would I wish to talk about their genitals or lost genitals all the time? There are so many harmful practices and alarming situations in the world, situations that cause people suffering, why does just this one worry us so and get headline attention in our newspapers? The situation described above captures the conflict between the general points of view concerning female circumcision among Westerners and those people practising female circumcision. In the West, the practice arouses intense emotions and it is

---

1. The chapter is based on experiences from my anthropological fieldwork that was conducted in the Lower Casamance region in the Fogny area during a period of 16 months between December 1997 and July 1999. I stayed in a small village of about 400 inhabitants, in the compound of an extended, polygynous Muslim Jola family. Interviews were conducted with people in different villages in the area, where I also attended several initiation rites for girls. The chapter is part of my PhD project financed by Sida/Sarec. A previous version of this chapter has been published in *Göteborg University in Africa—Africa at Göteborg University* (Närman and Ewald 2001).
    Internationally, 'female genital mutilation' (FGM) is the generally accepted term used by Western as well as many African activists working against the practice. Until the 1970's, the concept 'female circumcision' was used, but has since come to be understood as an euphemism. However, in a local context the concept FGM is conceived of as insulting; no parent would agree with the statement that they are *mutilating* the daughters, which is why I do not use this term other than in referring to a Western context of understanding. The Jola generally refer to the practice, which among them comprises clitoridectomy, as 'circumcision' and 'excision'. As this chapter is about Jola conceptions of the practice, these are the concepts I will use. It is important to note that the non-Muslim, foremost Christian, Jola do not practise female circumcision (Linares 1992, Thomas 1959, Friebe 1996), while male circumcision is practised by both Christian and Muslim Jola (Linares 1992, Mark 1992). This chapter deals exclusively with the Muslim Jola population..

assumed by many that the procedure is an ancient, un-changing custom intro-duced by men in order to control women's reproduction and deny them their sex-uality. In this paper I will show that from a local perspective in Senegal, the cul-tural interpretations of female circumcision are very different from these Western assumptions. My study of the Jola shows that the local meanings of excision are neither monolithic nor static, but are contested and constantly negotiated and re-negotiated by various social groups and actors: women and men, young and old. Regional ethnic relations and the political situation, which often pits the Jola against the Senegalese state and the South against the North, further contribute to a dynamic situation that influences and affects local negotiations on the mean-ing of female circumcision. I will also show that in contrary to general Western beliefs on the antiquity of 'harmful traditions' such as female circumcision, the Jola accepted excision as part of modernity.

From this, one can draw certain theoretical conclusions that challenge the common Western stereotypes of those people that practise female circumcision, particularly women who have gone through a circumcision, and by extension have important implications for the formulation of future interventions.

Women fighting for their rights

The Jola, a small ethnic group of about 500,000 individuals who subsist mainly on rice paddy farming in Lower Casamance, pose an intriguing challenge to the com-mon Western understanding of female circumcision as an un-changing, deeply rooted custom introduced by men in order to control women's sexuality. Since the middle of the twentieth century, the practice of clitoridectomy has been spreading among the Muslim Jola, allegedly as part of Islam.[1] My study shows that women not only defend the practice but, more importantly, that they have played an active role in the processes leading to the recent introduction of female circumcision[2] and that female circumcision is now an important aspect of women's initiation rit-uals and their secret society. Jola women, of course, form a heterogeneous cate-gory, but regardless of the differences within this category, excision is crucial to Muslim Jola women's religious identity, initiation, and a female collective identity.

Excision is regarded as "the most important ritual activity" (Bledsoe 1984:457) of many West African female secret societies, which is why anti-excision activ-ities meet with strong resistance. In the middle of the 1990s, for example, mem-bers of the influential women's society, Sande, in Sierra Leone started a fierce

---

1. Excision has come to be associated with Islam among many practising and non-practising people. The custom predates Islam by at least 2,500 years. It is unknown in Saudi Arabia, the cradle of Islam and the majority of Mus-lims in Africa do not practise it. Female circumcision is a local tradition and not a universal Islamic practice (Kas-samali 1998). It is not mentioned in the Quran, nor in the Bible or in the Torah. It is, however, practised and commonly used as a religious marker by certain Muslim, as well as Christian, Jewish, and 'animist' ethnic groups in different parts of the world (Dorkenoo 1994; Toubia 1995). Considering the high prevalence of excision in the African continent, the practice is foremost an African phenomenon.
2. See also Alice Joyce Hamer (1983).

counter-offensive that reached the headlines of the international press.[1] The same is happening in Casamance. These campaigns are generally perceived as part of imperialistic strategies counteracting local culture and women, in particular, suspect the campaigns of being attempts to abolish the secret societies. In contrast to Western belief, excision in the context of secret societies forms the foundation of a certain power base, especially for older women. The Jola perceive imperialism in two ways; on the one hand it is power felt to be exercised by the Western world and the *toubabs* ('the whites') over Africa, and on the other, and more directly, it is the power felt to be exercised by the Senegalese state over Casamance. Since Senegal's independence in 1960, the separatist movement has grown strong in Casamance. The political situation that often pits Casamance against the rest of Senegal has contributed to a social and political process of creating and strengthening a common Jola ethnic identity (Mark 1992). The female circumcision ritual seems to be gaining a particular role in this process. In the last ten years, many men have joined the Senegalese government's action against excision[2] on the grounds that female circumcision is neither a Muslim nor a Jola custom and that it ruins women's health, sexuality, and fecundity. Women, on the other hand, especially married ones, fight against their fathers, brothers, and husbands for what they perceive as their right to be excised and initiated (Dellenborg 2000).

The importance of an inner perspective

This ethnographic account stands in sharp contrast to the Western public debate on female circumcision, according to which the practice is to be understood in terms of male domination, mutilation, and sexual control.[3] The discrepancy between the Western and the Jola cultural understandings of excision presents the researcher with an ethical problem. As an anthropologist living in the field with people who were defending excision, I had to struggle with this discrepancy in my everyday life. I was constantly torn between my role as a scientist trying to catch the 'native point of view' and my personal feelings of indignation and frustration, as well as my feelings of respect and love for the people I came to know in Casamance, people who so generously shared their life, thoughts, and experiences with me. It is obvious that they love their daughters and circumcise them with good intentions. With this insight as a point of departure, I try in my research to grasp the inner rationality of the practice, the reasons that are so important for

---

1. See *Newsweek* October 1994; *New African*, January 1997; *The Democrat*, September 26, 1996.
2. In January 1999 the Senegalese government passed a law against female genital mutilation.
3. In an article in Le Monde (June 2000) a male journalist writes on female circumcision in Senegal. He draws the conclusion that: "Excision … simply seems to be an expression of men's will to control their wives' and daughters' sexuality by mutilating them" (my translation). This sentence, written in one of Europe's most renowned newspapers, can be seen as representing the deeply prejudiced assumptions commonly held by many in the Western world on practising people and, by extension, people in the Third World. The important distinction between structure and actual individuals is missing and this evokes an image of all women as powerless victims in the hands of men, who are egocentric monsters (cf. Mohanty 1999).

people that they will actually expose their children to the pain and risks related to excision.

Anthropologists are often accused of cultural relativism. This, however, is not the same as moral relativism. It is important to emphasise that the inner understanding I am advocating does not imply acceptance, or refusal to take a stance. In D'Andrade's (1995:408) words, it all "comes down to a choice: whatever one wants in the way of political change, will the first priority be to understand how things work?" For interventions to be effective, it is a prerequisite that they are socially grounded and formulated with knowledge and understanding of the custom's socio-cultural context, a context that in the Jola case, clearly involves female agency. Using a method based on the inner (emic)[1] perspective is, in my opinion, the best way to grasp such a complex cultural context.

The Jola cultural and historical context of female circumcision

Making women religious persons

According to the Muslim Jola, circumcision is a religious recommendation for women and an obligation for men. Both male and female circumcision is referred to as *sunnaye*,[2] and in practice it is an obligation for women as well. The prayers of a woman who is not circumcised will not 'take' as well, they will not give her as many 'points' as had she been excised. Far from being just a physical alteration, the genital cutting essentially transforms a girl in the deepest sense of the word. A circumciser told me that it is sufficient for a circumcised girl to put her front to the ground for God to take it as a prayer. A circumcised woman is considered a better Muslim. A Jola religious leader told me that circumcision, male and female, is not only the mark of belonging to Islam, but of having a religion itself. All followers of the religion of Abraham—Jews, Christians, and Muslims—should be circumcised. In discussions with Senegalese friends, colleagues, and informants on the secularisation of Europe, I have understood that not having a religion is, in a sense, considered tantamount to not being human and fits a common assumption of 'white people' as anti-social individualists. The religious leader's statement can, in this context, be understood as implying that to be circumcised is to have a religion, and by extension, to be human.

Social change and female agency

The relatively recent adoption of female circumcision was due to complex cultural and socio-economic influences from the neighbouring ethnic group Mandinka,

---

1. An *emic* model explains the ideology or behaviour of members of a culture according to indigenous definitions, whereas an *etic* model is based on criteria from outside a particular culture (Barnard 1996).
2. The Jola word for circumcision, *sunnaye* comes from the Arabic word *sunnah* which means 'tradition'. Within Islam, *sunnah* is the generic term for the Hadiths (the accounts of the Prophet Mohammed's life, his sayings and doings). Acts that are considered religiously advisable are called *sunnah*, which is a subject of local variation (e.g. Abu-Salieh 1999). There is no Islamic consensus on female circumcision being advisable (see footnote 1 on p.80).

with whom the Jola have been in close social interaction (trade, slavery, intermarriage) for at least three centuries (Mark 1992). The Mandinka proselytised their style of Islam among the Jola, proclaiming female circumcision to be a Muslim custom. The Jola conversion in the middle of the 20th century and their acceptance of the custom of female circumcision was the result of several coinciding factors. The dramatic social and economic changes that took place after the turn of the century, involving French colonialism, taxation, military conscription, and the use of forced labour, coupled with a series of natural calamities that afflicted Jola society, influenced people heavily and made them more open to alternatives to their indigenous religious rituals (cf. Baum 1986). The French colonial administration promoted peanut cultivation and to meet the demands of colonial taxation, the Jola, who were mainly rice cultivators, introduced cash crops, which, in turn, put the Jola and the Muslim Mandinka into closer social contact. At first, Islam attracted mainly young Jola men who went to sell their labour on groundnut fields in the Gambia usually staying with a Muslim Mandinka family. Cash crop cultivation gave these young men a certain financial independence and put them in a position to free themselves from the authority of their elders, an authority that was based on control over the traditional rituals. To be awarded adult status and gain the right to marry and start a family, a man had to go through the male initiation rite, *bukut*, which was held every 25–30 years. In short, Islam "offered a more rapid means of attaining adulthood" (Mark 1978:11). Soon young women joined in the seasonal migration to the Gambia (Hamer 1983). Women, in the current debate and academic studies on belief and practice in Muslim societies, are seldom described as persons taking an active part in processes leading to Islamisation (Ask and Tjomsland 1998; Ahmed 1992; Frisk 1998). However, both Hamer's and my study of local oral history and interviews with old women who were young at the time of Islamisation, reveal that even though women initially were more reluctant towards conversion than men, young women, in particular, were active in introducing female circumcision and the ensuing initiation (*ñaakay*) into a 'new' form of female secret society associated with Islam and the Mandinka.

Female strategies for empowerment?

The dramatic social changes of the last century, with influences from the Mandinka, the local version of Islam, and French colonialism have affected Jola women and girls in a very specific way. In addition to the introduction of female circumcision, the Mandinka social system, with its crucial separation of the sexes, in many ways reinforced an asymmetrical relationship between women and men, as did the weight of French colonialism. For instance, the ignorance showed by the colonial administration of the crucial roles that women played in agriculture implied that "the selection of people to introduce agricultural innovations was, for the most part, exclusively male" (Hamer 1983:94). Researchers have emphasised that these changes implied a general social and economic depression of the position of Jola women in society. Women's workloads increased, their burden as breadwinners became heavier at the same time as their economic independence, religious, and ritual authority decreased (Hamer 1983; Journet 1981, 1985; Linares 1992; Pélissier 1966; see also Weil 1976).

Before the introduction of peanut cultivation, at the beginning of the twentieth century, the Jola took part in the rubber and palm oil trade on a family basis. During the dry season, husband and wife migrated to the Gambia where they sold what they had produced and shared the incomes (Hamer 1983; Mark 1977). With peanut cultivation this migration pattern changed. Women had little to gain from assisting men in this trade and thereby lost their most important avenue for gaining cash. Women were, and still are, virtually excluded from peanut cultivation that by the 1930s already had become the principal rural cash mainstay. But young women soon found an alternative income, less lucrative, however, in working as domestic servants in the Gambia. Hamer (1983:280) points out that no matter how meagre their earnings "Without rural-urban migration as an option, women would be more victims of, as opposed to participants in, the new economic order". In addition to a certain economic independence they won a new freedom of movement. In the Gambian cities the migrating Jola women were exposed to urban life styles and brought new ideas, behaviour, and bodily practices back to the village, such as gestures, walking-style, language, clothing, and female excision.

With the declining importance of indigenous religion, according to which women are ascribed a ritually central role as guardians of agricultural and human fertility (Linares 1992; Journet 1983, 1985), women had to find new strategies for ritual and religious authority. Circumcision as a way for women, as well as men, to become religious persons within the Mandinka form of Islam, and the 'new' form of female secret society associated with Islam, may have opened up empowering possibilities for unmarried young women and childless married women. Traditionally, it is through marriage and motherhood alone that women achieve social status. Motherhood per se constituted, and in many ways still does, a veritable initiation rite for Jola women (Journet 1983, 1985). But whereas only those women who have given birth to a child have the right to be initiated into the indigenous form of female secret societies, the prerequisite for initiation into the 'new', 'Muslim' form of female society is excision. In a sense, Muslim Jola women are no longer dependent on their relation to men (traditionally marriage is the precondition for motherhood) for ritual authority, and the risk of exclusion is not only under female control, but more importantly under a certain individual control practically as any woman is free to choose excision.[1]

Paradoxically, the active role that women played in the introduction of and their current defence of excision, must be understood in the light of these radically changing gender relations. Women, both young and old, had to cope with economic, social, and religious changes at the turn of the last century. Understood in relation to that complex cultural and historical context, the female circumcision ritual might have been a strategy of empowerment for young women caught up

---

1. Christian Jola women who convert to Islam and choose to undergo excision usually have to cope with their family's dislike, which means that their freedom of choice is relative.

in a changing social system that in many ways has led to a general social and economic lowering of women's position in society.

Excision, initiation and knowledge

At present, excision is generally performed when a girl is about four and the initiation rite into the secret society is ideally carried out at puberty. Some decades ago, excision was performed at puberty, in direct connection with the initiation ritual. People told me the wound heals better on little girls and they therefore circumcise at a younger age nowaday (cf. Skramstad 1990). The initiation ritual is elaborate, time consuming, and costly, gathering family and friends from all over Senegal. It is an occasion that girls look forward to with fervour.

In addition to religion, excision is connected to 'knowledge' (cf. Johnson 2000). An excised girl knows something a non-excised girl does not, no matter her age. The circumcision ritual is a socialisation process and an important education for girls. This knowledge—a practical, theoretical, and corporeally 'magical' knowledge—can only be transferred from older women to girls through the excision ceremony and the subsequent initiation ritual. The uncircumcised girl or woman is called *solima*, which is Mandinka and means not only 'uncircumcised' but also 'the one who knows nothing', 'rude', 'ignorant', 'immature', 'uncivilised', and 'unclean' (cf. Hernlund 2000; Johnson 2000).[1] The word is strongly judgemental and is commonly used to insult girls with bad manners, excised or not. However, an un circumcised woman is considered *solima* no matter her social behaviour. With few exceptions, all women in the village are initiated and form a sort of secret society, an association through which much of women's social and religious life is organised. An uninitiated woman is not allowed to participate in the ritual activities of this female society and is socially excluded in many respects.

Different voices in the negotiation

In Casamance, views on female circumcision are many and conflicting. In my experience, it is primarily older women who defend the practice. Only a few middle-aged women told me that they would not have excised their daughters if they had been faced with the choice today. Many of the old women were among the first Jola to go through excision and convert to Islam and to be initiated into the 'new' form of secret society. Genital cutting is an important mark of their ritual authority and religious identity. Older women often reacted with aggression when I posed questions about their opinions of the recent Senegalese law against excision. They were well aware of the law and answered with indignation that Islam demands excision and education. Frustrated, they posed the rhetorical question: "How are we to educate the girls in the future if they are not excised?" One of the

---

1. According to Skramstad (1990:12), *solima* means 'uncircumcised person'. Weil (1976:187), who has done fieldwork in the Gambia as Skramstad, says it means 'sexually licentious person'. Skramstad (1990) critisises him for not explaining how he comes to this conclusion. Her study does not support his interpretation and neither does mine.

oldest female circumcisers in the region told me she would save (sic) all the girls in her family and excise them before she died. Then she added that she would gladly do her next excision-ceremony in the middle of the street: "And they may arrest me! They can't prevent me from following the Prophet's recommendations".

As I mentioned above, women who are not initiated into the female society are socially excluded in many respects. But as long as they are excised, they are not insulted or subjected to other women's harassment as uncircumcised women generally are. Men who are critical of uncircumcised women would not express their critique in public, but more likely in paraphrases and tacit disapproval; it is considered indiscreet and shameful for a man to talk of 'women's matters'. However, I have noticed that people are tolerant vis-à-vis those un-excised women who have immigrated and are not married to one of the local men. Those who did marry a local man however, seem to have been more or less forced to go through the procedure in order to be socially accepted, especially by the women.

Young women and teenage girls rarely expressed any doubts concerning excision in front of me. A few whom I know well told me that they were considering not excising any daughters that they might give birth to in the future. But they would not tell their mothers and grandmothers about their thoughts. Respect for elders is an important element in the education of young people. Respect explains why the young local *imam* I came to know in Casamance could not express his criticism of excision in front of his mother, who is a circumciser.

It is rare to hear old men speak out against excision. In fact, I never met an elderly male villager taking an open stance against excision. Like the old women, they say it is a religious recommendation and a prerequisite for the initiation ritual and education of the girl.

Young men, on the other hand, are generally more critical and curious to know what excision is, what it does, and if it really has consequences for women's health. Most questions concerned women's sexual health and whether non-excised women take more pleasure in sex than excised women do. The villagers I met that were outspoken against female circumcision were all young and middle-aged men; those in the latter category were all educated.

In interviews concerning the growing criticism of excision, the older women ridiculed men and said they are 'only thinking of sex'. It is interesting to note how they dismiss men's talk of sex as childish and irresponsible. An old woman told me that she knows why nowadays a man does not like female circumcision: "He plays with 'that' and if he doesn't find it he will not be pleased. But that 'thing' is exactly what we don't want and have to remove, because it is *kosaye*". *Kosaye* is the word used for the ritually unclean state from which one has to be cleansed through a ritual purification (*ghusl* in Arabic) in order to pray, as for instance, after sexual intercourse (concerning both men and women) and during the menstrual period. Just like the female circumciser cited in the introduction, this old woman put emphasis on the religious importance of excision, to be ritually pure in prayer, interpreting men as irresponsible and more concerned with their own pleasure than with religion.

This points to an internal dynamic involving not just men's relationship to women, but also and perhaps more importantly, the power relationship between old and young women. Obviously, there are several social actors and rival discourses claiming authority. Most visible is the younger and middle-aged men's Western-influenced discourse on sexuality and the older women's discourse on ritual purity and religion. Among the various representations of the meaning of female circumcision, these younger men's voices stand out as especially interesting.

Younger men and the discourse on sexuality

At first, I was surprised to learn that the local understanding of excision did not include the idea of sexual control. As Skramstad (1990:3) contends, it may be valid to argue on an analytical level that the practice is intended to control female sexuality, but the question is whether such an argument is relevant towards understanding the actual social significance of the practice. Among the Jola, sexual control is not mentioned as a reason for women to be excised, neither did people think that circumcised women could more easily control their sexual behaviour than uncircumcised (cf. Skramstad 1990). To my understanding, people are little concerned with women's chastity; and since chastity is not a cultural problem, neither is virginity. Even though parents prefer their daughters to be virgin at marriage this is not always the case and it does not cause a scandal. Before Christianisation and Islamisation, Jola teenagers were allowed to engage in sexual relations, but a child born to an unmarried mother was usually killed at birth, and abortion was severely punished. The taboo was on pre-marital reproduction but not sexual relations (Thomas 1959). I would say that people do not spend a lot of time worrying about women's sexual behaviour, neither is women's sexual pleasure conceived of as a problem. This does not mean, however, that women and men's sexual pleasure are equally valued, nor that women are free from sexual control.

Those women I heard expressing doubts about excision did not specify why. Some just said they had heard that 'it is not good'. Although they do not have unified ideas about the circumcision, men critical to the practice usually have many arguments: excision is not a Jola custom, is not recommended by Islam, and is detrimental to women's health, sexuality, and fertility. Young men particularly dwelled on the subject of sexuality and said they would prefer to marry an uncircumcised woman, assuming that these women take more pleasure in sex, and are more 'tasty'. The way they discussed the subject reveals a certain reification of sexual enjoyment. They did not speak of sexuality in relational terms, and did not consider their own behaviour in relation to women, but focused on the absence or presence of a clitoris. Many of these young men seem to be constructing a dream image of uncircumcised women, a fantasy of how sex with non-excised women would be. From talking to women, I got the impression that their sexual response, or lack of it, had more to do with men's sexual behaviour than with the clitoridectomy. In talking with men who had experienced sex with both excised and non-excised women, they usually could not tell if it made a difference.

The cultural construction of sexuality

From a contemporary Western point of view, it is difficult to conceive of female sexuality when parts or all of the outer genitalia are missing. Without trivialising the harmful effects of different forms of excision, it is important to emphasise that "Western theories do not prove that the biological base for sexual satisfaction is completely removed by female circumcision" (Skramstad 1990:14). In conversations with close female friends in Casamance concerning sex and romantic relations, I understood that they do take pleasure in sex. They did not express any feelings of being denied sexual pleasure and the clitoridectomy is not mentioned as a problem. To understand circumcised women's statements about their sexual experiences, sexuality has to be related to the particular cultural and historical context. Besides being a very individual experience that is difficult to measure and compare, sexuality and sexual pleasure are culturally and socially constructed (Caplan 1987). What is conceived as sexual pleasure is to a high degree dependent on what is defined as such within one culture. "What people want, and what they do, in any society, is to a large extent what they are made to want, and allowed to do" (Caplan 1987:25). In each society this changes with time, as "sexual behaviour and practice, morality, and ideology are constantly in a state of flux". (Caplan 1987:1). Although far from defending female excision, I wish to emphasise that we cannot talk of pleasure and sexuality as something solely biological and dependent on anatomy (cf. Ahmadu 2000).

Questioning Western stereotypes

The discrepancy between the Western and the Jola understanding of female circumcision is striking. In considering the custom from an emic, or inner, point of view, the common Western stereotyped representations of those people that practise female circumcision are immediately challenged. We need to pose the question: if they are not reflected in ethnographic and empirical data, on what then are the common Western assumptions concerning female circumcision based? What emotions underlie the great concern and interest that the practice of female circumcision/female genital mutilation arouses in the Western world? Using a reflexive approach, I suggest that far from being based on investigations conducted in a 'scientific' or 'neutral' way, Western reactions to excision are founded on a Western cultural and historical model of sexuality (cf. Parker 1995).

The shifting significance of the clitoris

Female circumcision has not always aroused the intense emotions we see in the West today. The first pressure on the World Health Organization (WHO) for action came in 1958. A year later, the WHO stated in a resolution that female circumcision is of a socio-cultural character and therefore not their responsibility. In 1975, the alarm was sounded again, and the same answer was given (Thiam 1978; Vichniac 1977). Not until the end of the 1970s did the WHO take action against excision (Coqiery-Vidrovitch 1994). This may seem late, but in fact coincided with the 're-discovery' of the clitoris in the West.

In the Western history of sexuality,[1] the clitoris has attracted special attention in varying ways. From having been considered in the 18th century medical literature with a matter-of-factness as "the main location for women's pleasure in sexual intercourse", the clitoris, together with the female inner sexual organs, had by the late 19th century become the focus of women's "illness" (Johannisson 1994:200, my translation). Masturbation in both boys and girls was understood as causing physical and psychological disorders. In the case of women, this even led certain physicians to prescribe clitoridectomy (Johannisson 1994:200). Although never practised broadly it was used in England and United States as recently as in the 1940s (Toubia 1995). Moreover, Freud's theory on sexuality can be said to have imposed a 'psychological clitoridectomy' (Toubia 1995:18) on Western women, as clitoral orgasm was labelled an 'immature' fixation, and the 'leading genital zone' of a sexually mature woman should be her vagina (Freud 1975:101). Not until the late 1960s, when Master and Johnson "proved that all orgasms in women are caused by clitoral stimulation" (Hite 1976:95), was vaginal orgasm dismissed as a myth and the clitoris again recognised as important to women's pleasure in sexual intercourse.

The time of the presentation of this theory coincided with the Sexual Revolution and the Women's Liberation Movement, a fact that is more than simple coincidence. Free sexual expression came to be regarded during the 1960s as antithetical to the exercise of power.[2] Consequently, Master and Johnson's report was used in the 1970s feminist debate on women's right to orgasm and sexual autonomy. The invention of 'the pill' was an important factor as it gave women the possibility to control and separate sexual activity from reproduction (cf. Giddens 1995). Female orgasm by clitoral stimulation became a prerequisite of 'good' sexual intercourse and linked to women's identity and liberation in a wider sense than the purely sexual. Shere Hite notes the "social pressure that says a woman who has an orgasm is more of a woman, a 'real' woman" (1976:131).

The loaded symbolic meaning the practice of excising the clitoris has in the West is then obvious. To cut a woman's clitoris not only means a mutilation of her body and a reduction of her capacity to feel sexual pleasure, but also deprives her of her femininity, since the capacity to experience orgasm from a Western point of view makes a woman more of a 'real' woman. Furthermore, given the importance attached to sexuality as closely related to personal identity and self-fulfilment, the excision of the clitoris also has the implication of a 'mutilation' of a woman's potential for liberation in a more extended sense.

1.   Cf. Foucault 1976.
2.   Cf. Wilhelm Reich and Herbert Marcuse using Freud's theory on sexual repression and neurosis for re-analysis.

This understanding of sexuality and the self is not universal, but a specific Euro-American culture model. By reacting according to this model, Westerners commonly draw conclusions that give rise to misleading implications of female circumcision. An illustrative example can be drawn from an advert found in a Swedish newspaper. Instead of 'Seminar on female genital mutilation', it said 'Seminar on mutilated femininity'. The Somali women present at the seminar were deeply humiliated and angrily pointed out that "It is our genitals that are mutilated, not our femininity."

Global power relations

This leads us to reflect on the context of global power relations. The Northern hemisphere's hegemonic position in the world gives it a monopoly, an ability to set the agenda, to formulate and decide the priority of problems to be settled in international political arenas. Western feminists have tended to act according to this power structure, and in their will to fight for the right of women in the Third World, have unreflexively reacted in paternalistic ways (Mohanty 1999). At the United Nation's Second World Conference on Women in Copenhagen in 1980, for instance, Western feminists vexed women from Third World countries by debating on the quality of clitoral versus vaginal orgasm. Finally, representatives of the Southern hemisphere protested, pointing out that the acute problems concerning the majority of women of the Third World are lack of clean water and fuel, and high maternal and child mortality (Bexar 1997). This criticism persists today (cf. Mohanty 1999). I do not wish to belittle or ridicule the struggle of Western feminists, but to draw attention to the problems that arise when agendas and research questions are not analysed in relation to global power relations.

A telling case in point is the contemporary practice of partial clitoridectomy that some 2,000 infants per year are subjected to in the United States since they are born with 'ambiguous genitalia'. Interestingly, people in the Western world have their own cultural reasons for trimming girls' clitorises and in Africa people have their cultural reasons too. The difference is that in the West the excision has an aura of scientific credibility and is therefore not considered a mutilation. However, American women who have been operated on began in 1997 to lobby the American Congress to apply the federal ban on female genital mutilation to put an end to this surgery. They argued that the clitoral reduction serves no purpose beyond the cosmetic one and has left many of them with physical, sexual, and psychological problems (*New Internationalist*, April 1998; *New York Times,* May 13, 1997).

Conclusion

Understood in its cultural context, excision among the Jola in southern Senegal is about much more than girls' clitorises. The practice is carried out so that a girl can pray and be part of the women's secret society, to acquire the practical, theoretical, and corporeally 'magical' knowledge that essentially transforms the girl into a real person, into a human being of female gender. In a way, the very same implications that the clitoris has come to have in the West, the absence of the clitoris seems to have among the Muslim Jola, particularly the older men and women.

It is interesting to note that, contrary to common Western assumptions, sexuality is not emically perceived as a cultural reason to excise women, but in the last ten years it has become a reason for younger men to react against excision.[1] In fact, sexuality and excision were only mentioned together in relation to men's critique of the excision. It is obvious that the local context of power relations is complex and involves many social actors, discourses, and agendas. Far from being consistent, views on the meaning of female circumcision are contested and in a constant process of negotiation and re-negotiation. Standing out most clearly in the struggle for authority is the older women's defence of the practice using a discourse on religion, ritual purity, and female education, and the younger and middle-aged men's critique on the practice using a Western discourse on sexual and reproductive health.

Contributing to the complex political context are the relations between Africa and the Northern hemisphere, and between the Jola and the Senegalese state. Accordingly, anti-excision campaigns have generally been interpreted as imperialistic strategies to counteract local culture. The reaction remains especially strong among married and older women. Since excision in the context of a female secret society provides a certain authority in society in general, Jola women commonly meet male actions against excision with suspicion of a hidden agenda. Without knowledge and understanding of the complex cultural and historical context, women's agency and struggle for what they perceive as a right to be excised and initiated becomes unintelligible (cf. Gruenbaum 1994).

From this, one can draw certain theoretical conclusions that will neutralise common stereotypes concerning those who practise female circumcision, especially women who have gone through a circumcision.

Interventions would most likely become more efficacious if consideration was taken of both the Western (etic) and the local socio-cultural (emic) meanings of female circumcision and its generally contested and multivocal character. While men should certainly be involved in anti-excision campaigns (as they commonly are nowadays), my experiences from Casamance suggest that it is also very important to consider why and how various categories of women interpret male resistance to excision in the manner in which they do.

During my time in Casamance, I came to realise that the deep moral indignation with which female genital mutilation, or sexual mutilation as it also has significantly been labelled, is met with in the West, is an expression of our emotions and not necessarily those of the circumcised women. Until we understand the source of these emotions and the way they influence fieldwork and data analysis, our understanding of female circumcision will remain inadequate and misleading

---

1. These findings on male resistance correspond with recent studies from other parts of Africa and from studies on Africans in Sweden (cf. Almroth & Almroth-Berggren 1998; Johnsdotter 2000a, 2000b, 2002; Skramstad 1990).

(Parker 1995). Adding to prejudiced assumptions about other people and societies, these misconceptions will impede adequate interventions designed to put an end to the practice of female circumcision/female genital mutilation.

References

Abu-Salieh, Sami A. Aldeeb, 1999, "Muslims' Genitalia in the Hands of the Clergy, Religious Arguments about Male and Female Circumcision", in George C. Denniston, Frederick Mansfield Hodges, Marilyn Fayre Milos (eds), *Male and Female Circumcision: Medical, Legal, and Ethical Considerations in Pediatric Practice*. New York: Kluwer Academic/Plenum Publishers.

Ahmadu, Fuambai, 2000, "Rites and Wrongs: An Insider/Outsider Reflects on Power and Excision", in Bettina Shell-Duncan and Ylva Hernlund (eds*), Female 'Circumcision' in Africa: Culture, Controversy, and Change*. Boulder: Lynne Rienner Publishers.

Almroth, Lars & Almroth-Berggren, Vanja, 1998, "Female Genital Mutilation in Sudan: A Literature Review and Field Study on Knowledge Of, Attitudes To and Practice Of Female Circumcision in a Rural Area in Sudan", *MFS-Report* No 6/98. Karolinska Institutet, Division of International Health Care Research, Stockholm.

Ahmed, Leila, 1992, *Women and Gender in Islam, Historical Roots of a Modern Debate*. New Haven: Yale University Press.

Ask, Karin & Tjomsland, Marit (eds), 1998, Women and Islamization, Contemporary Dimensions of Discourse on Gender Relations. Oxford: Berg.

Barnard, Alan, 1996, "Emic and Etic", in Alan Barnard and Jonathan Spencer (eds), *Encyclopedia of Social and Cultural Anthropology*. London: Routledge.

Baum, Robert Martin, 1986, *A Religious and Social History of the Diola-Esulalu in Pre-Colonial Senegambia* (Senegal; Slave Trade). Ann Arbor: UMI.

Bexar, Katja, 1997, "Från en Svensk Horisont i Kairo", *Kvinnovetenskaplig Tidskrift*, 3–4, 1997.

Bledsoe, Caroline, 1984, "The Political Use of Sande Ideology and Symbolism", *American Ethnologist*, vol. 11, no.3, 1984.

Caplan, Pat, 1987, "Introduction", in Pat Caplan (ed.), *The Cultural Construction of Sexuality*. London: Routledge.

Coqiery-Vidrovitch, Chaterine, 1994, *Les Africaines, Histoire des Femmes d'Afrique Noire du XIXe au XXe Siècle*. Edition Desjonquères.

D'Andrade, Roy, 1995, "Moral Models in Anthropology", *Current Anthropology,* vol. 36, no. 3.

Dellenborg, Liselott, 2000, "Women Fighting for Their Rites or How Female Circumcision was Made Possible in Casamance, Southern Senegal". Paper presented at the *U-landsforskning 2000 Conference*, Göteborg, Sweden 13–15 January 2000, arranged by Sida/Sarec and Göteborg University.

The Democrat. September 26, 1996, Freetown, Sierra Leone.

Dorkenoo, Efua, 1994, *Cutting the Rose: Female Genital Mutilation: The Practice and Its Prevention*. London: Minority Rights Publications.

Foucault, Michel, 1976, *Histoire de la Sexualité, 1. La Volonté de Savoir*. Paris: Gallimard.

Freud, Sigmund, 1975 (1905), *Three Essays on the Theory of Sexuality*. New York: Basic Books, Inc., Publishers.

Friebe, Jens, 1996, Altern im Senegal: Gesellschaftliche Transformationprozesse am Beispiel der Situation der Alten in einem Dorf der Unteren Casamance. Saarbrücken: Verlag für Entwicklungspolitik Saarbrücken GmbH.

Frisk, Sylva, 1998, "Kring Moskén, Kvinnlig Religiös Praktik och Nätverk med Moskén som Bas", *Feministiskt Perspektiv,* no. 4, 1998.

Giddens, Anthony, 1992, *The Transformation of Intimacy: Sexuality, Love and Eroticism in Modern Societies*. Stanford: Stanford University Press.

Gruenbaum, Ellen, 1994, "Women's Rights and Cultural Self-Determination in the Female Genital Mutilation Controversy". Paper presented at a symposium on Women and Human Rights, American Anthropological Association Annual Meeting, Atlanta, Georgia, December 1994.

Göteborgs-Posten, May 22, 1996, Göteborg, Sweden.

Hamer, Alice Joyce, 1983, Tradition and Change: A Social History of Diola Women (Southwest Senegal) in the Twentieth Century. Ann Arbor: UMI.

Hernlund, Ylva, 2000, "Cutting without Ritual and Ritual without Cutting: Female 'Circumcision' and the Re-Ritualization of Initiation in the Gambia", in Bettina Shell-Duncan and Ylva Hernlund (eds), *Female 'Circumcision' in Africa, Culture, Controversy, and Change*. London: Lynne Rienner Publishers.

Hite, Shere, 1976, *The Hite report: A nationwide study on female sexuality*. New York: Macmillan.

Johannisson, Karin, 1994, *Den mörka kontinenten: kvinnan, medicinen och fin-de-siècle*. Stockholm: Norstedts Förlag.

Johnsdotter, Sara, 2000a, "The Pros and Cons of Female Circumcision: The Views of Swedish Somalis". Paper presented at the Sexual and Reproductive Health Workshops at Rute, Gotland, 23–27 August, 2000, arranged by ICHAR, Sweden.

Johnsdotter, Sara, et al. 2000b, "Som Gud skapade oss: Förhållningssätt till kvinnlig omskärelse bland Somalier i Malmö". Report. Malmö: Malmö Stads Program Sexuell Hälsa.

Johnsdotter, Sara, 2002, "Created by God, How Somalis in Swedish Exile Reassess the Practice of Female Circumcision". Doctoral Thesis. Lund: Dept. of Sociology, Lund University.

Johnson, Michelle C., 2000, "Becoming a Muslim, Becoming a Person: Female 'Circumcision', Religious Identity, and Personhood in Guinea-Bissau", in Bettina Shell-Duncan and Ylva Hernlund (eds), *Female 'Circumcision' in Africa, Culture, Controversy, and Change*. London: Lynne Rienner Publishers.

Journet, Odile, 1981, "Les Femmes Diola Face au Développement des Cultures Commerciales", in A. Michel, F. A. Diarra, H. Agbess (eds), *Femmes et Multinationale*. Paris: Karthala.

Journet, Odile, 1983, "La Quête de l'Enfant, Représentation de la Maternité et Rituels de Stérilité dans la Société Diola de Basse-Casamance", *Le Journal des Africanistes*, Vol LI. No 1–2.

Journet, Odile, 1985, "Les Hyper-Mères n'ont plus d'Enfants, Maternité et Ordre Social chez les Joola de Basse-Casamance", in Nicole-Claude Mathieu (ed.), *L'Arraisonnement des Femmes, Essais en Anthropologie des Sexes*. Cahier de l'Homme. Nouvelle Série XXIV. Paris: Éditions de l'École des Hautes Études en Science Sociale.

Kassamali, Noor, 1998, "When Modernity Confronts Traditional Practices: Female Genital Cutting in Northeast Africa", in H. L . Bodman & N. Tohidi (eds), *Women in Muslim Societies: Diversity within Unity*. London: Lynne Rienner.

Linares, Olga, 1992, *Power, Prayer and Production, the Jola of Casamance, Senegal*. Cambridge: Cambridge University Press.

Marcuse, Herbert, 1970, *Eros and Civilization*. London: Allen Lane.

Mark, Peter, 1977, "The Rubber and Palm Produce Trades and the Islamization of the Diola Boulouf (Casamance)", *Bulletin de l'IFAN*. T 39. Serie B. No 2:341–361. Dakar.

Mark, Peter, 1978, "Urban Migration, Cash Cropping and Calamity: The Spread of Islam among the Diola of Boulouf (Senegal), 1900–1940", *African Studies Review*, vol. XXI, no 2, September 1978.

Mark, Peter, 1992, *The Wild Bull and the Sacred Forest, Form, Meaning, and Change in Senegambian Initiation Masks*. Cambridge: Cambridge University Press.

Mohanty, Chandra Talpade, 1999, "Med Västerländska Ögon: Feministisk Forskning och Kolonial Diskurs. (Under Western Eyes)", in Catharina Eriksson, Maria Eriksson Baaz, Håkan Thörn (eds), *Globaliseringens kulturer: den postkoloniala paradoxen, rasismen och det mångkulturella samhället*. Nora: Nya Doxa.

Le Monde, June 2000. Paris, France.

Newsweek, October 14, 1994. New York, USA

New African, January 1997. London, UK.

The New Internationalist, April 1998, issue 300. Oxford, UK. (www.newint.org)

The New York Times, May 13, 1997. New York, USA.

Närman, Anders & Jonas Ewald (eds), 2001, *Göteborg University in Africa—Africa at Göteborg University*. Göteborg: Centre for Africa Studies, Göteborg University.

Parker, Melissa, 1995, "Rethinking Female Circumcision", *Africa* 65 (4):506–523, 1995.

Pélissier, Paul, 1966, *Les Paysans du Sénégal, Les Civilisations Agraires du Cayor à la Casamance*. Saint-Yrieix: Imprimerie Fabrègue.

Reich, Wilhelm, 1961, *The Sexual Revolution*. New York: Farrar, Straus and Giroux.

Skramstad, Heidi, 1990, "The Fluid Meaning of Female Circumcision in a Multiethnic Context in Gambia: Distribution of Knowledge and Linkages to Sexuality". Working Paper D 1990:12. Bergen: Chr. Michelsen Institute.

Thiam, Awa, 1978, *La Parole au Negresses*. Paris: Éditions Denöel/Gonthier.

Thomas, Louis Vincent, 1959, Les Diolas: *Essai d'Analyse Fonctionelle sur une Population de Basse Casamance*. Tome I & II. Dakar: IFAN.

Toubia, Nahid, 1995, *Female Genital Mutilation: A Call for Global Action*. United Nations, New York: Women Inc.

Vichniac, Isabella, 1977, "Des Millions de Fillettes et d'Adolescents sont Victimes de Mutilation Sexuelles", *Le Monde*, April 29, 1977.

Weil, Peter, 1976, "The Staff of Life: Food and Female Fertility in a West African Society". *Africa*, vol. 46, no. 2.

Photo: El Hadj Bassirou Sanni, 1982

4. Preventing HIV? Medical Discourses and Invisible Women

Katarina Jungar and Elina Oinas

Introduction

Ever since the global panic around HIV/AIDS started, Africa has been represented in extremely catastrophic terms as the lost continent (Patton 1997). There is now growing attention to the fact that young women (and babies) are the major HIV risk group in Africa (UNAIDS/99.2, UNAIDS/99.16E). In both research literature and popular media the striking statistics of Sub-Saharan Africa are presented at the beginning of each article: for example that almost one fourth of pregnant mothers in South Africa are infected (Gilbert and Walker 2002). In this study we ask if this new emphasis in media reports has, in fact, any impact on HIV/AIDS prevention strategies, and whether women are actually taken into account. We focus on one debate, that of male circumcision as prevention strategy in Africa.

We analyze the male circumcision texts in medical journals by tracing stories about two themes: *gender* and *race*. Regarding *gender*: How are women and girls represented in the texts? If the suffering of women is the new AIDS icon, are real women taken into account? Our approach to the theme of *race* is inspired by Cindy Patton's work on "African AIDS" as a social construct (Patton 1997). If the suffering of Africa is reproduced (again), what kind of representation of Africa is at work?

During the last few years male circumcision has become intensely discussed as a new possible strategy for HIV prevention in Africa. This chapter focuses on this discussion, in medical media and also to some extent in popular news media. We will show that the contemporary debate on male circumcision bases its questions and research interests on a mythological understanding of HIV/AIDS as something specific for Africa, and that these assumptions and questions are based on and reproduce colonial imaginations of 'African sexuality'. Further, we ask what the implications of this are for women. The background for this study is an interest in the concerns raised by women's activism and HIV activism in Southern Africa. We wish to explore how the debate on male circumcision relates to the concerns of activists, who point to the urgency of protecting women from HIV and to the importance of changing sexual power relations in order to do so. Our conclusion will be that the male circumcision debate not only completely ignores women and girls but also maintains a (hetero) sexual politics of male power, in tune with the idea of 'different' African sexualities and 'different' African AIDS (cf. Patton 1997; Ratele, this volume).

The material for this study consists of articles in medical journals, primarily journals like the *Lancet* and *British Medical Journal* that popularize and debate research findings and health care policy, but also journals of stricter academic style reporting research and findings.[1] We deliberately blur the difference between media texts and scientific texts. Medicine, as no other human enterprise, cannot represent a level of knowledge that can raise itself above 'culture' and thus address the HIV epidemic 'objectively' (cf. Foucault 1973). That medicine is just another social institution and an integral part of contemporary media society is not as such a problem. A problem and indeed a very lethal problem for women is however the *sexism* and the *constructions of 'Africa'* inherent in medical accounts of male circumcision and HIV/AIDS.

Inventing 'African AIDS'

The theoretical frame of reference within which the analysis is conducted draws from postcolonial feminist theory (Mohanty 1991; Spivak 1988) and feminist deconstructive readings of AIDS. According to Paula Treichler (1999) AIDS should be viewed as constructed through language—in particular through the discourses of medicine and science. This construction according to her is 'true' or 'real' only in certain specific ways—for example, insofar as it guides research or facilitates clinical control over the illness. The name AIDS in part constructs the disease and makes it comprehensible (Sontag 1991). Treichler argues that while it is not possible to look behind language to determinate what AIDS 'really' is, it is of importance to explore the sites where such conclusions and fixing occur (cf. Epstein 1995). Treichler, among others, assesses that the social dimensions of AIDS epidemic are marginalized in the biomedical discourse. In this chapter we will show that the social construction of AIDS is a complicated matter: in a paradoxical argumentation the medical media maintain a representation of HIV/AIDS based on simple biological determinism while, in the very same texts, the constructions of HIV/AIDS are based on stereotypical ideas of Africans and 'African culture'.

Patton claims that "Western science today is slowly consolidating around a particular construction of 'African AIDS', which elaborates on the colonialist mystifications of the past century"(1997:387). One important part of this construction is the idea that Africa and Africans are already lost to the pandemic. Another widely spread thought is that AIDS in Africa is spreading in a different way than in the West. Patton maintains that the idea of 'African AIDS' is very much connected to constructions of 'African sexuality', which stem from Western colonial imagination of African sexuality as closer to nature and therefore different to the West's. Frantz Fanon's classic work (1971) demonstrates how the black

---

1. According to different review articles and a MEDLINE search conducted by us in March 2001, male circumcision and HIV have been discussed in approximately 40 articles since 1986, with a peak from 1999 onwards. These articles in the *Lancet, British Medical Journal, AIDS, International Journal STD AIDS, Clinical Infectious Diseases, New England Medical Journal* and *International Journal of Epidemiology* (and to some extent other media following up the medical reporting) constitute the material of this study. The debate has continued since this study was concluded.

man/black penis is used as the uncivilized imagery in the service of white sexuality (see Ratele, this volume). What does this mean for women in the specific context of HIV/AIDS prevention?

In 1988 a new theory was put forth: Africans are afflicted by genital ulcers that can increase transmission of the virus from women to men: "Conference visual aids during the genital ulcers era were never complete without pictures of diseased genitals—projected to 6 or 8 feet high to get over the point that the equipment of men and women in Africa is 'different'" (Patton 1997:398). It is around this time that for the first time in medical media speculations about the connection between male circumcision and HIV transmission are mentioned (Fink 1986). As in the genital ulcers theory, here too the focus is on genital 'difference'. There is a clear parallell here to what Eisenstein calls "a phallocratic construction of racism" (Eisenstein 1996: 38) where 'different' penises are needed to represent 'race'. We argue that the male circumcision debate operates within this same logic, "disguised as Western altruism"—as Patton characterizes Western attempts to 'help' the Africans (1997:387). We continue from Patton's point by asking how women are situated in the discourse on male circumcision.

Activists addressing HIV/AIDS

In this chapter we contrast the male circumcision debate with activists' work that connects HIV/AIDS to questions of historically specific patterns of colonialism, apartheid, capitalism and a global economy with its powerful pharmaceutical corporations. HIV activists have to deal with the Western constructions of 'African AIDS' on the one hand, and the realities of HIV/AIDS in women's lives, on the other. One strategy has been to highlight the importance of women's empowerment in fighting HIV/AIDS (Abdool Karim 1998; Gilbert & Walker 2002). Activists in Africa have, like other activists worldwide, emphasized the impossibility of fighting HIV/AIDS without addressing HIV/AIDS in gendered terms. They look for ways of pointing out that women are more vulnerable to become infected both socially and physiologically, and that this should not be disregarded in HIV prevention work. Gilbert and Walker (2002) emphasize that addressing women's specific situations should not be understood as a further victimization of African women, nor as an essentializing view on gender.

A notion that can be helpful when trying to understand the specific situations of African women without reproducing victimization is *vulnerability* (Delor and Hubert 2000). The notion enables a social analysis of infection patterns: while anyone is biologically susceptible to infection by different diseases such as HIV/AIDS, certain social and economic factors place some individuals and groups in situations of increased vulnerability (Kalipeni 2000:966). Kalipeni (2000) refers to vulnerability as consisting of entitlement, empowerment and political economy. Doyal's (1995) general claim that the disadvantageous social position of women and girls places them in a vulnerable position with serious health consequences, is applied by Gilbert and Walker (2002) on the South African HIV/AIDS situation. On the basis of statistical information, they assert that despite the problems of reliability of statistics, it seems clear that women, especially young women, are the group that should be given the highest priority in HIV prevention work. Further, they conclude that this work should focus on political and social issues rather than individual issues; addressing social inequalities, education, poverty and employment (Gilbert and Walker 2002).

Local grass-root activism and especially women's activism are growing to powerful political movements in Sub-Saharan Africa (Mama 1997), addressing HIV/AIDS alongside other social and political issues. Of importance in most movements is to situate HIV/AIDS into a wider social context. In South Africa, for example, grass-root organizations involved with women's empowerment and HIV prevention represent a wide scale of social activism and differing awareness of gendered power relations in the society. The starting point of this activism is often the very statement we began with, that women, especially young women, are becoming infected in greater numbers than men. This statement, as we indicated earlier, can be explained in terms of Western constructions of 'African AIDS': AIDS in Africa as something radically different, with different transmission patterns having to do with dramatic differences in Western sexual practices and mystified 'African sexuality'. Emphasizing that more women than men are dying of AIDS in Africa can, however, also be seen as a way of legitimating women's political mobilization, especially when it is used by activist women themselves.

Women who are working in organizations dealing with empowerment of women, men's sexualized violence and issues around women's health, emphasize the connections between HIV, gender power relations and (hetero)sexuality. For example the Musasa Project in Zimbabwe highlights the difficulties most women face in negotiating safe sex in heterosexual relationships. This project is concerned with the connections between violence against women and HIV: "There is a strong link between women's low position in society, male violence against women, and the spread of HIV/AIDS" (PACSA factsheet 1999). Women's lack of voice and power as sexual subjects has also been highlighted as the major obstacle hampering safe sex practices among young European women (Holland et al. 1994).

The global fight for the right to medication for people living with HIV can be seen as an important part in the empowerment of women. The South African *Treatment Action Campaign* (TAC), along with other HIV-activism, is raising the issue of HIV from the personal to the political level of global resistance.[1] Access to health care and medical treatment is one important part of this battle, but the social empowerment that such 'medicalization campaigns' mean for women also poses a challenge towards other forms of social inequalities (see also Sewpaul and Mahlela 1998). For example in Khayelitsha in South Africa a mother-to-child transmission prevention project that was run in close connection with TAC's

---

1. TAC is a noteworthy health movement with its emphasis on generating political mobilization in society. It deserves a more thorough examination than what is possible here (Jungar and Oinas 2003).

HIV-activism, focusing on women's own initiatives and informed choices, has created a political consciousness among women about their health rights, and ultimately a political consciousness about global politics. These women are raising questions on women's health rights and situate these questions into a larger context of economical exploitation and global capitalism. Interestingly, the obvious point that TAC emphasizes—that the availability of drugs is a human rights issue *and* an effective tool in HIV prevention—is little mentioned in otherwise socially aware research (e.g. Gilbert and Walker 2002).

Feminist research and the feminist movements in the West have been peculiarly silent about HIV/AIDS as a key feminist issue. According to Treichler (1999) feminism has failed to influence the direction of the epidemic or challenge the stereotypes in AIDS discourse. African feminist scholars are, however, changing this picture (Sewpaul & Mahlela 1998; Tallis 2000; Moletsane et al. 2002; see also Machera, this volume). HIV research and feminist theory in general share conceptual interests—e.g. on power, control and change—and we argue that stronger links could challenge Western views in productive ways. Discussions on power and control involve a whole variety of issues ranging from macro level political questions of social inequalities, poverty and employment, to a symbolic level of gendered constructions of sexuality (Mama 1997; also Gilbert and Walker 2002; Kumar et al. 2001). Ratele's (2001) important note, that sexualities are always political, and involve political questions of power and racism, is highly relevant in the context of gender and HIV prevention. Grass root women's activism, however, shows that the questions of sexuality and power are concrete reality that must be addressed, and they are not giving up on the (utopian?) wish that such power relations can be changed.

Male circumcision in medical media

Against the background of what Patton calls constructions of 'African AIDS' and the knowledge continuously produced among HIV-activists, we want to explore the debate around male circumcision as a means of fighting HIV/AIDS in Africa. The argument in the texts that promote male circumcision is that the removal of the foreskin may reduce a man's susceptibility to HIV infection (Szabo and Short 2000a; Halperin and Bailey 1999; Weiss et al. 2000; Bailey 2000).[1] The pro-circumcision texts are mostly reviews of other medical articles. For example, Szabo and Short popularize selected research findings and conclude with a strong pro-circumcision statement: "The majority of men who are HIV positive have been infected through their penis. There is conclusive epidemiological evidence to show

---

1. Mainly two explanations are given as to why uncircumcised men would be more vulnerable to HIV infection. Firstly the foreskin contains HIV target cells. During intercourse the foreskin is pulled back and the highly vascularised part of the foreskin, which contains a high density of HIV-target cells, is exposed. The other explanation is that the foreskin during intercourse may be more sensitive to trauma, which could cause tearing and bleeding, which means additional vulnerability to HIV. Finally it is explained that circumcision may reduce the risk of STDs, which act as co-factors for HIV infection (Weiss et al. 2000; Szabo & Short 2000a).

that uncircumcised men are at much greater risk of becoming infected with HIV than circumcised men" (2000a:1592). Weiss and colleagues (2000) conducted a "meta-analysis" of previous research on connections between male circumcision and HIV infection rates. This article concludes that "the data from observational studies provide compelling evidence of substantial protective effect of male circumcision against HIV infection in Sub-Saharan Africa, especially in populations at high risk of HIV/STD" (Weiss et al. 2000:2369).

These texts point out that there are problems—for example that there is no evidence that male circumcision performed on adult men has any positive impact—but their conclusion is clear: *lack* of male circumcision is a health risk in Africa and male circumcision should be promoted as a means of HIV prevention:

> The hour has passed for the international health community to recognize the compelling evidence that shows a significant association between lack of male circumcision and HIV infection. It is time to take the following actions: to provide communities with accurate, balanced information so that individuals can make informed choices; to provide the training and resources needed to offer safe, voluntary male circumcision in which pain is kept to a minimum; and to begin investigations of the feasibility of acceptable male circumcision interventions in communities with large HIV and STD seroprevalence where circumcision has traditionally been practised (Halperin & Bailey, 1999:1814–1815).

Voices against the practice of male circumcision are raised in the journals, too (Van Howe 1999). In fact, strong opposition follows any article presenting male circumcision as a HIV/AIDS prevention strategy. Szabo and Short's (2000a) article, mentioned above, provoked more than 50 replies to the *British Medical Journal*. These replies argued, for example, that the review did not hold scientific standards, did not present enough evidence, did not take into account the risks of complications involved in circumcision etc. Van Howe's (1999) meta-analysis concludes that medical research does not show conclusive evidence on the protective effect of male circumcision.

Those researchers who in their empirical studies have most data on circumcision and HIV infection rates are the ones most cautious in promoting male circumcision as a preventive measure. It is more frequently the popularizing media texts that highlight and promote male circumcision as a preventive measure. In the following discussion it seems necessary first to deal with the issue of scientific evidence for male circumcision promotion, in order to show that what is discussed in these studies is above all the issue of scientific uncertainty as to whether male circumcision can reduce risks for male infection. The major concern of this study, the race and gender discourse in male circumcision promotion, will be discussed afterwards.

Scientific uncertainty

What is evident is that the male circumcision research has been conducted on a macro level of large populations of men, often involving whole societies. Different infection rates in different countries are explained by the rate of male circumcision in different areas (Halperin and Bailey 1999). In an often cited study by

Moses and colleagues (1990) infection rates in populations are explained in terms of male circumcision, while other factors such as access to health care, HIV drugs, gender inequalities, money spent on prevention programmes and availability of condoms, that could be seen to influence the different infection rates in different countries, are unaccounted for. The social, cultural, economic, religious, and other differences within different countries are disregarded—and only the foreskin of the black penis prevails as a way to explain difference.

During the 1990s the research on male circumcision takes regional and cultural differences in African societies more seriously, and detailed studies within local communities are conducted (Urassa et al. 1997; Quinn et al. 2000; Gray et al. 2000; Oliver et al. 2000). The Rakai study in urban Uganda (Quinn et al. 2000; Gray et al. 2000) is the only one where a clear pattern is found: but this only in as small a "population" as 50 men. The Rakai researchers themselves do not, however, promote male circumcision in their conclusions (Quinn et al. 2000:928), but maintain that the issue is too complicated—for example by social factors—for any recommendations. Yet, this study is continuously used as a basis for male circumcision promotion (Szabo and Short 2000a:1592; Ford 2000:9).

The only certain result our examination of the pro-circumcision texts found is the uncertainty regarding scientific proof of whether male circumcision is related to HIV infection rates among men. In studies where a weak connection is found it is still unclear at which age the procedure should be conducted and how much of the foreskin must be removed. Most studies conclude with a statement that more research is needed. "Randomized trials are needed to determine the utility of circumcision as an HIV preventive measure" (Gray et al. 2000:2380).

No texts promise anything close to total protection for men. The studies are conducted on the level of populations, and social aspects, such as differences in behavior between different social groups—not to mention monitoring for individual behavior such as actual sexual practices—cannot be sufficiently accounted for. Based on populations it should be clear that these studies do not offer evidence on the level of the individual, even if they had found a connection between male circumcision and male infection—which they did not. Yet, the highly regarded medical journals publish texts where male circumcision is strongly promoted. The article titles describe the political agenda: "How does male circumcision protect against HIV infection?" (Szabo and Short 2000a:1592)—the question is how, not whether. In their article, Harper and Bailey phrase the problem as a *lack* of circumcision as if circumcision would be a natural and unproblematic procedure.

Even when skepticism or reluctance is expressed, the common conclusion is that more research should be conducted. Our question is: *why?* In addition to the highly problematic ethical issues involved in any medical trials and research in developing countries (see Benatar 2002; Pang 2002) HIV prevention trials highlight some specific problems. When studying the effectiveness of one prevention strategy, others may be neglected. Even the promoters conclude that people would still need other prevention measures, like condoms—but the role of condoms becomes unclear if male circumcision is promoted.[1]

One answer to the question of why there is such urgency in promoting such procedures, is that the 'dark continent discourse' is at work here: it can only be on a continent that is seen as already lost, that such a preventive measure can make any sense at all. It does *not* make any sense if the realities of HIV infection in Africa are in focus, but they are not. As we will discuss further on, male circumcision promotion draws from the image of 'Africa as different', creates a boundary between Africa and the West, and thus protects Western white heterosexuality.

Africa is lost anyway

In all the articles male circumcision is being promoted only to non-Western countries. The first question we need to ask is why male circumcision is researched and promoted as a method to prevent HIV transmission in the South, but not in Europe or the United States? How can medical researchers argue that male circumcision can offer some immediate protection against the spread of the disease but not promote circumcision in the West? Even the most enthusiastic pro-circumcision researchers keep the 'developed' world out of the discussion:

> Other than recommending that male circumcision should be seriously considered as an additional means of preventing HIV in all countries with a high prevalence of infection, we have avoided all discussion about the relative advantages and disadvantages of neonatal male circumcision as a routine procedure in developed countries, where the prevalence of HIV infection is low. We do not intent to enter that debate, where objectivity is hard to find (Szabo and Short 2000b:1469).

Nowhere in the articles is the construction of this clear cut "difference" between the developed countries and Africa explained however strongly it is assumed to exist. It seems clear that this unexplained "difference" is the bottom line of the whole argumentation for male circumcision. HIV/AIDS in Africa is something special, an issue different from HIV/AIDS in the West. Imagery of a dark continent on the brink of disaster, as pointed out by Patton (1997:391), is invoked, for example: "The heterosexual spread of HIV-1 in some regions of Sub-Saharan Africa has been *explosive*" (Tyndall et al. 1996:449). Africa is constructed as a lost continent where people are dying anyway, which is why different preventive measures must be implemented and can be afforded. Africa being the dark continent, Africans cannot afford "opinions" the way the West can in the quote above.

The argument of Africa as 'different' is intertwined with that of *Africans* as different. The underlying assumption is that promotion of condoms and changes in sexual behavior—elsewhere seen as the primary mode of HIV protection—do

---

1. Another problematic issue is the objectification of participants during a research process. Concerning male circumcision trials the researchers point out that men's own accounts of whether their penises are sufficiently circumcised cannot be trusted but their penises should be examined by experts to see whether at all, and to what extent, the foreskin is removed (Weiss et al. 2000:2368). We find such examinations extremely humiliating. They resemble examinations conducted on mine workers in South Africa, which violate basic human rights and the bodily integrity of workers (Butchart 1998).

not solve the problem of 'African AIDS'. Male circumcision promoters do not question condoms as the primary measure of HIV/AIDS prevention, but they argue that in Africa condoms do not suffice. Condoms cannot be enough in Africa because Africans will not use condoms, or cannot use them properly. Access to condoms is not even always accounted for in the texts that seek explanations for regional differences in infection rates:

> Although condoms must remain the first choice for preventing the sexual transmission of HIV, they are often not used consistently or correctly, they may break during use, and there may be strong cultural and aesthetic objections to using them (Szabo and Short 2000a:1593).

In their article, published in *Clinical Infectious Diseases*, Tyndall et al. write:

> However, in the view of the rapid spread of HIV-1 and the *lack of effective prevention strategies* currently available, circumcision indeed may offer one of the few effective means of slowing the spread of HIV-1 in some countries (Tyndall et al. 1996:453, emphasis ours).

Why would not condoms be a currently available, effective means of prevention of HIV/AIDS in Africa? Why is antiretroviral therapy—that has made a huge difference in the West—not even mentioned as a (at least partial) remedy for Africa? Our interpretation is that in these texts Africa is represented as poor and hopeless, and Africans themselves cannot be trusted to bring about a change. Therefore surgical measures directly on their bodies[1] are most effective. In this discourse the black penis that needs to be altered is an appropriate means of addressing a mystical catastrophe in Africa.

Following Patton's argument, it should be no surprise that male circumcision as HIV prevention resonates with Western fantasies about African sexuality and, unlike more mundane prevention campaigns actually taking place in Africa, attracts the interest of the media in the West. "In Western eyes, Africa's problems can only be solved through civilizing forces—or in the romantic version, through a withdrawal from civilisation and a return to pristine 'tribal ways'" (Patton 1997:391; cf. Treichler 1999:99). The medical promotion of male circumcision is a graphic illustration of what 'tribal ways' can mean. In several texts it is suggested that male circumcision is, anyway, already a part of African culture, at least in many areas. Male circumcision may be a more 'natural' method of prevention to Africans than the plastic device, a condom that is a Western technological invention and difficult to use for Africans.

Male circumcision and invisible women

The most important aspect of the male circumcision debate we wish to highlight is the way in which women are rendered invisible in the entire debate. Not even the opponents of male circumcision raise the issue of women becoming infected too. Instead, women are totally marginalized rendering them to nothing other than sources of infection and objects of male heterosexuality.

---

1. In many ways the medical argument for male circumcision resembles medical texts on female contraceptives that are implanted under the skin or in the womb, so that they work independently of the patient.

The Weiss, Quigley and Hayes (2000) review on male circumcision and HIV prevalence restricts itself to female–male transmission in Sub-Saharan Africa (Weiss et al. 2000), with the explanation that in Sub-Saharan Africa heterosexual transmission is the predominant mode of transmission. They ignore the figures that the primary mode of heterosexual transmission is male to female transmission. The research agenda around male circumcision is focused solely on protecting the man from becoming infected.

The research reports state that "HIV transmission to the female partner was not significantly reduced if the male was circumcised" (Quinn et al. 2000:924) or that "the overall effect of circumcision on HIV transmission from infected men to their HIV-negative partners was modest and not statistically significant." (Gray et al. 2000:2380). In other words, women become equally infected by HIV-positive men regardless of whether they are circumcised or not. We argue that when making the gender dimension of heterosexual transmission invisible and at the same time focusing on the protection of men, gendered power relations are in fact strengthened.

Our first concern is the question of how HIV prevention research can still work from a hypothesis that ignores women. Even if the discourse of biological reductionism was accepted as a starting point for discussion, the issue of women getting infected should be the central one as women, especially young girls, are claimed to be physiologically more vulnerable to HIV infection than men due to the composition of female sexual organs (Gavey and McPhillips 1997). Especially young women's tissues are argued to be more easily penetrable by the virus even in sexual acts with their consent, not to mention acts of violence where ruptured tissues are a specific risk factor for the woman rather than the man (Gorna 1996).

Second, what these studies do not account for is that if the 'news' of men being protected by circumcision spreads, HIV transmission to women may increase significantly. If circumcision were seen as a way of prevention it would probably decrease women's possibility to negotiate safe sex as the whole discourse is built upon male power in heterosexual practices. The real risk for women is that the medical 'knowledge' of the protective effects of male circumcision may lead to neglect of other prevention measures. This worry is not unwarranted since the media seems eager to publish any news on progress in HIV prevention, and scientific news must be simplified in popular media.

On the basis of statements in many pro-circumcision texts, the idea that male circumcision may protect men from HIV has already become known and influences lay people. Szabo and Short state that "it is pleasing to note that organizations are now beginning to give serious consideration to the policy implications arising from the protective effect of male circumcision against HIV infection" (Szabo and Short 2000b:1467). An article on a Tanzanian study reports that male circumcision has become popular among educated, urban men regardless of their ethnic or religious background (Urassa et al. 1997). Halperin and Bailey present the following:

> In east and southern Africa, increasing numbers of people are becoming aware of the differenc-
> es in prevalence of AIDS and STDs between circumcised and uncircumcised men, and they are
> taking action. Male circumcision is increasingly recommended by traditional healers. Private
> clinics that specialize in male circumcision, many of which are run by people with minimum or
> no medical training, are sprouting up in Tanzania, western Kenya, Rwanda, and Uganda, and
> many advertise their services as a way to alleviate chronic STD infection and AIDS. Young men
> and adolescents in east and southern Africa are increasingly electing circumcision—both the
> medically safe procedure and more precarious non-clinical methods—in regions where tradi-
> tionally they have avoided the practice (Halperin and Bailey 2000:1814).

Instead of enhancing women's possibilities for demanding safe sex in relationships, avoiding sexualized violence and reducing the lack of control over their
health risks, the male circumcision strategy seems likely to increase all these risks
for women, as it completely ignores the needs of women and, in our view, recasts
them as objects.

Our worry about decrease in condom use by circumcised men may be unwarranted. The idea that African men would not use condoms if they did not have to,
but would rather practise promiscuous sex without any interest in the partner's
health, resonates with colonial, racist ideas of African masculinity—that will,
surely, affect sexual practices (cf. Mama 1997).

Media needs 'African news'

The medical news media seem to have become especially attached to the idea that
male circumcision may provide something new to write about in the, for news
media, rather eventless battle against AIDS in Africa. The XIIIth International
AIDS Conference in Durban, South Africa, gained a lot of media attention and
here too male circumcision was presented as a possible new hope for Africa. For
example, The *Lancet* in June 2001 in an article titled "Male circumcision could
help protect against HIV infection", maintains that despite problems some conference delegates agreed on the importance of continuing research on male circumcision:

> ...Buvé pointed out, however, that to substantially reduce HIV transmission, men would need
> to be circumcised before they reached sexual maturity. Furthermore, since there are doubts
> about the safety of circumcision procedures in parts of Africa, implementation of this policy
> would also have important practical and ethical implications. Most importantly, the delegates
> were concerned that safe sex practices might decrease if circumcision became perceived as pro-
> viding full protection against HIV infection. Despite indecision about the appropriate popula-
> tion studies that need to be done, all the speakers agreed that randomised controlled trials ex-
> amining the effect of male circumcision on HIV transmission are needed (Clark 2000:225).

In popular media the news is visibly highlighted. This study, however, did not attempt to cover all popular media reporting on the matter, but some examples may
be worth mentioning. In the main South African newspaper *The Mail & Guardian's*
special issue on World Aids Day, the 'news' was reported in a lengthy article that
was also concerned about male circumcision becoming used as a 'natural condom', but it ends as following: "Circumcision is only one of many complex ways
of stopping transmission. South Africa, with the fastest growing and largest population of HIV patients in the world, needs them all. And fast" (Ford 2000:9).

A BBC documentary was made about the Rakai research. The documentary was reviewed in the British Medical Journal in the following way:

> [The TV-programme] turned out to be a first-rate virological detective story. […]An impressive array of witnesses—doctors, scientists, anthropologists—were lined up to present the evidence, which seemed to suggest overwhelmingly that having a foreskin could make men more vulnerable to HIV. It all hinged on the natural protection offered by keratin, found in much lower quantities in the foreskin, and so making uncircumcised men much more vulnerable to heterosexual transmission of HIV. There was a wonderfully dramatic white coat and Petri dish moment when an American scientist used a live foreskin taken from a just circumcised adult male to test the rate at which HIV invaded the cells. They changed colour in a jiffy, proving they had succumbed to infection. This was television science at its best (Jackson 2000:1419).

There are examples of success in risk reduction programmes in several African countries (Waldo and Coates 2000). Women's grass-root movements in Africa are very clear about there already being enough knowledge on ways to prevent HIV transmission. Access to health care and antiretroviral drugs, support groups for women, and promotion and availability of (female) condoms are among prevention strategies that are known to work effectively—and are crucial for women's empowerment. Such projects, however, are less likely to gain news attention. Even less likely to gain visibility are projects that focus on *not* specifically 'African' problems, but feminist political issues like power dynamics in (hetero)sexual encounters.

Conclusion

The male circumcision debate seems more involved in reproducing imagery on 'African sexuality', than in envisioning actual change. In our analysis, the media interest in male circumcision research is connected to, first, medicalization, and second, a media fascination by 'African news' that feeds the Western fantasy about 'African sexuality'. Medicalization has been described as a typical feature of modern Western societies: it is easier to see social problems in terms of medical, preferably clinical, problems than in terms of social power relations (Conrad 2000). It is obvious that Waldo and Coates' (2000) statement about the bias towards individual-level solutions and randomized clinical trials in prevention research applies in this case too: "HIV prevention scientists are not connected to prevention efforts outside their own academic lives. Community-based interventions have been occurring in affected communities since the beginning of the epidemic, but HIV prevention scientists are frequently not involved in them" (Waldo and Coates 2000:24–25). In this chapter we have wished to turn the attention to the constructions of 'Africa' and the marginalization of women in the male circumcision debate.

Neither medical articles nor media reports on male circumcision discuss the question of what the consequences of possible male circumcision campaigns will be for women. The writers do not consider how a promotion of male circumcision as HIV/AIDS prevention may affect infection rates for women. Women's organizations, in contrast, have focused on the social conditions that make women more vulnerable to becoming infected with HIV. When considering social and economic circumstances, gender inequalities and sexism, it becomes quite clear that young women should be the main targets of interest in HIV/AIDS research and media attention (Gilbert and Walker 2002).

Women's organizations promote a change in power relations between men and women, and a radical change in how heterosexual relations are perceived. The male circumcision model, on the contrary, reproduces a stereotypical assumption of heterosexual practice where the involved parties are an active male penetrator who will not take an interest in his (passive female) partner's health and safety— indeed a rather stereotypical and offensive representation of 'African masculinity' that resonates with colonial imageries (cf. Mama 1997). The texts display a consistent inability to reflect on the politics involved in representations of sexualities and race as well as a belief in their enterprise as being objective, neutral science— and it is this combination that makes the male circumcision research highly problematic.

Patton (1999) maintains that in media AIDS is constructed through a deadly set of assumptions about cultural and political difference. She is concerned with the way scientists and policy makers have the power to produce "masks of otherness". This article shows that unfortunately Patton's concern is valid even for recent expert accounts on how to deal with HIV/AIDS in Sub-Saharan Africa. In face of the knowledge of how the virus actually is spread in Africa, there is every reason to be alarmed about the promotion of male circumcision (as an already available strategy, or in the form of "more research needs to be conducted") that may actually *increase* the spread of the virus.

The tragic of the medical construction of 'African AIDS' is that it *hampers* the implementations of effective prevention programs. Local HIV activists are among the most important forces for changing deadly[1] discourses around HIV and AIDS, and to provide resistance on a global scale. Having contrasted local activism with the 'heroic' stories of an assumed medical breakthrough, we argue that the understandings of HIV in medical research and medical media, as well as in popular news media, remain seriously distorted if they do not make use of the knowledge that activism generates.

---

1. According to current medical understanding HIV infection is no longer a life threatening condition but, *with continuous treatment*, leads to a manageable chronic disease.

References

Abdool Karim, Quarrisha, 1998, "Women and AIDS. The Imperative for a Gendered Prognosis and Prevention Policy", *Agenda* 39, 15–25.

Bailey, Robert C., 2000, "A Study in Rural Uganda of heterosexual Transmission of Human Immunodeficiency Virus", *New England Journal of Medicine,* 343 (5), 364.

Benatar, S.R., 2002, "Reflections and recommendations on research ethics in developing countries", *Social Science & Medicine*, 54 (7), 1131–41.

Butchart, Alexander, 1998, *The Anatomy of Power—European Constructions of The African Body.* London: Zed Books.

Conrad, Peter, 2000, "Medicalization, Genetics, and Human Problems", in Cloe E. Bird, Peter Conrad, Allen M. Fremont (eds), *Handbook of Medical Sociology.* 5th edition. Upper Saddle River, N.J.: Prentice Hall.

Clark, Stephanie, 2000, "Male Circumcision Could Help Protect against HIV Infection", *Lancet* 356 (9225), 225.

Delor, F. and M. Hubert, 2000, "Revisiting the concept of 'vulnerability'", *Social Science & Medicine,* 50(11), 1557–70.

Doyal, Lesley, 1995, *What Makes Women Sick: Gender and the Political Economy of Health.* Houndmills: Macmillan.

Eisenstein, Zillah, 1996, *Hatreds: Racialized and Sexualized Conflicts in the 21st Century.* New York: Routledge.

Epstein, Julia, 1995, *Altered Conditions: Disease, Medicine and Storytelling.* New York: Routledge.

Fanon, Franz, 1971, *Svart hud, vita masker.* Göteborg: Daidalos. (Orig. *Peau noire, masques blancs.* Éditions de Seuil, 1952.)

Fink, Aaron J., 1986, "A Possible Explanation for Heterosexual Male Infection with AIDS", *The New England Journal of Medicine,* 315 (18), 1167.

Ford, Denise, 2000, "Circumcision: The Kindest Cut", *Mail & Guardian*, December 1, 2000.

Foucault, Michel, 1973, *The Birth of the Clinic.* New York: Vintage Books.

Gavey, Nicola and Kathryn McPhillips, 1997, "Women and Heterosexual Transmission of HIV: Risks and Prevention Strategies", *Women and Health*, 25 (2), 41–63.

Gilbert, Leah and Liz Walker, 2002, "Treading the Path of Least Resistance: HIV/AIDS and Social Inequalities—a South African Case Study", *Social Science & Medicine,* 54 (7),1093–1110.

Gorna, Robin, 1996, *Vamps, Virgins and Victims: How Can Women Fight AIDS?* London: Cassell.

Gray, Ronald H. et al., 2000, "Male Circumcision and HIV Acquisition and Transmission: Cohort Studies in Rakai, Uganda", *AIDS,* 14 (15), 2371–81.

Halperin, Daniel T. and Robert C. Bailey, 1999, "Male Circumcision and HIV Infection: 10 Years and Counting", *Lancet,* 354 (9192), 1813–15.

Holland, Janet et al.,1994, "Desire, Risk and Control: The Body as a Site of Contestation", in Lesley Doyal, Jennie Nardoo and Tamsin Wilton (eds), *Aids: Setting a Feminist Agenda.* London: Taylor & Francis.

Jackson, Trevor, 2000, "No News Is Bad News", *British Medical Journal,* 321, 1419.

Jungar, Katarina and Elina Oinas, 2003, "Treatment Action Campaign—HIV activism transforming the notion of medicalization". Paper presented at *Vital Politics: Health, Medicine and Bioeconomics into the 21st Century*, London School of Economics and Political Sciences, 5–7.9. 2003.

Kalipeni, E., 2000, "Health and Disease in Southern Africa: A Comparative and Vulnerability Perspective", *Social Science & Medicine,* 50(7–8), 965–983.

Kumar, Nikki, June Larkin and Claudia Mitchell, 2001, "Gender, Youth and HIV Risk", *Canadian Woman Studies*, 21 (2), 35–40.

Mama, Amina, 1997, "Sheroes and Villains: Conceptualizing Colonial and Contemporary Violence against Women in Africa", in Alexander, Jacqui M. and Chandra Talpade Mohanty (eds), *Feminist Genealogies, Colonial Legacies, Democratic Futures.* New York: Routledge.

Mohanty, Chandra Talpade, 1991, "Under Western Eyes: Feminist Scholarship and Colonial Discourses", in Mohanty, Chandra Talpade, Ann Russo and Lourdes Torres (eds), *Third World Women and the Politics of Feminism*. Bloomington: Indiana University Press.

Moletsane, Relebohile et al., 2002, "The School Setting: Opportunities for Intergrating Gender Equality and HIV Risk Reduction Interventions", *Agenda* 53, 11–21.

Moses, Stephen et al.,1990, "Geographical Patterns of Male Circumcision Practices in Africa: Association with HIV Seroprevalence", *International Journal of Epidemiology,* 19 (3), 693–7.

Oliver R.T.D., Josephine Oliver and Ron C. Ballard, 2000, "More Studies Need to Be Done before Widespread Circumcision Is Implemented", British Medical Journal, 321, 1468–1469.

PACSA factsheet, 1999, "Gender, Violence and HIV/AIDS", no. 46.

Pang, T, 2002, "Commentary on 'Reflections and Recommendations on Research Ethics in Developing Countries' by S. R. Benatar", *Social Science & Medicine,* 54(7), 1145–6.

Patton, Cindy, 1997, "Inventing 'African AIDS'", in Roger N. Lancaster and Micaela di Leonado (eds), *The Gender/Sexuality Reader: Culture, History, Political Economy*. New York: Routledge.

Quinn, Tomas C., Maria Wawer, Nelson Sewankambo, David Serwadda, Chuanjun Li, Fred Wabwire-Mangen, Mary O. Meehan, Thomas Lutalo and Ronald Grey, 2000, "Viral Load and Heterosexual Transmission of Human Immunodeficiency Virus Type 1", *New England Journal of Medicine,* 342 (13), 921–9.

Ratele, Kopano, 2001, "Between 'Ouens': Everyday Makings of Black Masculinity", in Robert Morrell (ed.), *Changing Men in Southern Africa*. London: (University of Natal Press), Zed Books.

Sewpaul, Vishantie and Thobile Mahlela, 1998, "The power of the small group: From crisis to disclosure", *Agenda*, 39, 34–43.

Sontag, Susan, 1991, *Illness as Metaphor, and, AIDS and Its Metaphors*. London: Penguin.

Spivak, Gayatri Chakravorty, 1988, "Can the subaltern speak?", in Cary Nelson and Lawrence Grossberg (eds.), *Marxism and the Interpretation of Culture*. Urbana: University of Illinois Press.

Szabo, Robert and Roger V. Short, 2000a, "How Does Male Circumcision Protect against HIV Infection?", *British Medical Journal*, 320, 1592–4.

Szabo, Robert and Roger V. Short, 2000b, "Authors' Reply", *British Medical Journal,* 321, 1469.

Tallis, Vicci, 2000, "Gendering the response to HIV/AIDS: Challenging gender inequality", *Agenda,* 44, 58–66.

Treichler, Paula, 1999, *How to Have a Theory in an Epidemic: Cultural Chronicles of AIDS*. Durham: Duke University Press.

Tyndall, Mark W. et al., 1996, "Increased Risk of Infection with Human Immunodeficiency Virus Type 1 among Uncircumcised Men Presenting with Genital Ulcer Disease in Kenya", *Clinical Infectious Diseases,* 23 (3), 449–53.

UNAIDS/99.2, 1999, "AIDS—5 years since ICPD: Emerging issues and challenges for women, young people & infants". A UNAIDS discussion document.

UNAIDS/99.16E, 1999, *Gender and HIV/AIDS: Taking stock of research and programmes*.

Urassa, Marc et al., 1997, "Male Circumcision and Susceptibility to HIV Infection among Men in Tanzania", AIDS, 11 (3), 73–80.

Van Howe, R.S., 1999, "Circumcision and HIV infection: review of the literature and meta-analysis", *International Journal STD AIDS,* 10 (1), 8–16.

Waldo, Craig W. and Thomas J. Coates, 2000, "Multiple Levels of Analysis and Intervention in HIV Prevention Science: Exemplars and Directions for New Research", *AIDS,* 14 (suppl. 2), 18–26.

Weiss, Helen A., Maria A. Quigley and Richard J. Hayes, 2000, "Male Circumcision and Risk of HIV Infection in Sub-Saharan Africa: A Systematic Review and Meta-Analysis", *AIDS,* 14 (15), 2361–2370.

Photo: Abderramane Sakaly, 1958

5. Whose 'Unmet Need'?
Dis/Agreement about Childbearing among Ghanainan Couples

Akosua Adomako Ampofo

"By God's grace I had a boy".

Introduction

Since the 1960s, when it became evident that the Third World,[1] Sub-Saharan Africa particularly, was undergoing a population transition different from the 'over-developed'[2] Western world, there has been a sustained interest in population growth and later fertility trends in the sub-region (Easterlin 1975). However, among this amazingly large body of literature, work produced by scholars on the continent, and especially work by feminist scholars, has not generally made its way into the dominant discourses.

This state of affairs is but a reflection of the cultural hegemony that has dictated the population agenda. Much of the early discourse is framed around excessive population growth, which was seen as a major cause of poverty. The lowering of fertility was, and still is, expected to promote prosperity; in other words the discourse surrounding fertility remains inherently neo-Malthusian.[3] Knowledge, Attitude and Practices (KAP) surveys, mainly the World Fertility Surveys (WFS) and later the Demographic and Health Surveys (DHS) were carried out to assess attitudes related to family size and fertility-related behaviour, and the results were used to document several demographic phenomena, including the existence of an 'unmet need' for family planning services in Third World countries, and hence a

---

1. I use the term "Third World" pointedly to refer to those countries and societies that have overtly experienced colonization, or covertly continue to experience different forms of exploitation. I do not use the term to denote hierarchy (the sense in which it was used in the 1970s development literature) relative to a "first" world, but rather to reflect the political, economic and cultural dominance that has divided the world, and which is implicit in many of the concepts and the discourse on population and demography.

2. Credit to Marilyn Waring (1999) who uses the term to reflect the over-consumption and waste in the industrialized nations. The resultant discrepancies that thus exist between these nations and those in the Third World cannot be overlooked in analyses of population discourse.

3. Even in Africa the trend continues. The stated goals of the revised 1994 Ghana population policy, for example, even though these include the pursuit of programmes and measures directed at promoting development, enhancing the status of women, and improving not only reproductive/maternal health, but also general health and nutrition, still maintain a fertility-reduction focus (Population Impact Project 1995).

115

ready market for contraceptives.[1] The basis of this conceptualisation was the fact that women interviewed in the DHS indicated, in response to standard questions on fertility preferences, that they had 'unwanted', 'unplanned' or 'mistimed' births. The standard formulation of 'unmet need' includes all fecund (not pregnant or amenorrhoeic)[2] women who are currently married or living in a union, who either want to postpone their next birth for two or more years (have an 'unmet need' for spacing births), or want to cease childbearing altogether (have an 'unmet need' for limiting births), but who are not using contraception. For example, the 1998 DHS for Ghana puts the total 'unmet need' for all women aged 15–49 in the country at 16.5 per cent and puts it at 23 per cent for married women in the same age group (Ghana Statistical Service and the Institute for Resource Development 1999).

In this chapter I take a critical look at this concept of 'unmet need' commonly used in population discourse and development efforts in the Third World. In the process I also address the underlying assumptions about 'agreement' between couples regarding reproductive issues that are implicit in the concept. For me it is important to take a closer look at the concept of 'unmet need' because my own research interests include the areas of population, and gender and reproductive decision-making. More importantly, the concept of 'unmet need' and concerns about African women's fertility remain at the heart of population and reproductive health discourse and programs in Ghana, and within the discipline of demography more generally. Within theoretical frameworks that continue to view 'rapid' population growth per se as a problem, the concept of 'unmet need' remains a very attractive one because it presents a practical approach to solving the 'population problem' by providing contraceptives for women and their partners (Bongaarts and Bruce 1995). The concept assumes that the reason women have an 'unmet need' is because they do not know about ways to meet this need, and/or do not have access to the services required to effect their fertility preferences, or, if they do have access to services, that these are inefficient (Bongaarts 1991).[3] While we can expect that better access to, and efficiency of programs and services will enhance contraceptive use, the important cultural and ideological aspects of fer-

---

1. The need for comparative fertility data on a global scale prompted the creation of demographic surveys that measure individuals' knowledge, attitudes and practices (KAP) related to a range of reproductive issues. The first, the World Fertility Survey (WFS 1972–1984) was carried out in more than 60 countries focusing primarily on fertility and maternal and child health. Contraceptive Prevalence Surveys (CPS 1977–1985) were designed to quickly provide basic indicators on family planning and fertility. Since 1984, when The Demographic and Health Surveys (DHS) program was established at The Institute for Resource Development, Inc. (IRD), over 100 surveys combining the qualities of the WFS and the CPS have been carried out in the Third World. The DHS include important questions on maternal and child health, nutrition, and HIV/AIDS (www.measuredhs.com/data/indicators/table_builder; accessed June 18, 2002).

2. Refers to the physiological cessation of menstruation such as during pregnancy or lactation, as well as the pathological absence of menstruation.

3. Belatedly the population establishment has also conceded that women may not be using contraceptives because of opposition from male partners, hence the new call to "focus on men" (Population Reference Bureau 1996). However, even here the emphasis has often been on disagreement about using contraceptives rather than on disagreement about fertility preferences.

tility behaviour in Africa have been neglected. The quote cited at the head of this chapter comes from a woman whose story I return to later. She was not, as might appear to be the case, anxious to have a son. On the contrary, she did not want to have any more children; however, her husband was insistent that she would continue childbearing until she had a son. And yet her 'unmet need' is not exposed in the survey I conducted prior to the subsequent interview. Broadening the understanding of the relevance of the social context for demographic processes will bring to the discipline issues of gender inequality, which should enhance our understanding of fertility behaviour generally.

I will argue that in its theoretical and methodological approach the concept of 'unmet need' is at best overly simplistic, and, at worst, neglectful of the dominant role of males in human reproduction. Thus the concept fails to take into account the gendered social context of reproductive decision-making and behaviour. I also question the (over) reliance on traditional KAP-style survey questions in the measurement of 'unmet need' by pointing to some of the inherent methodological limitations of this approach. Specifically, I will show how the survey method *overstates* the level of 'agreement' between couples about past fertility behaviour, and also, fails to take into account the outcome of *potential past childbearing that did not occur* (i.e. in the case of induced abortions).[1] This approach of measuring 'unmet need' may account for the failure, over three decades, of family planning programs to have significantly reduced the high level of 'unmet need' in Africa (see Dodoo 1993; Dodoo and van Landewijk 1996). I base my arguments on available literature, the DHS, as well as data from my fieldwork among Ghanaian couples with reference to the last born child.

Background to conceptualising and measuring 'unmet need'

Traditionally 'unmet need' was defined on the basis of women's responses to particular survey questions.[2] If a woman reports in a survey that she does not want to have any more children, or wants to postpone the birth of her next child, and is neither breastfeeding nor pregnant, but is not using any form of contraception, she is defined as having an 'unmet need'. Even the most general among the early models explaining fertility behaviour focused on a female perspective (Davis and Blake 1956; Easterlin 1975). The entire family planning movement and consequent programs were also based on a female model/framework—i.e. women (and initially only married women, as defined by Western concepts of marriage) informed the focus of research, information and service efforts (Hodgson and Watkins 1997; Simmons et al. 1992). Yet women's own perspectives were not considered in its formulation. Women were the target group, not agenda setters. This model was based in part on the assumption that the ones who do the actual child-

---

1. Hereafter referred to simply as abortion.
2. Some of the DHS carried out since the mid-1980s also include similar questions for smaller (sub-) samples of male respondents.

bearing are more knowledgeable about their past (and future) fertility behaviour than their male partners (Blood and Wolfe 1960).[1] Furthermore, since the woman is the child-bearer, her attitudes about proscriptive fertility-related events were felt to be more logical predictors of future behaviour (Mott and Mott 1985). The model implicitly assumes that women generally take decisions about childbearing alone without consideration of the cultural context of childbearing in Africa where children belong to lineages, and not individual couples, let alone individual women. Indeed the concept of an 'unmet need' (for contraception) generally still refers to the discrepancy between *women's* expressed fertility goals and their contraceptive practice. Continued childbearing, in the face of reported desires to stop, led demographers to describe African women as inconsistent, irrational, or simply ignorant (see Casterline et al.'s critique, 1996), and yet when men's preferences are included in analyses, many children cease to be 'unwanted' or 'mistimed' (Bankole and Ezeh 1997; Dodoo 1993).

The concept of 'unmet need' was first explored in the 1960s when data from KAP surveys of contraceptive use showed a gap between women's intentions and behaviour. The term that was used to describe this apparent discrepancy was 'KAP-gap' (Bogue 1974). In 1974 Freedman and Coombs used survey data from several countries for the first time to identify the size of the group of women who experienced such a gap; they found this gap to be considerable. Freedman and Coombs (1974) coined the term 'discrepant' behaviour to describe women in this group. One of the first published works to refer to 'unmet need' was by Stokes (1977), who, citing evidence from KAP studies in Third World countries, and from fertility surveys in the US, notes, "in disparate ways, the number of ill-timed pregnancies and widespread reliance on abortion among all social classes and groups signal an 'unmet need' for contraception" (Stokes 1977:4). Between 1972 and 1984 World Fertility Surveys (WFS) carried out in several countries were the first to report extensively on 'unmet need'. Caldwell and Ruzicka (1978) note that 'unmet need' was so important that once such data became available to demographers this became the first variable to be analysed in any fertility-related study. Based on comparative estimates from five Asian countries in the WFS, Westoff published articles on 'unmet need' for limiting births (Tsui 1985; Westoff 1978).[2] Subsequently, Westoff and Pebley (1981) recommended that the concept of 'unmet need' be extended to include the desire to space births. Contraceptive Prevalence Surveys (CPS) carried out from the mid-1970s to 1984 added questions about women's interests in postponing their next birth, thus making it possible to include measurements of the 'unmet need' for spacing births.[3] Other demographers, for example Boulier (1985), argued that if 'unmet need' measured the proportion of women who were supposed to be using modern contraceptives but

---

1. There were also important political and epistemological reasons for this historical trend, which this chapter cannot take up, but which are addressed elsewhere (see Adomako Ampofo 2002).
2. The WFS did not ask women about their desire to space births.
3. This was found to be useful in distinguishing between women who needed temporary methods (for spacing) from those who needed permanent or long-term methods (to stop childbearing).

were not, then the concept should be extended to include users of traditional methods as having an 'unmet need'. His argument was that traditional methods could not be considered to be reliable, hence women in this category had an 'unmet need' for more reliable contraception, or in Foreit et al.'s (1992) formulation 'appropriate contraception'. Finally, the DHS that have been carried out in 44 countries since 1985, have allowed further refinements of the measure;[1] the DHS now also ask pregnant women whether their current pregnancy is "wanted then (planned or intentional), not wanted then (mistimed), or not wanted at all (unwanted)" and whether they were using contraception at the time of the pregnancy. This allows for the measurement of 'unmet need' among pregnant women as well. Clearly, the measurement of 'unmet need' has undergone a lot of refining since it was first conceptualised; however, limitations persist. In the next section I turn to an assumption that is implicit in the conceptualisation of 'unmet need'— the assumption that a woman's reproductive behaviour is a reflection of a couple's intentions or preferences.

Whose 'unmet need'?

As pointed out, the DHS indicate that women in Africa want to have fewer children than they are having, or would have preferred to increase the space between their children. Despite these desires, after two decades of the promotion of family planning programs on the continent, contraceptive use generally remains low and hence women's 'unmet need' remains significant (Bongaarts 1991).[2] Yet the conceptualisation of 'unmet need' does not allow for the fact that a child (conceived by, and born to a woman) could be wanted by her partner even if *she* does not want it. Is this child still unwanted, and hence does this woman still have an 'unmet need'? This question is extremely relevant given the acknowledged dominance of men in reproductive decision-making. The reverse situation obviously also holds true; that is, that a child could be wanted by a woman but not by her partner—is this child unwanted and does the woman's partner in this case have an 'unmet need'? Would a woman's reports about an 'unmet need' really reflect her own preferences? For almost three decades 'unmet need' has been conceptualised and measured taking women into account as though women had children on their own, and as if their 'unmet need' represented a couple's need for contraception.[3] And yet, it is entirely conceivable, and indeed is often the case, that spouses do

---

1. 20 in Africa, 5 in the Near East and North Africa, 8 in Asia, and 11 in South America.
2. In some countries, contraceptive use rates in the 1990s have remained under 5 per cent (DHS/Macro International 1995).
3. An important exception are the Contraceptive Prevalence Surveys carried out in the Caribbean region in which male respondents were also considered as potentially having an unmet need. Men were included in this category if they were sexually active, their partners fecund and not pregnant, they did not want their partners to become pregnant but neither was using contraception (see McFarlane et al. 1994).

not have a joint 'unmet need' because they have discrepant preferences (Dodoo et al. 1977).[1]

It would seem obvious that individuals' and couples' decision making about whether to have a child, and when, may be influenced, at least in part, by the gender-power relations that pertain. Yet, while the sociological and anthropological literature on marriage and the family is replete with studies of power differences between spouses in the area of decision making, since gender differences are not what demographers traditionally sought to explain, the input of feminist discourse in population and fertility studies has been minimal (Watkins 1993). Susan Watkins (1993) carried out a study of articles on population-related issues in the official journal of the Population Association of America, *Demography*, from 1964 through to 1992, and found that while women's fertility behaviour forms the focus of research, few articles pay attention to cultural or women's concerns, nor to the relative well-being of women and men. When the focus on women's position and well-being entered the discourse it did not come without challenge. Harriet Presser (1997) comments on Charles Westoff's article in the *New York Times Magazine*, in which he argues that the feminist agenda is a divisive issue in the population field. He rightly notes the feminist agenda as including "women's rights; making women the subjects and not the objects of population policies …the inadequacies of reproductive and women's health services in general…the empowerment of women in the economic, social and political arenas" (Westoff 1995:178–179). Yet, while he acknowledges these as legitimate concerns, he argues, "they (feminists) ignore or minimize population growth and its presumed consequences." (Westoff 1995:179). According to him the 'real problems' to feminists are "gender inequality and poverty" while in his view the "real problems are population growth in less developed countries which threatens the basic condition of life" (Westoff 1995:181). By locating such a distinction Presser argues that Westoff sets up a spurious "opposition between gender and population issues." (Presser 1997:315).

The manifestation of power within the marital dyad is evidenced by the ability to influence decision-making and behaviour according to one's wishes (advance one's objective position) even when this may be detrimental to the other partner. The gap in the discourse on fertility behaviour exists partly because the large fertility data sources used for reproductive behaviour analyses do not elicit information on gender relations or decision-making power, in itself an outcome of how fertility behaviour has generally been conceptualised within demography. When disagreements between spouses have been argued in relation to women's 'unmet need' the implicit assumption has essentially been that men are pronatalist and desire more children than women (Kannae and Pendleton 1994; Khalifa 1988; Mustafa and Mumford 1984) hence men prevent women from using modern contra-

---

1. Sexually active unmarried adults or adolescents form another group, who have generally been neglected in the conceptualisation and measurement of unmet need. These groups, if they are sexually active, are obviously at greater risk of having unwanted or mistimed pregnancies. Westoff himself (Westoff et al. 1994) observes that this is a serious omission.

ceptives. Alternatively, men are said to be opposed to modern contraception (supposedly out of fears that their wives will be unfaithful). Analysis of what happens when the situation is reversed, that is when a man wants his wife to practise family planning (he has an 'unmet need') but his wife wants more children, does not appear in the literature. Yet abortion statistics have been described as indicating the ultimate 'unmet need' for family planning (Coeytaux 1992). What we also do not know is the extent to which men persuade, coerce, or even force their partners to have an abortion because the men have an 'unmet need'. I return to this in my analysis and discussion.

Childbearing in Ghana

It is not possible to provide a summary of 'traditional' norms regarding childbearing here; however, since fertility issues are central to an understanding of conjugal relations and reproductive behaviour in Ghana I will point to some issues of general significance.[1] Women generally looked to marriage for children, economic support, and sexual satisfaction within a respected union. On the other hand they brought to a marriage sexual and domestic 'services', and the birth of children. The rights acquired by a husband differ between patrilineal and matrilineal societies. Among patrilineal groups, such as the Ewe, for example, a wife's sexual and procreative services are said to be given to her husband in exchange for maintenance (Nukunya 1966, 1991). Among the matrilineal Akan, however, although a woman provides sexual and domestic services for her husband, Oppong argues that the rights over her own sexuality, "her body, while alive and reproductive or dead, belongs to her lineage" (Oppong 1980:201). Generally children bring prestige to the lineage, whether matrilineal or patrilineal, and in the past they were considered important economic assets, ensuring the lineage's continuity. Among the matrilineal Akan bearing and raising children are said to be a woman's most important contribution to her lineage since they provide assurance of its continuity, and a woman's family actually thank her husband for giving them children. Among all groups special public honour is bestowed on a woman at the time of the 'outdooring' of her baby.[2] Prolific childbearing is honoured, and mothers of twins, triplets, and a tenth child are held in special esteem (Sarpong 1977). Fertility is so important that most ethnic groups have special ceremonies to commemorate a girl's 'entry into womanhood'. A good portion of the period spent on the initiation of girls used to be taken up with instructions on the secrets of sexuality, how to be a good wife, and rudimentary aspects of mothering.[3] Post-partum abstinence was traditionally practised in order to achieve spacing of births and women typically went to live with their natal families for periods up to two years until the baby was weaned. The practice was in order to ensure the survival and health of the baby. Women who resumed sexual relations with their

---

1. Many useful, thorough accounts exist (see the work of Fortes, Nukunya, Oppong, Sarpong to name but a few).
2. New babies are usually 'outdoored' presented to the families in ritual celebrations, about a week after they are born.
3. The performance of initiation rites, however, has declined markedly over the last few decades.

husbands 'too soon' after the birth of a baby were teased as feeling insecure in their marriages—i.e. they were afraid that their husbands would take another wife during their period of abstinence. Older females were the ones mainly responsible for ensuring that this sort of 'family planning' was practised. They would offer advice about herbs and sexual practices which could ensure birth spacing. Traditionally husbands had a limited role, if any, in reproductive decision making.

Fortes (1948) observes that there is a deeply-ingrained idea that 'normal' men and women should continue to bear children throughout their reproductive years. Hence, when couples remarry after divorce or the death of a spouse, subsequent marriages are likely to produce offspring (Anarfi and Fayorsey 1995). Childless individuals, on the other hand, are scorned and despised. Among the Akan an impotent (and, hence, a childless man) is given the name *kte krawa*, or inadequate penis. Among the Akan an infertile woman is referred to as *boni*, a term used to describe brackish water in which no fish can thrive. Sarpong (1977) also indicates that because the survival of the matrilineage depends on its female members, childlessness in a woman is viewed as the ultimate betrayal. The importance of children makes childlessness an important reason for divorce, although husbands are more likely to seek an additional wife or have children outside the marriage than to choose this option. Since Ghanaian customary law recognises polygyny, although marriages contracted under the ordinance must be monogamous, since almost all marriages are preceded by customary procedures, they are potentially polygynous.[1] This has implications for the security of the wife, especially if she 'delays' childbearing. Anecdotal evidence suggests that many marriages become polygynous as a result of the 'infertility' of the wife, or, among some patrilineages, her 'inability' to bear sons.

A comment on method

Before I describe the data that I rely on it is important to make a comment on methodological issues associated with the measurement of 'unmet need'. I have used surveys to assess reproductive processes in my own work, however, because of my experiences with surveys, I find it important that careful consideration be given to the usefulness of surveys (alone) for the measurement of processes involved in (reproductive) decision-making. While surveys are useful for providing cross-sectional data (and even longitudinal data), they have limitations when it comes to providing insights into what goes on between couples and how. The discrepancies between survey and interview responses among the same sample highlight these limitations. In the ensuing discussion I use the example of my own survey data, modelled along the lines of the DHS, as well as case stories, to show how surveys can both over- and understate the extent of 'unmet need', as well as reverse the identity of the partner who actually has the 'unmet need'. The case of

1. In 1958 the Native Authority Courts were officially abolished; however, certain customary laws have been incorporated into judicial laws. Furthermore, traditional courts still have limited jurisdiction in domestic issues especially pertaining to marriage and the family.

one couple, Nana and Nortey is especially revealing (and poignant) in that it reveals the couple-based dynamics involved in Nana's decision to have an abortion, presumably to meet an 'unmet need' for spacing. To date statistical analysis of the relationships between levels of 'unmet need', levels of abortion and contraceptive prevalence provide ambivalent findings. In 1996, the year before my study, the UNFPA estimated that about 45 million induced abortions took place worldwide (UNFPA 1996). A 1994 USAID report suggests that abortion remains a common way for women to control their fertility (USAID 1994). As Nana and Nortey's story will show, it is really Nortey, and not Nana, who had the 'unmet need', and yet the survey does not capture this.

Between June 1997 and January 1998 I carried out a census among the junior staff workers of the University of Ghana and their spouses; my final sample size included 125 men (husbands) and 140 women (wives). The resulting couple sample eventually contained 110 dyads. The survey instrument I used was modelled along the lines of the Ghana DHS (GDHS) as far as background and family planning questions were concerned. However, additionally, the survey included a series of questions on family decision-making, financial support, and access to resources not contained in the GDHS.[1] The survey was interviewer-administered, conducted in the respondents' homes, separately for men and women, and interviews on average lasted between 30 and 40 minutes.

From the survey respondents who had agreed to be re-interviewed I short-listed 30 couples for re-interviewing, who reflected the range of attitudes and behaviours:1) couples in which husbands are advantaged in reproductive outcomes; 2) couples who express conjugal 'jointness' or agreement about reproductive outcomes; and 3) couples in which wives are advantaged in reproductive outcomes. I eventually interviewed 12 husbands and 11 wives (hence 11 couples) that reflected such a range.[2]

Although I did not prevent interviewees from diverging from my script, and I myself also probed respondents when they went off on an interesting path, I did adhere to my fixed set of questions thereby systematizing the collection of this qualitative material. Each respondent was interviewed separately from her or his spouse. Generally interviews lasted between one and one and a half hours; a few took as long as up to two hours or longer; however, I never observed respondents getting bored or tired, and no one ever suggested terminating the interview (see Appendix for a summary of respondents' characteristics).

---

1. See Adomako Ampofo (1999) for an analysis of the effects of these variables on what I refer to as individuals' gender orientations, and how this is associated with reproductive decision-making.

2. A 12th wife could not be interviewed as her schedule did not seem to make this possible, hence my ending up with 11 and not 12 dyads.

Whose 'unmet need'?—Issues of dis/agreement

Reproductive decision-making is a complex process, differing from one couple to the next, as the ensuing analysis illustrates. Generally, even though the large scale surveys that have interviewed both husbands and wives can be used to assess differences in preferences for children and attitudes to family planning, the underlying processes, and often the real preferences, are lost. In this section I focus on husbands' and wives' responses to a question on the 'wantedness' of their last child to show the discrepancies that can emerge between a survey and an interview. This is not to suggest that surveys are unreliable, but to indicate that a question as sensitive as one dealing with feelings about past childbearing (i.e. a living and breathing person and not an abstract idea) is often so political, and so tied up with personal and gendered identities that a survey item (alone) may not be the best way of capturing the phenomenon.

The data from my survey allow us to identify 8 childbearing preferences[1] related to the last child. These can further be divided into two categories—couples who were in agreement, and those who were in disagreement about wanting the child:

Agreement:
Both partners wanted the child then (Both then)
Both did not want then (Both wait)
Both want no more (Both stop)

Disagreement:
Wife wanted then/Husband not then (Wife then-husband wait)
Wife no more /Husband not then (Wife stop-husband wait)
Wife wanted then/Husband no more (Wife then-husband stop)
Wife not then/Husband wanted then (Wife wait-husband then)
Wife no more /Husband wanted then (Wife stop-husband then)

Among the 107 eligible survey respondents (i.e. excluding three couples where one or both partners have not had a child) almost 78 per cent indicate they were in agreement about wanting or not wanting the last child at the time s/he was born, with most (66.4 per cent) agreeing that they both wanted the child and 10.3 per cent revealing the existence of a joint 'unmet need' (Table 1). The bottom half of the table describes the couples in which one partner had an 'unmet need'. In over 20 per cent of cases one partner had an 'unmet need' for spacing or limiting (combined 'unmet need' for spacing and stopping for husbands is 8.3 per cent while it is 13.9 per cent for wives).

---

1. A possible ninth category, "Wife not then/Husband no more" (Wife wait—husband stop) was not represented in my data.

Table 1. Wantedness of last child among couples (couples N=107*)

Couple (joint desire)	%	No.
1. Both wanted then	66.4	(71)
2. Both did not want then (wait)	0.9	(1)
3. Both want no more (stop)	10.3	(11)
4. Wife then—husban wait	1.8	(2)
5. Wife stop—husban wait	1.8	(2)
6. Wife then—husband stop	4.7	(5)
7. Wife wait—husband then	1.8	(2)
8. Wife stop—husband then	10.3	(11)
Wife no reply—husband then	1.8	(2)

* While there were 110 couples in the overall sample, three couples where one or both partners have never had a child are excluded from the analysis.

A comparison of the responses to both survey and interview questions among the re-interviewed couples allow us to tease out some of the nuances involved in 'unmet need'. Among the 11 couples I interviewed interesting discrepancies emerge between the survey and interview responses. What is even more interesting is the analysis of which couples fall into the respective categories. When we remove one couple where the wife had a child prior to the marriage and the couple have no children together (yet), out of the remaining ten couples only four maintained the joint positions they had offered in the survey when they were interviewed. In two cases husbands and wives reversed their positions from 'wife then and husband wait' and 'wife wait and husband then'. In one case where both indicated 'stop' in the survey this changed to 'both then' in the interview. And in three cases it would appear that during the survey one partner gave a response that matched what he or she believed the other's position to be; this was borne out in the interviews. In the first of these three both indicated 'stop' in the survey, but the wife said 'then' in the interview while her husband maintained 'stop'; in the second both said 'then' in the survey but in the interviews the wife said 'stop' while her husband said 'then'. In both these cases it would appear that the wife did not reveal her 'real' preference until the interview. In the third case both also said 'then' during the survey but during the interview while the wife still said 'then' her husband said 'stop'.

How can we explain these discrepancies? Firstly we should note that these are *stated* preferences. Individuals may be presenting what they believe to be the socially acceptable responses on the survey. More importantly, some respondents may be reflecting the extent to which individuals who 'lost' out in a disagreement present the preferences of their spouses who 'won' in a survey where no attempt is made to explore processes. In such cases levels of disagreement about reproductive decision-making are understated and decision-making dynamics are masked. For other couples it is possible that a *stated* preference may be accurate at the time of the survey but may be revised later; some of the wives' and husbands' revisions may in fact cancel each other out depending on who does more of such 'revising' of preferences.[1] In the next sections I focus on the cases of three couples that show how 'unmet need' can be masked or overstated.[2]

Nana and Nortey: When 'unmet need' is not really unmet need

Nana is a 44 year-old middle-management employee and has been married to Nortey, a 53 year-old accountant for over 12 years. Together they have a 13 year-old daughter. In the survey Nana says that at the time of her last pregnancy she wanted to 'wait' to have the child while Nortey says he wanted the child 'then' indicating that Nana had an 'unmet need' for spacing. In the interview Nana says, however, that the last time she got pregnant she did want the child 'then' while Nortey says he wanted to 'wait' indicating that in reality Nortey was the one with an 'unmet need' (for spacing). Nana's story is a sad one. Over a year after the birth of her daughter she became pregnant again, and, she explains, decided to have an abortion for a number of reasons. First, her first daughter had been born by Caesarean section, which scared her. She clarifies further, "I was not ready and I thought it was too early". Yet her daughter was one and a half at the time she became pregnant, meaning that the culturally acceptable gap of two years between siblings would have been met by the time the next child was born. As we talk further the real reason why she had the abortion surfaces; her husband was very angry that she had become pregnant when he had 'instructed' her to use family planning. In other words, it was Nana's failure to use contraception that resulted in the (for Nortey) 'mis-timed' pregnancy. Nana now reveals that for her the pregnancy was not mistimed when she concludes, "If he wanted it I would have just carried it".

> I: *What you are saying is that if he had said go ahead you would have had the baby?*
> R: *(sadly) Yes.*

Nortey did not specifically ask Nana to have an abortion; however, his response to the news of her pregnancy was so severe and hurtful that she went and had one based on her interpretation of his response. Sadly for Nana, she has not been able to become pregnant since then. Sadder still for her, Nortey has since then had a son with another woman (and had his need for a child met). It was not that Nana's husband, Nortey did not want any more children when Nana had the abortion. His ideal number, he says, would have been three, "plus a mistake, four at most". I ask Nortey why Nana had an abortion since she has clearly articulated she would have wanted more children, and since Nortey himself seemed not to have achieved his ideal number at the time of the abortion either. Apparently the timing of the pregnancy was inconvenient for Nortey. This was conditioned by his

---

1. In the case of one particular couple (not discussed in this chapter) the wife indicates she wanted the child "then" during the survey but revises her position during the interview to say she did not want the child at all. What I assess has happened in the intervening period is that she believes her husband to have taken a second wife, and that this new relationship causes him to neglect his family. She now says she wishes her young daughter had never been born and insists that she did not want to get pregnant at the time.
2. All names have been changed.

beliefs that the husband is the one with the primary responsibility for providing for the family. He and Nana were not living together at the time (she was living with her parents) because Nortey was not yet able to provide the family with an adequate place to live. Further, he argues, their first daughter, who was experiencing some developmental delays, was not independent enough to take second place for her mother's care.

> *R: We were all saying that that shouldn't happen because the child needed time to grow up, and all that. So when it came we were all upset, in fact I was more than she was [...] because I had advised her earlier on to go for this family planning, and apparently she didn't even consider it [...] because she thought she was already late in starting childbearing, so probably her friends were saying have it, have it, that kind of thing [emphasis added].*
>
> *I: So were you both satisfied with the decision to terminate?*
>
> *R: I was okay with it, but she was not happy about it. It was a messy situation, because I wasn't expecting it [...] my reaction was so bad and the next time I came she had gone for it. And what I asked her to do before and she didn't do (laughs) now she went there.*
>
> *I: Has she never complained subsequently?*
>
> *R: Both of us have complained; she would have wanted more kids, indeed I would have too, I had an ideal number, but I took it that if I didn't have I wouldn't worry too much. But she felt bad, because she knows how much I love kids. So we discuss it occasionally, she expresses her desires, wishing it were still possible, but all attempts have been futile, we just pass it off as a joke and carry on.*

It is interesting that Nortey views the abortion as a consequence of Nana's failure to practise contraception when he had instructed her to do so. That Nana's disappointment at not being able to have a child subsequently could be passed off as "a joke" also seems particularly insensitive given that Nortey has had a child outside the marriage, while he himself expresses intolerance for adultery. However, Nortey simply reveals his view that he has the right to determine his and Nana's reproductive behaviour. What the data reveal are that if a husband feels strongly enough about not having a child, and the husband is the dominant partner, he has the option to suggest that his wife have an abortion. Further, in such a situation, during the survey the wife may rationalize the action taken by indicating the child was unwanted at the time of the pregnancy. She is measured as having an 'unmet need', when the 'unmet need' is really her husband's. The fact that I modelled my survey instrument on the GDHS allows me to point to some limitations in the survey questions, as posed, for the measurement of 'unmet need'. The fact that no question is asked about past preferences regarding pregnancies which were terminated is an important gap in the measurement of 'unmet need'. While anecdotal evidence suggests that most abortions are performed on young, single women,[1] the possibility of terminating an unwanted pregnancy cannot be ruled out for married persons. It would be useful for future surveys to ask—in cases

---

1. There is very little accurate data on the incidence of abortions in Ghana; however, a study of complications arising from incomplete abortions carried out at the nation's major hospital in the 1980s suggests that the incidence is high among women in their late teens and early twenties (Ampofo 1993).

where pregnancies were terminated—whose decision it was to opt for an abortion.

Grace and Akwasi: What happened to Grace's 'unmet need'?

Grace is a 48 year-old assistant head cook in one of the student halls of residence and her husband Akwasi is a 55 year-old laboratory technician. Grace has one daughter and a son by a previous partner and together the couple have three daughters and a son. Akwasi typifies the type of behaviour regarding reproductive decision-making that is conjured up by the literature on the 'male role' and male dominance in childbearing behaviour. Akwasi feels he came to the marriage disadvantaged. Of Grace he says, "she has the upper hand" as he puts it, because Grace already had two children from a previous relationship. Indeed, at the time Grace got married to Akwasi she did not really want any more children—neither to prove her fertility, nor to experience the so-called resource-related or emotional benefits of having children. In this sense we might argue that her last four children (with Akwasi) were all 'unwanted'; however, during the survey both Grace and Akwasi say that at the time of Grace's last pregnancy the child was wanted 'then'. Hence, Grace's 'unmet need' is not exposed. It is only during the interview that Grace laments about the repeated pregnancies she has had to go through to satisfy Akwasi's fertility aspirations. Akwasi's responses, of course, are consistent for both the survey and the interview, especially since the last child was the son he had so long desired.

According to Grace, when her third child with Akwasi turned out to be a third girl he was unhappy, and she became very worried. Although she insisted to Akwasi that it is "God who gives children", and Akwasi acknowledged that "girls can do all that boys do" Grace still felt concerned and wanted to 'give' Akwasi a boy. When the third girl was born Akwasi refused to go to the hospital to see mother and child until he had to bring them home. After the birth of her fifth child, and third child (daughter) with Akwasi, Grace started using contraceptives, but Akwasi wanted Grace to have yet another child. She told him that if he insisted on having another child he would have to get another woman to have it with since she did not "need any more children". Further, she explained to me that all her pregnancies and deliveries had been difficult ones and her doctor had advised her not to have any more children. However, Grace did become pregnant a fourth time in her marriage. Initially Akwasi did not say much, but after some months he began to speculate, or wish aloud, that it would be a boy, and told Grace that if she had another girl she would definitely have to have another baby subsequently. Several years after the birth of this child Grace is still affected by the telling of the story, and sighs, "by God's grace I had a boy".

This story points to an important issue in the designation of reproductive outcome categories, i.e. the shortcoming of the so-called 'agreement' category. Grace and Akwasi's story shows that this category does not necessarily really reflect agreement, rather that one partner (in this case the husband) coerces, convinces or suggests a reproductive outcome for the other to follow. Further, the failure of the survey instrument to capture the process that led to the child's birth masks Grace's 'unmet need', not for contraception, but to be able to effect her reproductive preferences. A couple may 'agree' to have (or as in Nana and Nortey's case, to not have) a child, not because both want the same thing, but both 'agree' that what the man wants holds; here an examination of gender power relations is crucial.

Delali and Kobla: Do husbands also have 'unmet needs'?

Kobla is a 45 year-old accounts clerk at the university and, at the time of the interview, Delali, his wife, aged 35, is not working outside the home. Together the couple have three children, a 9-year-old daughter, Esi, a 7-year-old son, Kofi, and a baby boy, Yao. Before Yao's birth Delali had worked as a hairdresser and she considered her exit from the labour market as temporary. Kobla had been content to have only two children. Indeed, he was also concerned about being able to meet the financial obligations of raising three children. Kobla also knew that a third child would take an additional toll on his free time, as he would have to be involved in the day-to-day care of three, and not two, children. Before the third child was born, however, Delali, felt that their son Kofi was "lonely" and needed a sibling playmate. In any case she wanted a third child. Delali approached the subject very tactfully, advancing all manner of 'scientific' reasons to convince Kobla, focusing on Kofi's loneliness. Kofi's teacher had told her, she argued, that boredom and loneliness caused Kofi's occasional tendency towards undisciplined behavior. This was a very strategic move as Kobla (and Delali) is very concerned that his children grow up to be well-behaved and responsible. Delali concludes, "finally he came to understand me".

Delali had an inherent desire for a third child. Kobla felt very strongly about providing his children with a good education and was concerned that three children would stretch the couple's ability to adequately provide this. Additionally, Kobla was concerned about the day-to-day demands having a third child would place on him, since he knew that he would be required to participate in the caregiving activities. Thus, in the traditional conceptualisation of 'unmet need' Kobla's last child was 'unwanted'. Delali, however, was able to push to have her way because she knew that she had the option to do this in her marriage; in other words it has a lot to do with the nature of the husband/wife relationship and their beliefs about female and male roles and identities. I argue elsewhere (Adomako Ampofo 1999) that the decision to *compromise* in the area of reproductive decision making may have more to do with *gender orientation* than issues of financial convenience (i.e. structural factors). Simply put, by gender orientation I refer to the expectations relating to roles, behaviours and rights that an individual has for women and men. A male dominant orientation, which can also apply to females, generally grants men more rights and approves of a hierarchical power structure that advantages males. Such an orientation may depress what might otherwise have been the empowering effects of a woman's structural resources (or a man's lack of these) by reducing a woman's sense of entitlement, in this case, to determine the couple's fertility regime. These power differences govern the resolution of decision-making, especially in instances of disagreement, and yet this aspect of compromise is not captured in the concept of an 'unmet need'.

Conclusions

Western epistemologies have largely failed to take into account local cultural realities in their explanations for phenomena which affect indigenous peoples. The concept of 'unmet need' in demography is one such example. In the foregoing analysis I have sought to show that an 'unmet need', where one exists, is often about power and gender relations. The measurement thereof also points to issues of methodology, linked to the broader questions about the relative importance of quantitative and qualitative data collection techniques and what sorts of evidence carry weight in development concerns. It also raises questions about the conceptualisation of fertility-related behaviour within traditional demography where women (and men) are seen as objects whose behaviour can be manipulated for larger development concerns.

For a KAP-based study on reproductive behaviour to have some usefulness it must be adapted to the particular social and cultural setting, and include questions on gender issues and power structures, building on the ethnography of that particular culture, society or group of people. Even though women are at the centre of the 'unmet need' concept, they are there without regard to the gender power relations that are always a part of women and men's lives. The model was not conceived from women's point of view but rather from a very instrumental, generally male-biased way of approaching development issues. Contraceptive behaviour is not only determined by the desire to space or limit births, nor even the motivation to use contraceptives, but also by the costs associated with their use (Easterlin and Crimmins 1985). Grace's story shows how these costs include social, psychological and cultural factors that sometimes act as disincentives to individuals or couples who may otherwise feel motivated to use contraception. For women these costs may be included in their inability to refuse to acquiesce to their husband's wishes. Thus the couples in the agreement category show that 'agreement' does not necessarily mean 'egalitarianism'; indeed, Grace's interview shows that 'agreement' can reflect acquiescence on the part of the wife rather than agreement between the spouses.

A partner's 'unmet need' can also be inadvertently measured as one's own if the right questions are not asked. While Nana tries to subvert Nortey's wishes to postpone childbearing by failing to use contraceptives she does eventually give in to *his* preference by having an abortion. Grace also tells her husband she will have no more children and that for all she cares he can have a child with whomever he wishes, but eventually she accedes and *does* become pregnant when she really wanted no more children. Thus it is certainly important to include the male partner's preferences in analytical models in order to arrive at a more realistic picture of fertility behaviour. Women's 'unmet need' is not likely to be met without reference to men's needs both conceptually and from a programme perspective.

On the other hand, men, who are rarely conceived of as having an 'unmet need' if their wives do not have an 'unmet need', are generally left out of the picture. Yet, some wives, like Delali, are able to effect preferences for a child based on more egalitarian gender relations. Unwanted (or mistimed) births are rarely simply indirect indicators of the extent of imperfect control over reproductive processes (Adetunji 1998), including social control. Thus, the 'unmet need' for family planning must be attributed to more than inadequate supply factors or ignorance about methods, and include the role of gender relations. More useful than simply examining women's stated family size preferences in relation to achieved fertility, then, is an examination of the relative preferences of individual spouses, and the ultimate reproductive behaviour of the couple. There are critics of 'male-inclusion' efforts who argue that 'male motivation' (family planning) campaigns simply reconfirm that men have control over women's bodies and their reproductive capacities (see Win 1998). I take the position that increasing male involvement should not, and need not, detract from efforts to improve the status of women, but should foster mutual respect and shared responsibility. Thankfully, some scholars have begun to look at developing a broader definition of 'unmet need'.[1]

However, there are limits to the extent to which surveys can capture these nuances and processes. Spouses may under or over ascribe their own reproductive preferences to their spouses, or they may ascribe more or less agreement than actually exists, though women are more likely to do so than men given the general trend of male dominance. The increasing acceptance of including qualitative and triangulation techniques in surveys, though more costly and time consuming, needs to make greater inroads in the population establishment. There are so many underlying concerns which individuals simply cannot, or will not reveal in a questionnaire survey. For example in the story of Grace and Akwasi, the latter's mother was an important player in questioning her daughter-in-law's (and son's) inability to bear a son. This had significant implications for Akwasi's gender identity, and his dominance over Grace (see Adomako Ampofo 2000). Yet, the role of the extended family in creating a 'need' for children does not feature in population discourse. Fertility and infertility are such important aspects of people's lives in Africa that examining people's decisions (or non-decisions) to have (or not have) children needs to be carried out, as with all research, in a careful, sensitive and, culturally-relevant manner, both in the design of concepts as well as in the field methodology.

---

1. For example Sinding and Fathalla (1995) proposed this at the ICPD (International Conference on Population and Development) held in Cairo in 1994.

References

Adetunji, Jacob A., 1998, "Unintended childbearing in developing countries: Levels, trends, and determinants." DHS Analytical Report, No. 8, June 1998, viii. 46 pp. Macro International, Demographic and Health Surveys [DHS], Calverton, Maryland.

Adomako Ampofo, Akosua, 1999, "Resource Contributions, Gender Orientation, and Reproductive Decision Making in Ghana: The Case of Urban Couples," *African Studies Research Review* 15(2).

Adomako Ampofo, Akosua, 2000, "Who Is the Driver and Who Is the 'Mate'? Gender Orientations and Household Decision Making in Ghana." Paper presented at the Annual Meetings of the African Studies Association, Nashville, Tennessee, 16–19 November.

Adomako Ampofo, Akosua, 2001, "Beyond Cairo: Gender, Sexual Behaviour, and Reproductive Health: Gender and Fertility," Paper presented at the CODESRIA Gender Institute, Dakar, Senegal, 2001.

Adomako Ampofo, Akosua, 2002, "Does Women's Education Matter? A Case Study of Reproductive Decision Making from Urban Ghana", *Ghana Studies* 5:123–157

Ampofo, Daniel A., 1993, *The Health Issues of Our Time. Philosophical Perspectives of Health and Social Problems of Procreation.* J.B. Danquah Memorial Lectures, 26th series. Accra: Ghana Academy of Arts and Sciences.

Anarfi, John K. and Clara K. Fayorsey, 1995, "The Male Protagonists in the 'Commercialization' of Aspects of Female Life Cycle in Ghana." Paper prepared for the Seminar on Fertility and the Male Life Cycle in the Era of Fertility Decline, Zacatecas, Mexico, 13–16 November 1995.

Bankole, Akinrinola and Alex C. Ezeh, 1997, "Unmet Need for Couples: A Conceptual Framework and Evaluation with Recent DHS Data." Paper presented at the 1997 Annual Meeting of the Population Association of America, Washington, D. C., March 27–29.

Blood, Robert O. Jnr. and Donald M. Wolfe, 1960, Husbands and Wives, the Dynamics of Married Living. New York: The Free Press.

Bogue, Donald, 1974,"Population Perspectives: Some Views from a Sociologist." Population Dynamic Quarterly, 292:2–20.

Bongaarts, John, 1991, "The GAP-Gap and the Unmet Need for Contraception." Population and Development Review, 17(2):293–314.

Bongaarts, John and J. Bruce, 1995, "The Causes of Unmet Need for Contraception and the Social Context of Services," Studies in Family Planning, 26(2): 57–75.

Boulier, B. L., 1985, "Evaluating Unmet Need for Contraception: Estimates for Thirty-Six Developing Countries." World Bank Staff Working Papers No. 678, Population and Development Series No. 3. Washington, D.C., World Bank.

Caldwell, J. C. and l. T. Ruzicka, 1978, "Demographic Levels and Trends," in Cleland, John, C. Scott and D. Whitelegge (eds), The World Fertility Surveys: An Assessment. Oxford: Clarendon Press, 741–772.

Casterline, J., A. E. Perez and Ann E. Biddlecom, 1996, "Factors Underlying Unmet Need for Family Planning in the Philippines." *Working Papers*, No. 84. New York: The Population Council.

Coeytaux, F., 1992, "Abortion: the Ultimate Unmet Need,"in Senanayake, P. and R. L. Kleinman (eds), *The Proceedings of the IPPF Family Planning Congress.* New Delhi and New York: Parthenon Publishing, 701–708.

Davis, K. and J. Blake, 1956, "Social Structure and Fertility: An Analytic Framework," *Economic Development and Cultural Change* 4:211–235.

Dodoo, F. Nii-Amoo, 1993, "A Couple Analysis of Micro-Level Supply/Demand Factors in Fertility Regulation," *Population Research and Policy Review* 12(2):93–101.

Dodoo, F. Nii-Amoo and Poem van Landewijk, 1996, "Women, and the Fertility Question in Sub-Saharan Africa," *African Studies Review* 39(3):29–41.

Dodoo, F. Nii-Amoo, Ye Luo and Evelina Panayotova, 1997, "Do Male Reproductive Preferences Really Point to a Need to Refocus Fertility Policy?" *Population Research and Policy Review* 16: 447–455.

Easterlin, Richard A., 1975, "An Economic Framework for Fertility Analysis," *Studies in Family Planning* 6: 54–63.

Easterlin, Richard A. and Eileen M. Crimmins, 1985, *The Fertility Revolution: A Supply-Demand Analysis*. Chicago: University of Chicago Press.

Foreit, Karen, P. Mostajo, E. Gamarra, and A. Padilla, 1992, "Unmet Demand for Contraception versus Unmet Demand for Appropriate Contraception." Paper presented at the 120th Annual Meeting of the American Public Health Association, Washington D.C, November.

Fortes, Meyer, 1948, "The Ashanti Sociological Survey: A Preliminary Report," *Rhodes Livingstone Journal* 6:1–36.

Freedman, Ronald and Lolagene C. Coombs, 1974, *Cross Cultural Comparisons: Data on Two Factors in Fertility Behavior*. New York: Population Council.

Ghana Statistical Service and the Institute for Resource Development, 1999, *Ghana Demographic and Health Survey 1998*. Columbia, Maryland: GSS and RD.

Hodgson, Dennis and Susan C. Watkins, 1997, "Feminists and Neo-Malthusians: Past and Present Alliance," *Population and Development Review* 23(3):469–523.

Kannae, Lawrence and Brian Pendleton, 1994, "Fertility Attitudes among Male Ghanaian Government Employees," *Journal of Asian and African Studies* XXIX(1–2):65–76.

Khalifa, Mona, 1988, "Attitudes of Urban Sudanese Men toward Family Planning," *Studies in Family Planning* 19:236–243.

Institute for Resource Development/Macro International, 2002. www.measuredhs.com/data/indicators/table_builder (accessed June 18, 2002).

McFarlane, C. P., J. S. Friedman, L. Morris, and H. I. Goldberg, 1994, *Jamaica Contraceptive Prevalence Survey, 1993: 3: Sexual Experience, Contraceptive Practice and Fertility*. Kingston, Jamaica: National Family Planning Board.

Mott, Frank L. and Susan H. Mott, 1985, "Household Fertility Decisions in West Africa: A Comparison of Male and Female Survey Results," *Studies in Family Planning* 16 (2): 88–99.

Mustafa, Mutasim Abu Bakr and Stephen D. Mumford, 1984, "Male Attitudes towards Family Planning in Khartoum, Sudan," *Journal of Biosocial Science* 16:437–449.

Nukunya, Godwin K., 1966, *Kinship and Marriage among the Anlo Ewe*. London: The Athlone Press.

Nukunya, Godwin K., 1991, "Tradition and Change: The Case of the Family." Inaugural Lecture Delivered at the University of Ghana, Legon, 14th February 1991.

Oppong, Christine, 1980, "From Love to Institution: Indications of Change in Akan. Marriage," *Journal of Family History,* 197–209.

Population Impact Project, 1995, *Introducing Ghana's Revised Population Policy*. Accra: PIP.

Presser, Harriet. B., 1997, "Demography, Feminism and the Science-Policy Nexus," *Population and Development Review* 23(2):29–331.

Quarcoopome, Samuel S., 1993, "The Impact of Urbanisation of the Socio-Political History of the Ga Mashie People of Accra: 1877–1957." Ph.D Thesis presented to the Institute of African Studies, University of Ghana, Legon.

Sarpong, Peter, 1977, *Girls' Nubility Rites in Ashanti*. Tema: Ghana Publishing Corporation.

Simmons, Ruth, Rezina Mita, and Michael A. Koenig, 1992, "Employment in Family Planning and Women's Status in Bangladesh," *Studies in Family Planning* 23 (2): 97–109.

Sinding, S.W. and M.F. Fathalla, 1995, "The Great Transition", *Populi*. Dec. 18–21.

Stokes, B., 1977, "Filling the Family Planning Gap." *Worldwatch paper 12*. Washington, D. C: Worldwatch Institute.

Tsui, A. O., 1985, "The Rise of Modern Contraception," in J. Cleland, J. Holcroft, and B. Dinesen (eds), *Reproductive Change in Developing Countries: Insights from the World Fertility Survey*. London, Oxford: University Press: 115–138.

UNFPA, 1996, *Follow-up actions to the recommendations of the International Conference on Population and Development: Reproductive rights and reproductive health*. Geneva: Population Information Network.

USAID, 1994, *Reproductive Health Baseline Survey: A Survey of Projects and Activities Implemented and Planned by USAID Missions and Cooperating Agencies*. Washington, D.C. August 1994.

Waring, Marilyn, 1999, *Counting for Nothing: What Men Value and What Women are Worth*. Toronto: University of Toronto Press.

Watkins, Susan Cotts, 1993, "If all we knew about Women was what we read in Demography, what would we know?" *Demography* 30(4):551–577.

Westoff, Charles F. ,1978, "Is the KAP-Gap Real?" *Population and Development Review* 14(2):225–232.

Westoff, Charles F., 1995, "The Feminist Agenda Detracts from Population Control Efforts," pp. 177–187 as reprinted in Hohm, F. Charles and Lori Justine Jones (eds) *Population: Opposing Viewpoints*. San Diego: Greenhaven Press.

Westoff, Charles F., Annklimas Blanc, and Laura Nyblad, 1994, "Marriage and entry into parenthood," *Health Surveys Comparative Studies 10*. Calverton: Macro International.

Westoff, C. F. and A. R. Pebley, 1981, "Alternative Measures of Unmet Need for Family Planning in Developing Countries," *International Family Planning Perspective* 7(4): 126–136.

Win, Everjoice J., 1998, "The Inclusion of Men: A Cry for Help or a Serious Strategy for Women's Advancement," *Women's Health News,* August 1998 (27): 4–6.

Appendix

Unlike the GDHS respondents, who are mostly younger than or 34 years of age, my sample is older; the mean age for women and men respectively is 40 and 47 (only 23.6% of female and 3.2% of male respondents were under the age of 34). In other words, most of the individuals in my sample are outside the considered ages of reproduction, thus past reproductive outcomes are more salient than are considerations about future births. While Akan (ethnic) representation closely reflects that of the GDHS, making up almost half of the entire sample, both Gas and Ewes are over represented. However, these three groups, the Akans, Ewes, and the 'indigenous' Gas of Accra, are the most common ethnic groups in urban centres in southern Ghana such as Accra (Quarcoopome 1993). Given the cultural importance attached to fertility it is not surprising that very few respondents have no children (3% of women, and 5% of men). The mean number of children in the sample is 4.0 for men, and almost 3.5 for women; lower than the national average, but almost equal to the average for the highly urbanized Greater Accra Region. However, it should also be pointed out that a considerable number of men (18.5%) and women (11%) have six or more children. The mean number of children for wives and husbands in the sub-sample is very close, 3.6 and 3.7 for wives and husbands respectively. The range for wives and husbands differs somewhat more, however, being 6 for wives but 11 for husbands.

Problems of Pleasure and Desire

Photo : Hamadou Bocoum, 19?

6. Kinky Politics

Kopano Ratele

Introduction

If 'the sexual superiority of the Negro' is not really 'real', as Fanon (1986:159) is at pains to show in his work on black and white sexual desire and fear, what propels or pulls questions about the bodies, skins, buttocks, penises, vaginas, and lips of Africans as interesting into our presence? Fanon's question—"is the sexual superiority of the Negro real?"—is the incitement for this chapter. In addition to this question this chapter asks whether issues of sexual superiority are actually worth our serious attention or whether they should they be left to women's and men's magazines, the back pages of newspapers, and living rooms. If questions about sex deserve any seriousness, even if it is only because many people around the world still find inter-racial, inter-cultural, inter-religious, or inter-ethnic coupling irritating or at best titillating, should critical scholars and activists not come out and advocate inter-group sex education as part of gender-conscious antiracism, multiculturalism, or religious and ethnic tolerance?

These questions are treated by examining discourses mobilised by young heterosexual African men in accounting for their own and others' sexual and racial identity practices within the changing cultural and political landscape of South Africa. The chapter is focused by a purposive selection of essays written by three part-time male students in the psychology of racism class of 1999 at the University of Western Cape. Students were asked for permission to use their writing for research purposes. Part-time students generally are older than the traditional university student by a few years as well as likely to juggle their studies with other life commitments such as a full-time job, marriage or other kinds of steadier relationships, and other activities. One of the requirements of this class has been that students write essays focusing on an event in their lives characterized by what they would define as racism. The essay task for the class from which essays used in this chapter are taken was the same, but, in addition, a student's work had to trace the colour line to where it connected to sexuality, without losing critical theoretical distance.

It is perhaps important to make a note of some of the objectives of this class. It is intended to expose students to the racism of the discipline of psychology; to sensitise students to the fact that as South Africans our lives and identities are intimately influenced by race and racism; and to bring students to an understanding of race and racism as they intersect with other discourses and practices of power and oppression. Furthermore, it should be noted that at the time of writing their essays the students who wrote the essays used here were supposed to be familiar with Fanon's question, Fanon being among the list of authors prescribed for the class.

The aim of this chapter is part of an ongoing project to think about practices surrounding the multiple, shifting, piled up, crosscutting divisions that re-write our identifications and relationships, in order to sharpen our appreciation of the histories of the current debates around the transformation of South African society. In spite of good intentions transformation debates and resultant policies, institutions and programmes have tended to re-produce certain old as well as creating new cultural, social, economic and political divisions. Specifically, these debates, policies, institutions and programmes have tended to gloss over certain blind-spots, to re-install particular inimical cleavages, and to follow certain lines of argument. Examples abound. One of these is that some political, business and cultural leaders, programmes and institutions continue to deploy ~~race~~ as a fact of nature, act as if sex and gender at some moments are ~~unraced~~, and almost always completely ignore desire, or at best keep it separate from, the politics of ~~race~~, and similarly sex and gender.

What this means is that while on the one hand these leaders and society need reminding of what the facts of being queer, being female, or being male might mean politically, economically and socially, on the other hand the attentions of sex and gender researchers and activists need to be drawn to the racialised troubles in the desiring practices of some men and women, lesbians and gays. I will try to do this by tracing moments of African identification, in particular of male identifying practices, from the one side, and sexual politics and masculine desire from the other side, and their connections to and disconnections from efforts at transforming South African society. As indicated above, I do this with the help of three purposively rather than randomly selected semi-autobiographical essays by African male students, Paul, Mzi, and Bo'nkosi. That is to say, the chosen essays are not representative but rather limited to only those that contradicted the objectives of the class in specific ways.

Discursive psychology and insubordinate practices

Elsewhere I have argued against engaging in regressive practices and representations in our pains to want to know ourselves and to find our homes again (Ratele 2001). Given the persisting, intractable white masculine traditions of depicting African, black and third world peoples, it is excusable, even understandable, when one comes upon a wish to overturn every last one of these traditions. The need to challenge western masculine traditions, and to work at changing our cultural and political economy, our societies and our identities, our self and our relationships is thus clear and constant. However, these desires to overturn these traditions and, perhaps, to know ourselves as we were, or could have been, should not be allowed to blind us to the fact that all of us are capable of oppressing others. The desire to transform ourselves and our conditions must in fact stimulate a heightened, reflexive and rebellious consciousness, in particular regarding those practices that are often explained as simply a self-evident part of us, part of our cultures or vanquished traditions. The need to remain vigilant against all dominant practices, particularly those that appear obvious and straightforward, thus continues to exist. I think where one finds or builds this insubordinate vigilance against simple categories, one is likely to find or develop the necessary, enduring revolt against naturalisations, against obvious and hence oppressive practices, identities, cultures, ways of being, realities. Against the backcloth of continuing 'nature' discourses, pushing for varied and more sophisticated positions (which are not confined to African bodies, black male identities, or sexual hierarchies) retains urgency.

The argument developed here derives from constructionist, and specifically discursive psychological dialogues. The range of dialogues referred to as constructionism revolves around ways by which individuals come to account for themselves and the world we live in. For example, constructionists frame the notion of identity as a project arising out of our relationships with others and these relationships as historically and culturally specific (Burr 1995; Durrheim 1997; Frankenberg 1995; Gergen 1985). Similarly, discursive psychologists maintain that how we make meaning for ourselves is made possible by language and accomplished in social interaction (Antaki 1994; Billig 1998; Danziger 1990; Duncan 1993). These psychologists study how objects of psychological inquiry which orthodox psychology says are entities or processes inside individuals, are produced through discursive activity (Durrheim 1997; Levett et al. 1997). Where the latter kind of psychologist treats, for example, feelings such as attraction or disgust, identities such as woman and 'coloured', and notions of beauty and difference as internal states or natural processes, discursive psychology has shown that feelings, social identities and views of beauty, difference and other things, are produced in relationships between people and are achieved through discourse. Feelings, motivation, racism and so on are activities. People should be understood as 'showing' love, 'acting' motivated, 'sounding' intelligent, constructing themselves or being positioned as beautiful, black, African, men, coloureds, white, women or European.

Heterosexual masculine desire and racialised difference

Paul is a twenty-something year old man. He works as a trainer in a non-governmental organisation. His essay is about his sexual affairs with "Coloured"[1] women. These affairs he opposes to his experience with African or black women. This means that Paul deploys apartheid identity categories where coloureds although they were not white were neither black nor African. Paul says some of the reasons "why black men" and specifically he "got attracted to Coloured women" are that

---

1. I write coloured, black, white or any ~~race~~ name in small letters but follow the usage of the students and other writers when quoting. However, African, Indians or European I capitalise as I take these to be more than strictly ~~race~~ identities.

"Coloured women are more exposed to making love" and "more open than black women". The phrase 'more open' is intriguing. It becomes clearer what Paul means by it later on when he says "Coloured women I went out with are more civilized when it comes to making love".

One must always be cautious when interpreting second or third language speakers, even when they are university students. Does Paul really mean 'civilized' or was he short of a more appropriate word? Still the word is there. Coloured women are more 'civilized' (than African/black women). This advanced civilisation of coloured females he deduces from their lovemaking as well as the fact that "they are more open discussing on how you performed". We could speculate if there is some anxiety buried in Paul's need to have women discuss his performance or if his interest to know is motivated by a desire to be a better lover for his partners?

Paul relates coloured women's civilisation to his view that "they are very romantic". Once again, what are we to understand by 'very romantic'? Is what Paul wants us to understand that they like walking hand in hand, candle-lit dinners, rose petals on satin covered beds, Taban La Liyong before and Marvin Gaye afterwards? Or are we to connect being 'more open', 'civilized' and 'very romantic' with his opinion that coloured females are "sexually … very stimulating and open minded to do and explore different types of sex positions".

These sentiments from Paul's essays of course beg Fanon's question. It may be important to note that that question, which Fanon was directing firstly at white French society and then educated blacks in France, gets complicated by the historical South African situation where, instead of two ~~races~~ there were, according to the Population Registration Act of 1950, three official racial categories and several ethnic and tribal categories. On the other hand, according to the national democratic movement, at least that led by Steve Biko and his associates, there were essentially two groups in South Africa: the black and the white. In his essay Paul, as we said, plays not in the re-defined identity field charted by Biko and his comrades, or that staked out by Fanon, but squarely within the official apartheid territory. He sees coloured women and coloured men as different from, and as not, black. They are also not African.

Closely tied to the deployment of the racial categories of the government, at the heart of Paul's text, lies what I mean by *kinky politics*. By kinky politics I want to indicate racial perversion. Kinky politics follows the fetish of, and refetishises, ~~race~~. There can be no racism without this constant re-fetishisisation. Indeed, one could say, racism is kinky politics as it always involves a sexual warping of identity politics. Racism, together with (hetero)sexism, then, is what keeps us in awe, or fear, or ignorance of black and white, male and female bodies and sexualities in this society. For example, Mzi, the second student whose essay I use, wrote that ever since a certain incident I will come back to later, he tries to avoid looking "at naked white women" when he is at the beach. As with Paul's words, caution is advised: I suspect nakedness here might mean dressed in a bikini. But even if it is it not complete nudity that he is talking about, it gives away a certain perception of what Mzi thinks about (white women in) bikinis. In any event, he writes that "whenever I happen to get an eye contact with a white body I always pretend as if I am looking somewhere to avoid eye contact". He says because of the incident "when my friends organize a date for me if it is a white lady I always come up with some excuses".

Kinky politics is personal and institutional practices, politics, programmes and cultures that naturalise, objectify, and stabilise difference, refusing to allow for its characteristic of movement and change. In respect to racial difference, kinky politics shows itself when that difference is held permanently constant and becomes an explanation of what the idea of race or the policy of racial domination generates in the first place. For instance, this is how Paul explains his attraction to the females of the coloured race: "There are certain features that turn me on when I look at Coloured women. They have beautiful legs and light in complexion". To put it a bit more bluntly, the light complected races are beautiful because a light complexion is more beautiful.

Notwithstanding the historical and geographic specificity of Fanon, the point of his question can thus be easily stretched to cover whether it is coloureds or Africans, as opposed to whites and Indians (that is in South Africa; elsewhere it could be some other races, ethnicities, religious, or other opposed groups), who are naturally more sexually superior. Or, to put it differently, why is the relation of sexual potency to political, social and economic power generally inverted? But, perhaps even more importantly, we must investigate what conditions make it possible for someone like Paul to talk in these sorts of ways, for anyone to talk in such ways in a specific cultural situation and period, about these kinds of things.

Social transformation and sexualised racial politics

At the centre of the texts by Paul and Mzi, as I have argued, as of Bo'nkosi's below, lies a kink, in two senses of the word: (1) a twist in a rope that causes an obstruction, a tight curl in human hair, a bend in a course or line, and (2) a mental quirk but now, chiefly, taken to mean a bizarre sexual quirk, taste, or practice. The kinks that can be read in the three essays reflect, or are reflected, in the histories of local and global politics of whiteness and blackness, as well as those of sex and gender (see e.g. Biko 1996; Epstein 1998; Frankenberg 1993; Mandela 1994; Morrison and Lacour 1997). The history of South Africa is full of kinks. South African institutions, policies and programmes have for the most part reproduced, redeployed and replayed these twists and quirky practices.

These reproductions and replays are, for instance, identifiable in a particular variety of debate, specific lines of argumentation and the regularity, if not fetishisation, of certain subjects. One area where the shape of debate, where one can trace the usual line of argument and observe the fetish in play is of course in government structures. For example, the government vehicle tasked with redressing gender inequality has tended to unrace its purview, largely steering clear of the racial troubles in its focus. On the other hand, the structure that is intended to pro-

143

mote a human rights culture, is known for its almost obsessive focus on ~~race~~, to the near exclusion of gender issues. There are exceptions to this. Individual members of the Commission for Gender Equality (CGE) and the Human Rights Commission (HRC) have spoken for pursuing a transformation politics that includes both ~~race~~ and gender (e.g. Lowe-Morna 1998; Pityana 2000). However, the CGE, as its name implies, was established to focus on the latter. The point is enlarged by considering the fact that even though its mission is human rights, the HRC, in particular in the person of its outgoing chairman, Barney Pityana, figures prominently in the public consciousness on its work around ~~race~~ and racism (e.g. Beresford 2000; Mahlangu 1999; Ka'Nkosi 2000; SAPA 2000). The HRC has investigated racism in the media, the investigation and the report turning into subjects of intense public argument; and recently, the commission hosted a national conference on ~~race~~ in Sandton, Gauteng Province. The two separate statutory organs, the HRC and the CGE, are among several moves aimed at transforming power relations in the country. This structural segregation might appear to some observers an inconsequential quirk at worst. But it actually has deep implications for how we account for ourselves, the routes of our identifying stories, day-to-day cultural practice, and our relationships to one another as citizens. Thus, in continuing to operate as separate entities the two commissions, rather than effecting change in the material discursive orders of ~~race~~ and gender/sex, might further entrench historical divisions and create new divisions in political society and cultural life.

The kink though that is most difficult to negotiate or undo is not that between black and coloured or white, or even that between men and women. Neither is it the widening gap between rich and poor. And it is not that existing among black people. The kink that is hardest is that re-produced in each of us, shown by Paul's and Mzi's accounts. On the other hand, this is nothing new: these are the curls, tears, twists, convolutions in identities and practices that black women activists and feminists have spoken so long about. What they have shown is that ~~race~~ politics are limiting and limited since they generally tend to be separated from feminist struggles, sex wars and other struggles, but also that colour-blind sex/gender activism is always likely to produce serious problems in the everyday lives of women who are not middle-class, heterosexual and white.

I am being mindful of this kind of thinking around these matters in South Africa and its taken-for-grantedness when I offer what might be seen as merely provocative advice: young men and women should be encouraged to have good, 'normal', sexual intercourse at the earliest opportunity with another person of another ~~race~~ or ethnic group before they reach a certain age. This is not only in the interest of a much more comprehensive sexual education. It may be one way of attaining liberated masculinities. Most crucial, though, good interracial sex could have deep significance for reconstructing our national politics. Perhaps, rather than remain unsaid, for once recommendations such as this should be stated in a book like this in explicit terms. But, as I suggested, this is supposed to be the terrain of pop culture, even pornography, and for anyone who does not want to be thought of as lacking in seriousness, out of bounds. Besides the glare of academic scholarship, there are a number of other reasons why no one has explicitly advised sex to combat some of our social and political ills. At best, any such advice might be regarded as just trying to be provocative. Educationally it might be criticised as having no pedagogical grounding. It may be thought to be politically naive, regressive, immodest, suicidal even. And sex, wrongly, is still widely taken to be private and having very little to do with political affairs.

However, beginning with Fanon's treatment of sexuality and ~~race~~, one already has a glimpse of what many intellectuals and activists would take up, in one guise or another, quietly or loudly, which is the fact that "the sexualisation of ~~race~~ is an artifact of white racism" (Zack 1997a:153). Racism produces or encourages kinky racial positions. Desire in racist cultures is misrecognised, that is to say 'perverted', and this can be seen in how ~~race~~ relations transmogrify into sexual relations. Speaking heterosexually, Fanon would argue that "the women among whites view the Negro as the keeper of the impalpable gate that opens into the realm of orgies, of bacchanals, of delirious sexual sensation" (1986:177). Even more hetero-masculine is Hernton (1988) who would take up the same point and contend that the taboo of the "other" woman eats into the psyche of the black man. The taboo of the other woman, he said, erodes portions of the black man's sexual development, creating in him an unconscious ambivalence towards women of the other ~~races~~ but also to those of his own ~~race~~. I think the larger point is that while African people's relations to whiteness do not have to be sexual they tend to be sexualised: that is to say, they always imply the production of desire and pleasure in a ~~race~~ defined culture.

Perhaps I should take one step backwards and note that if one makes an argument that unsexed or genderless ~~race~~ politics produces kinky relations, others might wish to know, what, to start with, is meant by ~~race~~. And if that is answered satisfactorily, the next question may be whether there is ever a possibility of 'normal' good sex between ~~raced~~ people. Shouldn't we rather stop this sex business and speak instead about love, friendship, working together in an antiracist, antisexist environment, it may be asked? How, anyway, would encouraging sex with other ~~races~~ and ethnic groups liberate men or women, or any other group of people? How is it of interest to projects of national reconciliation, African Renaissance, or the New Partnership for African's Development?

Eroticising ~~race~~ in Cape Town, South Africa

Bo'nkosi was nearing thirty in 1999 when he wrote his essay. Among the many, complicated emotions revealed in Bo'nkosi's essays is anger. It is clear from reading the essay that his anger is imbricated with desire. He tells us that in his "township" they "usually saw a couple of beautiful ladies who were called prostitutes". The sentence seems strange. One does not usually see beauty and prostitution in one line. Moreover, but perhaps ironically, these beautiful prostitutes he refers to as "ladies". But Bo'nkosi is not taking the whole blame, if any, for what these women were called. He uses the plural voice—"we usually saw"—and the passive voice to distance himself from much of the happenings. Why were the "beautiful ladies" "called prostitutes"? The assumption you have of what prostitutes do is overturned in the next few lines. He writes that "they were called names by the community because they were sleeping with white men". Having sex with white men, in other words, is what turned these women into prostitutes. True, there is a sentence about monetary exchange, but it comes later, and it is suspect. The sentence follows after Bo'nkosi tells us that because of their relations with white males these women "were regarded as outcasts in our society". After this line, it is then that he says "they were selling their bodies to white men for the sake of money". It is important to note that Bo'nkosi sees what was happening in his townships, more likely in a neighbourhood in a township, as affecting all black men. "Black men in South Africa", he writes, "were furious because they could not have sex with white women whereas their sisters were having fun with white guys". Once again, this becomes complicated because 'fun' is not one of the things we always associate with prostitution.

One of the questions we have to ask at this stage after reading Bo'nkosi is whether the women he is talking of actually sold sex to white men (only), or were they said to sell their bodies because they preferred to have relations with white men? The latter would seem to be the case. It seems to me easier and more lucrative for black and African women, if they are going to work as prostitutes, to work in town and city streets, hotels and clubs than it is in townships. And I think it is easier for a white man to know where to find a sex-worker, get a lap-dance or visit a strip-joint if they are in a town or city than to go all the way into a township for coition. But it is Bo'nkosi who wraps the whole thing up for us:

> The ladies perceived themselves as moderately different from others. Black men who were neighbours were calling them names and the ladies were careless about those nasty words. They perceived themselves as different from others as they knew they will not be accepted by black guys anymore ... Black brothers and sisters had an attitude towards each other ... For the love of money people end up having sex with whites. They are not sexually harassed. There is an agreement between them they are not forced to go to bed. White men are willing to and always want to have sex with black women. But the laws and regulations of the country did not allow that. Black women were sexual slaves of whites. Our sisters become victims because they are poor and unemployed. Having sex with a white man is a job for them which generates income. The black brothers cannot touch or have sex with white women as they are protected and they are not easy targets like our sisters are. It is not easy to approach them and they cannot be lured by money as they have everything money can buy.

What Bo'nkosi's words point to is the enduring kinky emotional and social complex of anger, disgust, powerlessness and fascination regarding the possibility of sexual congress between people of different colours. This socialised emotional labyrinth lies at the core of sexist, racist cultures. This emotional structure plays a significant part in the reduction of all black and white relations to bodies, sexuality, and especially, to perversion. Scholars and activists have shown that sexualised anxieties and fantasies about ~~race~~ run deep within such cultures and societies, and that in accounts of people opposed to racial mixing sex tends to have a privileged place (Fanon 1986; Hernton 1988; Gordon 1997; Zack 1997a, b). From Bo'nkosi's text, as from the other students', it is evident that these associations of sex and ~~race~~ persist up to today in South Africa. Individuals leap from ~~race~~ to sex and backwards in what seems to be very easy movements, but the leap at times appears to be strange and inexplicable. Yet it is because of the deep-running love-hate historical relationship between the two that it is both easy and somewhat odd. It is odd that other, unknown persons' practices and relationships can evoke such strong emotions in observers. It is easy because the unfavourable connections between sex and ~~race~~ have been naturalised over centuries and people in these sexist, racist societies inherit these connections with their histories and cultures.

The historical eroticisation of ~~race~~

The eroticisation of 'the other' has come full circle it seems. The earliest point in circle is the sort contained in Anton Gill's work on the sexual side of British imperial history. In his work Gill refers to Edward Sellon. Sellon was an officer in the 1840s in the British Indian Army. He was also an anthropologist. Gill quotes the anthropologist-officer on his views about the joys of the colony: "I now commenced a regular course of fucking with native women. They understand in perfection all arts and wiles of love, are capable of gratifying any tastes, and in face and figure are unsurpassed by any women in the world …. It is impossible to describe the enjoyment I have had in the arms of these sirens" (1995: 37). It is uncanny how this sounds almost exactly like parts of Paul's essay. For the white army man and anthropologist it is native women who understand the arts and wiles of love and it is their figures that are beautiful. For the young African male student it is coloured women who are sexually better than black and African women, being more willing to give feedback on his performance, besides being romantic and beautiful.

The reference to anthropology leads Gill to discuss another 'scientist', Richard Burton. He was a "great explorer and linguist" and "one of the leading lights in the nascent science", according to Gill. Besides telling us, as we have been told before, that Burton "discovered" Lake Tanganyika, Gill states that Burton reached a scientific conclusion that "debauched women prefer Negroes on account of the size of their parts". Burton's purpose in describing those women who might prefer Negroes as debauched is of course not concealed at all. It works to the same intended effect as this sentence: "I measured one man in Somaliland, who, when quiescent, numbered nearly six inches" (Gill 1995:39). From this scientific sample of black penises Burton does not blink as he makes the incredible claim that the one Somali man is clear evidence of the length of penises of the Negro ~~race~~. The problem with this may not be clear until where he says that this is also a characteristic "of African animals; e.g. the horse". The aim in this proof is contained in the reference to the size of the genitals of African animals immediately after the spurious evidence of the size of Negro penises. Fanon, among many others, has shown that in white minds the black is penis and an animal. Also of interest here is Gill's comments on all this "scientific" work: Burton's "observations are not wrong", Gill is moved to tell us. "The science of penis-measuring is called phalloplenthysmography, and it has established that the black penis is indeed on average a little larger than the white" (1995:39).

Obsessions inherited from apartheid

Let us take Mzi's essay as an example. Mzi had gone with four friends from his work, "three whites, one coloured, and myself", to Sandy Bay Beach for a braai. Sandy Bay was a nudist beach. Under apartheid beach laws, it was restricted for the white group. It seems as if at some point the beach had a controlled access point. At the access point the group were ordered to stop the car by a security man because he wanted to do a thorough check. "To my surprise", Mzi writes, "the other vehicles with white people [only] were allowed free access". The group asked the security guard if they could see his seniors. They were told they could not. After a couple of hours one of the student's "white friends decided to call the police" to intervene. It was then that the man allowed the group to go onto the beach provided that they did "not look at the naked white bodies".

One of the things that can be made of this is that the incident was socially and emotionally important for Mzi. When read with other parts of the essay we can go further and infer that the kinds of views he holds on social, political and cultural relationships are shaped by what he sees as emotionally significant interactions, in this case the exchange with a white security man. But why was this particular incident available to memory? Because, as we suggested earlier, the relation between race and sex is emotionally significant as it is a crucial part of antiblack, antiwomen societies. Emotions, that is to say, are not inner states but things we do rhetorically and accomplish in social relationships. What is viewed as an emotionally significant interaction is produced in the context of relationships with other people and not merely personal. Personally emotionally significant events have extra-individual antecedents and implications, deriving in part from what is emotionally important for a society or culture and in turn having consequences for subsequent views held by individuals.

In South Africa this production of emotion and memory plays out against an historical antagonistic masculine ideology. One of the reasons for the sorts of accounts that, for instance, we read in Mzi's essay, is largely because of this antagonistic masculine ideology and particularly its obsessions. Apartheid obsession takes many forms. The obsession can be seen in the state's penchant for division and surveillance. Racialised and ethnic divisions produced under the policy of apartheid were spectacular. This obsession extended to private life. For this reason, sex came to mean much in South Africa. That is to say, not only did sex obsess apartheid ideologues insofar as sexuality tends to be one of the readily vexing questions. It becomes extra-special, taking on added meaning because within social and cultural systems deeply divided on one or another characteristic, private life is not beyond the severe control and surveillance of the state. Thus sex in the

South Africa of *Slegs Blankes* toilets was a sometimes flagrant, often thinly disguised motive through which to view ~~race~~ relations. In segregated South Africa sexuality came to possess a fascinating, outrageous character which is yet to be unravelled.

Yet, of course, apartheid sexuality had to do with much more than separate bathrooms and segregated beaches. In a very simplified form, the sexuality of apartheid policy had to do with at least three key facts of white ruled South Africa. The first fact is that of ~~race~~, of course. This is commonly known and we have dealt with it to some extent. The second is that the ideas of ~~race~~, racial hierarchy, domination and segregation have *a masculine character*. Apartheid was a masculine ideology in the sense that Susan Bordo (1987) makes of Cartesian thought. But this masculine thought and practice was inflected by "the problem of the native". White men worried greatly about the matter of the 'other' man, the native. The neglect by many pro-liberation writers, especially, to see apartheid as a sexualised male ideology stems in part from the fact that the struggle for South Africa was also masculinised. The national struggle was cast primarily as a ~~race~~ struggle between black and white *men*, and less as a radically exhaustive struggle between all those with power and those without. Because of the privileging of the racial struggle, the liberation project tended to overlook, for instance, the right of the father to rule. Within such a framework of what it was we were struggling for, and, in fact, supported by legislation on property and marriage, it became easy to see how women became the spoils of the war between white males' idea of a perfect society and black males' quest for freedom. This leads to the third related fact of apartheid sexuality: its *heterosexual orientation*. Heterosexuality has been viewed as a kind of control males have over female bodies, and sex between men and women as the eroticisation of unequal gender power relations. Heterosexuality fits snugly within the framework of patriarchy. The essence of patriarchal sexual relations is heterosexual. Heterosexual sex is almost always focussed on penetration, and males sometimes liken the act of penetration to conquest, an extension of domination, imperialism, colonialism, and power in general. Since heterosex has been largely for the benefit of men's pleasure, apartheid and antiapartheid became phallocratic contests with women being the stakes.

All of this is evident in all the essays. In Paul's essay the coloured women are the stakes. In Mzi's essay black men are prohibited from seeing white women "naked". Bo'nkosi says black women who sleep with white men are prostitutes. Thus, although apartheid immorality laws might have been read by some analysts as out to thwart all interracial coupling, what white males set out to do was really to prevent sexual relations between white women and black men. This, to be sure, is not an original Afrikaner taboo. Preventing sex between women of one's group and other men is a widespread taboo in male dominated cultures and societies.

The body of culture

The common answer to the question by Fanon is likely to be and has historically been that the man and woman of colour are sexually superior. Darker people, that is to say, have better, tighter, more supple, bigger or wilder genitals. The size of their penises or the elasticity of their vaginas and the way they use their body parts elevates them over their lighter counterparts. The answer, that is, always refers back to nature, to biology, to bodies. Even when cultural accounts are deployed, culture is naturalised, inserted into the biologies of individuals and groups. The answer for males and females is different about specifics but all in all similar. The black woman's sexual puissance, like the black man's, centres on her body. But as we are dealing with men's accounts, it is not the bodies of women but those of men, particularly the size of certain parts of the bodies of some men that we concentrate on.

Concerns about the large size of African penises, and the sexual superiority of Africans and other colonised peoples in general, occur against particular political, social, economic and cultural histories. These are histories of power relations. Because of these histories of domination, there continues to exist an engrossing discursive relation between ~~race~~ and sexuality affecting the ordinary moments of everyday life and relationships between individual Africans and members of other social groups in, for instance, South Africa. The discourse of powerless but well-endowed African males arises out of historical colonial and racist relations. As we saw, this discourse has in fact been supported by a particular 'scientific' enterprise beginning from around the middle of the nineteenth century (see Dubow 1995, Gill 1995, Gould 1981).

In his essay Paul reveals and seems to revel in the discourse of sexually powerful African males. He writes that when he started working where he ran workshops, he was a bit uneasy with "the ladies' reaction" to him. "This made his job difficult", he says. He then mentions the fact that as he is fluent in Afrikaans this made it easy for "coloured ladies to communicate with [him] and to start a relationship". This facility with language made his sexual rapport with coloured women (not difficult as he started out saying) but easy, he also experienced this outside the work situation: in "taverns" and "shebeens". The conclusion he draws from this is that:

> Coloured women get attracted to black men very easily if communication is not a problem. On many occasions I will ask them what they like about me. The reply differs from one person to another. But many say that I am different and they find it easy to speak to me. They do want to speak to more black men but communication is always the problem.

From the matter of language, Paul then proceeds to comparing males of different ~~races~~. The comparison in this case is between black men and coloured men. Paul says coloured women he has known say "there is something about black men that coloured men don't have". But what is this that coloured don't have but black males have? Paul says from his experience and the 'research' he has conducted it comes down to two things: "The first one being what they have heard about black men. The second being what they experience with their own brothers (coloureds).

The second reason is composed of comparison between black men and coloured men". It is now that Paul reveals the cult of the body. Coloured females, he writes, want black men because "black men have big penises". Something interesting that he adds, which is obviously part of the sexual stuff, is that "black men take long to ejaculate".

However, against the predominantly racist, hetero-masculine anxieties about penis size there is a newer and increasingly popular discourse. This set of views gathers momentum in the latter part of the twentieth century. It is inspired in contradictory ways by both parts of the women's liberation movement and feminist theory on the one hand and sexology on the other. This is the discourse that size does not matter which in effect challenges the notion of sex as located in genitals. This new discourse exhorts men and women that to worry about size is misplaced vanity.

Given these two competing discourses, I can hear myself being asked, how come size does not matter now, when African men (like Paul) are beginning to revel in it? Is this new discourse liberating? Why, if this has always been the case, was it not always common knowledge? And, it should be asked, is the answer simply a colonial, racist science and society even when a somewhat sympathetic writer like Anton Gill seems to be convinced of the facts of black sexual superiority?

Race and the construction of threat and desire

In his analysis of desire in an antiblack world, Lewis Gordon, like Fanon, destroys the link between the penis and the phallus. His response to "the extensive literature on the reduction of black males to their penis" is that to deal effectively with the link between black genitals and black powerlessness we should attend to the significance of not just penis size but penis colour also. "Penises of equal length", he argues, "are not of equal length significance when they are of different 'colours'. For, in an antiblack world, a black penis, whatever its size, represents a threat" (1997:128). Gordon argues that a black penis spells threat because it is a declaration and a demand of masculinity that is denied by white society. Thus, to put it in another way, the penis of the black man does not have to be longer or thicker to pose a threat to white society. Fanon had revealed and cut down in a highly perceptive manner this constructed threat of the black penis. After showing that the black person is "the incarnation of a genital potency beyond all moralities", Fanon would simply state, "we have shown that reality destroys all these beliefs" (1986:177). But it appears that the threat of the black penises is deeply embedded in many societies, as evinced in this next extract:

> Mzi: I could not understand why because everybody was wearing underwear and we were also prepared to wear the same. The security personnel escorted us to our braai space. Whenever my coloured friend and I looked at bypassing women he would ask what are we looking at because we were there only for a braai and nothing else. The other guys would pass some remarks when seeing women and this guy keep quiet. This security showed us the place, which is about a kilometre away from everybody else.

151

One interpretation that can be made from this extract is that for an African to be thought capable of giving sexual pleasure or posing a sexual danger he does not have to be biologically well-endowed or sexually skilled. As in the case of Paul's othered females, the African male plays into the sexual anxieties generated by a racist history by simply being there. It may help, but in fact it is not necessary that he speaks Afrikaans or the language of the women. In both the cases of Mzi and Paul, Gordon's hypothesis about penis colour is germane. Furthermore, as one can read in Sellon's account of his sexual escapades, and the accounts of both students' more recent personal relations, racial masculinities specifically and racialised identities generally tend to contain voyeuristic or fetishistic elements.

Colours of bodies used to produce and govern social relations point to spectacle. The spectacle is one of difference. In other words, differently ~~raced~~ bodies are the narrative motif, and possibility of physical relations between them is spectacularised. The spectacle, Toni Morrison has said, monopolises appearance and social reality. There is therefore an unmistakable and prurient fascination with the colour of bodies of others. For the dominated the fascination can be dangerous to the point of self-hate, at least hating oneself for being fascinated in the first place with such bodies, with colour, with the strangeness itself.

Voyeuristic/fetishistic racial masculinities thus refer to the fact that a man like Sellon, as an example, views women of other colours as offering a sexual trip, or that someone, like Paul, constructs himself (or other African males) as capable of offering adventure to people of other ~~races~~ simply because he is of a different ~~race~~. In the case of African men this is another version of the "cold black hustler" who "claws his way into the whiteness of his desire" chanting, "brother, sister, revolution, power to the people" (Kgositsile 1975:90). In the practices of racial voyeurs or fetishists sexual desire tracks the desire for 'othered' objects. In Paul's case, for instance, sex cannot be understood without looking at how it follows a colonial or colonised attitude towards 'othered' female bodies. In both Sellon and Paul's cases sex relations are interesting insofar as they are exoticised, fetishised, that is, objectivised.

But to say sexual desire tracks racial practices and identification is only partly true. It is very difficult, except only for the aim of analysis, to separate what originates together. Sexual and racial differences are almost inseparable in real life. Desire for sexual identity is interwoven with the work people put into other kinds of identity making. Desire in racially segregating cultures is made from its birth by both elements of attraction for othered skin colour and sexuality. Racial voyeurism and fetishism are precisely about histories of social hierarchies, about what social life in these cultures makes us put first. Racialised sexualities are constructed such that young heterosexual males like Bo'nkosi and Paul want to have females of other ~~races~~ because the females are of other colours, and not just female. The females are desirable because they are white or coloured first, and this makes them sexually attractive. What makes the women attractive is not their figure but the colour of their bodies, not their individuality but the colour of the genitals.

Conclusion

In addition to the question about the sexual superiority of black people, this chapter was prompted by the question whether issues of sexual superiority are worth our serious attention. In responding to the question, the chapter used three purposively selected semi-autobiographical essays on ~~race~~ and sexual practices and identities written by African male students for a psychology of racism class in 1999 at the University of the Western Cape. The essays were analysed using discursive psychological understandings for how individuals' practices and identities are produced, naturalised and what gets left out and how they are related to racialised hetero-masculine desire. The accounts of these males showed themselves to be anything but straightforward, revealed by often contradictory discourses of sexual and racial identities and practices. Sexual and racial identities and practices, it was argued, are founded within and must be seen as part of complex economic, sociopolitical, cultural and interpersonal histories.

References

Antaki, Charles, 1994, *Explaining and arguing*. London: Sage.

Beresford, David, 2000, "Into the HRC confessional", *Mail & Guardian* (weekly), 8–14 September.

Biko, Stephen, 1996, *I write what I like*. London: The Bowerdean Publishing Company Limited.

Billig, Michael, 1998, "Keeping the white queen in play", in M. Fine, L. Weis, L. Powell & M. Wong, (eds). *Off-white*. London: Routledge.

Bordo, Susan, 1987, *The Flight to Objectivity: Essays on Cartesianism and Culture*. Suny Press.

Brewer, Susan, 1997, *Better sex*. London: Marshall Publishing.

Burr, Vivian, 1995, *An introduction to social constructionism*. London: Routledge.

Butchart, Alexander, 1998, *The anatomy of power: European constructions of the African body*. Pretoria: Unisa.

Danziger, Kurt, 1990, *Constructing the subject: Historical origins of psychological research*. Cambridge: University Press.

Dubow, Saul, 1995, *Illicit union: Scientific racism in South Africa*. Johannesburg: Witwatersrand University Press.

Duncan, Norman, 1993, "Discourses of racism". Unpublished doctoral dissertation: University of the Western Cape, Bellville.

Durrheim, Kevin, 1997, "Social constructionism, discourse, and psychology, *South African Journal of Psychology* 27(3), 175–182.

Epstein, Debbie, 1998, "Marked men: Whiteness and masculinity", *Agenda*, 37, 49–59.

Fanon, Frantz, 1986, *Black skin, white masks*. London: Pluto Press. (Orig.1952, *Peau noire, masques blancs*. Éditions de Seuil.)

Frankenberg, Ruth, 1995, *The social construction of whiteness*. London: Routledge.

Gergen, Kenneth, 1985, "The social constructionist movement in modern psychology", *American Psychologist* 40(3). 266–275.

Gill, Anthony, 1995, *Ruling passions: Sex, race and empire*. London: BBC Books.

Gordon, Lewis, 1997, "Race, sex, and matrices of desire in an antiblack world: an essay in phenomenology and social role", in N. Zack, *Race/sex: their sameness, difference and interplay*. New York: Routledge.

Gould, Stephen, 1981, *The mismeasure of man*. London: Penguin.

Kgositsile, Keorapetse, 1975, "Notes from no sanctuary", in W. Soyinka, *Poems of black Africa*. Nairobi: Heinemann.

Hernton, Calvin, 1988, *Sex and racism in America*. New York: Doubleday.

Ka'Nkosi, Sechaba, 2000, "A problem cannot be solved until it's acknowledged", *Mail & Guardian* (weekly), 8–14 September.

Levett, Ann, Ann Kottler, Erica Burman & Ian Parker, 1997, *Culture, power and difference: Discourse analysis in South Africa.* London: Zed Books.

Lowe-Morna, Coleen, 1998, "Discrimination wears familiar faces", *Cape Times,* 13 August.

Mahlangu, D, 1999, "Racism still entrenched in SA", *City Press,* 20 June.

Mandela, Nelson, 1994, *The struggle is my life.* Cape Town: David Phillip.

Morrison, Toni, & Claudia Lacour, 1997, *Birth of a nationhood: Gaze, script, and spectacle in the O.J. Simpson case.* London: Vintage.

Pityana, Barney, 2000, "Side by side, we shall overcome", *Mail & Guardian* (weekly), 28 July–3 August.

Ratele, Kopano, 2001, "Between ouens: making black masculinity everyday", in Morrel, R. (ed.). *Changing Men in Southern Africa.* Durban: Zed/University of Natal Press.

Zack, Naomi, 1997a, "The American sexualisation of race", in N. Zack, *Race/sex: Their sameness, difference and interplay.* New York: Routledge.

Zack, Naomi, 1997b, *Race/sex: Their sameness, difference and interplay.* New York: Routledge.

SAPA, 2000, "Legislation to combat racism in South Africa pending", *Cape Times,* 2 August.

Photo: Abderramane Sakaly, 1958

7. Opening a Can of Worms: A Debate on Female Sexuality in the Lecture Theatre

Mumbi Machera

Introduction

The term sexuality elicits images of belongingness, physically and emotionally. Sexuality is a complex term with a multifaceted meaning referring to deep emotional feeling as well as to issues of power and vulnerability in gendered relationships. The feelings and power dynamics seem to be linked to the biological existence of an individual as either male or female. Nonetheless the scope of sexuality is socially constructed—i.e. sexual feelings and behaviour are influenced and constrained by cultural definitions and prohibitions rather than by physical possibilities for sexual indulgence.

In this paper, I will critically analyze a number of issues related to female sexuality. I will move beyond conventional boundaries to engage in a discussion of the female genitalia as an area of struggle. I will argue that the construction of female sexuality is influenced by the meanings attached to the female genitalia. With examples from Kenya and other parts of Africa I will show that the female genitalia are often downgraded, but also at the same time powerful. The naming or not naming is significant, as is the imposed dilemma of procreation or pleasure. In this context I will discuss issues of 'bi-curiosity' and 'multiplicitous sexualities', before returning to issues of pleasure, safe sex and 'bedroom power'. Finally I will highlight the policy dimension of the discussion by providing possible linkages between the constructions of the female sexuality and the prevalence of the HIV/AIDS pandemic.

The discussion is largely informed by observations made by students during lectures. Throughout my teaching career at the University, I have had interesting discussions with both female and male students on issues connected to female sexuality. I teach courses on 'Gender and Development' and 'Demography' to undergraduate students and 'Gender and Society' to postgraduate students. Both female and male students attend these courses. A lot of views brought to the lecture theatre by students originate from their diverse modes of socialisation (they come from different ethnic backgrounds); meanings and values, which they connect to the female body, are thus socially engineered. Our discussions range from getting familiar with the female genitalia to analysing the power dynamics in sexual relationships and how these affect women's socio-political realities in a changing world. Issues like society's perception of female sexuality and the limitations surrounding female sexual expression in sexual relationships are frequently discussed.

What is in a name? Representation and symbolization of female and male genitalia

It is apparent that pronunciation of the name of the vulva is generally avoided. During our seminar discussions, students have categorically told me that it is not conventional for people in their communities to identify "that part" of the female body by its "name". Why? The shame linked with various vernacular terms used to describe the vagina is evident. Some students say that one has to be out of one's mind to be able to use "that term". Some of the responses I get range from: "that thing is dirty, it is not referred to in its original name… you cannot name it in public….". One male student told me "the term is an insult … even when men are making love to their wives … they use symbolic terms in reference to the vulva". Another student observed that "if someone calls you 'it' … you can easily murder them because calling someone 'a vagina' is such a terrible thing". A female student conclusively stated that it is not pronounceable.

In my vernacular the vulva is called *nvini*. This term can only be used publicly as an insult. This happens especially when two adult men are fighting or if one really wants to hurt the opponent deeply. Ardener's study of the Bakweri, Balong, and the Kom tribes of Cameroon shows that names used to describe the female genitalia also refer to an insult (1975, 1987). Similar observations have been made among the Azande (Evans-Pritchard 1929), among the Meru and Kikuyu of Kenya (Lambert 1956) and among the Pokot (Edgerton and Conant 1964).

The feelings attached to names for the male genitalia are very different. The information that I have collected from students originating from different ethnic backgrounds shows that names used to describe the male genitals are characteristic of the shape or sexual functions of the penis. For example, among the Kikuyu, the male penis is called *mucuthe* which means 'tail', among the Embu it is called *muthino* and *mucino* among the Ambeere, both of which mean something used for pricking or digging or something that is meant 'to go into something else'. Interestingly, the majority of my audience do not find it as shameful talking about the penis as it is to talk about the vagina. Evidence from our discussions shows that children are taught names of different body parts except the vagina. Different pseudonyms exist for the male genitalia. In my community the male genital is called *karamu* which is the vernacular name for a 'pen', the female genital has no pseudonym. Similar patterns exist in other parts of the world. Significantly, the Holy Bible establishes the wickedness of the vagina. The text of the Old Testament compiled in the third century BC explicitly refers to the sexual cravings of the vagina. The book of Proverbs 30:15 explicitly states: "There are three things that are never sated, hell, the vagina and the earth." A pattern emerges where female sexuality is inhibited by society's definition of it, whereas male sexuality is punctuated with performance and achievement.

I have wondered for quite some time now why the feminist movement has not attempted to change these negative stereotypes associated with the vagina. While I was writing this paper, I had personal discussions with a number of European women (from Sweden, Finland and Norway) and they felt that the vagina is still a "shameful" thing to talk about in the western world.

Shirley Ardener, in *Perceiving Women* (1975), uses ethnographic examples to illustrate how women from West Cameroon, Bakweri and Kom, react and deal with sexual insults from men. The women's associations in western Cameroon use direct collective action to resolve disputes, which has proved to be both a strong and powerful form of social sanction: the women from Bakweri will respond to scornful lewd comments from men, particularly those about the smell of female genitalia, in a specific way. Ardener states that "if such an insult had been uttered to a Bakweri woman before a witness, she is supposed immediately to call out all other women of the village" (Ardener 1975). The women of Bakweri perceive this form of insult as an affront not only to the individual but also to their gender as a whole. The women will collectively confront the male offender expecting an apology to, and compensation for, the affronted women. Even when the accused man has admitted to the offence, the women will continue their protest and will encircle him singing "abusive songs accompanied by obscene gestures" in order to emphasize the gravity of the offence. The behaviour of the women is seen as highly embarrassing for men to witness and while the protest is taking place the other male villagers will move away from the scene, meanwhile the offender tries to avert his eyes as the protest continues. In Kom similar forms of female militant corporate actions occur, and "when the women of a village wished to resort to disciplinary action against a man … they assembled as *anlu*[1]". The women of Kom have a similar way of calling together the females of the village as in Bakweri. As a high pitched call to assemble is sounded, females around the village will stop their daily tasks and join the growing throng of women. The nature of the offence will be relayed and frenzied dancing adds to the atmosphere. To add to the solemnity of the offence the ancestors are called upon to join the protest (Ardener 1975).

While such militancy demonstrates that women are not just passive recipients of verbal violence, their dramatic strategies do not seek long-term solutions to the negative images associated with the female genitalia. To support this statement, I will give an example of the Kikuyu, the largest tribe in Kenya. I am familiar with this ethnic group who are my close neighbours and some of my students are Kikuyu. Lambert's 1956 ethnographic analysis details pre-colonial female militancy among the Kikuyu. Here women show their displeasure by 'cursing' the offender. A form of curse employed by women involves deliberate exhibition of their private parts towards the person being cursed. Usually the aggrieved women remove their undergarments, stand in line with their backs towards the offender, bend forward and lift their backsides in unison (1956:99).

In the post-colonial Kikuyu such vulgar resistance has been overtaken by 'modernity' and by the impact of Christian religious teachings on modesty. In contrast, use of 'insults' related to the female genitalia continues in contemporary so-

---

1.   *Anlu* refers to the act of female militancy.

ciety. The most widely used is a Swahili word *kumamamako* which means 'your mother's vagina'.

Procreation, pleasure and the power of the erotic

The term vulva, originally a Latin word meaning 'sheath' or 'scabbard', has been the standard name for the female passageway since the mid-sixteenth century. To this day, the standard view focuses on the reproductive function of the vagina. According to the standard medical opinion the main functions of the vagina are to receive the penis during sexual intercourse and provide a passageway for the sperm; to provide a passageway for the baby during birth and to serve as a duct for menstrual fluid. Several studies have been done to establish whether the vagina serves a direct pleasurable purpose in female human beings (Kinsey et al. 1953; Masters and Johnson 1966; Sevely 1987). Most of these studies reported variability on vaginal responses in females. I argue that women's potential pleasure from the vagina is purposefully distorted through the process of socialization.

To support this argument I present a childhood experience, which is still vivid in my mind. In my community girls are reproved for wanting to peep at their genitals. Infantile masturbation is highly restricted. When I was about nine years old, my mother caught me red-handed looking at my 'private parts' through a mirror. I guess I was just curious to know what this very private part looked like. Mother gave me a severe beating and warned me never to do that again. It is "bad manners" she said. A good girl never looks at that place; a good girl sits properly (with her legs drawn together) and never talks about issues regarding the vagina. Whether such experiences generate feelings of sexual inferiority and female social subordination is an issue for further investigation.

On the contrary, the boyhood experience is entirely different; at the time when I was getting lashed for wanting to know my genital form; boys of my age would have what the community refers to as a 'urinating contest'. This game involves boys standing on a line struggling to pump their urine to the furthest point possible. Both adults and children would find this game very interesting. The boys were not reproached, instead the applause would increase their pride, making them proud of their little penises, while girls walked around with something between their legs which they would not dare look at! The genesis of sexual gender socialization is configured around approval and disapproval.

In a cross-cultural examination, Elena Bellotti notes that in Italy, both girls and boys play with their genitals at the same stages of development and get obvious pleasure out of doing so. But while in a boy this activity is regarded with a certain indulgence, it is rigidly suppressed in a girl. She further notes:

> Already present in these diverse attitudes towards a baby's earliest sexual activities is the prejudice that boys are endowed with much stronger sexual instincts than girls, and that therefore any erotic activity in them should be tolerated if not exactly encouraged. A girl who indulges, on the other hand, is deviating from the norm and must be restrained. It is quite possible to grow into a woman without ever living one's own sexuality, but one cannot become a man without living it fully. This is part of the creed created by stereotyping (Bellotti 1975:44).

In the African diaspora women face similar constraints. Bell Hooks urges black women to

> ... reconsider our relation to our bodies ... all our eroticism has been shaped within the culture of domination. Despite our choices and preferences, we act in an erotic and liberatory way toward ourselves and others only if we have dared to break free from the cultural norms (Hooks 1993:114–115).

The provided cross-cultural evidence is obviously not sufficient to establish whether the suppression of female sexualities takes place universally. Further research especially in Africa may divulge interesting information. For example, the Baganda of Uganda are known to have a practice known as 'pulling of the labia minora' aimed at enhancing sexual pleasure. Arnfred (1990) noted a similar practice in Mozambique. On female initiation rites, Arnfred notes that

> ... in the proper course of events, the women's initiation rites would be preceded by the small girls (some 8–10 years) learning how to manipulate their small vaginal lips in order to pull them longer. This preparation previously was an integrated aspect of becoming a woman all over Mozambique (1990:71–107).[1]

The Baganda and Mozambique cases are a direct reverse of those ethnic groups that practise female circumcision. The practice of female circumcision, or Female Genital Mutilation, occurs in different forms, often including removal of the clitoris. Masters and Johnson (1966) established that the centre of female sexuality is the clitoris; female orgasm they confirmed, is achieved through the stimulation of the clitoris, whether or not accompanied by vaginal penetration.

My discussions with students have gone further to confirm that in most ethnic groups the clitoral ability to give a woman sexual pleasure is perceived negatively. One of the reasons given for performing circumcision on girls and women is the reduction of sexual desire (cf. Kenyatta 1962:132; Mbiti 1969:123). Some students feel that in their communities, the priority is to control women so that they cannot indulge in immoral sexual behaviour and to prepare girls for marriage. This take precedence over sexual pleasure in those ethnic groups where sexual intercourse and its completeness is defined in terms of vaginal penetration and the ultimate ejaculation by the male in disregard of the female orgasm.

In her novel *Possessing the Secret of Joy* (1992), Alice Walker explores the life of a daughter whose culture demands the literal destruction of the most crucial external sign of her sexuality: the vulva itself. Below I quote from the novel, a response from Tashi the genitally mutilated woman from Africa, to Raye her African-American psychiatrist:

> Yes. My body was a mystery to me as was the female body, beyond the functions of the breasts, to almost everyone I knew ... Everyone knew that if a woman was not circumcised her unclean

---

1. The author provides a description from Gaza where groups of girls would go to the dense bush about 3 o'clock in the morning, each of them carrying a *capulana* (a coloured piece of cloth, normally used as a skirt) to be used as cover once the work started, because they would be sitting like somebody giving birth to a child. On the first day they would be given instructions by the *madrinhas* (older women in charge) about how to procede, and after that each of the girls would continue on her own, using a certain pomade to facilitate the process. In the course of this work the *madrinhas* would check each one of the girls in order to see if they had been pulling satisfactorily, at the same time verifying that some of them had been doing too little work.

parts would grow so long they'd soon touch her thighs; she'd become masculine and arouse herself. No man could enter her because her own erection would be in his way (Walker 1992:54).

One of the students, whose Aunt is a circumciser, reported that sometimes married women are forced to get circumcised by their husbands: "I know my aunt has circumcised married women occasionally. Husbands send such women to her. Their husbands claim that the labia makes penetration difficult during sexual intercourse".

Nici Nelson (1987) found that among the Kikuyu, sexuality for women has more to do with procreation than with pleasure; and more specifically procreation for the patrilineage. Her findings show that female circumcision in this ethnic group is also done to control women's sexual drive and to keep them under control. In this respect, female genital mutilation must be understood as a practice that is meant to enforce the subordination and suppression of women. The alteration of the vulva is supposed to facilitate other avenues of masculine domination in the sexual and social sphere. Studies have shown that most practising communities circumcise girls in preparation for marriage; circumcision symbolically ensures that a woman will remain faithful to the husband and other male relations (Toubia 1995; Walker 1992, 1993; Lightfoot-Klein 1989; Kenyatta 1975; Thiam 1986; El Dareer 1982; Dorkenoo 1994).

Beyond cultural dictates there is nothing to affirm that something is wrong with a woman being erotic and conscious of the physical and emotional presentations of their sexuality. In *Sisters of the Yam* (1993), Bell Hooks notes that,

> when I speak of eroticism ... it is not meant to evoke heterosexist images. I want to speak to and about that life-force inside all of us—there even before we have any clue as to sexual preferences or practices—that we identify as the power of the erotic (1993:113).

In my opinion sexual arousal, pleasure and orientation goes beyond geographical boundaries; eroticism is not a Western thing, it is a life-force inside of every individual, like the G-spot.[1] But many women may not be aware of this life-force, until sexual meaning is effectively constructed around it. This explains why some women enjoy the pleasures of the erotic and bodily zones such as the G-spot while others do not. The erotic is innately biological but the outcome is shaped and reshaped through societal norms. Until our cultures recognize the power that lies within female eroticism, then we shall continue to watch helplessly as women mutilate and maim their own kind and as men kill the female spirit through acts of sexual and physical violence and as hypocrisy builds up even within scholarly realms where denial of the fact that there is pleasure and freedom in the variety of sexual identifications for both women and men can be read in the silence regarding these issues.

In recent years, feminist perspectives have focused more on a discussion of sexual pleasure. Richardson (1993) notes that this is often portrayed as a response to the emphasis on the dangers of sexuality during the 1980s, in particular debates

---

1. G-spot is a region of the wall in front of the vagina which swells during sexual arousal and is highly sensitive to stimulation.

about the meaning and effects of pornography and sexual violence. Carole Vance believes that "feminism must speak to sexual pleasure as a fundamental right" (1984:24). I share Vance's stand but this does not tell us much about the opinion of other women especially African women. Further investigations are necessary in this area. In the West, several feminists have observed that the issue is not finding out how women get sexual pleasure but of asking what constitutes 'sexual pleasure' and what functions it serves? Nici Nelson (1987) studying Kikuyu notions of sexuality notes that "the paucity of data on this subject in the literature is indicative of the reluctance of both anthropologists and their informants to discuss sex and sexuality" (Nelson 1987). Similarly, Signe Arnfred (in this volume) observes that "discussions of sexuality are remarkably absent in analytical works of African feminists". She notes the contrast to the Western women's movement and feminist studies where analysis and critique of discourses on female sexuality were key issues right from the start.

'Bi-curiosity' and 'multiplicitious sexualities'

Whenever I raise the issue of homosexuality in class, students are up in arms. They say "it is not African, that it is purely a Western development", "our cultures do not condone such behaviours", "it is deviant behaviour", and so on. I often ask them: "what would you do if your own sister is 'a lesbian'? Or if your brother chose to be gay?" This always elicits another onslaught on me: "that is impossible!", "it can't happen!", "if it does, they will be cast out!", "I would advise them to go to America"... the suggestions are endless—no compromise. What does this tell us? That the belief that heterosexuality is the only natural form of sexual expression is rooted in a cultural framework that defines heterosexuality as compulsory and homosexuality as deviant or pathological. The question of sexual identity has been debated upon actively in the West but not without controversy. Jeffrey Weeks observes that:

> [T]he very idea of sexual identity is an ambiguous one. For many in the modern world, especially the sexually marginal, it is an absolutely fundamental concept, offering a sense of personal unity, social location, and even at times a political commitment ... Not many say 'I am heterosexual' because it is the taken for granted norm, the great unsaid of our sexual culture (1987:31).

In most African countries homosexuality is suppressed as an alternative expression of sexuality though isolation and a conspiracy of silence (Pisani 2001:169). The social sanctions brought against women who are not identified as attached to men in African societies show how heterosexuality is maintained through social control. For example even if women remain single and couple with no one, they are ridiculed and ostracized. My female students frequently complain that men (and society) do not respect single women, poor or rich, literate or illiterate. In fact such women are easily labelled negatively as rebels or prostitutes. In Nairobi, it is not uncommon that single women out for some fun will be accosted and sexually terrorized for being unaccompanied by men. Thus phallocentricity advances sexual terrorism against women. Moreover, if women love other women, they are seen as deviant or sexually pathological.

In the course of writing this paper, the *Daily Nation*, a daily newspaper published in Kenya, put out an article entitled: "Bi-curious: An emerging trend." The article (published on November 17, 2001) addressed an "emerging breed of young Kenyan women who are choosing a different kind of sexual relationship— they love occasional dalliances with other women, which is considered a bit of fun". What I found very curious about the bi-curious girls is the difficulty they face in self-defining their new sexual identities. The girls interviewed reiterated that they are not lesbians; so what are they? They admitted having sexual intimacies with their girlfriends "but they do not consider these trysts as cheating on their boyfriends." The girls interviewed also said that they are not bisexual.

Jeffrey Weeks asserts that emerging sexual identities should be seen more accurately as a powerful resistance to the organizing principle of traditional sexual attitudes (1987:42). Though a discussion of sexual identities is beyond the scope of this paper, after reading the bi-curious article I noted that the girls interviewed did not identify themselves either as lesbians or bisexuals. This brings up the issue of sexual identification as a choice. Weeks observes that

> sexual identification is a strange thing. There are some people who identify as gay and participate in gay community. And there are homosexually active people who do not identify as gay. The development of a homosexual identity is dependent on the meanings that the actor attaches to the concepts of homosexual and homosexuality (1987:42).

However, he goes further to argue that these processes (of identity) depend on the person's environment and wider community.

Gloria Wekker introduces the subject of *multiplicitous sexualities*. By analyzing 'mati work',[1] an institution with its own rules and rituals, Wekker demonstrates that women may be in a variety of relationships with men (e.g. marriage, concubinage, visiting relationships) and also have sexual relationships with women. She contends that "the distinctions often made in a Western universe between heterosexual and lesbian women—based on women's sexual identity and the supposed underlying psychic economy—do not correspond with realities in the Afro-Surinamese universe" (1997:336–337).

The tendency to single out heterosexuality as the acceptable mode of sexual relationship is reflected in the students' belligerent responses to the issue of homosexuality in a class discussion. It is a well known fact that sexual orientation as a discursive issue is closely linked to radical feminism. Regrettably, feminism is a very controversial subject in scholarship today especially among African female

---

1. Wekker explains that 'mati work' is an institution in which Creole women openly engage in sexual relationships with men and with women, either simultaneously or consecutively. *Mati* is the Creole word for friend used by and for males and females. Mati work is called work by insiders because it involves obligations between two female partners in nurturing, social, sexual and economic spheres. In the Afro-Surinamese construct, these women share the values of a working class culture that stresses the importance of motherhood, emotional and financial savvy, and a sharp presentation of the self. And it is a culture where importantly, sexual activity is considered healthy and in itself more interesting than the gender of the object of one's passion (Wekker 1997; also in Wekker 1992).

scholars. Feminism (speaking out against women's rights abuse) is confused with 'man-hating'. Quoting Ama Ata Aidoo, Mary Kolawole in *Womanism and African Consciousness* (1997) posits some of the sentiments African female scholars bear towards feminism: "Feminism. You know how I feel about that embarrassing Western philosophy? The destroyer of homes. Imported mainly from America to ruin nice African homes" (1997:11).

I strongly feel Bell Hooks in *Feminist Theory—from margin to center* (1984) provides a broader view of the link between feminism and sexuality:

> All women need to know that they can be politically committed to feminism regardless of their sexual preference. They need to know that the goal of feminist movement is not to establish codes for a 'politically correct' sexuality. Politically, feminist activists committed to ending sexual oppression must work to eliminate the oppression of lesbians and gay men as part of an overall movement to enable all women (and men) to freely choose sexual partners (1984:152).

Whose body is the female body?

Two years ago I was assigning seminar tasks to a group of graduate students in Gender Studies. One of the articles on my agenda bore a provocative title *Whose pussy is this?* A feminist comment from Hooks' book entitled *Talking back—Thinking feminist, thinking black* (1989). The article as I had anticipated stimulated a lot of controversy. A male student whom I asked to make a presentation based on the article said he simply could not do it. In his opinion, the title sounded vulgar, and according to his cultural norms, he simply did not want to work on an essay which deal with the 'female genitalia'.

To provide a brief summary of this article, Bell Hooks makes a feminist comment on Spike Lee's film *She's Gotta Have It*. Her analysis focuses on whether the film depicts a radically new image of female sexuality. Nola Darling, the main character in the film, is depicted as the perfect embodiment of woman as desiring subject—a representation that does challenge sexist notions of female passivity. Ironically and unfortunately Nola Darling's sexual desire is not depicted as an autonomous gesture, as an independent longing for sexual expression, satisfaction and fulfilment. Instead her assertive sexuality is most often portrayed as though her body, her sexually aroused being, is a reward or gift she bestows on the deserving male. Nola believes in 'pussy power'—while this character is not sexually passive, her primary concern is pleasing each of her partners. Though Spike Lee leads the viewer to believe that Nola enjoys sex, her sexual fulfilment is never the central concern. She is pleased only to the extent that she is able to please. Then Bell Hooks drives the point home. As Jaime (one of the male characters) rapes Nola and aggressively demands that she answer the question, "Whose pussy is this?"—this is supposed to be the moment of truth—the moment when she can declare herself independent, sexually liberated, the moment when she can proudly assert through resistance her sexual autonomy (for the film has highlighted her determination to be sexually active, to choose many partners, to belong to no one). Ironically she does not resist the physical violence; when Nola responds to the question "Whose pussy is this?" by saying "yours" it is difficult for anyone who has fallen for the image of her as sexually liberated not to feel let down, disappointed both in her character and in the film (Hooks 1989:139).

My urging that students must discard their cultural inhibitions if they are to engage in useful discussion dissolves most of the social cultural eccentricity among them. So this male student did the presentation. The discussion was rich and it led us into analyzing our own African cultures and how the female body is located in the social milieu. Some of the conclusions we arrived at explicate that the female body is owned, it belongs to the social entity mainly for reproductive purposes and Man has been commissioned to oversee this 'noble function' by subjecting the female to close scrutiny throughout her lifetime. Thus childhood and adolescent socialization in most African communities do not embrace the pleasurable aspects of sex. Girls are told that sex is only good in marriage, that a woman should not have sex with any other man except the husband, one should not deny the husband his right to sexual intercourse and most importantly one should preserve one's virginity and look forward to bearing many children for the husband. Such societal expectations show the extent to which women are detached from their sexuality. Like Nola Darling most women (some female students supported this) have sex to please their partners with total disregard for their own pleasure. This to a certain extent explains why women fail to resist harmful practices such as FGM and sexual violence in marriage simply because sexual fulfilment is not their central concern. On the other hand, men go to such extremes in a bid to control women's sexuality.

In a research report entitled "Domestic Violence in Kenya" I cite a not-so-uncommon case of a man who "... dismembered a month-old baby before chopping off the wife's arm with an axe following a bitter quarrel over the paternity of the child" (Machera 1997:47). These are issues, which I hope to explore in later works on the social construction of the female sexuality and the reproduction of gender violence in African communities.

Of safe sex and 'bedroom power'

There is a perceptible link between women's sexual helplessness in most developing countries and lack of control over their sex lives and reproductive behaviours. For a long time, African countries have continued to record very high rates of fertility and currently there are soaring rates of HIV/AIDS infection. Demographic literature indicates that global efforts have been directed towards fertility regulation by targeting female reproductive functions, but fertility rates have continued to be persistently high. Betsy Hartman in "A womb of one's own" (1995) quoting the sentiments of Rene, a 29 year-old Peruvian woman, demonstrates that most women lack bargaining power over sex and reproduction:

> There isn't much understanding in some marriages. My sister has six and another one has eight. And I said to one of them that she shouldn't have any more. And she said, 'what can I do? When my husband comes home drunk, he forces me to sleep with him and that is what happens to a lot of women. And if the women don't do it, the men hit them, or treat them badly, or the men

get jealous and think their wives must be with other men. And the women have to do whatever they say. I think it is changing a little because the young women are more aware (1995:41).

Demographic trends in Kenya point implicitly to this kind of helplessness. Even with availability of contraceptive technology since 1967, women seem to have been very reluctant in accepting contraceptive use. One female student shared her experience: "My husband insists that I should not use contraceptives. He says that women who use these devices are promiscuous and can easily cheat on their spouses … ". These experiences reflect a common plight: lack of 'bedroom power'; lack of control by women over their own reproduction. This means that lack of reproductive rights and rights over one's sexuality have deprived millions of women the right to decide if and when to have sex, a child, access to safe and voluntary birth control and abortion. Lack of 'bedroom power' means women cannot decide whether to have safe sex or not. Some students shared with me a new terminology *condom-phobia*. This is an apparent fear of men of condom use. Some men feel that using condoms with their spouses is less manly. "It's like begging for what belongs to you", "it's like eating a sweet with the wrapper on, and you cannot get the true taste of sex with a condom". Pitted against women's control over their own reproduction are a number of obstacles, economic discrimination, subordination within the family, religious and cultural restrictions, the nature of health care systems and the distortion of family planning programmes. In this respect, gender-power inequalities in the negotiation of safe and satisfactory sex have to be acknowledged.

UNIFEM's Biennial Report (2000) shows that HIV/AIDS is the fourth most common cause of death world-wide. Women experience a double burden as a result of the spread of HIV/AIDS; a burden of suffering and a burden of caring for those who are suffering. Though HIV/AIDS infection takes place through different ways, it is the coercive gender relations existing in most of Africa that predispose most women to infections. The gender dimensions of the pandemic, focusing on women's lack of knowledge of or control over their own bodies and the terms on which sex is negotiated all relate to how the female sexuality is perceived. That means if more women have the power to 'say no' to unwanted and unsafe sex, the HIV infection rate would dramatically decline in Africa. Further there would be a notable decline in fertility rates. Thus more and more women would realize greater social and economic goals.

Summary and Conclusions

Sexuality is a social-political arena constantly reshaped through cultural, economic, familial and political relations, all of which are conditioned through prevailing social organizations of gender, race and class relationships at given points in time.

In Africa male and female sexualities have been patterned by cultural definitions of masculinity and femininity. Female sexuality is seen as something to be contained and controlled; this can be traced in the well known dichotomy of labelling 'good' women as virgins and 'loose' women as whores. Such labels depict female sexuality as evil and dangerous if not constrained and imply that 'good females' should repress their sexual feelings.

Even though people like to think of sexuality as a private matter, social institutions (the family, church, schools) direct and control sexuality. For example, some forms of sexual expression are seen and treated as more legitimate than others. In Africa, heterosexuality is a more privileged status in society than is homosexuality. In general, heterosexuality is justified from a religio-cultural perspective. Because cultural proscriptions define sex primarily in terms of heterosexual monogamy or polygamy, our orientation of sexuality has fused sexuality and reproduction. More recently the separation of sexuality from procreation through widespread availability of birth control is revolutionizing sexual behaviour. This means that gradually women can focus their attention on pleasure rather than on possible conceptions. However, some African scholars and politicians are not comfortable with notions of 'sexual liberation' fearing that this would promote homosexuality, which is 'unafrican'. One of the arguments posited in this paper is that sexual preference should not be regionalized. Individual freedoms should include freedom of sexual choice without fear of social ridicule. Across cultures, human expression includes a range of behaviours and attitudes. Although society tends to think of sexuality as internally situated, sexuality also involves a learned relationship to the world. The feminist movement has inspired a new openness about women's and men's sexualities—and to a large extent has helped free some women's sexual behaviour from its traditional constraints. Yet the persisting beliefs in Africa that heterosexuality is the only natural way of expressing sexual feeling need further probing.

To wrap up this presentation, I need to state that writing this paper was rather unnerving. Issues of sexuality in Africa, especially when they touch on the pleasurable aspects of sex are rather touchy, most of the reasons have been provided in the discussion. The paper title was derived from this apprehension, the fact that I geared up to *Open a Can of Worms* not because I think that female sexuality stinks—far from it, I enjoy my own sexuality to the fullest—but because of the reactions I expect from the readers, scholars and lay people alike. I am enthusiastic that society, as a result of the feminist movement must envision new sexual paradigms to change the norms related to female sexuality. Such paradigms should enhance the value of female sexuality, including issues of sexual pleasure and well-being, thus promoting basic sexual freedoms.

References

Ardener, S., 1975, "Sexual Insult and Female Militancy", in Ardener, S. (ed.), *Perceiving Women*. London: JM Dent and Sons Ltd.

Ardener, S., 1987, "A Note on Gender Iconography: The Vagina", in Caplan, P. (ed.), *The Cultural Construction of Sexuality*. London: Tavistock Press.

Arnfred, S., 1990, "Notes on Gender and Modernization: Examples from Mozambique", in Bentzon, Agnete Weis (ed.), *The Language of Development Studies*. Copenhagen: New Social Science Monographs.

Belloti, E., 1975, *Little Girls*. Boston: Little Brown & Company.

Bible, The Holy, Proverbs 30:15.

Caplan, P., 1986, *The Cultural Construction of Sexuality*. London: Tavistock Press.

Daily Nation Saturday Magazine, 2001, "Bi-Curious: An Emerging Trend", *Daily Nation Saturday Magazine* (Nairobi), 17 November, (p. 6).

Dorkenoo, E., 1994, Cutting the Rose: Female Genital Mutilation. The Practice and Its Prevention. London: Minority Rights Publications.

Edgerton, R. B. and Conant, F. P.,1964, "'Cultural' vs 'Ecological' Factors in the Expression of Values, Attitudes, and Personality Characteristics among the Pokot of Kenya", *American Anthropologist* 6: 442–447.

El Dareer, Asma, 1982, Woman, Why Do You Weep?: Circumcision and Its Consequences. London: Zed Books.

Evans-Pritchard,1929, "Some Collective Expressions of Obscenity in Africa", *Royal Anthropological Institute of Great Britain and Ireland Journal* 59: 311–331.

Freud, S., 1953, *Three Essays on the Theory of Sexuality. Standard Edition*. New York: Random House.

Hartmann, B., 1995, *Reproductive Rights and Wrongs: The Global Politics of Population Control*. Boston, MA: South End Press.

Hooks, B., 1993, *Sisters of the Yam: Black Women and Self-Recovery*. Boston, MA: South End Press.

Hooks, B., 1989, *Talking Back: Thinking Feminist, Thinking Black*. Boston, MA: South End Press.

Hooks, B., 1984, *Feminist Theory: From Margin to Center*. Boston, MA: South End Press.

Kenyatta, J., 1962, *Facing Mount Kenya*. New York: Vintage Books. (First published in 1938).

Kinsey, A. C. et al., 1953, *Sexual Behavior in the Human Female*. Philadelphia: W. B. Saunders Co.

Kolawole, M., 1997, *Womanism and African Consciousness*. Trenton, NJ: African World Press.

Lambert, H. E.,1956, *KIKUYU: Social and Political Institutions*. London: Oxford University Press.

Lightfoot-Klein, H.,1989, *Prisoners of Ritual: An Odyssey into Female Genital Circumcision in Africa*. Binghamton, New York: Harrington Park Press.

Lips, M., 1988, *Sex and Gender: An Introduction*. Mountain View, CA: Mayfield.

Machera, M., 1997, "Domestic Violence in Kenya: A survey of Newspaper Reports", in Oyekanmi, F. (ed.), *Men, Women and Violence*. Dakar: CODESRIA.

Masters, W. H. and V. E. Johnson, 1966, *Human Sexual Response*. Boston: Little Brown.

Mbiti, J., 1969, *Concepts of God in Africa*. London: SPCK.

Nelson, N.,1987, "Selling Her Kiosk: Kikuyu Notions of Sexuality", in Caplan, P. (ed.), *The Cultural Construction of Sexuality*. London: Tavistock Publications.

Obiora, L. A., 1997, "Bridges and Barricades: Rethinking Polemics and Intransigence in the Campaign against Female Circumcision", Case Western Reserve Law Review 47(2): 275–378.

Pisani, Kobus Du, 2001, "Puritanism Transformed", in Morrell, R. (ed.), *Changing Men in Southern Africa*. London: Zed Books.

Rich, A., 1980, "Compulsory Heterosexuality and Lesbian Existence", *Signs: Journal of Women in Society and Culture* 5 (Summer): 631–660.

Richardson, D., 1993, "Sexuality and Male Dominance", in Richardson, D. and V. Robinson (eds), *Thinking Feminist: Key Concepts in Women's Studies*. New York: The Guilford Press.

Sevely, J. L., 1987, *Eve's Secrets: A New Theory of Female Sexuality*. New York: Random House.

Thiam, A., 1986, *Black Sisters Speak Out: Feminism and Oppression in Black Africa*. London: Pluto Press.

Toubia, N., 1995, *Female Genital Mutilation: A Call for Global Action*. New York: Rainbo.

Vance, C., (ed.), 1984, *Pleasure and Danger: Exploring Female Sexuality*. London: Routledge and Kegan Paul.

Walker, A., 1992, *Possessing the Secret of Joy*. New York: Harcourt Brace Jovanovich.

Walker, A. and P. Parmar, 1993, *Warrior Marks: Female Genital Mutilation and the Sexual Binding of Women*. Florida: Harcourt Brace and Co.

Weeks, J., 1987, "Questions of Identity", in Caplan, P. (ed.), *The Cultural Construction of Sexuality*. London: Tavistock Publications.

Wekker, G., 1997, "One Finger Does Not Drink Okra Soup: Afro-Surinamese Women and Critical Agency", in Alexander, J.M. and T.C. Mohanty (eds), *Feminist Genealogies, Colonial Legacies, Democratic Futures.* London: Routledge.

Wekker, G., 1992, "I Am Gold Money (I Pass Through All Hands, But I Do Not Lose My Value: The Construction of Selves, Gender and Sexualities in a Female, Working Class, Afro-Suranamese Setting." Unpublished PhD Dissertation. Los Angeles: University of California.

UNIFEM, 2000, *Progress of the World's Women.* Biennial Report. New York: United Nations.

Photo: El Hadj Bassirou Sanni, 1982

8. Paradoxes of Female Sexuality in Mali
On the Practices of *Magonmaka* and *Bolokoli-kela*

Assitan Diallo

Introduction

According to what is perceived as 'tradition' in Mali, open discussions about sexual issues are taboo and often perceived as a lack of virtues. Till recently, interests in sexuality and sexual behaviour among Malians have only been found among a handful of foreign writers. With extended campaigns against the practice of 'female genital mutilation' (FGM) and actions for the prevention of AIDS, there have been increasing media programs, advocacy initiatives and new writings about male and female sexuality. However, these debates are often tailored according to specific topics. For example, feminist writers and activists, who made most of the discourses on 'female genital mutilation', have emphasized that this practice is an expression of women's sexuality being oppressed on the behalf of the patriarchal society (Famille et Développement 1991; Hosken 1994). They were neither interested nor motivated to find out whether the same society would also consider promoting women's sexual behaviour at some points in their life cycle.

The leading idea in the present study is that in Mali there is a paradox in how society deals with female sexuality. There are ingredients in the prevailing norms and practices with regard to both enhancing and hindering women's sexuality. The *magnonmakanw* are nuptial advisors whose role is to teach, promote and sustain healthy and enjoyable sex among couples and adult members of communities. At the same time, there are *bolokoli-kêlaw* who are traditional or modern practitioners entrusted with carrying out female circumcision for many reasons, among which one is to diminish women's sensuality. This practice refers to various forms of cutting the female genitalia (Diallo 1978). In Mali, it is most commonly called 'excision'. However, knowing with cerainty the harm that these practices do to women's health and sexuality, I shall use the terminology 'female genital mutilation' (FGM) throughout this text, except where I talk about it in the context of local Mali understandings. This fits well with my conceptualisation in terms of hindrance mechanisms, and expresses more accurately in my view the reality of these practices.

This chapter includes a double-focus analysis that shifts between the issues of 'sexual mutilation' and 'sexual pleasure', in a social setting where sexuality is crafted around specific notions of social identity. It aims at highlighting the complex construction of female sexuality. The discussion is meant to be a contribution to the discourses on 'female genital mutilation' that allow for new insights for the fight against the practice. It is a theoretical discussion, which is embedded in statements gathered through an exploratory study on *magnonmakanw* and *bolokoli-kêlaw* in Mali. In this regard, I have conducted in-depth interviews with ten (10) *magnonmakanw* and seven (7) *bolokoli-kêlaw* in Bamako, the capital city of Mali. The paper starts with a description of the two parallel mechanisms of influencing women's sexuality. The analytical section addresses the following questions regarding the cultural construction of female sexuality in Mali:

— What motivates a society to value both sexual mutilation and sexual enhancement?

— How do these apparently contradictory sexual systems manage to co-exist and make sense among the same social groups?

— What reading can be made of this paradox, from a feminist perspective?

Hindrance of women's sexual behaviour

Chastity is the norm of premarital sexuality among most of the social groups in Mali. It is perceived as the result of a good family upbringing, which fostered obedience to ethical norms and strengthened individual value systems. Girls' virginity is a source of respectability because it proves self-mastery, maturity and decency. That is why virgin brides receive generous gifts (gold, cows or money) for their achievement and the honour that it brings to their family. However, the importance attached to girls' virginity no longer corresponds to disgrace and social exclusion that were traditionally the punishments held in reserve for girls who are sexually active prior to their wedding. As elsewhere in Africa, there are currently more exceptions to the rule than compliance with the normative sexual abstinence before marriage (Locoh 1996). Interestingly, the ascribed codes of conduct persist despite extreme changes in individual sexual behaviour.

The practice of excision/female genital mutilation

Excision/female genital mutilation is still omnipresent, in urban as well as rural areas, as a regulator mechanism of female sexuality. It includes several types of cutting the female genitalia. A small sub-group of the population submit girls to the 'sunna-circumcision', which involves only the removal of the skin covering the clitoris. The clitoridectomy, called 'excision', is a more common practice, which consists of cutting parts or the entire clitoris along with an incision in the small lips (labia minora) of the female genitalia.[1] These centuries old practices are performed by traditional or modern practitioners, usually in homes, on girls in a wide range of age cohorts. In cities, the age at excision has dropped drastically from adolescence to early childhood, being performed on infants and newborn babies. The rites and rhythms, which were an important part of these practices, are almost non-existent today because of their irrelevance due to the younger age

---

1. This practice is worsened sometimes by a cutting and sewing of the large lips (labia majora). This latter procedure is called "infibulation".

at excision. Moreover, many justifications of excision are no longer used as valid rational explanations of these practices. The belief that the clitoris can harm the young girl, the childbearing woman or her male sexual partners, is among those disappearing rationalizations. Instead, conformity to traditional or Islamic teaching, clarification of individual sexual identity and control of sexuality are the most frequent reasons for submitting women and girls to the practice (Diallo 1978; Toubia 1993). Usually, people give more than one reason why they approve of these practices, often combining other justifications with the recurrent motive of diminishing women's sensuality and sexual activities. For example, all the nuptial advisors and practitioners of excision, who are included in the present study, have asserted that the primary function of current practices of female genital mutilation is to diminish women's sensuality. They believe that the induced decrease in the libido is a sure method of preventing sexual permissiveness among boys and girls, ensuring faithfulness among couples and reinforcing the respectability of older women. However, it is no secret today that female genital mutilation is a source of intense suffering and health hazards for many Malian women. Its effects may be devastating for women's sexuality, ranging from painful intercourse, risky childbearing, to misshapen and dysfunctional genital organs (Koso-Thomas 1987).

Why go along with FGM when it is known to be harmful?

Those who favour the practice of excision/female genital mutilation often deny its harmful consequences or are stubborn enough to find a way around eventual problems. Indeed, many followers of these practices rationalize their positive attitude by the fact that they have never experienced or seen any of the presumed inconveniences of female genital mutilation. Moreover, some individuals, city natives with higher education, even assert that a good alternative to eradicate these practices would be the promotion of 'sunna-circumcision' against other types of female genital mutilation, and the use of modern health facilities. For many of them, they are not mutilating or denying human rights, they are following a cultural tradition, while willing to modify it to avoid hurting their children whom they love and want to see well integrated in the society. Among the *bolokoli-kêlaw* included in our study sample, two who are also midwives claim that they only circumcise girls who are their own or their friends' relatives. Their services are free, and are meant to prevent these girls from being submitted to a full clitoridectomy or to some malpractices, if they were taken to traditional practitioners. One of these midwives asserted that she is against these practices, and she always tries to convince the parents not to do it, before offering her help. Another practitioner, who is aware of the hazardous nature of the profession, confessed that she is only doing it under the threat of her mother who handed the practice to her, and would curse and reject her if she gives it up. Similarly, many traditional practitioners, made aware and convinced by NGO agents to 'let down their knives' and start a new occupation, may resume their practice under social pressures (CNRST 1991). These dissonances in individual behaviours may simply be summed up into 'it is hard to say no' to the rule of norms in Malian society. Furthermore, the price of refusing or confronting the will of the elderly is often perceived as more destructive than putting one's children through female genital mutilation. That is why many surveys have shown that conformity to tradition is currently the number one justification of this practice.

From the above information you would think that the bottom line of this social system is the mutilation of girls and adult women. So, why bother assisting women with the means of enjoying their sexual life?

Enhancement of women's sexual behaviour

Similarly to *bolokoli-kêlaw*, the *mmagnonmakanw* come from caste[1] groups and are the designated gatekeepers of traditional practices and rites of initiation. For both, their roles are social obligations handed down through several generations, through training and personal coaching. From our discussions, we gathered that both practitioners still enjoy social approval for their activities, and that they are in great demand for their services. Their remuneration varies from one client to the other. In urban areas, these occupations come as secondary activities, parallel to a main income-generating occupation.

The *magnonmakanw* usually insist on the fact that their services are not meant for the promotion of adultery, they are particularly denied to girls involved in premarital sex. The *magnonmakanw* do not want to be associated in any way with what they perceive as abnormal sexual behaviours. They are usually the care providers to couples, throughout the lifespan of the marriage.

Assistance during the wedding period

The work of the *magnonmakan* begins three days before the wedding ceremonies. During that period, referred to as *konoboli-so*[2], the nuptial advisors have the assignment to prepare the bride for the intense sexual activity that will take place in the following week. The main assumption being that the bride is a virgin who may resist a fast attempt to remove her virginity in the course of one night. This special treatment seeks to diminish her strength to resist sexual intercourse.

On D-day, after a variety of marriage ceremonies and festivities, the *magnonmakan* discreetly brings in the bride to the nuptial room[3]. Before leaving, she will ask the couple to be mutually respectful and call on her help if needed. Currently, few couples need the involvement of the nuptial advisor due to a high prevalence of premarital sex, and a scarcity of arranged marriages in which her assistance is often needed to break the ice beforehand. The *magnonmakan* is particularly helpful

1. Castes are social groups with lower status, resulting from a hierarchical stratification of society.
2. *Konoboli-so* refers to the process of submitting the future bride to a special liquid diet, which constantly purges her, and to light daily meals.
3. Nuptial rooms are set up as seclusion spaces in which the bride and groom are kept inside, all week long, to start their intimate life as a couple.

in cases where there is a large age gap between the groom and bride or when the bride has been infibulated to prevent earlier sexual acts.

In the morning following the celebration of the marriage, a group of 'bride's mothers' greets the new couple, to the sound of various musical instruments. This customary visit aims at finding out whether the bride was 'found home' (i.e. a virgin). If the answer is in the affirmative, there will be songs thanking her and exalting the merits of her upbringing. If the opposite is the case, her reputation and that of her family will be spoiled forever. Currently, the usual response to such disappointing behaviour is a 'collective denial'. The bride and her parents would still be congratulated in public, through songs and implicit compliments. Sometimes, the pretence goes as far as giving the traditional gifts to the bride, suggesting that she has met the social expectation.

All week long, the couple indulge themselves with multiple visits from relatives and friends, who bring in unusually enriched meals, sweets and drinks. Traditionally, the bride's peer group give daily entertainment through songs that celebrate womanhood and motherhood. The groom may come out to greet or sit down with visitors, whereas the bride is confined inside a mosquito-net for the whole week, wearing a light white veil *(payini)* to ensure a good tan of her body and face when she is released from seclusion. Her immediate needs are taken care of by a *kognio wuluni*[1] whose role is to run her errands, maintain the premises, and help in food preparation for the bride.

With regard to services rendered, there is a wide range of actions undertaken by the *magnonmakan* to create an atmosphere of enchantment and leisure around the new couple. She is believed to have outstanding skills entrenched in a large base of knowledge and supernatural power. She is the real master of the nuptial ceremonies in charge of preparing, protecting and supervising the couple during the seclusion period and thereafter. She fixes the time and length of visits to the bride, and watches her behaviour closely. The bride should not talk much, should eat moderately, and be quiet about what goes on 'behind the curtains'. The *magnonmakan* is the principal entertainer of the couple, which allows her to teach and discuss with them a variety of subjects. She informs them about their social status and family roles, stressing the importance and norms of marriage in society. She gives advice about many aspects of a married woman's life: domestic obligations, behaviour towards the husband, his relatives and friends, and the neighbours. In the case of a Muslim couple, she is also in charge of the spiritual education of the couple by maintaining a routine of prayers done on time and correctly, after teaching them the purification methods required after sexual intercourse.

Sexuality is never discussed as much and as openly as in this period of women's life. The nuptial advisor teaches the virgin bride how to give pleasure to a man or help the already sexually active bride to improve her sexual performance. She puts in daily meals and drinks special herbs, roots and plants, known for their aphrodisiac effects. She also prepares and gives to the bride a set of specially

---

1. *Kognio wuluni* is the nickname given to the young female relative of the bride, who stays with her during the week of the marriage and often lives with her afterward.

mixed lotions and ointments that lubricate, cleanse and smooth the female genitalia. Different types of these 'love concoctions' are put, usually secretly, in the groom's daily food to boost sexual desire and reinforce sexual performance. The purpose of all these products called *maya-dyalan*[1] and the matching erotic behaviours, is to make the bride sexually attractive and sustain the groom's sexual pleasure. This practical assistance is backed up by a psychological preparation of the virgin bride to discover and enjoy sex. For the sexually active bride, the mental preparation seeks to influence her sexual behaviour and her perception of a sexual partner.

These practices of the nuptial advisor vary slightly when the bride is already pregnant, due to the delayed traditional ceremonies which takes place well after the celebration of the civil or Islamic marriage. Pregnant brides are exempted from the purging and special diet, and they are kept in seclusion for three days only. There are some other modifications in the care provided to new couples, when the groom has already one or up to three other wives in conformity with his option for a polygamous marriage. In such a case, the coaching of the bride stays as it is normally, and the husband still get his revitalizing potions. In addition, he is reminded of the rules of the game: night shift among his wives and attending correctly to each one's economic and sexual needs. Meanwhile, he is required to stay three straight days in the nuptial room with his new wife. The bride may stay on, to continue the process of initiation into married life. In general, the *magnonmakan* focuses her actions on the bride's needs and behaviour. The groom benefits mostly from the advice on good marriage relationships and the add-on virility received through the concoctions put in his meals. Some grooms or brides give feedback, for the *magnonmakan* to take into account their hints and complaints. When the groom is a first-timer, he benefits from more guidance and supervision from the nuptial advisor. There are a few cases of male *magnonmakan* whose role is to coach the groom, and work hand in hand with his female counterpart.

Assistance beyond the nuptial room

At the end of the week-long seclusion, the bride joins her conjugal home, loaded with bedding, kitchen-utensils, a new wardrobe, and a stock of incense and *maya-dyalan*. Usually, the *magnonmakanw* stay in touch with the couples that they have coached. They supposedly continue to protect them against witchcraft and bad spirits. Many of their protégées are said to have come back for more aphrodisiac substances, throughout their reproductive life and even beyond. *magnonmakanw* have reported that some of their ex-clients have called on their services, from abroad, to get some products or to have them travel to Europe and America in the company of brides-to-be. They claim that women need this support to their sexual life because men may remarry, but women have only one partner to attend to their sexual needs.

---

1. This is Bambara terminology, which means ingredients to sweeten human relationships.

Usually, the *magnonmakan* is the first one to hear of and deal with cases of sexual incompatibility or other types of intimate problems among "her couples". She will then check and advise the woman about her nightwear, night diet, and communication with her husband, etc. The *magnonmakan*'s role may go as far as getting in touch directly with the spouse or asking assistance from the in-laws. In some cases, she will take the woman to healers or advise her to go to modern health providers. However, she usually knows enough about plants and other medicines to try to take care of the problem herself. In particular, the *magnonmakanw* are well known for their successful treatment of minor gynaecological problems and temporary women's sterility. However, the common expectation is that the bride will get pregnant immediately after the nuptial room. Such an event would be interpreted as *galama kounandi*[1], an indication that the nuptial advisor should take credit for it. Sometimes, the *magnonmakanw* serve as intermediaries between husbands and wives in their discussions about delicate matters, such as the use of contraception or the probability that the couple's infertility may be the man's responsibility. Their mentoring of the couple may extend to the promotion of healthy maternity, child survival and assistance during women's menopause.

In contrast, the *magonmakanw* are less involved in unmarried women's sexual life. They may sometimes come to the rescue of divorcees and widows who are striving to remarry. They would then provide advice, support to their sexual life or even "work the targeted man" to have better feelings for the woman concerned. In general, there is no nuptial seclusion for a woman's remarriage. In some cases, a *magnonmakan* will be just in charge of preparing and taking the 'adult bride' to her new residence.

These nuptial practices, as described, are very much alive in most parts of the country. The seclusion is still compulsory among many ethnic groups, although some urban couples reduce the length of their stay in the nuptial room to three days only. The use of *magnonmakan* to solve personal problems, once the nuptial room is over, is also on the decrease among the urban population. There are newcomers in the job, without much expertise or know-how but the cities still offer a large pool of clients, enough to ensure regular gifts and cash remuneration to sustain interest in the practice.

Paradox of female sexuality and gender identity

Traditionally, individual sexuality was dealt with step by step in conformity with male/female physiological and psychological development, through various rites of initiation and an elaborate system of gendered socialisation. Learning about sexuality was mostly a collective event organized by age groups and led by an elder. This formal teaching about sexuality is progressively disappearing in many parts of the country. However, the underlying perception of the individual life cycle as an upward scale of events is still omnipresent. A person is seen as not need-

---

1.   Which means that the big wooden spoon, containing the concoctions served to the couple, was a lucky one.

ing much information or even autonomy at an early age, while allowed to exercise self-agency and leadership in old age. Marriage is the dividing line on this continuum. Consequently, there is a conceptualisation of sexual behaviour as being immature and disrespectful before marriage, and it as afterward presumed to be at its full potentials and legitimised by its conjugal functions. This vision of individual sexuality explains the existence of parallel systems that are complementary means of managing individual sexuality at different periods in the lifespan. Hence, nuptial advising and the practice of excision have the common objective of establishing a normative sexual behaviour, which aims at preserving the established social order. Individuals might ignore the incentives and actions taking place, but it is all part of a well-structured system set up to assert social identity and collective welfare. The praised social values of self-discipline and accountability in individual behaviour help in keeping secret and taboo a lot of information, and tasks performed in society.

Perceptions and norms of female sexuality

Sexuality is monitored throughout women's life cycle

At a younger age, girls' socialisation is more focused on learning their gender roles. Later on, sexual education is given incidentally, through older siblings and grandmothers, on a basis of need. However, the learning of body language is constantly promoted through daily remarks, criticism and guidance on how a woman should look, walk, laugh, and interact with men. Participation in life events (e.g. excision, weddings and naming ceremonies) offers additional opportunities to become acquainted, in a subtle way, with existing sexual norms and practices. Strict control on girls' mobility and social contacts is still the norm in most rural areas. In cities and towns, networking at school and marketplaces, an increasing number of nightclubs, and a greater access to sex-orientated information through movies, videotapes and connections to the internet, constitute serious challenges to normative sexual behaviour.

Marriage is still the only suitable entry to a sexually active life. Getting married is almost universal in Mali, although the forms of marriage might vary from one ethnic group to the other. Wives are expected to be attractive, to know how to prepare themselves to deliver and enjoy pleasurable sex with their spouses. There are a great deal of products to support sexual activities. These may be nicely coloured and flavoured bead belts, short wrap-around pieces of cloth, body ointment, incense,[1] etc. The use of each of these items is often surrounded by myths, ceremonial gestures and postures. For example, the incense should be burnt on live coals in a way that it sends into the air a nice smell of mixed perfume. Young girls learn how and when to use incense by often being in charge of that chore. The reason for using this mixture is revealed progressively to girls mainly through

---

1. Incense, the Malian style, is made of a mixture of flavored roots and grains, high quality Arabic gum and various perfume fragrances. The whole thing is kept tightly closed in order to obtain a strong pleasant scent.

observation and noting that only adult cloths and rooms are incensed, only during certain times of the day, and particularly at night. The aphrodisiac function of incense is confirmed by its constant use in nuptial rooms. Without any explicit statement, girls learn to view incense and similarly other things as sexual tools. Regarding the bead belts and the short wrap-around cloth, they are meant to provoke sexual desire. The beads are worn on the lower body with the intent to make small noises leading the vigilant watcher to search for their origin, admire the body shape and elegant walking of the woman who is wearing them. The short wrap-around piece of cloth, called *pintélounin,* is an item of the traditional underwear, which may be given an enchanting power in some magic ways or used to trigger a co-wife's jealousy by insinuating a multiple use of it overnight. As a general rule, intimate relationships between the couple should unfold in a judicious way, through body language and coded messages that are likely to be missed by an external eye.

A greater concealment is imposed on sexual behaviour outside wedlock, due to its prohibition by society. The gender bias, in this case, lies in the degree of tolerance allowed to deviant behaviour. Premarital abstinence is a must for girls and just an aspiration regarding boys. Sexual activities among unmarried adults are usually perceived as adultery. Divorced or widowed men unwilling to remarry are simply viewed as stubborn, whereas women's preference for remaining unmarried is usually understood as a tendency towards prostitution. Remarriage is often arranged for or even imposed on women. The hostility to sexual activities among unmarried women is matched with a great control on their behaviour and a clear reluctance to promote their sexual life.

Sexuality is conceived as a source of pleasure and power

For many, the practice of excision/female genital mutilation deprives women of important means of sexual pleasure, because scientific research has ascertained the primary role of the clitoris in women's achievement of orgasm (Zwang 1972; Koso-Thomas 1987). Some people have quickly inferred from those findings, without further scrutiny, that all women who undergo these practices are doomed to be frigid. Bitter written or verbal exchanges have been taking place on this subject (Leuliette 1980; Gunning 1992; McFadden 1994). Consequently, many African scholars and feminist activists have refrained from writing or dealing with the issue of 'female genital mutilation' due to what they perceived as the Western world's fascination and aggressive discourses about sexuality in Africa. Societies, which condone these practices, have been perceived as oppressing women's sexuality and violating their rights to sexual pleasure. However, the cultural context in many of these practising societies acknowledges individual sexual pleasure, as a vital part of human life, for men as well as for women. In Mali for example, there are a great deal of coded messages in popular songs talking about individual sexual needs, feelings and episodes. These are folk songs that are often whispered during women's housework or danced to during events such as harvesting in groups, marriage ceremonies or other types of social gatherings. Individual sexual talents are often associated with a strong hold that some women, particularly those involved in polygamous marriages, have over their husbands. There are also persistent stereotypes about women's sexual performance, based on specific physical characteristics. The fact that a husband's impotence is a valid cause of divorce in Mali, according to both custom and civil laws, denotes the importance attached to women's sexual needs.

Sexuality is a cornerstone of women's family role as wife

A healthy sexual life is said to be the guarantee for a good marriage. For some, the prevailing norms endorse the perception of wives as sexual objects. This view is based on many existing facts and practices. For example, a man may "own" more than one sexual partner through the system of polygamous marriage, in which husbands' pleasure and gratification are at the centre of women's sexuality. In general, wives' sexuality is based on values and practices that aim primarily at satisfying their spouses' needs. Worse, husbands have the implicit right to impose sexual intercourse on them. There is even a common saying that suggests ignoring all conjugal quarrels, particularly those that occur at night. In fact, the notion of 'marital rape' is just laughed at, as nonsense coming from elsewhere and irrelevant in this cultural context. The prevailing norms of moderation, discretion and obedience surrounding wives' sexuality safeguard the status quo. However, there are also people who believe that beyond this apparent inequality in sexual relations among couples, marriage provides women with a respectful context and means for sexual fulfilment. For them, married women have the rights to request and enjoy sexual intercourse, in perfect harmony with religious and customary requirements.

Sexuality is valued through the importance granted to procreation

The end in mind regarding women's sexuality is its reproductive component. Procreation is the most celebrated function of female sexuality in Mali. To this extent, a woman's recurrent concern about sexual pleasure is often misinterpreted as her possible deviance from reproduction. Such a presumption has led some people to believe that the practice of excision/female genital mutilation seeks to displace women's libido from self-gratification to the social obligation of childbearing.

The inequality context of the paradox around female sexuality

Gender inequality is the norm among all ethnic groups in Mali with a variation, in the nature and areas of discrimination, due to differentials in the life style and social values that are emphasized in individual behaviours (Rondeau 1994). Inequality among generational groups is common to all components of the Malian society. *Age* is a definite determinant of gender roles and relations. In particular, women's age and family position, as mothers in-law or grandmothers, provide them with substitutes in their domestic obligations, greater decision-making power and more participation in public affairs.

With regard to sexuality, the elderly watch both men and women closely. Couples' decisions on having children, using contraception or circumcising their offspring are greatly influenced by their own parents and older relatives. Gatekeepers, such as the *magnonmakanw* and *bolokoli-kêlaw*, are traditionally old women aged 60 years and over. Their main collaborators are aunts and grandmothers who are the usual decision-makers concerning nuptial ceremonies and excision. Together they constitute the hardcore group sustaining these practices. For example, they often prompt or vigorously influence parents to carry out excision. There are even some cases in which girls have been circumcised, in spite of their parents' rejection of these practices, by some older relatives in the name of tradition. Women *not* men are in the forefront of nuptial and FGM practices.

How do both social practices validate gendered sexuality?

Basically, the norms of chastity and abstinence apply to both men and women, when they are not married, at any stage of their life cycle. There is a net preference for 'social sex', in which the final goal is procreation, as opposed to the promotion of 'personal sex' that focuses on self-gratification. Hence, regularity of intercourse in wedlock, childbearing and her husband's satisfaction are the conventional indicators of a woman's healthy sexual life. The concern for optimum pleasure in the sexual act, for men and women, is neither emphasized nor displayed due to a limited access to relevant information, the expectation of reserve in individual behaviour in public, and the taboo around sexual issues. However, both the practices of excision/female genital mutilation and nuptial advising express gendered sexuality. Both systems of influencing individual sexuality fit well in the prevailing context of gender inequality. Women's sexuality is about giving and pleasing, whereas men's sexuality emphasises experience and power. Men have greater sexual freedom due to more tolerance for their misbehaving, and the fact that they are permanently on the marriage market thanks to the option of polygamous marriage. Women have limited power of sexual negotiation, in conformity with the social values of submission, patience and endurance that characterize ideal femininity, as defined in the Malian society. However, men's virility is praised and also presented as something out of their control: it is up to women to avoid being victims of their own sexual impulses, and to use the necessary means to enhance their own sexual capabilities. Gender relations in this context are about women demanding less due to excision/female genital mutilation, and knowing enough to satisfy their legitimate sexual partners with the support of the *magonmakan*.

There is no explicit intent of hindering men's sensuality through male circumcision, which consists of taking off the prepuce from the male organ in order to keep it clean, obeying the rules of tradition. In contrast, female genital mutilation may be seen as corresponding to men's castration due to the fact that it consists of cutting the clitoris, the small and large lips of the female genitalia. The parallel is more explicit when looking at an infibulated woman: no sign of genitals!

However, there is a high probability that 'mutilation' is not what people have in mind when they submit their daughters to the practice of female genital mutilation. The expectations and impact that *magnonmakanw* claim on women's sexual behaviour leads to thinking that the mutilation aspect of the practice is not a conscious act. Indeed, the assumption behind the practice of nuptial advising is that the effects of 'female genital mutilation' on women's sexuality are reversible. Women are believed to get back from one practitioner what they lose with the other one. An interesting finding of our research is that both the *magnonmakanw* and *bolokoli-kêlaw* pretend that the final goal of their respective practice is to empower women for self-agency. For the nuptial advisor, her products and teaching enable women to acknowledge and possess their sensuality, and to perform their role of wife well. Where others see 'mutilation', the *bolokoli-kêlaw* see empowerment: they claim that their act has a positive impact on women's status. They believe firmly that it allows women to have self-mastery and capabilities to have power over men, who are perceived as slaves of their own sexual desire. In other words, the belief is that with excision women will be in a better position to protect themselves, and successfully negotiate their sexual encounters based on their needs and interests.

Why hinder women's sexuality not men's?

Excision/female genital mutilation is a decisive aspect of the construction of gender identity. A woman is a cultural creation and female circumcision is normatively obligatory as part of this creation in many cultures (Nypan 1991:42). In Mali, male identity is glorified through its "innate" ability for leadership and its ascribed role of economic provider. Female identity is centred on domestic and reproductive roles, which are exalted and looked down upon at the same time. Wives are viewed as "the pillar of families", responsible for the basic needs of the family but also for their husbands' reputation, the implicit assumption being that women have greater influence on men than appears to be the case in public. Being a mother is the preferred and cherished self-identity of many African women (Oyewùmí 2000:1096). The role of mother is also highly appreciated due to the centrality of families in the functioning of society. A common belief in Mali is that 'women hold the community's destiny in their hands' through their innate capability of procreation, their ascribed role of socialisation of younger members of the community, and their de facto status as role models for future mothers. In other words, they are at the centre of family formation and continuity.

The implicit reason for hindering women's sexuality at an early age is probably to shift the instinctive fascination with sexual gratification among young adults to a commitment to family roles and obligations. Up to the menstruation period, the young girl has no explicit access to information on sexuality. Instead, she is voluntarily kept in the dark on that subject, while fully involved in learning her gender roles through an active participation in domestic chores. Therefore, the primacy of women's roles, as wife and mother, is precisely what underlines the greater attention to her sexuality, relative to men's. A woman's focus on sexual pleasure is seen as a threat to the priority that should be given to motherhood, whereas men's pursuit of greater sexual fulfilment is often viewed instead as a will to take on more responsibilities as a father. Flirting is sometimes rationalized as the necessary step for a married man to take on a new wife in order to increase his offspring. The hindrance of women's libido may then be understood as a social device meant to reinforce differentials in gender roles.

The system of enhancing female sexuality looks as if it is set up to compensate the physiological damage caused by the parallel mechanism of hindrance. Yet, there is no work relationship between *magnonmakanw* and *bolokoli-kêlaw*. With regards to the relationships between these practitioners, all the persons interviewed in the present study have confirmed that there are hardly any interactions between the two sets of practitioners. They know well each other's mission and roles but do not collaborate directly, except in cases where there is a need to 're-open' an infibulated bride, in the nuptial room. They describe their tasks as social obligations that are independent, stressing that one is a system for preventive measures against 'abnormal' sexuality and the other is a support system to adult sexuality. Interestingly, the *magnonmakanw* grant the same care and services to brides, regardless of whether they are circumcised or not. This is so because the enhancement of female sexuality is framed in the overall process of socialisation into gender roles.

Paradox of female sexuality and social change

Collectivism and interdependency are strongly favoured in Malian culture, which despises individual uniqueness and commitment to personal interests. An assertion such as "I have never seen someone like you, you are one of a kind!" is understood in the Malian context as a very insulting statement, which insinuates ignorance and selfishness in the person in question. The common belief is that the prevailing elaborate sexual socialization of men and women has the altruistic goal of promoting collective well-being through strengthening social identity and cohesion. Therefore, excision is viewed as only the first link of a chain of community interventions in individual existence. This perception is opposed to the claim that this practice ensures that female sexuality exists only through men, and is part of the agenda of serving the patriarchal interests of female oppression (McFadden 1994).

Ambiguities of female sexuality

The usual feminist model, for explaining 'female genital mutilation', stresses women's lower status in patriarchal societies. The woman in feminist theory is a wife, the subordinated half of a couple (Oyewùmí 2000:1094). For the *magnonmakanw* and *bolokoli-kêlaw*, wives have better social status and greater autonomy than appears to be the case. They give cosiderable credit to their practices for safe-guarding women's power in society. The presumed impact of 'female genital mu-tilation' on husbands' sexual performance has been inconsistent, ranging from an increase to no effect (Toubia 1993). Based on our exploratory research, social norms, not men's preferences, are the origine of these practices. The *magnon-makanw* affirm that many men would accept their wives as they are, at least in ur-ban areas. They did not recall any cases of husbands who gave up their spouses just because these women were not circumcised, not even in a polygamous mar-riage in which the other wives had been through these practices.

This debate, on the society's handling of female sexuality, is all but settled. Meanwhile, 'ambiguity', not 'just plain oppression', would better describe the weight of gender relations regarding the practices of *magnonmakanw* and *bolokoli-kêlaw*.

Another ambiguity in Malian society concerns the smooth co-existence of the commitment to tradition and the willingness to accept changes in individual atti-tudes and behaviours. Hence, the practice of excision/female genital mutilation in the name of sexual morals persists despite widespread pre-marital sex, increas-ing teenage pregnancy and prostitution. The proponents of this practice are aware of current discrepancies between social expectations and individual behaviours. They are going along with changes in individual sexual behaviours, often over-looking the normative sanctions of deviant actions. Yet, conformity to tradition remains the guideline of individual perception and decision-making. Is the per-sistence of the status quo, within this ambiguous social context, a collective hy-pocrisy or an expression of resistance to social change?

Resistance to notions of gender equality

Throughout history, subgroups of the African population have renounced the practice of female genital mutilation for one reason or the other: be it the death of a whole cohort of circumcised girls or a prolonged contact with non-practising societies. In Mali, efforts to fight this practice started in the late fifties, evolving into the current strong forces that combine governmental, NGO, and private in-itiatives and resources. However, external attempts to stop the practice date from early encounters with the Western world, before and during the colonisation of the continent. Recently, the whole world seems to have joined the Western femi-nists in their decades long advocacy against female genital mutilation. However, their long and strong dissuasive campaigns, often in collaboration with local forc-es, have only achieved limited impact on popular adherence to this practice. The feminists' call for an end to female genital mutilation through appeals for gender equality or women's rights seems to have created more problems than it has in-duced changes.

Promoting any form of equality in the context of a highly stratified society is an overt attack to its foundation. Indeed, the quest for more freedom, control and autonomy of decision to benefit women is often viewed as a goal greater than fighting female genital mutilation. Voices have been raised against the quest for gender equality, which is believed to bring along the rejection of feminine identity and roles, as they currently are. This expresses a fear about the destruction of morality in Malian society. In contrast, there is a claim that a genuine and better alternative to gender equality would be complementarities in differences. This would allow relative power among all social groups based on gender, age or socio-economic status. The difference between these standpoints has to do with the dichotomy that is often linked to social change: individual versus collective decisions and actions. Similarly, advocating women's rights has often been viewed as promoting individual decision-making to overrule the existing social order of interdependency and primacy of the elderly.

The fight against female genital mutilation in a feminist perspective is understood as women's intention to break away and 'own themselves'. Indeed, the emphasis on privacy and personal interests is discouraged among both men and women, because it is perceived as a threat to families in conformity with the social norms. In the Malian context, each family member is seen as a representative in his/her own right: honour or disgrace for one person is respectively a boost or a problem for the entire extended family. This strong sense of individual accountability remains, despite increasing individualism regarding economic welfare among family members. With regard to excision/female genital mutilation, it is frequent to hear that someone is or is not from a 'practising family'. A relative's self-given right to circumcise a girl without even asking for her parents' permission or those parents' incapacity to bring that person to court is all related to the primacy of family bonds over individual welfare. Thus, resistance to campaigns against female genital mutilation come down to being anxious about social identifiers, such as kinship affiliation and gender identity. In many ways, the widespread conformity to this practice subscribes to the strong fear of losing oneself.[1] The tenacity in holding on to the status quo, for the sake of a code of conduct, may then be perceived as a mechanism for self-preservation and an indication of a strong hold on social identity.

The threat of losing one's identity has been dealt with, for some time now, by a few African NGOs who have tried to discover and diffuse existing positive traditions, to convince their target population of their good intention. Recent involvement of the *bolokoli-kêlaw* in the fight against female genital mutilation, through NGOs' initiatives, is also an effort toward finding better strategies to communicate, convince and change attitudes and behaviours among the population concerned. To the best of my knowledge, no attempts have been made, so far, to use the *magnonmakanw*'s knowledge, experiences and products in fighting this practice. Sisterhood, between *bolokoli-kêlaw* and *magnomakanw* in fighting female genital mutilation, is likely to be seen as an agenda for collective welfare, contrary to those agendas perceived as individualistic means of social change. Their combined efforts would be an original way of addressing this particular legacy of African sexuality. It would be a good test of the 'women's asset approach',

---

1. Illustrated by this common Bambara saying: *"Sódon, djidon, yérèdon gnonkontè!"* (The best of all is knowing oneself!)

so praised lately in development projects, to achieve a paradigm shift in the struggle against female genital mutilation.

Concluding remarks

This paper includes a theoretical re-thinking of 'female sexuality', rooted in an empirical inquiry about 'excision/female genital mutilation' and nuptial advisors. The purpose of such an approach is to bring about elements of discussion that reveal the cultural basis of these practices as much as possible. In Mali, the social construction of individual sexuality is everything but a simple paradigm, which clearly states the justifications of gendered norms, values and practices in the matter. The usual causal linear model of explanation falls short of the complex motivations and mechanisms, which rationalize the decisions, attitudes and behaviours pertaining to individual sexuality. The established social order includes parallel systems, which are often contradictory if not confusing for an unfamiliar onlooker. Hence, there are social practices in Mali that promote women's sexual enjoyment while others hinder it, at different points in their life cycle.

I have attempted to conceptualise and put in context the sexual socialization and mentoring of girls and couples. I have shown that excision/female genital mutilation is a social system, which has its own logic, different paradigms, and different means to achieve what some people believe to be a means of women's empowerment. This is not to deny that 'female genital mutilation' is harmful to women's health and sexuality, but to show that this practice is also claimed to enhance female empowerment.

The analysis points to a consensus around the control of women's sexual behaviour. It shows that collective welfare, which is at the core of the two contradictory practices, is placed above individual interests. The discussion underscores the difficulties in trying to change the well-established and synchronized social order that sustains this peculiar construction of female sexuality in Mali. In reality the paradox around female sexuality reveals a social context of gender inequality and resistance to change of women's status in the society.

References

CNRST/Centre National de Recherche Scientifique et Technique, 1991, "Evaluation de la Stratégie de Reconversion des Exciseuses, au Mali". Rapport de Recherche. The Population Council, RO/AT, Projet Afrique II, New York, USA.

Diallo, Assitan, 1978, "L'excision en milieu Bambara du Mali", *Mémoire de Fin d'Etudes*, Ecole Normale Supérieure du Mali, Bamako.

Famille et Développement, 1991, "Pour la Dignité de la Femme Africaine—Halte aux Pratiques Traditionnelles Néfastes", *Revue Trimestrielle Africaine d'Education et de Coopération Technique,* no. 59, December 1991.

Gunning, Isabelle R., 1992, "Arrogant Perception, World-Travelling and Multicultural Feminism: The Case of Female Genital Surgeries", *Columbia Human Rights Law Review,* vol. 23.

Hosken, Fran P., 1994, *Hosken Report on Genital and Sexual Mutilations of Females.* Lexington, Massachusetts, USA: WIN News.

Koso-Thomas, Olayinka, 1987, *The Circumcision of Women: A Strategy for Eradication*. London and New Jersey: Zed Books Ltd.

Leuliette, Pierre, 1980, *Le viol des viols*. Edition Robert Laffont.

Locoh, Thérèse, 1996, "Changement des rôles masculins et féminins dans la crise : la révolution silencieuse", in Coussy, J. et Jacques Vallin, *Crise et Population en Afrique*. Les Etudes du Centre Français sur la Population et le Développement (CEPED), no. 13:445–49, Paris.

McFadden, P., 1994, "African female sexuality and the heterosexual form", *Southern Africa Political and Economic Monthly*, Mar. 7(6): 56–8

Nypan, Astrid, 1991, "Revival of Female Circumcision: A Case of Neo-Traditionalism", in Stolen, Kristi Anne et al. (eds), *Gender and Change in Developing Countries*. Oslo, Norway: Norwegian University Press.

Oyewùmí, Oyèrónké, 2000, "Family Bonds/Conceptual Binds: African Notes on Feminist Epistemiologies", *Signs: Journal of Women in Culture and Society*, vol. 25, no. 4.

Rondeau, Chantal, 1994, *Les paysans du Mali—Espaces de liberté et changements*. Paris: Editions Karthala.

Toubia, Nahid, 1993, *Female genital mutilation: A call for global action*. New York, USA: Women Ink.

Zwang, Gérard, 1972, *La Fonction Erotique*. France: Edition Robert Laffont.

Female Agency

Photo: El Hadj Bassirou Sanni, 1982

9. Understanding Sexuality in Africa: Diversity and Contextualised Dividuality

Jo Helle-Valle

Introduction

This chapter is basically an argument about how to understand and explain sexuality in Africa. It is, needless to say, a highly complex and controversial issue and hence needs some initial qualifications. First, is it at all reasonable to speak of an 'African sexuality'? Some say yes, others heatedly no. My position is somewhere between these absolute stances. On the one hand there seem to be certain aspects of sexual practices and ideology that are widely shared among Africans (in contrast to other regions of the world) but on the other hand we also find such diversity that simple and conclusive statements about 'an African sexuality' must by necessity be oversimplifications and essentialisations.

The stances taken on this issue are many but I contend that they all share one common theme; the controversies about variation vs. homogeneity are all linked to geography and ethnographic place. The advocates for the 'African sexuality'stance document that this or that sexuality trait can be found in such and such a place, tribe or culture, while critics have often argued from a 'not in my tribe' point of view.

In this paper I will take a radically different argumentative stance. I suggest that however large the culture-as-place variations are it is more ethnographically realistic and hence analytically rewarding to treat variations as contextual. By this I mean that although sexuality is meaningful practice, meanings are not unitary, invariable and geographically delineated wholes but linked to practically motivated social contexts—a term I will elaborate on below. Social contexts are often linked to places but not territorially delineated and people move in and out of them routinely. My argument, therefore, is that sexuality, both as practice and as a discursive theme, is (in Africa as elsewhere) many different things depending on the contexts it is part of and must hence always be analysed as part of such communicative contexts.

This perspective has many implications, some of which I will relate to in this chapter. It does not provide any conclusive argument in relation to the 'African sexuality-thesis', rather it might help to downsize the importance of that debate. More importantly however, is that this perspective implies not only that sexuality, as an aspect of a group's social life, should be a term used in plural but that different sexualities—because they are necessarily linked to persons through identity—are found within each individual. Hence it is, I claim, analytically appropriate to apply the term 'dividual' alongside the more commonly used 'in-dividual' as a means for linking sexuality to personhood (cf. e.g. Strathern 1988). In short, 'dividual' is meant to lead our attention to the fact that human beings, irrespective of ideas about 'indivisibility', have different perspectives and in a sense are different persons depending on the communicative contexts they are parts of. This perspective has, in its turn, consequences for the relationship between gender and sexuality.

The line of reasoning put forward in this paper is apparently inductive, emerging out of a narrow empirical foundation. This is especially conspicuous in the way I present it here—drawing generalisations basically from one case. This case is, however, meant as an illustrative example of insights I have gathered as a fieldworker in Botswana during the 1990s. From this experience, as well as from working as an academic within the field for many years, I know that the relevance of my arguments is much wider, partly because they are based on socio-cultural and economic mechanisms that can be found over most of Africa, and partly because they point to theoretical perspectives that have nothing to do with geography. But in any case the fact remains that the arguments presented are of course contentions and not conclusions.

Ethnographic and analytical background

All arguments have a biography and I owe the readers a brief outline of this one. My ethnographic foundation is first of all fieldwork in a medium-sized, semi-peripheral Botswana village situated on the fringes of the Kalahari. The village consists of about 4,500 inhabitants, is populated mostly by people from the Kgalagadi ethnic category, and serves as a sub-district administrative centre. Most villagers belong to multiactive peasant households, i.e. a majority of the households practise agriculture and/or animal husbandry, but almost all also have incomes in cash from wage work, small-scale business etc. (Helle-Valle 1997:118ff.). During my fieldwork I unexpectedly stumbled on a theme that I was not at all prepared for. I found, in my efforts to gather data about socio-economic characteristics of households, that a significant number of young and middle-aged women engaged in informal sexual relationships that were locally termed *bobelete*. These are sexual relationships that in their core imply that men and women establish more or less lasting sexual relationships, that these relationships are informal, and involve a transfer of economically signicant gifts from the man to the woman. The rationale behind these exchanges is that women 'give' men sex, hence the men have to reciprocate by giving her gifts. These gifts take many forms; as cattle or the building of houses but also food, clothes and cash are common.

These sexual practices are 'new' and hence a historical perspective is needed. During the colonial era it was the younger men who were the main agents of change. Their labour migration to the mines in South Africa gradually gave them control over cash as well as exposing them to new masculine ideas. In short these new ideals implied conspicuous consumption of 'Western' goods, and an increasing focus on sexual seduction of young, unmarried women (Schapera 1947). The result was a steadily increasing number of pregnant and deserted women in the villages. A core element in the men's seduction strategies was to enter into secret betrothals with the girls. By way of betrothals they followed traditional ways of establishing sexual relationships but the secrecy of the agreement personalised the relationship and hence gave them leeway to pursue their own sexual goals.

The young deserted mothers, who were one conspicuous result of these strategies, were obviously losers in these relationships. Due to the traditional roles of women they did not have the economic or social position to rectify the wrongdoings of the seducing men (Comaroff and Roberts 1977; Molokomme 1991). However, as the social framework gradually changed, new opportunities were made available to women and they were to an increasing extent able to turn disadvantages into advantages. Alongside new opportunities that had nothing to do with sexual practices (like education, new jobs, etc.) unmarried women found that the cultural logic of the marriage process—that the men had long been exploiting—could be manipulated by them also. The traditional marriage process implied a steady flow of gifts from the man's family to the woman's family, but as the young men had personalised these relationships by entering into secret betrothals directly with the women, this implied that women had potential incomes by way of the gifts men gave them. This possibility—together with all the other opportunities modernisation has generated—has given the unmarried woman the means to decide whether she will marry or not. And it is obvious that more and more women decide not to marry, or at least postpone marriage plans indefinitely (cf. also Haram's chapter in this volume). Moreover, as these informal sexual relationships are not confined to unmarried people, they also imply a lot of infidelity. Both wives and husbands engage in extra-marital affairs—to the extent that it is considered one of the main drawbacks of married life. Thus, by way of sociocultural entrepreneurship young men and women have changed the social landscape of Botswana. One conspicuous expression of this change is that between one third and a half of all households in Botswana are female-headed.

In various works I have described changing sexual practices and sexual mores in Botwana and explored various social implications of these changes (Helle-Valle 1994; 1997; 1999; 2002a; n.d.-a.; n.d.-b; Helle-Valle and Talle 2000). What I wish to do in this paper is to apply a perspective on this ethnography in which social context and dividuality are core concepts. I contend that this analytical approach provides a fruitful framework for understanding and explaining some of the hows and whys of domestic conflicts and gendered antagonisms—phenomena that many observers of African social life find conspicuously present. What such a perspective can provide is an analytical treatment of diversity; it deals with the fact that landscapes of sexual mores[1] are many-faceted and contradictory, that conflicts therefore constantly erupt and ambivalence is hence a common experience

---

1. Significantly 'mores' is the plural form of 'mos'—meaning morally laden attitude.

for both men and women. A case will provide the empirical foundation for these arguments.

A case

In 1998 I witnessed the dramatic effects of a domestic dispute. I was present during parts of a funeral process in which a husband, his wife and his lover were central participants. The man was dead and as a significant part of the funeral process the closest family underwent certain purification rituals (cf. Schapera 1994:163ff.). What was special with the performance of this specific purification ritual was that in addition to the participation of the wife and their two children, his lover too, together with her two children participated in the ritual. Basically the ritual involves different steps that are meant to lead the participants out of the impure (hot) state that results from the death of a person that one is closely linked to. Traditionally, the rules for who should take part in the purification ritual were fairly straight-forward; it was those who had a socially accepted sexual relationship with the deceased as well as the offspring (Schapera 1966:310ff.). However, as informal, but not necessarily secret, sexual liaisons have become increasingly common those responsible for such rituals have a more difficult time deciding who shall take part in the purification ritual. Most love relationships involving married men and/or women are covert liaisons and although few of them are actually secret it is important to be discreet (an ideal that is highly valued among most Batswana). Thus, in situations involving infidelity and deaths—of which there are many—those taking care of the ritual and practical sides of the deaths face a dilemma between living up to the ideal of discretion and following the rules of involving those sexually involved with the deceased. My impression is that discretion usually wins over ideas about blood and sex—that is as long as the lover relationship has been discreet.

Thus, the reason why the lover and the children she had with the deceased man were involved was that he had been indiscreet about the relationship to the point that he had actually told his wife that he intended to take the lover as his second wife. Although groups in Botswana traditionally have valued polygyny, it is today extremely rare for a man to marry more than one woman, and this therefore provoked and distressed the wife. She therefore went to a traditional doctor—a *ngaka*—and asked him if he could help her. He said that he could give her some 'magical' herbs that, if she put them in her husband's tea, would cause him to lose all interest in his lover. So she did, but the effect was devastating—he died. After a while another traditional doctor established the cause of death. It is not uncommon that witchcraft *(boloi)*—which this was a clear case of in the eyes of villagers—leads to revenging witchcraft. This did not happen in this case and it seems that the reason for this was that people found that her actions were reasonable and that it had to be treated as an accident. Thus, the family group decided to leave the issue of witchcraft aside and go on with the required purification rituals. In addition (and more untypically), they decided that since the lover was a significant part of the incident and openly included by the deceased, she and her children should also take part in the rituals.

The significance of contexts

The first analytical line to draw from this case is that it illustrates well what happens when social contexts become mixed. By social context I here mean more or less institutionalised frames that contain not only certain types of practices but also—as a consequence of this—certain ways of thinking. I have elsewhere discussed the term in detail (cf. chapters 2, 8 and 9 in Helle-Valle 1997) and will here only give a brief outline of the term. 'Social context' relies heavily on, and is closely related to Wittgenstein's concepts of 'language game' and 'forms of life' (Wittgenstein 1968), but also akin to Bourdieu's 'field' (Bourdieu 1991) and Goffman's 'frame' (Goffman 1974). For the present purpose the main relevance is that the term provides a way of treating cultural diversity analytically. In the late 1980s it was pointed out by many academics that our conventional idea about 'culture', although useful in many ways, gave a false impression of homogeneity and unity. 'One society, one culture' was the underlying assumption and although most have treated the term sensibly there are imbued connotations that create a tendency of reification and homogeneity (Appadurai 1986, 1988; Keesing 1987, 1990). The realisation that conventional conceptions of 'culture' are flawed is, however, only a first step. As long as one is not a radical postmodernist advocating non-systematic, impressionistic presentations there is need for finding new ways to grasp the undeniable regularities that after all characterise social life.

A central contention in my argument is that meanings are products of the practical tasks they by necessity are parts of. The argument is philosophical and logical and holds, at its core, that language, symbols and other expressions of meanings cannot be self-containing, consistent wholes whose tangible expressions only re-present this totality through application of rules: "Our rules leave loop-holes open, and the practice has to speak for itself" (Wittgenstein 1979:139, cf. also Malinowski 1974; Searle 1992; Taylor 1993). Practice is logically prior to meaning in the sense that meaning is about something (Bourdieu 1990), thus different meanings go along with different practices. That meanings normally have systematic qualities (i.e. constitute cultural patterns) is therefore caused by routinisation of practice, not by the existence of some transcendental langue. However, since practice is genuinely novel—being enacted in new ways on new situations involving different subject-positions—systems of meaning cannot be consistent and logical, rather they are fuzzy and routinely contested (Bourdieu 1977, 1998).

This implies an ontological claim: people think differently in different contexts, and therefore it is unrealistic and hence analytically unfortunate to talk of 'one culture' as if a group had one, unified way of thinking—irrespective of the practical contexts it accompanies. One reason for the hegemonic position of the conventional idea of culture is the Western propensity for creating an 'illusion of

199

wholeness' (Ewing 1990). This illusion springs from the normative idea that we are whole, consistent selves; we are in-dividuals. Ewing argues that non-Western and Western selves alike are contextual and shifting, and that the idea of 'whole-ness' related to the self is illusory. In all societies "people can be observed to project multiple, inconsistent self-representations that are context-dependent and might shift rapidly" (Ewing 1990:251). This argument can then be linked to Strathern's concept 'dividual' (Strathern 1988). Although her argument is about Melanesians, it might well be argued that the Melanesian case is just one variant of the more general argument that "persons emerge precisely from that tension between dividual and individual aspects/relations" (LiPuma 1998). The in-divid-ual aspect of persons is especially salient in language (the "I") and in its physical shape of a body (Lambek 1998). The direct extension of this line of thought is that as we speak of many facets of a person, then we also must speak of many sex-ualities in one person, a point I shall return to shortly.

From within this perspective it can be argued that the crisis—not only the death but also the events that led to the man's death—is the result of the man in-sisting on drawing together events that most villagers feel belong to different so-cial contexts. The widespread extra-marital sexual networking that takes place in the village constitutes (together with practices such as beer-drinking) a social con-text that for villagers is defined and recognised as distinctly different from the marital setting. The latter is part of what can well be described as being part of a traditional context—a context that all in all is dominated by a perspective that, al-though not a replica of, has its roots in the past. This perspective (in Wittgen-stein's term, language-game) contains fairly unambiguous ideas about gender roles and relative social positions, defined by kinship ideology. The former con-text, on the other hand, is infused by an 'ethos' that is in many ways the opposite of the kinship-dominated context. To some extent it is constructed and gets its legitimation by being an alternative, opposing sociality; blurred and even inverse hierarchical structures, alternative gender roles, etc. (Helle-Valle 1997:ch. 8). In short, the context is in many ways a manifestation of Bakhtin's carnevalesque so-ciality (Bakhtin 1984).

Thus, the man and his lover established a relationship, and hence paired iden-tities, that was seen by villagers as belonging to a social realm conventionally de-fined as being apart from the realm of kinship and marriage (Helle-Valle 1997:ch. 8). By being villagers living village lives they of course also routinely took part in other social contexts. Cultural competence thence consists not only of knowing the meaning-contents of different contexts but also knowing how to combine and make relevant contexts in proper ways. Every villager is, in other words, an embodiment of dividualities that are institutionally organised in different social contexts.

The initial transgression was not that the man had a lover but that he ex-pressed a desire to make public a 'promiscuous' relationship by taking her as a second wife. This decision was not based on cultural incompetence but grew out of a strong desire to make his relationship public. He might have had a hope of having two wives but his actions could just as well have been a way to provoke his wife into wanting a divorce.[1] Thus, apart from the fact that most people felt that this was a provocation that compelled the wife to act, it also provoked people because it implied that the man threatened to conflate borders. That is, he attempted to in-dividualise a dividually defined social constellation. In short, his actions were seen as threatening cultural order since his plan would mix contexts that should not be mixed.

What eventually heightened the moral crisis in this situation was the death. On the one hand most people involved evidently thought that the wife had not acted out of evil, but was only responding to a provocation. However, the death of a husband and father requires a ritualised response, and hence the mobilising of kinship networks. Furthermore, since the lover was more or less official and a possible wife-to-be, since she had children by him, and since she was a vital factor in the death of the man, the elders felt that she had to be involved. If not, the purification rituals that were needed in order to restore cultural order would not have the desired effect. But the uneasiness everyone involved felt was caused by the fact that she belonged to another context; thus she both should and should not be there—she was herself 'matter out of place' (Douglas 1966).

This event clearly shows that African sexuality is not as plain and straightforward an affair as some have claimed (Caldwell and Caldwell 1987; Caldwell et al. 1989). Different social contexts involve different rules and taboos associated with sex, i.e. different sexual mores and practices. It is therefore not appropriate to talk of one (African) sexuality, rather there are several sexualities linked to different contexts and hence different dividualities. But in the daily life and the pragmatic ways of much African sociality this sexual multiplicity is not seen, and often not reflected on by the participants themselves (cf. Ahlberg 1994; Heald 1995). By framing different practices in different settings people manage to live lives that appear as rather ordinary and uncomplicated but which owe their smoothness to the extent the participants manage to frame sociality in practical ways (Ewing 1990). An additional case should illustrate this well; a middle-aged man in the village had a father who became seriously ill. The norms required that he abstained from sex as long as his father was seriously ill. The problem was, however, that he remained ill for years. And the son was a man who greatly enjoyed keeping lovers. So after a while he decided that the rules were not really that strict, that it was just superstition, etc. This worked well for the man until, after eight years, the father died—a death that resulted in a pathological psychological crisis for the son. He became seriously depressed and blamed himself for the death of his father. It took many months before he became more or less his old self again, and it was obvious that his father's death had caused his compartmentalised framing of

---

1. His interest in provoking his wife into asking for a divorce was related to the issue of bridewealth (*bogadi*). If he demanded a divorce because he wanted to marry another woman he would have no possibility of reclaiming his marriage payments. If, on the other hand, the wife wanted a divorce because he planned to take an additional wife he might be able to reclaim his payments since taking another wife is not grounds for divorce (cf. Helle-Valle 1997:155).

practices and norms to collapse. The death forced a causal link between his own sexual behaviour and the death of his father, a link that he had managed to keep at bay by contextualising his different sexualities as long as his father was alive.

Reactions to social contradictions: Conflicts and ambivalence

The case of the dead man and his wife and lover also illustrates several important points related to individuals and their reactions to contradictory aspects of sociality. Obviously the man's sexual infidelity provoked the wife. A man who keeps a lover (or lovers) has to spend a lot of time and resources on her (them) and these are resources and attention that both his wife and their children rightly feel belong to them. The lover, on the other hand, is at the receiving end: as he had to provide her with a steady flow of gifts in order to keep her she had a net economic gain. Thus, although the fact that the cultural logic of traditional sexual mores compels men to give and women to receive, it does not follow from the gendered positions in the transactions that the results of these exchanges can be understood only by looking at gender. A first clue here is of course whether the woman is a wife or a lover. In a situation where the man is married the wife is perhaps the principal loser, while the lover (at least in the short run) is the winner. In such a perspective the transfer of goods is not so much a transfer from men to women as it is a transfer from married women to unmarried women. Or, to be more precise, it is a transfer from the wife of the man to the lover of the man—since the lover may very well be married to another man. Thus, we find that there are crossing lines of conflict here; there is a conflict between wife and lover (and one woman might well hold both positions here), as well as a conflict between men and women.

A love affair obviously creates frustrations in the married woman. Since the husband is obliged to give the lover gifts she rightfully blames him for letting his own carnal needs go before the needs of his children and family, hence draining dearly needed resources from the household. Such complaints from the wife are common. However, her grudges against the husband are not always accompanied by a clear conscience and a single thought. First, it is not infrequent that wives cheat on their husbands and although this gives her just as good reason to blame him for draining the household's resources she does not have the same moral weight when she blames him for being a sexual cheater (normally based on Christian ethics). Secondly, in cases where the wife does not have lovers the moral indignation might also be hampered by the fact that there is a good chance that she has had a phase in her life when she was the receiving lover. These conditions not only give the wife less moral credibility if she blames him for being unfaithful but it also makes the cheating easier for the husband and the lover. Lastly, even though she might have every moral right to be angry with her husband, it is not always easy for her to do anything practical about it. She can of course threaten to leave him, but that might well turn out worse for her than for him. And to engage the family group *(losika)* as a moral power to straighten him out is often not effective. As the kinship group loses more and more of its economic and political strength and relevance its power over individuals' conduct becomes less effective (Helle-Valle 2002b).

If we turn to the lover we find some of the same dilemmas and frustrations. Although she is on the receiving end she can, if she is married, easily identify with the wife of her lover, and hence feel bad. If she is unmarried her dilemmas are different but in no way less compelling (cf. Haram's chapter in this volume). By choosing not to marry and rather be a receiving lover she definitely gets some economic and practical advantages (gifts as income as well as not having to obey a man; as a lover she has a freedom that many married women envy her). However, it is a risky strategy (and not always one that is voluntarily chosen), and the older she gets the greater the risks are because being young a woman can postpone the question of life-style because she will stand a good chance of having a suitor, while older women will normally not find men who will want to marry them. Thus, her very life-style is a constant reminder for her of the risks she faces.[1]

Nor do men have singular thoughts on infidelity. Apart from the obvious difference in attitudes between cuckolded husbands and seducing lovers (again one man might hold both roles simultaneously), most men have conflicting thoughts on the matter. Not only does the role as a breadwinning head of household conflict with the generous lover but most men are seriously torn between, at least, two masculine ideals that are to a large extent mutually excluding. On the one hand he can 'make himself' as a man by following the traditional ideals where being a husband, a father and a significant participant in the local political game are core elements (Alverson 1978; Comaroff and Roberts1977). These ideals are, however, gradually becoming marginalised ideologically, politically as well as economically (Helle-Valle 2002b, cf. also Silberschmidt's chapter in this volume). On the other hand he might find the seducing male to be a more immediate and pleasant way to express his manhood. By keeping lovers (married or unmarried) he finds that whatever else happens he has had a good time. But this way of living obviously is not productive—as the costly gifts to lovers seldom provide any tangible repays—and his actions obviously generates a lot of conflicts (Helle-Valle n.d.-a). Thus, either way frustrations and ambivalence is generated also in the man.

The new sexual practices are thus expressions of new and contradictory socio-cultural forces but are simultaneously also instrumental in bringing about these changes. Of course, every social reality contains contradictory elements but contemporary African sociality is probably special in this respect. Old and indigenous practice and ideology exist alongside modern ones, and it is up to each and every member of society to 'reconcile' these conflicting socio-cultural elements—to in-

---

1. A small elaboration would not be out of place here. There is one category of older women who have suitors, the rich ones. Many of these have laid the foundation for their wealth by being *mabelete*. However, these women are most often unwilling to marry because they already possess the security, wealth and social position a man could offer. Wealth, as well as grown-up children, generate security and often also social position. The poorer, older women, on the other hand, are not desirable marriage partners since they lack all of these qualities, as well as beauty.

tegrate them into their life-projects in ways that are existentially and practically acceptable. On a personal, individual level this involves both frustrations and ambivalence—ambivalence because a person's individual qualities forces her/him to strive for a wholeness that social reality does not easily provide, and frustrations because being able to succeed in this wholeness-project requires not only skill but also power—something he/she will often lack. Hence, that outcomes are often dramatic is not difficult to see. While the death of a husband by witchcraft is not an everyday event, domestic fights are.

A perspective that links meaningful practice to contexts and dividuality has the advantage of lifting ambivalence from a private level—being a personal issue related to doubt, uncertainty and weak wills—to a social level. The advocated perspective demonstrates how private ambivalences are socially shaped and hence a core issue for the social sciences. However, in contrast to Bauman (1991), who sees ambivalence as originating in language and its inability to classify the world properly and which hence leads to indeterminacy and inability to act (cf. "Ambivalence, the possibility of assigning an object or an event to more than one category, is a language-specific disorder"— Bauman 1991:1), my perspective gives precedence to practice. Bauman states: "No binary classification deployed in the construction of order can fully overlap with essentially non-discrete, continuous experience of reality. The opposition, *born of the horror of ambiguity*, becomes the main source of ambivalence" (Bauman 1991:61, my emphasis). To me this amounts to putting the cart in front of the horse. Language gets its meaning and structure from human practice, and I contend that the ambivalence considered problematic by people themselves is that which is related to practical dilemmas. As such linguistic indeterminacy is only the *symptom* of this more fundamental practical indeterminacy (cf. Douglas 1975:252ff.). And this practical indeterminacy can best be grasped by understanding meaning as related to social contexts. Ambivalence results from the person's responsibility to handle their various interests in ways that are culturally acceptable. This involves the need to acknowledge and relate to communicative contexts in adequate ways, which also implies a proper balancing between acting dividually (confining aspects of one's personality to their appropriate contexts) and being individuals.

This perspective on the case described also shows how contexts, however cunningly they are kept apart by the actors, tend to collide due to practical matters (e.g. the draining of household resources in order to keep a lover). Thus, whatever types of choices individuals make the contradictory aspects of social organisation and cultural values are such that they constantly create conflicts and often also violence (either as wife-beating, as witchcraft or in other forms). These new socialities not only cement but in fact aggravate the lack of trust and intimacy that characterises many conjugal relationships in Africa. Although weak ties between husband and wife have been an ingrained part of African social organisation (Coquery-Vidrovitch 1997) the changes the African societies have gone through during the last 100 years have exacerbated these tendencies. This does not, however, imply that all social mechanisms have the same centrifugal effect. What seems to be a new, emerging centripetal force is the growing relevance of romantic love. There are signs that romantic and erotic feelings are increasingly being acknowledged—and increasingly used as a legitimate reason for pairing. But so far romantic love has not been a force that has had measurable effects on conjugal bonds and whether it will become such a force in the future is another, and uncertain, issue.

Some final comments

The advocated perspective also suggests some other views on gender. As Strathern repeatedly points out, gender does not have a simple, one-to-one relationship to persons (e.g. 1988:14ff.) but is cultural constructions that are, strictly speaking, only indirectly linked to persons. One implication of this view is that studies of gender necessarily have to involve both sexes. Gender—being collective (although contested) ideas about men and women as well as identities linked to selves—is created in social dialogical relations through different forms of externalisations and internalisations (Strathern 1988:14ff.). Thus, the results of restricting the issue of gender to studies of women are as tangible as the sound of one hand clapping. Moreover, modern societies are always class-divided in various ways. Hence the issue of power—which is an ingrained part of treatments of gender—is way more complicated and fuzzy than a simple dichotomous opposition between men and women. Differentiating forces criss-cross in various ways, thus requiring relating gender to other forces, which again requires a treatment of gender as relational. To be simple: not only are there educated and wealthy women who are more powerful than many men, but they probably also have little in common with the poor and uneducated women. But the most important implication in relation to the arguments put forth here is that the context/dividuality perspective provides the issue of gender—especially in its function as identity—with the tools that are necessary in order to treat it as the complicated issue it is. By deconstructing the person along the lines of context and dividuality gender is opened up in new ways that can fruitfully complicate not only the relationships between men and women but also between masculine and feminine aspects of singular persons.

To end this paper I want to retrace the issue of generalisation and culture, and I wish to do it by briefly discussing the infamous 'African sexuality' thesis. Many Africanists with a 'Western' background, including myself, feel that there are significant differences between sexuality in 'the West' and in Africa. Perhaps it is not so much a question of African permissiveness, or people's preoccupation with it—we certainly find similar traits in certain social groups in 'the West'. The regional difference is maybe more a question of sexual mores than sexual practice. Perhaps the most significant difference is the Western strictness about sex and motivations: romantic love and/or personal pleasure (physical and psychological) are the 'proper' motives for engaging in sex, while strategic, materially oriented uses of sexuality are strictly tabooed—being forcefully embodied in our image of 'the prostitute' (Helle-Valle 1999). When many of us feel uneasy about the contentions put forward by Caldwell and associates, this has a lot to do with the essentialisations that follow from an academic ambition like theirs. Many have rightfully criticised them for this. The 'not in my tribe' arguments are, however, equally essentialistic. The arguments presented in this paper contain a different type of criticism, namely that sexuality is many different things within the same socio-cultural group. Not only that different people relate to and practise sex in different ways, but that sexual mores and practices in fact mean many different things for each and every individual, depending on the socio-cultural contexts they take place within. (This, however, does not necessarily preclude the idea that there are regional differences.) This perspective has, among other things, direct implications for how we treat 'culture'. Instead of thinking of cultures as territorially delineated we might discard the spatial connotation altogether and think of culture in a plainly practical way—as that which enables people to communicate (Eriksen 1994). In this way we do not need to chase blurred borders but rather see cultural congruence as a matter of degree, appearing in many forms.

There is, however, a need for a qualification at the end: although this paper might be read as a general argument against generalisations, I want it to be read as a warning against putting too much faith in concepts and analytical models in general. Generalisations—including those that are territorialized—might sometimes be fruitful but so can 'deconstructions' all the way down to the level of dividuals.

References

Ahlberg, B. M., 1994, "Is There a Distinct African Sexuality? A Critical Response to Caldwell", *Africa*, vol. 64, no. 2, pp. 220–242.

Alverson, H., 1978, *Mind in the Heart of Darkness. Value and Self-Identity among the Tswana of Southern Africa.* New Haven: Yale University Press.

Appadurai, A., 1986, "Theory in Anthropology: Centre and Periphery", *Comparative Studies in Society and History,* vol. 28, pp. 356–361.

Appadurai, A., 1988, "Putting Hierarchy in Its Place", *Cultural Anthropology,* vol. 3, no. 1, pp. 36–49.

Bakhtin, M., 1984, *Rabelais and His World.* Bloomington: Indiana University Press.

Bauman, Z., 1991, *Modernity and Ambivalence.* Cambridge: Polity Press.

Bourdieu, P., 1977, *Outline of a Theory of Practice.* Cambridge: Cambridge University Press.

Bourdieu, P., 1990, "The Scholastic Point of View", *Cultural Anthropology* 5, 380–91.

Bourdieu, P., 1991, *Language and Symbolic Power.* Cambridge: Polity Press.

Bourdieu, P,. 1998, *Practical Reason.* Cambridge: Polity Press.

Caldwell, J. C. and P. Caldwell, 1987, "The Cultural Context of High Fertility in Sub-Saharan Africa", *Population and development review,* vol. 13, no. 3, pp. 409–437.

Caldwell, J. C., P. Caldwell, and P. Quiggin, 1989, "The Social Context of AIDS in Sub-Saharan Africa", *Population and development review,* vol. 15, no. 2, pp. 185-234.

Comaroff, J. L. and S. Roberts, 1977, "Marriage and Extra-Marital Sexuality. The Dialectics of Legal Change among the Kgatla", *Journal of African Law,* vol. 1, pp. 97–123.

Coquery-Vidrovitch, C. 1997, "Research on an African Mode of Production", in R. R. Grinker and C. B. Steiner (eds), *Perspectives on Africa. A Reader in Culture, History, and Representation.* Oxford: Blackwell, pp. 129–141.

Douglas, M., 1966, *Purity and Danger: An Analysis of Concepts of Pollution and Taboo*. London: Routledge & Kegan Paul.

Douglas, M., 1975, *Implicit Meanings: Essays in Anthropology*. London: Routledge & Kegan Paul.

Eriksen, T. H., 1994, *Kulturelle veikryss. Essays om kreolisering*. Oslo: Universitetsforlaget.

Ewing, K. P., 1990, "The Illusion of Wholeness: Culture, Self, and the Experience of Inconsistency", *Ethnos*, vol. 18, pp. 251–278.

Goffman, E., 1974, *Frame Analysis*. New York: Harper Torchbooks.

Heald, S., 1995, "The Power of Sex: Some Reflections on the Caldwell's 'African Sexuality' thesis", *Africa*, vol. 65, no. 4, pp. 489–505.

Helle-Valle, J., 1994, "Bobelete—en Kvinnestrategi?", *Norsk Antropologisk Tidsskrift*, vol. 5, pp. 14–26.

Helle-Valle, J. 1997, *Change and Diversity in a Kgalagadi Village, Botswana*. SUM, University of Oslo, Oslo.

Helle-Valle, J., 1999, "Sexual mores, promiscuity and 'prostitution' in Botswana", *Ethnos*, vol. 64, no. 3, pp. 372–396.

Helle-Valle, J., 2002a, "Når kvinner ikke lenger vil (gifte seg): noen følger for samfunnsorganiseringen i Botswana", *Tidsskrift for samfunnsforskning*, vol. 43.

Helle-Valle, J., 2002b, "Seen fromBelow: Conceptions of politics and the state in a Botswana village", *Africa*, vol. 72, no. 2.

Helle-Valle, J., n.d.-a, "Seduced by seduction: Aspects of male identity in a Kgalagadi village" (in progress).

Helle-Valle, J., n.d.-b, "Social change and sexual mores—a comparison between pre-20th century Norway and 20th century Botswana" (accepted for revision in *Continuity and Change*).

Helle-Valle, J., and A. Talle, 2000, "Moral, marked og penger: komparative refleksjoner over kvinner og sex i to afrikanske lokaliteter", *Norsk Antropologisk Tidsskrift*, vol. 11, no. 3, pp. 182–197.

Keesing, R., 1987, "Anthropology as Interpretive Quest", *Current Anthropology*, vol. 28, no. 2, pp. 161–176.

Keesing, R., 1990, "Theories of Culture Revisited", *Canberra Anthropology*, vol. 13, no. 2.

Lambek, M., 1998, "Body and Mind in Mind, Body and Mind in Body: Some Anthropological Interventions in a Long Conversation", in M. Lambek and A. Strathern (eds), *Bodies and Persons: Comparative Perspectives from Africa and Melanesia*. Cambridge: Cambridge University Press.

LiPuma, E., 1998, "Modernity and Forms of Personhood in Melanesia", in M. Lambek and A. Strathern (eds), *Bodies and Persons: Comparative Perspectives from Africa and Melanesia*. Cambridge: Cambridge University Press, pp. 53–79.

Malinowski, B., 1974, "The Problem of Meaning in Primitive Languages. Supplement 1", in C. K. Ogden and I. A. Richards (eds), *The Meaning of Meaning. A Study of the Influence of Language upon Thought and of the Science of Symbolism*. (With supplementary essays by B. Malinowski and F. G. Crookshank). 8th edn. New York: Harcourt, Brace and World, pp. 296–336.

Molokomme, A., 1991, *Children of the Fence. The Maintenance of Extra-Marital Children under Law and Practice in Botswana*. Leiden: African Studies Centre, 1991/46.

Schapera, I., 1947, *Migrant Labour and Tribal Life: A Study of Conditions in the Bechuanaland Protectorate*. London: Oxford University Press.

Schapera, I., 1966, *Married Life in an African Tribe*. Evanston:Northwestern University Press.

Schapera, I., 1994. *A Handbook of Tswana Law and Custom. 2*. Hamburg: LIT Verlag.

Searle, J., 1992, *The Rediscovery of the Mind*. Cambridge, Massachusetts: MIT.

Strathern, M., 1988, *The Gender of the Gift: Problems with Women and Problems with Society in Melanesia*. Berkeley: University of California Press.

Taylor, C., 1993, "To Follow a Rule", in C. Calhoun, E. LiPuma, and M. Postone (eds), *Bourdieu: Critical Perspective*. Cambridge: Polity Press.

Wittgenstein, L., 1968, *Philosophical Investigations*. Oxford: Basil Blackwell.

Wittgenstein, L., 1979, *On Certainty*. Oxford: Basil Blackwell.

Photo: Hamadou Bocoum, 19?

10. 'Prostitutes' or Modern Women? Negotiating Respectability in Northern Tanzania

Liv Haram

Introduction

The migration of women into East African towns has always generated particular moral discourses on women's life and particularly, their sexual behaviour. Even during colonial times, urbanisation was considered to affect Africans badly by separating them from rural life, family, clan or tribal authority. It also was thought to severely disrupt their social codes of behaviour, discipline, custom and maybe religion, which originally guided their thought and behaviour. Such stereotypical views of the good 'rural ways' and the bad 'urban ways' of life were also strongly reflected in the scholarly debates and theories of urbanisation during colonial times (cf. Ferguson 1999 for an in-depth critique). This was, and still is, particularly the case with 'single' women—also referred to as 'free', 'unattached' or 'husbandless'—who move to town. Studies of town women often focused on their sex role, and their more or less short-terms and transient relationship with men and they were often labelled 'prostitute'. The focus on townswomen as 'prostitutes'—an essentialisation of their sex role—is, of course, a crude generalisation of the female body and a neglect of these women's own life projects as well as of their economic role.

This chapter is based on long-term fieldwork among the ethnic Meru in Arusha town and the surrounding rural hinterland in northern Tanzania.[1] Drawing on the life histories of 50 women, this paper aims to describe some common traits in their life projects. Although their life-situations, such as their family background, educational level, access to scarce resources as well as their individual personalities, vary, their ways of life still share many common traits. The paper focuses on their relationship with their male partners and how they negotiate, albeit under considerable constraints, new identities as 'modern' women (*-ya kisasa*, literally meaning 'of now' in Swahili) and how they forge new futures for themselves. My particular concern is to discuss how they challenge normative expec-

1. Although most material for this chapter is from my fieldwork between 1991 and 1995, I have been in the field intermittently ever since. Grateful acknowledgement of funding is extended to the Tanzania-Norwegian AIDS project (1989–1972), the Norwegian Research Council (1992–1995), and the Nordic Africa Institute (2001–the present). Special gratitude goes to the field assistants Mrs. Elimbora Ayo Laiser, Mrs. Asinath Sumari and Mr. Jehova Roy Kaaya.

tations of 'respectability' *(heshima),* transgressing the norms of 'proper' daughters, and wives.[1]

First, however, I shall give some ethnography with a focus on how the gendering of space, in this particular local area, affects women's movement and their respectability.

The gendering of space and women's mobility

The Meru (100,000 to 150,000 people) live on the eastern and southern slopes of Mount Meru some ten km east of Arusha town. Understanding processes of urbanisation and peoples' spatial mobility as well as their economic adaptation to modern changes, the close proximity between the Meru land and Arusha town must be understood as a symbiotic relationship rather than a distinct rural–urban adaptation. Although most people are smallholders, cultivating coffee, maize, beans, bananas and vegetables, as well as keeping some livestock, an ever-larger number of households also draw home income from activities outside their home area. In addition to male labour out-migration, trade, transport and tourism are the most common income generating activities. Thus, dual or rather multiple household-economies have increasingly become a main characteristic of Meru households.

Whereas Meru men have been involved in urban migration for decades, women are now gradually taking part in a wide variety of market-oriented activities and are participating in different income generating activities from outside the mountain farming system.[2] This is particularly the case among young and as yet unmarried women and among women, who for various reasons have remained unmarried.

This gender difference is, in part, a result of socio-economic changes, such as integration into the modern market economy, transformation of the agricultural sector, and overpopulation with a resulting land shortage. But it is also closely associated with the moral principles inscribed in the local conception of space, which tends to curb women's spatial mobility compared to men. Although Arusha town is close to the homesteads on the mountain and many travel to and fro on a daily basis, the perceived gulf separating the socio-cultural construction of the two areas is considerable—the simple and morally esteemed life of the (rural) Meru versus the immoral and corrupting life of townspeople and town women in particular.

It is also obvious that the (Lutheran) Church, which has had a strong stand ever since the (German) missionaries arrived in northern Tanzania more than a hundred years ago, has had a crucial role in forming gender roles and the notion of a 'proper woman'. Claire Mercer, writing on the neighbouring Chagga women

---

1. All local terms are in Swahili, the national language in Tanzania.
2. As in much of East Africa, the migrating Meru men have been slow to take their wives along to the towns (Obbo 1981; Swantz 1985; Setel 1999).

and their participation in 'development' *(maendeleo)*, argues that the church has strongly promoted the idea that proper women should shun private business and rather participate in development through village-based women's groups where they are educated "about their roles as house-wives, mothers, and being useful community members" (Mercer 2002:112).

Thus, geographical mobility involves, particularly for women, much more than a shift in physical location. In terms of the gendered dimension of space, unmarried women in towns are conceived of as being socially and economically misplaced and are commonly seen as sexually loose. Studies from other parts of East Africa describe situations which very much resemble the Meru-Arusha area (cf., for instance Obbo 1981; White 1990; Ogden 1996; Wallman 1996). In her recent paper on town women in Kampala, in Uganda, Paula Jean Davis, argues: "The identity of 'town women' is constructed by means of a dual process of 'othering' engaging two sets of binary oppositions: married woman/prostitute and town/country" (2000:29). Such perceptions are also commonly voiced among people in the Arusha-Meru area. Whereas men can freely go to town and take on a modern town life, women, on the other hand, are seen as the upholders of traditional ways of life and should be protected from the negative influence of town life. In contrast to the rural wives, idealised as hard-working women and the caretakers of the family and children, townswomen, on the other hand, are stereotyped as 'bad', wasting time just gossiping, dancing, and drinking, and often using their bodies immorally to support themselves (Obbo 1981).[1]

As in much of Africa, an increasing number of Meru women are remaining unmarried (cf. Helle-Valle, this volume). Whereas some simply wish to postpone marriage, because they, for instance, wish to pursue further education, or initiate business activities, others have a child (out of wedlock), and thus they often fall outside the rather narrow standard prescription of a 'marriageable woman' or a 'proper wife'. However, whereas some fail to get married, others choose not to. For some the option 'not to marry' is part of a more general quest for freedom and a desire to pursue their individuality and to live a modern life in town. By avoiding marriage, women refuse to comply with gender ideology, which subordinates women to men, in their capacity as fathers, brothers and husbands.

Nevertheless, in their pursuit for self-fulfilment and economic independence, they become dependent on another type of attachment to men by tapping into informal loose 'conjugal' relationships which are often both fluid and transient. Although such a male–female union may resemble the formalised marriage, it is structurally very different. There is no 'bill of rights' (Giddens 1992) sanctioned by parents and kin to rely on, only the commitment of the partners. Yet, trust of-

---

1. Another view, cast in the urban-rural dichotomy, is, for instance, the distinction between 'work' *(kazi)*, on the one hand, and 'business' *(biashara)*, on the other. Whereas *kazi* is perceived as hard, physical work, such as farming, and thus something that rural people engage in, *biashara*, on the other hand, is not proper work. Accordingly, those who do *kazi*, the logic goes, get tired and thus cannot be involved in promiscuous sexual activities. Townspeople, on the other hand, who merely do *biashara*, do not get physically tired and thus have the energy for promiscuous sexual behaviour.

fers no permanent support; it must be developed on the basis of intimacy between the two and trust between partners is a scarce resource.

To break away from the (rural) well-known way of life into the less known world of urban life is, of course, exciting but it is also very precarious for most of the women. It requires new types of knowledge, skills and experiences. Furthermore, in the presence of AIDS, women's spatial mobility and their respectability are at stake. As I have described elsewhere, the single and 'unattached' women are faced with yet another threat to their socio-economic and emotional well-being (Haram 1999, 2001).[1] Although much research shows that young women are much more likely to get infected compared to men their age, the stereotypical idea of the single, unattached town woman as sexually loose and thus to be blamed for the spread and infection of HIV/AIDS, is more or less uncritically reflected in HIV/AIDS research and AIDS campaigns.[2] Before I further explore these problems, I will present cases that amplify these issues.

The life of single mothers

Anna

When I became acquainted with Anna, some ten years ago, she was 29 years old and worked as a secretary in a private European coffee company in Arusha town. She was unmarried and the mother of a 10-year-old daughter who lived at her grandparents' in Meru.

When Anna was roughly 19 years old, she worked as an accountant at a tourist hotel in the north-western part of Tanzania and she developed a sexual relationship with her boss. He was unmarried and worked as a hotel manager. They did not marry, but, according to Anna, "we lived together as a married couple and we planned to have a child." Anna became pregnant, but soon after she gave birth, their relationship began to dissolve. "He had other women and some of them he even brought to our home!" Anna suffered emotionally and, disappointed, she decided to leave her 'husband' (i.e. *mume* or *mzee*, the latter term also means 'the old' and is used by both sexes to express deference and respect to males) and her job, and she went with her seven-month-old daughter to her parents in Meru. Strongly supported by her mother, she left her daughter in the care of her mother and went to Arusha town to look for a job. She soon got a well-paid job at a Eu-

---

1. The latest UNAIDS reported AIDS cases in Tanzania, for the age group between 20 and 24, show that whereas the infection rate for men is 7.7 per cent, the rate for women is 17.9 per cent. The AIDS prevalence is also much higher among women in the age group between 15 and 19 compared to men—respectively 4.8 per cent for women and 1.5 per cent for men (UNAIDS/WHO 2002). Thus some of these young women have most likely been infected in their teens. These statistics also point to the fact that young women have sexual relationships with relatively older men—in the literature, commonly referred to as 'sugar-daddies' (Haram 1995; Silberschmidt and Rasch 2001).

2. Much research has focused on so-called risk groups, such as, prostitutes, bar-women—often neglecting the users/buyers of sex—and long-distance truck drivers. These groups had a high infection of HIV in the West, but in much of Africa they are increasingly irrelevant in the spread of HIV (Wallman 1996; Heald 2001).

ropean-run coffee company and the company also supplied her with a modern-standard house situated on the company estate.

Soon she developed a more or less steady love affair with a married man. *Babu*, or 'grandfather'—as she usually calls her lover—"is 60 years old and rich." Anna first met Babu through work:

> [H]e offered me beer, and soon we became lovers. Usually he comes to visit me late in the evening. If he provides me with money, I buy beer and food and prepare a nice meal for him. He usually gets very drunk. At times he is even drunk when he comes to visit me. After the meal, he goes to my bedroom and calls for me. Whether I feel like it or not, we make love and soon he is snoring.

Listening to Anna's story about Babu, it is not difficult to understand that her feelings towards her lover are very ambivalent. Besides being unsatisfied with him as a sexual partner, there is another quality in their relationship that Anna strongly misses: "[A]t times when he is not so drunk, he can satisfy me sexually, but he does not give me a happy heart. He is not the right one. I pray to God that He will send me a husband—the right one". Referring to her friend, Elimbora, who joined us in our conversation that day, she added, "I wish I had a 'husband' like hers!" She asked me: "Have you seen him? He is tall and handsome and he is a 'gentle person' [*mpole*]!" The woman who has joined us is herself a townswoman from Meru. For several years she has been an informal 'second wife' (referred to as a *mke mdogo*, literally 'small wife') to a married Meru and for the last three years they have been living together in Arusha town.

Like most single women, Anna is constantly searching for 'Mr. Right'. Although she does not believe in finding a faithful and devoted husband, she is constantly looking for a better option. "The man of my choice", she explains, "should be tall and handsome, young and unmarried. Like myself, he should be well employed and have more or less the same salary as myself". Anna is very conscious of her privileged economic position as well as her freedom compared to most women. "Because I have money I am free to do what I want to. I am free to go out with (male) friends. I can even invite them for a beer and if the man is not of my choice, I am still free to go home—on my own."

To my question why she keeps on seeing Babu, she gives me a clear-cut answer: "If not, I would not get any money from him. I need his money!" Perhaps Anna noticed my surprise upon her frank answer, and somewhat uneasy, she tells me about the high cost of living. She also informs me in detail about the house which she, for the past four or five years, has been struggling to build. Anna's relatively high salary puts her in a favourable economic situation compared to most, but to build a modern brick building is both a time-consuming and costly affair and after five years Anna has just about reached the roofing.

Anna returns to her relationship with Babu and explains why she always accepts him even when he is drunk, "I will take his money. Sometimes 5,000 [Tzs] and at times 10,000.[1] He is usually so drunk that he doesn't manage to keep a record of the money he spends." Then, referring to what she has just told me about Babu's money, she asks me: "Does that make me a thief?" And as if she wishes to clear herself, she continues, "You know, sometimes his breath is so intolerable that I have to hold my hands before my nose—while making love! Besides it is mainly I who satisfy him. So it is my right, isn't it? Life is hard!" Obviously, both parties benefit.

When I returned to the study area in 1999, Anna had left her job at the coffee estate in Arusha town. Actually, just before I left in 1995, she told me about her new plans and her wish to initiate her own business activities and was seriously considering taking up the gem-stone business in the southern parts of Tanzania. A close friend of hers informed me that Anna had finally managed to complete her house. Before she left Arusha, she had rented it out. She had also bought a big estate—a bar and restaurant with an attached guesthouse.

Nora

When I first met Nora, in 1991, she was a 29 years old single mother living at her mother's place in Meru together with her two children—from different fathers. Ever since Nora, at the age of 14, gave birth to her first born child out of wedlock, she has supported herself and her children through various forms of petty trading.

Like most unmarried women who give birth at home, Nora was strongly urged to fend for her child herself. She recalls how difficult it was: "My daughter was hardly four months old when my father forced me to 'try my luck' in business. Who else should care for my child and me? If I were to rely on my father, I would still be wearing the same dress!" Like a few other young and unmarried women in Meru at that time, Nora purchased goods in Kenya or more commonly at Namanga, a fast expanding town at the border between Tanzania and Kenya, and returned to Arusha where she sold her goods for a good profit. During the late 1970s and early 1980s the most common goods, such as soap, butter, flour, sugar, and factory textile products such as *kanga* and *kitenge*, for women's clothing, were hardly available in Tanzania. Since most people were in need of such commodities it was easy to make a profit, but since this business was illegal it also had a high risk. Thus, Nora has several times returned home empty-handed after the police confiscated the goods she had purchased illegally.

Later, when the border reopened, in 1985, Nora began to trade in sugar, another scarce commodity, by buying it directly from the sugar-factory at Moshi. Here Nora met a man, a young and unmarried Pare [i.e. an ethnic group originally from the eastern part of Kilimanjaro region]. "We planned to have a child together and soon I conceived." The man wished to marry her, but when Nora discussed it with her mother, the mother gave her a clear-cut answer: "If you leave me alone, you will be called home very soon [i.e. to bury me]."[1]

---

1. The standard exchange rates for 1US$ in 1991 and 1994, were Tzs 246 and 385, respectively. In 2002 the standard exchange rate for 1US$ had increased to Tzs 962.

Although Nora maintained the relationship with her son's father, she had additional short-term affairs at the same time. Recalling those days, she explains:

I used to be a malaya *[a sexually promiscuous woman, sometimes used synonymously with 'prostitute'] and I 'moved around a lot' [meaning that she had 'many lovers']. Before AIDS, life was not so complicated. If you quarrelled with your boyfriend, you just left him for another. These days, however, it is difficult because of AIDS and other sexually transmitted diseases, and I was therefore forced to change my life. You see, in 1988 I, along with some other unmarried mothers in the neighbouring village, was accused of having AIDS. The rumour said that we were* malaya *with AIDS. My boyfriend at that time insisted that I should defend my reputation. Along with the two other women I brought the case to [the local] court and we got some compensation.*

The person spreading the rumour was fined a total of Tzs 25,000, which was distributed among Nora's clan elders. The offender also had to slaughter a sheep 'to ask forgiveness'. Although Nora won her case, and thus regained some respect, the rumour still circulated. She had lost weight and people questioned her health condition; some remained convinced that she was infected with AIDS.

Because of the AIDS incident and the rumours about her, plus the fact that Nora considered herself too old to have sporadic and multiple love affairs, she decided to take on another life. Towards the end of 1989, she had a relationship with Mal who worked in Arusha town as an accountant when they first met. When he and Nora met he was married, but later he divorced his wife. Due to a poor salary, Mal quit his job and like many others in this area he initiated, more or less successfully, small income generating activities, including a poultry project, mining and trade in gem-stones. Mal openly told Nora that he had a wife who now lived in Dar with their five children. He did not, however, tell Nora that he was involved with another (informal) 'wife'—living some seven kilometres from Nora's home—and that they had two children together.

As mentioned above, Nora and her children were living at her mother's place. For Nora, as for most unmarried (Meru) women, to live at their parents' is rarely a good solution. Once the parents die, brothers will inherit the land and often force out their unmarried sisters. For single mothers, like Nora, this means very few opportunities for economic survival. Thus, fully aware of her situation, Nora managed, through Mal, to obtain one acre of land close to her natal home. She began growing vegetables for sale and also began to build a house. Thus, with additional support from her lover, Nora was now in a position to plan a life economically independent of her brothers and their wives. Nora was fully aware that this represented a unique opportunity for her and her children. Through her relationship with Mal she could strengthen her position both economically and socially and, more critically, she could remain with her children as well as care for her old mother. There was, however, one big problem with Nora's plan. Mal

---

1. In fact, Nora's mother is cursing her daughter, or, as Nora explains it: "Without my daily care, my mother fears that she may die and thus, she threatens me."

wanted a child, and although Nora had tried to conceive during their three-year-relationship, Nora had not yet conceived.[1] Mal therefore suspected her of not wanting his child, and Nora feared that their relationship would fizzle out and that Mal would take back the land he had bought for her. During this time, however, she got pregnant twice and since she miscarried, she strongly suspected her jealous sisters-in-law to be the cause. "They don't want me—a *malaya*—to have land, house and even a caring 'husband'!"

Nora and Mal started meeting more regularly; she became pregnant and gave birth to a baby girl. Nora continued with her business activities until she gave birth. When the child was five months old, Nora asked Mal for financial support to initiate a gem business—which soon proved a profitable enterprise. A few months later Mal joined her and he also temporarily moved into Nora's place.

Roughly two years later, Nora's mother died and while Nora was pregnant with Mal's second child, she finished her house and moved to her one-acre farm (*shamba*) together with her three children. Mal, however, was still coming and going. Soon after Nora gave birth to her fourth born, she was informed by her relatives about Mal's love affair. She now gave him an ultimatum: either he would stick to her and they would jointly raise their children, or, he could leave them and she would remain with their children. Nora told him straight forward that he had to make a choice between her and the other woman, with whom he also had two children. Besides reminding him about the danger of AIDS, she also told him that the land, the house, and the children, including his, belonged to her, to her alone. If he wanted to remain he had to contribute to the household, if not he was free to go. Obviously, Nora was neither willing to accept him having another love affair, nor to economically support his two children born in that union. According to Nora, Mal has not slept outside since then.

When I last visited Nora, in April 2002, she and Mal were still living together. Nora's first born, Eli, is now 24 years old and is attending a school for hotel management. Her 17-year-old son is, as most young men in this area, looking for a job and is meanwhile growing vegetables for sale. Mal has also changed job, but for some time now he has been doing leatherwork. Helped by Nora and Nora's first-born son, he buys leather locally and prepares it before he makes belts, bags and sandals for sale. After years of practice, it is slowly turning into a profitable business. Mal's and Nora's two daughters have turned seven and five. Like Mal, Nora has changed business activities several times, but for the last four years she has been building up her own business, partly helped by a male cousin, and she is now selling clothes and various commodities to tourists visiting Arusha town.

---

1. Although Nora had had several partners some time back, she had never had any sexually transmitted diseases (STDs). Maybe she had used the pill for too long, she worried. She resorted to all kinds of treatment alternatives including a gynaecology examination at the regional hospital and a handful of local healers. Nora was also treating herself with local medical herbs—knowledge she inherited from her father.

Rachael

Rachael and Nora had known each other since the time when they both had been involved in petty-trade, commuting between Arusha town and the Kenyan border in the late 1970s and early 1980s. When Nora introduced me to Rachael in 1991, Rachael was 34 years of age, and had become a relatively well-established shop owner. Her shop was close to the market at Tengeru, a rapidly growing small-town about seven km east of Arusha town and situated along the Arusha-Moshi main road. She had given birth to nine children, with four different men, but two died in early infancy. While Rachael lived in the poorly equipped backroom of her shop, all her children stayed with Rachael's (paternal) grandmother, less than two kilometres from Tengeru.

Unlike Nora, Rachael had the opportunity to pursue her education, but according to her she was not interested. Instead, Rachael ran off from home for the town, because "I did not want to live like my mother. My father has ruined her life." Hence, while Rachael was still doing her second year in secondary school, she escaped to Dar-es-Salaam and when she later that year became pregnant with a Pare man, they 'married' (i.e. cohabited). Hardly two years later, she left her 'husband' because she felt restricted by him, and along with her child she returned to her parents. For a short period of time she was employed as an office assistant at Tengeru, but owing to a very meagre salary, she decided to move to Arusha town and to earn a living by brewing and selling beer. She left her child in her grandmother's care.

Recalling her life at the time, she says:

I lived with many men, but they only messed up my life and gave me problems. At the time I was young and stupid and I therefore accepted men [i.e. sexually] too easily. I met men in bars or along the road; they approached me and I accepted them. That is why I have given birth to so many children. I did not think of my future. I would join a truck-driver or any man that came around. I travelled with my lovers to different places, such as Dar-es-Salaam and Bukoba [a town in the north-western part of Tanzania]. You know, I used to be a ma-laya, *but my* mradi *['project' or 'business'] did not run with profit.[1] Often I did not even bother to ask my various lovers for personal help or money. Therefore, I never prospered. Whenever I got some money I would usually give it to my grandmother who took care of my children.*

During my first research period, from 1991 until 1995, Rachael did not have a steady lover or someone she referred to as a 'husband'. Whenever this topic was raised, she referred to her past experience and strongly argued, "I know men's behaviour. They will only add problems to my otherwise difficult life." Just before I left the field in 1994, however, she resumed a relationship with one of her previ-

---

1.   The Swahili term *mradi* commonly refers to a means of supplementing income. Men and women are commonly engaged in one or more such 'projects'. As illustrated by Rachael, women also commonly refer to a man who supports them economically like any other income generating activity.

ous lovers and the father of her eight year old son. She was very excited about the reunion, and she proudly showed me a picture of her previous lover portraying him together with his (legal) wife and their five children. Soon Rachael got increasingly involved with her previous lover and she began to refer to him as her 'husband', and proudly she told me about her plans: "My 'husband' has asked me to look for a plot of land and has promised to help me to erect a house." Ever since Rachael settled at Tengeru, she has been planning to build a house, but she has been unable to purchase a plot of land at a reasonable price. She explained: "You see, my 'husband' is wealthy, he has cars, guesthouses, and he owns farming-land." Rachael's 'husband' was also a driver for one of the tour-companies situated in Tengeru. After his frequent trips to the Kenyan border, where he collected tourists travelling to Tanzania via Kenya, he brought crates of Kenya beer to Rachael's shop.

When I returned to visit Rachael in 1995, she had managed to build a 'modern' brick house and she had finally become a bar owner. Annexed to her house, she had built a bar. She was still involved with the same lover and was regularly visited by him, but, as she argued, "I do not want to live with him. Now I am old [34 years old] and I have learnt my lesson. I know men and I do not want to lose my freedom!"

When I visited Rachael in 1999, I found her busy and hardworking as usual, pursuing goods for her shop and keeping her customers company in the bar. She was still commuting to Namanga, buying Kenyan goods and commodities, but she had also extended her business activities to include more luxurious commodities which she purchased from Zanzibar. However, Rachael's 'husband' or long-term lover had died the year before. He actually died at Rachael's house. He took Rachael by surprise when another lover visited her. During the fight that consequently evolved between the two men, Rachael's 'husband' died of a heart-attack.

Women and men: Different dreams and expectations

Based on the life histories of 50 women, and illustrated in the above cases, most women attach themselves to multiple lovers or temporary partners of various types and durations, but frequently they are transient. While they are still young, most women, more or less deliberately, get involved in temporary alliances as a way to test a potential partner and conjugality. Once their expectations fail, they can now more easily end the union compared to a formalised marriage. Whereas some women such as Rachael turn to multiple and occasional lovers with no long-term plans, it is also obvious that many women hold unrealistic ideals of marriage. Women like Anna, for instance, are searching for a young, handsome and faithful partner who will respect them.

Anna often complains about the lack of sexual satisfaction in her relationship with Babu and temporarily turns to younger lovers not only for sexual pleasure, but also in pursuit of her own dream of a more intimate relationship based on equality and compatibility. "Otherwise, he will not respect me." And she adds,

"He must be faithful. We should have a nice house with a garden and, if everything works out, I would have another child." Although Anna often talks about meeting the right man, to marry and even to have another child, she has not yet met anyone who, as she puts it, "satisfies my needs". On the contrary, Anna has frequently experienced that such young and handsome men soon turn out to be the wrong choice. "Once, for instance, I tried to establish a relationship with a young and unmarried man, but very soon we quarrelled over money. He very much resented that I spend money on my child and my mother. He did not only interfere with my spending of money, but he even wanted to control it! I therefore decided to leave him. Perhaps I am too selective in my choice of men."

Anna, and many with her, share the same dreams and expectations about their male partners as described by Carmel Dinan in her study of unmarried women in Accra: "Men should be egalitarian, intimate, [and have a] companionable nature, involving trust, affection and shared intimacies" (1983:350). Although some women, like Rachael, are very sceptical about marriage while they are still young and marriageable and typically refer to their mother's miserable marriage, most become sceptical through their own experience with men.

In spite of 'modern' and romantic ideas of partnership and intimacy, most women soon realise that such notions are unrealistic and they often choose men with other qualities, namely the married, well-settled and generous men, whenever such possibilities are available. Men, for their part, are for various reasons willing to take on the extra economic burden to maintain such relationships. Obviously, elderly men are sexually attracted to young women. For some men, such love affairs may also be a means to advance socially and in their careers, since the number of girlfriends, temporary lovers or one or more 'small wives' are signs of a man's wealth and prestige. In the literature such men of means are commonly referred to as 'sugar daddies'. Locally they are referred to, for instance, as *buzi* (a 'billy goat'), *mwingi* (literally 'a man of many', that is, lovers), *mshefa* (a colloquial term which no one was able to translate, but which might derive from the French word 'chauffeur') a 'driver', or given the nickname 'tycoon'. The terms refer to a man's promiscuity, virility and thus his masculinity. Since it is commonly recognised that the only means to get access to a woman's sexuality is to give her some form of compensation, a man's lovers thereby become an attestation of his virility or wealth. Thus men with several partners are given prestigious names stressing their virility and strength, and above all, their wealth. Whereas women search for intimacy, faithfulness and equality, men rarely express such ideas. Women have always had a 'healthy' mistrust in their husband's or partner's outside love affairs. With the increasing emancipation of women, this 'healthy' mistrust is also becoming more common among men—a trend accompanied by a rising antagonism between the genders (Bujra 2000; Silberschmidt 1999).

"Love comes with money"

Disillusioned in their search for an egalitarian and faithful husband, women rather opt for a generous man who is willing to support them. Although some women stick to their lovers, even in times when they have less to offer, most women are likely to terminate such affairs when their temporary lovers or more stable partners suffer financial setbacks. Such a money-oriented characteristic of male–female relations is widely reported from much of Africa. In her study of single women in Kpelle society, Bledsoe notes, "Women compete for rich lovers, and usually drop men who cannot afford gifts in favour of those who can" (1980:160). As illustrated in the case of Anna, if Babu does not give Anna sufficient economic support willingly, she 'steals' and considers it even her right to do so. In fact, ideas of personal love are seldom expressed. This is not to say that love and passion between the partners does not exist. However, when women speak of love and respect in a love affair, it is closely linked to money, or as they generally put it, "Love comes with money", and commonly add, "That is the power of money" *(hii ni ngu-vu ya pesa)*. Single Meru women frequently attach themselves to a well-established man simply because he is the best *mfadhili* (literally 'donor') or the best 'project' *(mradi)*, terms commonly used to refer to generous lovers. It must be noted that such economic motives in male-female sexual relationships are intermingled with social emotional bonds. Such a notion of love and affection which is closely associated with money is in part based on the notion of the providing male but also in part on the transactional character of female sexuality. The fact that women can use their sexuality in bargaining is a well-recognised feature in male–female sexual relationships among the Meru (Haram 1995, 2001). Female sexuality is not something that should be given free of charge; men have to earn it.

Obviously, women draw on their sexuality not only for personal sexual satisfaction but, more importantly, for economic reasons. Thus, women use men to link into social networks using them as 'patrons', for example to find employment, to cover for illegal business activities, to advance their economic careers, to purchase a plot of land, to erect a house or they may use them simply as cash-paying boyfriends. Needless to say, in a society where most resources are owned and even monopolised by men, they exercise considerable power. For many women the only means to get access to such resources which they need for living (house, plot, arable land or a job) and to cover for illegal business activities is to build relations with men. The best 'projects' for these women are those married and relatively wealthy men since they can provide more than the young and poor who are still saving money to marry a woman in keeping with the notions of a 'proper woman'.

'Any man's woman' and the problem of female respectability

For a woman to live on her own without male protection and control is not only an alien idea to most people in the study area, but it even rebels against prime gender notions. Since she lacks male protection, the cultural logic goes, she becomes easy prey of men, who notoriously see an unmarried woman and single mother to be, as they say, 'any man's woman' and thus sexually available. As noted by Håkansson, the situation of single Gusii women tallies with that of my findings, "Behind their backs, single women are called harlots *(omotayayi)* or women who move from place to place *(omotangatangi)*, epithets which are not removed until such women are either properly married or permanently cohabiting with a man" (1988:185). Like the single Gusii women, Meru women also seek more stable relationships with men as a means to protect their respectability.

The most favourable relationship for a single mother is a 'small house' arrangement *(nyumba ndogo)* with a visiting 'husband', in which the woman , usually referred to as 'small wife *(mke mdogo)* can maintain some degree of social independence and avoid the severe control often exercised by a true husband. A 'small wife' usually receives a flat, a plot of land to build on or even a house, sometimes furnished, depending on the wealth of her partner. Such an arrangement also seems, at least to a certain degree, to cater for a woman's respectability. Based on a historical study from Rhodesia, now Zimbabwe, discussing informal conjugal unions *(mapoto marriage)*, Diana Jeater also argues that such alliances allow a woman "to retain her independence, while gaining male protection" (1993:179). It seems that female respectability can only be fully obtained through male protection.

Men, for their part, notoriously argue that a single woman has a particular *tabia* or 'nature'/'behaviour' which is beyond male control and therefore she is neither capable nor willing to stay with a husband (Haram 1995,1999).[1] Most women reject the authoritarian role adopted by most men, but at the same time, they commonly act in accordance with such accepted gender roles and frequently use them as a means to get access to strategic resources held by men. Such female compliance is, for instance, illustrated in the case of Anna, who often feels humiliated by Babu, when he expects that she will be willing to satisfy him sexually, even when he is drunk. Still, she does not speak up, but takes on the roles of female submission and virtue whenever he wants her sexually. Women are fully aware of the importance of taking on such a docile role or as Anna puts it herself, "Otherwise I will not get his money!" Women also camouflage their intelligence and ambition by playing along with expected female behaviour—being extremely docile or taking on a 'soft tongue' *(sauti laini)* when beguiling men. To have a 'soft tongue' or to act out such feminine qualities as shyness expresses humbleness and confirms the male-constructed gender notions that females should be inferior to men.

---

1. Assessing the person and the (Meru) notion of personhood, the concept of *tabia* is central. It is also gender specific, but suffice it here to say that it strongly impinges on the notion of a moral person as well as his or her sexual behaviour.

Childbearing in transient sexual unions and the importance of motherhood

It is reported from many parts of Africa that women may manipulate their child's identity, i.e. fatherhood, to improve their social and economic positions when such options are available to them (cf. for instance, Bledsoe and Pison 1994).

In her study of single mothers among Yoruba-speaking groups of Western Nigeria, Jane Guyer developed the conceptual framework of *polyandrous mother-hood*, which captures the particular life situation of the unmarried mothers in a more fruitful way than does the concept of 'prostitute' which reduces them to im-moral sexual beings: 'Polyandrous motherhood' is a liaison consisting of women "cultivating co-parental ties with more than one father of their children" (1994:230). Such multiple-partner unions, where women bear children to several men, Guyer argues, "set the primacy of parenthood over marriage" (1994:231). Childbearing, she argues, creates a longer and more "sustainable union" com-pared to marriage because the child links the mother and the father into life-long networks. Actually, she argues that "children are the main means of giving some solidity to old relationships without foreclosing new ones" (1994:237). According to Guyer, polyandrous motherhood is particularly beneficial for women:

> [A]lthough a woman cannot have concurrent husbands she can have concurrent recognized fa-thers to her children, men whose lineal identities are different from each other and whose chil-dren therefore tap into different kinship networks. In terms of resource access and daily needs for herself and her children a woman may be managing several men at once (Guyer 1994:250; cf. also Bledsoe and Pison 1994).

Guyer's description from Nigeria tallies with the life of most single mothers in my study. Childbearing is valued among both men and women. Rachael, for instance, had nine children (two of them died in infancy) by various men. Although she had children because she wanted to, she also gave birth to many children to comply with the wishes of her various partners. Similarly, Nora considered her two chil-dren to be sufficient, but she made great efforts to become pregnant when Mal, her current partner, wanted another child. Before Nora became pregnant, her re-lationship with Mal was about to fizzle out, but when she later gave birth, Mal showed more responsibility. Thus, as noted by Guyer, the child is "stabilizing an otherwise fleeting relationship"(1994:237). But a common child also bolsters the mother's right to ask for economic support from the child's father. In line with Guyer's argument, we have also seen that even though a sexual relationship may gradually fizzle out, a common child often cements the relationship between par-ents. Sometimes the father, who has neglected the child for years, may re-establish the relationship with the child's mother. Thus a child may create a lasting relation-ship between the parents.

Yet, for a woman to have children by many men or, as Guyer says, "concur-rent recognised fathers to her children", is not without difficulties. As often ar-gued by the single mothers themselves, to bear children with different fathers, may backfire. To raise and educate children is expensive and some fathers may therefore lose interest or, in times of economic hardship, they simply cannot afford to support them. Consequently, 'polyandrous mothers', like Nora and Rachael, often have to turn to other men for economic assistance and are faced with a demand for more children to maintain a new relationship. There is also another risky twist involved in 'polyandrous motherhood', which is often voiced by the women themselves. Although many are offered help and support by their children's fathers, at least for some periods of time, to use the child to claim more long-term assets, to paraphrase Guyer (1994:237), may be risky. For a woman to receive economic assistance from previous lovers and fathers may, in fact, endanger her role as a custodial mother, i.e. her right to remain with her children. Nora's experience, mothering children by three different men, speaks for most: "If he [the child's father] offers me help, I will usually accept it, but I will never ask him for any support." Thus, there is a delicate balance to be maintained by single mothers between their need for economic assistance and their wishes to keep the children and be a good and caring mother. As further asserted by the same woman, "Once I ask for help, he may later claim the child."

Thus, some single mothers lose the custody of their children. Whereas some turn to their natal family in times of crisis and thus secure their role as good mothers, some do not have such options. Their respectability is further marginalized when they are deprived of motherhood. Since the respectability of a single woman very much hinges on her performance as a mother, once she is deprived of motherhood, she is further marginalized as a loose woman. Thus, 'polyandrous motherhood' is not a real option for the poorest or for those who cannot turn to their natal families in times of crisis.

It should also be noted that 'polyandrous motherhood' is not always planned. Whereas some have an unwanted pregnancy, others struggle to become pregnant. The way single mothers manage their reproductive capacity also depends on the woman's age. Whereas younger women more often become pregnant without any plans and may have children by any men, older women are frequently more conscious about how they allocate their fertility. These older women may strive to fulfil their own desire for children or to obtain respected motherhood, but they may also bear children to concede to their lovers' wishes.

Although the women in my sample are still of reproductive age and are likely to have more children, the fertility rate among 'polyandrous mothers' is lower compared with married women. Among the upper classes in Lagos, Wambui Wa Karanja found that fertility patterns among 'outside wives' differ from those who are properly married. She argues, "outside wives, because of the fundamental instability of most outside unions, seek to keep their options open to establish new unions, if necessary, by having just enough—but not too many—children within their current unions" (Karanja 1994:194). In other words, in case the current relationship fails, the woman must restrict her fertility for future options.

Negotiating male authority and female freedom

Most single women who are involved in a more steady relationship, and particularly with a cohabiting partner, are gradually faced with the ultimate dilemma between, on the one hand, social respectability and economic security provided by the partner and, on the other hand, the increasing control exercised by a steady and more present partner which will consequently reduce their autonomy and freedom to pursue their own economic careers. Rachael, who for years has been running her own shop, highlights the problem faced by most single mothers who want to maintain economic independence: "You know, a businesswoman does not want to marry [meaning both a formal marriage and a cohabiting partnership] because a husband controls his wife's freedom, her movements and her money!" When Rachael continues her argument, she speaks for most single women: "A husband will exercise control and consequently he will limit my freedom. I do not want to marry since a husband keeps his wife under his control and rules [*Sitaki kuolewa kwa sababu wanaume wanawaweka wanawake wake chini la masharti yao*]. I do not want to be in a situation whereby I have to ask my 'husband' for money!" Hence, to maintain a certain level of independence, Rachael has to maintain her business.

Men as lovers or as temporary partners are often crucial in helping women to pursue their economic activities, but once the relationship becomes more permanent and particularly, if the two share a household, men wish to curb and control the women's economic activities. Thus to maintain a certain degree of independence, a woman is faced with a dilemma: she has to balance between, on the one hand, the authoritarian role of a 'husband' which provides for her respectability and, on the other, her desired autonomy which she needs to fulfil her obligations towards her children. Therefore, it seems to me that most women can only solve or rather reduce the bad influence of an oppressive and authoritarian 'husband' by shuttling in and out of such loose and temporary unions with men, frequently changing partners and mothering children by two or more men.

Conclusion: Modern women

As pointed out in the introduction, often research on single women, and particularly studies of single townswomen, has focused on how they utilise their sexuality for material gain and, more or less unproblematically, they have been labelled 'prostitutes'.

In this paper, I have tried to draw a more composite picture of single mothers, showing that these women are trying to survive socially and emotionally as well as to develop strategies to support themselves and their children. I have explored why some women, more or less consciously, choose more short-term unions with men and, adding to this, why they frequently are reluctant to convert such relationships with men into a formalised marital union. Although both women and men may attach themselves to each other temporarily for sexual pleasure, the production of children in such unions is crucial. Men and women alike value children, but frequently men value children for other reasons than women. Often it is the men who desire children and the women usually comply. Men's desire for children does not, however, necessarily mean that they will meet the responsibility to raise a child born in such unions. Rather, men consider a woman's willingness to have their child to be proof of her love and commitment, as well as of her subordination to male control and authority. In line with Guyer's thesis on *polyandrous motherhood*, I have shown that such modes of 'serial monogamy' or multiple and concurrent partnership, combined with childbearing, are also commonly practised among single Meru mothers. I have, however, argued that a 'polyandrous mother' has to be careful when she draws upon support from her previous lovers and fathers of her children. For a woman to remain with her children, she must restrict such economic, social and emotional support lest she be deprived of motherhood and, ultimately, of respectability.

Thus women must portion out their fertility and attach themselves to other men in a repertoire of new sexual and reproductive unions. They employ their sexuality and childbearing capacity to develop new forms of kinship and marriage systems. The notion that female sexuality can be bartered for economic gain, gives women the right to negotiate with men to secure their own economic and social security. Female sexuality and reproductive power is not free of charge; men have to earn it.

These forms of 'conjugal' union, are, however, transient and short-term and do not involve authorised ties. In sharp contrast to the formalised conjugal union, which involves negotiation between the couple's parents and is in keeping with their interests, the informal and temporary sexual relationship is negotiated, entered into, maintained and terminated by the two partners and is in accordance with their personal interests. The duration of such unions is therefore mainly based on the commitment of the partners. Yet, trust offers no permanent support; it must be developed on the basis of intimacy between the two. And trust between partners is a scarce commodity. Thus such male–female transient unions, including polyandrous motherhood, have no 'bill of rights', but rather a 'rolling contract' (Giddens 1992). They are not only open to negotiation, but actually require negotiation to be ongoing. A modern Meru woman who pursues her individual wants—sexually, emotionally and economically—has a high consumption of men.

An unmarried woman is faced with a dilemma: she has to balance between, on the one hand, submitting to a 'husband' to gain a certain amount of respectability; and, on the other, retaining her autonomy in order to fulfil her obligations to her children. Men as friends and lovers are 'patrons', assisting them economically and linking them to resource networks. At the same time, however, men also restrict their female partners' independence since increasing economic support entails more exclusive rights to a woman's sexuality. In the life of most Meru single mothers, the only means to get a certain share of both is simply to go in and out of temporary unions with men.

The fact that these women go to town in search of a better life and thus become exposed to different ways of life, not only indicates that they have 'broken out' of the customary pattern but also that they are future oriented. These women are commonly said to have 'intelligence' and 'consciousness' (*akili*). An experienced woman knows how to 'get around'—including how to manoeuvre male control. They acquire new strategies; they learn how to do things in the modern world and, albeit by taking a great risk, how to fend for themselves. This is the knowledge they bring back home with them, thus challenging the customary ways of life. According to most men and (married) women, however, women who have 'acquired experience' have become 'too clever'. Such 'wicked' women are commonly referred to as '*wajanja*' (*mjanja*, singular) a term which can be translated as 'a sly, smart and deceitful person'. They are seen as a threat, if not an outright danger, to male control and authority. They cannot be trusted and are apt to play tricks on men.

Moving on the margins of the socially and culturally acceptable, they are frequently stigmatised as sexually loose *malaya* and are commonly seen as 'wicked' women by others in society. First, they choose sexual partners and build serial and even concurrent sexual relationships with men. Secondly, they have children by men of their own preference. Thirdly, and more exceptional, once the partnership ceases, contrary to 'proper wives', they take their children with them.

Unmarried women and single mothers are becoming more numerous and even though they are frequently hampered in pursuing their ambitions, they are ploughing new paths to more or less successful alternative ways of female living. By transcending the roles and ways of life of their mothers, they are prime agents in negotiating and reworking gender roles and thereby they become role models for their younger sisters.

References

Bledsoe, Caroline H., 1980, *Women and Marriage in Kpelle Society*. Stanford: Stanford University Press.
Bledsoe, Caroline and Gilles Pison (eds), 1994, *Nuptiality in Sub-Saharan Africa. Contemporary Anthropological and Demographic Perspectives*. Oxford: Clarendon Press.
Davis, Paula Jean, 2000, "On the Sexuality of Town Women in Kampala", *Africa Today* 47(3–4): 28–62.
Bujra, J. M., 2000, "Risk and trust: Unsafe sex, gender and AIDS in Tanzania", in Caplan, P. (ed.), *Risk revisited*. London: Pluto Press, pp. 59–84.
Dinan, Carmel, 1983, "Sugar Daddies and Gold-Diggers: The White-Collar Single Women in Accra", in Oppong, Christine (ed.), *Female and Male in West Africa*. London: George Allen and Unwin, pp. 31–48.
Ferguson, James, 1999, *Expectations of Modernity. Myths and Meanings of Urban Life on the Zambian Copperbelt*. Berkeley, Los Angeles, London: University of California Press.
Giddens, Anthony, 1992, *The Transformation of Intimacy. Sexuality, Love and Eroticism in Modern Societies*. Cambridge: Polity Press.
Guyer, Jane I., 1994, "Lineal Identities and Lateral Networks: The Logic of Polyandrous Motherhood", in Bledsoe, Caroline and Gilles Pison (eds), *Nuptiality in Sub-Saharan Africa*. Contemporary Anthropological and Demographic Perspectives. Oxford: Clarendon Press.

Haram, Liv, 1995, "Negotiating Sexuality in Times of Economic Want: The Young and Modern Meru Women", Chapter 3, in Klepp, Knut Inge, Paul M. Biswalo and Aud Talle (eds), *Young People at Risk: Fighting AIDS in Northern Tanzania*. Scandinavian University Press.

Haram, Liv, 1999, "'Women out of Sight': Modern Women in Gendered Worlds. The Case of the Meru of Northern Tanzania". PhD thesis. Bergen: University of Bergen, Department of Social Anthropology.

Haram, Liv, 2001, "'In sexual life women are hunters': AIDS and women who drain men's body. The case of the Meru of northern Tanzania", *Society in Transition*. Journal of the South African Sociological Association 32 (1): 47–55.

Heald, Suzette, 2001, "It's Never as Easy as ABC: Understanding of AIDS in Botswana", *African Journal of AIDS Research* 1 (1): 1–11.

Håkansson, Thomas, 1988, *Bridewealth, Women and Land. Social Change among the Gusii of Kenya*. Uppsala Studies in Cultural Anthropology, 10.

Jeater, Diana, 1993, *Marriage, Perversion, and Power. The Construction of Moral Discourse in Southern Rhodesia 1894–1930*. Oxford: Clarendon Press.

Karanja, Wambui Wa, 1994, "The Phenomenon of 'Outside Wives': Some Reflections on Its Possible Influence on Fertility" (194–214), in Bledsoe, Caroline and Gilles Pison (eds), *Nuptiality in Sub-Saharan Africa. Contemporary Anthropological and Demographic Perspectives*. Oxford: Clarendon Press.

Mercer, Claire, 2002, "The Discourse of Maendeleo and the Politics of Women's Participation on Mount Kilimanjaro", *Development and Change* Vol. 33, 101-127.

Obbo, Christine, 1981 (1980), *African Women. Their Struggle for Economic Independence*. London: Zed Press.

Ogden, Jessica A., 1996, "'Producing' respect: The 'proper woman' in postcolonial Kampala" (pp.165–192), in Werbner R. and Terrence O. Ranger (eds.) *Postcolonial identities in Africa*. New Jersey: Zed Books.

Setel, Philip Wittman, 1999, *A Plague of Paradoxes: AIDS, Culture, and Demography in Northern Tanzania*. Chicago and London: The University of Chicago Press.

Silberschmitdt, Margrethe, 1999, *Women Forget That Men Are the Masters. Gender Antagonism and Socio-Economic Change in Kisii District, Kenya*. Uppsala: Nordiska Afrikainstitutet.

Silberschmidt, M. and Rasch, V., 2001, "Adolescent girls, illegal abortions and 'sugar-daddies' in Dar es Salaam: Vulnerable victims and active social agents", *Social Science & Medicine* 52 (12), 1815–26.

Swantz, Marja-Liisa, 1985, *Women in Development: A Creative Role Denied?* London: Hurst, and New York: St. Martin's Press.

UNAIDS/WHO, 2002, "Epidemiology Fact Sheets on HIV/AIDS and Sexually Transmitted Infections", p. 6. 2002 Update. United Republic of Tanzania.

Wallman, Sandra, 1996, *Kampala Women Getting By. Wellbeing in the Times of Aids*. London: James Currey.

White, Louise, 1990, *The Comforts of Home. Prostitution in Colonial Nairobi*. Chicago and London: The University of Chicago Press.

Photo: El Hadj Tidjan Shitou, 1977

11. Masculinities, Sexuality and Socio-Economic Change in Rural and Urban East Africa

Margrethe Silberschmidt

Introduction

The AIDS epidemic in Sub-Saharan Africa has thrust sexuality, sexual practices and sexual behaviour into the spotlight as a major public health issue. However, although sexual and reproductive health behaviour in Sub-Saharan Africa is attracting increasing attention there is an inadequate understanding of the structures and processes influencing sexuality and sexual behaviour in general and male sexuality and male sexual behaviour in particular. [1] Issues of sexuality have been considered too private and not a public matter to be discussed, and the fact that sexuality is vested with symbols with often opposite meanings for men and women has not been considered. Moreover, the complex and changing social and economic contexts and how they interact with sexual conducts, in particular those of men, have not been addressed by these efforts.

Research by this author in rural and urban East Africa suggests that HIV/AIDS prevention campaigns have missed the point by neglecting the above issues and concentrating their efforts on the promotion of ABC-efforts (Abstinence, Be faithful, Condom use), women's empowerment and women's ability to negotiate safe sex. The need for a much wider understanding of the dynamics of HIV/transmission, sexuality and sexual behaviour in a Sub-Saharan context has become increasingly crucial as a direct consequence of the escalating HIV/AIDS epidemic (UNAIDS 2001).

Sexuality is not a 'biological given', it is socially and culturally constructed and in a constant state of flux (Caplan 1991; Ortner and Whitehead 1989). Moreover,

---

1. Before the ICPD (International Conference on Population and Development) in Cairo, September 1994, men, their role as (responsible) partners and also their own sexual and reproductive health needs had not received much attention—in spite of men's prominent sexual and reproductive role. The final ICPD document (1994), however, clearly recognised the need to address and involve men, in order to improve women's reproductive health. With deteriorating sexual and reproductive health, particularly in Sub-Saharan Africa, with more women than men being HIV infected (often by their own husbands), male involvement, men as responsible partners, and not the least male sexuality and sexual behaviour have become increasingly unavoidable issues on the sexual and reproductive health agenda. This was clearly reflected in the Cairo + 5 meeting in The Hague in February 1999. The 'male issue' is gaining in importance. This has been clearly demonstrated in the document 'Men make a difference' (2000) presented by UNAIDS at the AIDS conference in Durban, SA (2000). Operational attempts, though, to reach men are very few, and have not yet been given high priority either by local governments, donor agencies or NGOs, or by researchers.

in order to understand sexuality and sexual behaviour in general and male sexual behaviour in particular, especially in an HIV/AIDS context, there is a need to focus not only on the incidence of particular attitudes and practices, but on the social and cultural context in which sexual activity is shaped and constituted (Gagnon and Parker 1995). Research attention should be directed not merely to the calculation of behavioural frequencies, but to the relations of power and social inequality within which behaviour takes place (ibid.). It should also be kept in mind that

> [m]en and women engage in sexual relations for an array of reasons that range from the pursuit of pleasure, desire for intimacy, expression of love, definition of self, procreation, domination, violence or any combination of the above, as well as others. How people relate sexually may be linked to self-esteem, self-respect, respect for others, hope, joy and pain. In different contexts, sex is viewed as a commodity, a right or a biological imperative; it is clearly not determined fully by rational decision-making (Carovano 1995:3–4).

Over the past three decades, it has been widely documented that socio-economic change and breakdown of traditional social institutions in Sub-Saharan Africa have left women in a disadvantaged and vulnerable situation with increasing burdens and responsibilities (Boserup 1980). In the development debate, though, and also in research, the situation of men and particularly the changes to which this situation has been subjected during the process of socio-economic development in the twentieth century has been seriously neglected—contrary to that of women. Hardly any attempts have been made to investigate and analyse in gendered terms the impact of socio-economic change on men's lives. Based on my research, this chapter pursues the following arguments: socio-economic change in rural and urban East Africa has increasingly disempowered men. This has resulted in men's lack of social value and self-esteem. With unemployment and men being incapable of fulfilling social roles and expectations, male identity and self-esteem have become increasingly linked to sexuality and sexual manifestations. Multi-partnered sexual relationships and sexually aggressive behaviour seem to have become essential to strengthen masculinity and self-esteem. Linked to this, this chapter shall address the following issue: To what extent are men in East Africa who are faced with marginalisation, lack of social value and disempowerment at all motivated for responsible sexual behaviour and HIV/AIDS prevention?

Thus, the aim of this chapter is twofold. First, to illuminate how socio-economic change has affected men's lives, masculinities and eventually men's sexual behaviour patterns. This requires an analysis of inherent meanings of masculinity (as opposed to femininity) in the East African context. However, as definitions of masculinity are also in flux and vary over time, there is a need not only to explore the current pattern of masculinity/ies, but also to look back over the period in which this pattern came into being. A second aim is to challenge conceptions based on gender stereotypes, neglecting the fact that male and female roles and relations have been submitted to profound changes during the socio-economic changes of the past century.

Research findings from Kisii and Dar es Salaam: Socio-economic change and changing gender roles and relations

As mentioned above, research—mainly based on qualitative interviewing with both men and women, case studies, life histories and focus group discussions— was carried out, first in rural and then in urban East Africa. The focus for the re- search was on changing gender roles and relations as well as sexual and reproduc- tive health and behaviour by men and women.

Research in Kisii was carried out at different periods from the mid-1980s to the mid-1990s. Research in urban Dar es Salaam took place during one year (1996–97). The initial field study (1984–86) in Kisii consisted of both survey data (723 women and 200 men of reproductive age) as well as qualitative data. The subsequent studies were based on qualitative data collection, life histories and fo- cus group discussions with a selection of men and women (Silberschmidt 1991, 1992, 1995, 1999). All interviewees belonged to the Gusii tribe, and were either Catholics or Seven Day Adventists. The vast majority had not completed primary education.

The qualitative data collection in urban Tanzania took place during a one year field study (1996–97) in three low income squatter areas of Dar es Salaam: Ma- bibo, Tandale and Vingunguti/Buguruni. In-depth interviews were carried out with 38 women and 53 men by means of structured, semi-structured, and open- ended interviews. In addition, and in order to discuss major issues that came up in the in-depth interviews, thirteen focus group discussions (each with 8–10 par- ticipants) were conducted with different groups of men (aged 16–65) and women (17–69). The interviewees had different religious and ethnic backgrounds—with a majority being Muslims. The majority had a primary education. 7 out of the 53 men had attended secondary school. Only one of the 38 women had attended sec- ondary school.

Findings from Kisii

Kisii is among the most productive cash and food crop regions in Kenya. In 1907 the population was estimated at 75,000. Since then the population has multiplied at least 20 times. HIV/AIDS infections are alarming with more women than men infected (UNAIDS Update 2002). Unemployment is a serious problem, because the land available is not enough to secure survival. Before colonial rule men were warriors, cattle herders and took active part in political decisions. Cattle repre- sented wealth and power, and constituted the major part of bride price. The more cattle a man had—the more wives he could marry, and the more land could be cultivated. Through marriage he controlled his wife's sexual and reproductive powers. Masculinity was closely linked to self-control and dignity.

The colonial power impacted significantly on the pre-colonial social and eco- nomic structure. Taxation was introduced, and men were recruited to construct railroads and urban centres. Many women were left for years to manage the farm.

235

After World War II, a shift towards production of industrial goods began. This created a demand for skilled and semi-skilled workers rather than for unskilled workers. Most Gusii migrants were unskilled and had to return home. In Kisii, though, men's activities had disappeared. No tribal wars to fight. No more cattle-camps because it was more profitable to use land for cash crops. Many returned to the urban areas—only to find that their labour was not needed. As a result, most workers returned again to Kisii.

In the 1940s and 50s the household became dependent on men's financial aid. Matching these changes men acquired a new social and ideological role—that of breadwinner. With the urban minimum wage only providing the barest essentials for a single man (White 1990) husbands' remittances were irregular or non-existent. The colonial power's introduction of migrant work initiated a shift from men's dominance and responsibility as head of household to a pattern of absent tax-paying men with responsibility towards the state rather than the household. The ideology of male breadwinner and household head survived, however.

Over the years new values were created—meshing with old ones. Men's difficulties in providing financial assistance to the household undermined their social roles and their social value. The disappearance of cattle camps had a negative effect on bride price payment. 'Unions' with no transfer of bride price were increasingly substituted for marriage. This made women's access to their means of production insecure. Moreover, women had to learn how to make ends meet—without any assistance from their husbands. And they did. Male control over women weakened.

Women have no illusions about men as providers. In my interviews in Kisii recurrent comments from the women were the following: "a woman is better off without a husband"; "if only he was dead"; "men are so delicate; they break so easily"; "our sons have nobody to take as a model". Men interviewed would immediately emphasise their status as head of household and their right to correct (= beat) an obstinate wife. However, typical comments by men (and also women) were that "men drink to drown their problems—and they are many", "men drink and are rude to women to forget that they cannot provide the family with blankets". Particularly striking was men's aggressive 'macho' behaviour, on the one hand, and on the other, men's complaints that "today women do not respect their husband"; "they humiliate the husband and tell home secrets to others". Some felt pursued and were afraid to get poisoned by food prepared by their wife (Silberschmidt 1999).

The intensification of their roles and responsibilities made women increasingly aware of their important position in the household. This nourished their sense of identity and their self-esteem. They complained about lack of male responsibility, lack of male assistance and the fact that having a husband was like "having an extra baby in the house". But when women complain they take a position of power (LeVine 1979). Thus, even though structurally subordinated, women have actively responded to the new situation. They have created new social roles for themselves. According to both men and women interviewed "more and more women have taken command of the home", and "harmony has gone out of the window". Thus over the past several decades, Kisii has been in an ongoing process of fundamental socio-economic transformation with escalating gender antagonism and domestic violence. Persistent rumours about men being poisoned by their wives circulate. Men's position as heads of household is challenged, and some women see men just as 'figureheads' of the household. However, land is still owned by men, and most men call themselves farmers (Silberschmidt 1999).

Findings from Dar es Salaam

In 1894, Dar es Salaam was a minor settlement with 10,000 inhabitants. By 1957 it had grown to 130,000 (Leslie 1963). Today, the population has grown to close to 2 million. In the 1950s men in the capital far outweighed women. Today there are only 0.9 men for every woman. About thirty per cent of the sexually active population is HIV positive (Tanzania Demographic and Health Survey 1996; UNAIDS Update 2002).

In 1978, 84 per cent of the men in Dar es Salaam had formal employment (Tanzania Population Census, 1982). In the 1980s large numbers of workers lost their jobs, and today only a small fraction are employed in the formal sector. Salaries, though, are far from enough to support a family. Thus, the informal sector has become overcrowded with myriads of market vendors—men and women. As in Kisii, the ideology of men as breadwinners is forcefully alive. Stereotyped notions shared by both genders are that "a man should be the head of his family"; "he should provide a house (and land), pay school fees and clothes for wife and children". Such a man has social value and respect. However, a majority of men suffer the same fate as those in Kisii: they cannot fulfil expectations and withdraw from household responsibilities. Even if many men use enormous amounts of energy and ingenuity to get an income, it is well known that it can only feed a family for a few days. Consequently, men cannot fulfil their breadwinning role, and men's status as head of household is seriously challenged. However, when asked about their 'status' in the household it was obvious to all 53 men interviewed that they were the 'born' heads of household. That was a 'God given' fact. Just like "women are like children and should be guided by men". "Men are the lions, and women are the sheep". Nevertheless, women accused men of being irresponsible husbands and fathers avoiding the claims of children.

As in Kisii, most men and women in my research areas also lived in more or less informal/passing unions. If a couple had lived together for two years they were registered as 'married'. A proper marriage, though, still requires the procurement of bride price. This was already a problem fifty years ago (Leslie 1963), when men at that time were also not able to pay the bride price. The implications are that women's security is at stake—and so is male control over women's sexual (and reproductive) powers. In Tandale—one of the study areas—'divorces' (changing registration) filed by women had become increasingly common. On the one hand, divorced women interviewed said that they felt much better off on their own even if they were then sole providers for their children. On the other, they also felt moral judgement and jealousy from other women. A few hopeful women would still maintain that it was better to have a husband 'in case of emergencies' (though they were perfectly aware that in such cases they could not count on 'husbands').

While women would often express self-limiting culturally accepted expectations of them as women, in practice, they would be very entrepreneurial agents struggling for survival. The majority who referred to themselves as 'housewives' were actively involved in the informal sector, baking and selling *mandazis* (small sweet buns), preparing 'lunches', selling second hand clothes etc. Both men and women interviewed agreed that women are much harder working and enduring than men. Therefore, when women enter the informal sector many are often able to earn more than their husbands. In 1993/94, contrary to expectations, female headed households in urban Tanzania constituted 18 per cent of the highest income households, and only 13 per cent of the poor households (World Bank 1995). The fact that women are becoming increasingly economically independent is a serious threat to men. "As soon as a husband starts declining economically, his wife will take advantage and go out to look for other men to satisfy her material needs", men would argue. Successful businesswomen in Dar es Salaam are even said to pay younger men for sex—a new situation and a new threat to men. Both men and women agreed that a man's honour, his reputation, his ego are severely affected if he cannot control his wife.

While most men, therefore, had a negative attitude towards women's activities most men and women interviewed agreed families cannot survive unless women contribute income. Most women would say that husband and wife should decide together on the use of 'household' money. In practice, though, what women had earned, they kept for themselves and they decided how to use it—not their husbands. Nevertheless, husbands would always be expected to provide rent, money for food and school fees even if this was honoured more in theory than in practice.

Male disempowerment and male sexual behaviour in Kisii and Dar es Salaam

Recurrent observations by men as well as women interviewed were that "a real man needs to demonstrate that he can handle more than one partner"—especially when a man needs to strengthen his self-esteem. According to men in Kisii "a man needs at least three wives: one to bear his children, one to work and one for pleasure". However, most men had not even been able to provide a bride price for their present 'wife'[1]. With one 'wife' only, a general observation by men was

---

1. In the 1970s, 33 per cent of the households in Kisii were still polygamous (Population and Development in Kenya 1980). Survey findings in 1986 by this author indicated that less than 10 per cent lived in polygamous unions.

that "a man needs to go outside to feel like a man"; "wives always complain. To get affection he has to go to his outside partner".

According to the Tandale ward officer in Dar es Salaam who constantly dealt with divorces filed by women, women are much more hard working, more inventive, and they have a strength that men do not have. Contrary to women, many men feel destitute and have "no tactics to deal with their problems". According to my male and female informants "when husbands are crushed down economically they suffer from feelings of inferiority"; "a man's ego is hurt". As a result, "men lose their vigour and women take over". And "when a man has lost control over his household and is humiliated by his wife his pride is hurt". In this situation, there was general agreement among men interviewed that in order to "build up our pride" and "boost our ego", we men need to 'relax' and to be 'comforted'. Relaxation and comfort are provided by 'extra-marital' partners.

Men as well as women also agreed that it is impossible for a man to stick to one partner only. Men have a constant need for sex—contrary to women. 'Outside partners' can be more or less casual partners, more permanent partners or *nyamba ndogos* (small houses) as they were referred to in Dar es Salaam. These latter partners are seen as serious threats by 'wives', as husbands tend to give whatever little income they may have to the *nyamba ndogos* and not to their own household.

Women's sexuality was not a neglected issue. Even if Kisii women were expected to be passive and sexually submissive, this was not a general feature, and women complained of men's inability to perform well sexually—often because they were 'weakened' by local brews. In Dar es Salaam 'Amazon women' who may even endanger men's physical health, strength and wellbeing were often heard of. Such women also have the capacity to drain a man of life and energy (by loss of semen). Similar observations are made by Haram (1997) in a study from the northern part of Tanzania. A man can be ambushed, lured and 'milked' by women. Women employ certain techniques to capture a man's mind—without them being aware of it. Women are like serpents. They create a certain smell when they are hunting for lovers, a smell which men cannot resist (Haram 1997). Hence—many men cannot resist and are drawn towards women whether they like it or not. From that point of view, women's sexuality also represents an active and threatening power. Therefore, men do not only have to be on guard, they also have to be in control. Such control increasingly seems to be manifested in aggressive behaviours, sexual violence and even rape—which were daily events both in Kisii and in Dar es Salaam.

Men and safe sex

Even if condoms are now more widely referred to and also used, in particular in the urban contexts, interviews also clearly demonstrate that when a man has had intercourse with a new partner a few times, that person is no longer a stranger, and condom use is stopped. It is a well-known fact that it is extremely difficult— not to say almost impossible—for women (married women in particular) to negotiate safe sex measures—even if women in many cases have the upper hand in the household. Women interviewed would all agree that to ask the husband to use a condom—when they know that he has been with other partners—would be to disclose their disrespect too openly. It was well-known that many *nyamba ndogos* gave comfort to more than one man because the financial assistance from one man was not enough to support the household. However, as relations with these 'outside' partners were considered permanent, condom use was not an issue. Besides, common arguments from both *nyamba ndogos* as well as 'wives' were that if they insisted on condom use, their partner/husband would be suspicious and then have a reason to accuse them of not being faithful. Thus, even if women have become much more self-confident and even independent, in sexual matters most women interviewed were not in a position to negotiate safe sex.

Risk assessment as regards contracting a STD or HIV infection is low by the men interviewed. "You never know if you will be run over by a *matatu/dala dala* (local bus in Kenya and Tanzania, respectively) to-morrow", men would argue, "Why should this prevent me from walking in the street?" A general attitude by men interviewed—who admitted having several partners at the same time, and who were well aware of the risk of contracting HIV/AIDS—was "why should it hit me?" Other reasons given were that "condoms hurt a man's ego"; "semen is valuable and should not be thrown away". Recurrent rumours met over and over both in Kisii and Dar es Salaam were that condoms had been infected with HIV/AIDS.

Male authority under threat

Although, the main axis of patriarchal power is still the overall subordination of women and dominance of men—my research from both Kisii and Dar es Salaam clearly indicates that the deteriorating material conditions have seriously undermined the normative order of patriarchy in both Kisii and Dar es Salaam. While men are in power structurally and in theory, men have become increasingly marginalised and disempowered in practice. While men do have a relative freedom, compared to women, particularly in sexual matters, lack of access to income earning opportunities has made men's role as heads of household and breadwinners a precarious one. Being reduced to 'figureheads' of households, men's authority has come under threat and so has their identity and sense of self-esteem.

According to Ortner and Whitehead social value and prestige are the domain of social structure that most directly affects cultural notions of gender and sexuality (Ortner and Whitehead 1981). Moreover, as noted by Kandiyoti (1988) and in agreement with my findings, the key to and the irony of the patriarchal system reside in the fact that male *authority* has a material base while male *responsibility* is normatively constituted. This has made men's roles and identities confusing and contradictory. Many men in my studies expressed feelings of helplessness, inadequacy and lack of self-esteem. They also increasingly seek psychiatric help (personal communication with heads of Psychiatric Department, Kisii District Hospital and Muhimbili Medical Centre, Dar es Salaam, respectively). Moreover, local newspapers are filled with advertisements from psychiatrists and herbalists offering to assist men with problems of depression and loss of sexual power. Local markets and traditional healers, of course, also sell a number of different herbs and roots to prevent impotence and to strengthen men's sexual powers.

As my findings show, contemporary and normative concepts of a 'real' man continue to be based on ancient beliefs, including male (sexual) control over women. As documented in numerous studies, in earlier times, households in East Africa were frequently polygynous. This permitted men to have sexual relations with several women. Men were not used to sexual abstinence, to be faithful or to practise safe sex. Such traditional norms and values are still deeply imbedded in most men interviewed. But today most men cannot afford several wives (lack of land, lack of money for bride price etc.). Most boys, though, grow up believing that they are not only the superior gender, but also that their identity as men is defined through sexual ability and accomplishment. "A man who cannot handle several women is not a real man", young and old men would argue both in Kisii and in Dar es Salaam. And women would agree. However, with an escalating HIV/AIDS epidemic, such beliefs cannot be legitimised today. Even if men know that, they are not ready to admit it. Thus, my findings raise the need to explore in more detail: What is masculinity? Why is it so valuable, and how do notions of masculinity relate to sexuality?

Masculinity/ies and sexuality

Masculinity (and femininity)—just like gender and sexuality[1]—does not simply reflect a biological 'given'—but is largely a product of cultural and social processes (Ortner and Whitehead 1981; Connell 1995; Gagnon and Parker 1995, Bourdieu 1998 and many more). Thus, neither masculinity nor sexuality are constant factors but change along with different historical and social structures, the complexity of contemporary life—and not the least when confronted with the effects of poverty—as underpinned by my research findings.

Drawing on the masculinity literature, masculinity, however, impinges on a number of different elements, identities and behaviours that are not always coherent. They may be competing, contradictory and mutually undermining. Moreover, masculinity is always liable to internal contradiction and historical disruption (Cornell 1995; Bourdieu 1998).

---

1. In the deconstruction of traditional sexology and sex research it has become apparent that these concepts are based on ideology and social coercion rather than necessity. Traditionally, sexual desire was assumed to be natural and automatic and heterosexual and universal. With the constraining frames of local marriage rules the male body responded to the presence of the female body, as if to a natural sign. In the most recent discussion of sexual desire the focus moves from inside the individual to the external environment. Rather than asking what internal forces create desire, the questions are: how is desire elicited, organized and interpreted as a social activity? Recent attempts to uncover local histories of desire have been closely linked to a fundamental concern with the relationship between sexual desire and identity (Gagnon and Parker 1995).

With the media celebrating violence to an extent where masculinity has almost become synonymous with toughness and aggression, boys/men in East Africa are socialised into a masculinity with the aura of violent and aggressive behaviour. As my research reveals, such behaviour has been reinforced by poverty, and by lack of access to education and employment. Men are, therefore, expected to perform certain roles, including being sexually aggressive, and they may not see anything wrong in sexual violence. They feel entirely justified—they are just exercising their right. They are authorised by an ideology of supremacy (Connell 1995; Lindsey 1994 and many more). As also observed by Morrell (2001) having several girlfriends establishes a young man's masculinity.

On the other hand, while masculinity is power, masculinity is also terrifyingly fragile because it does not really exist in the sense we are led to think it exists, that is, as a biological reality ... it exists as ideology; it exists as scripted behaviour; it exists within 'gendered relationships' (Kaufmann 1993:13). This is because the male gender is constructed around at least two conflicting characterisations of the essence of manhood. First, being a man is natural, healthy and innate. But second, a man must stay masculine. He should never let his masculinity falter. Masculinity is so valued, so valorised, so prized, and its loss such a terrible thing that one must always guard against losing it (Connell 1995). As a result, men should always be on guard and defend and demonstrate their masculinity. It is worth noting, though, that male honour is dependent on women's appropriate behaviour (Ortner and Whitehead 1981). Therefore, women and female sexuality represent an active and threatening power to male identity and masculinity (Silberschmidt 1999).

While, on the one hand, masculinity—almost world-wide—has increasingly become constructed from men's wage-earning powers, on the other—and more fundamentally—notions of masculinity are also closely associated with male virility, sexuality and sexual performance (Connell 1995; Bourdieu 1998; Morrell 2001). Men (and also women) in both Kisii and Dar es Salaam would certainly agree. The same observations are made in many other parts of the world (Lindisfarne 1994).

However, as has also been widely observed, whereas for men there is a strong correspondence between masculinity, sexual activity and status, this is the inverse for the female system (Ortner and Whitehead 1981; Connell 1995; Bourdieu 1998). In fact, research findings from both Kisii and Dar es Salaam clearly indicate that while *sexual potency* gives social potency, value and self-esteem to men, *sexual modesty* gives social value to women—but certainly not to men (Silberschmidt 1999, 2001a,b).

While masculinities and femininities are historically and socially constructed they are also relational constructs; the definition of one depends on the definition of the other. This is in line with my research findings as well as those of Bourdieu (1998) based on his studies among the Kabyles in North Africa. His categorisations of basic gender constructs and gender differences are useful in order to understand the persistence of such constructs and differences as well as present contradictions and confusion that East African masculinities (and femininities) are faced with.

According to Bourdieu, the basic notions of femininity and masculinity as well as female and male sexuality reflect a number of fundamental and competing oppositions and differences. Even if there is no set of characteristics that universally defines notions of femininity and masculinity, according to Bourdieu there are nevertheless some enduring and pervasive features that continue to persist. Bourdieu claims that ideas about femininity are associated with the private sphere and with traits that suggest passivity and subordination; ideas about masculinity, on the contrary, are associated with the public sphere, and with authority and dominance. With female sexuality being linked to modesty, restraint and secrecy and male sexuality to the opposite, there are different norms, values and expectations that are associated with being a woman and being a man. Moreover, and in particular in relation to sexuality, what gives social value to a man does not give social value to a woman.

Bourdieu's 'model' reflects static/universal features[1]. As such it does not allow for a multiplicity of masculinities (and femininities). But it does show why men and women may constitute two groups with different interests. It almost legitimises the existence of gender stereotypes—which is however not Bourdieu's purpose. Nevertheless, relating Bourdieu's categorisations to my research findings is enlightening. It reveals that men and women in Kisii and Dar es Salaam both fit and do not fit into these categorisations. Or rather: *they fit ideologically—but not in practice.* As my research findings show, women and femininity in today's rural and urban East Africa cannot be limited to the private sphere, to passivity and subordination. Moreover, while men and masculinity/ies may be associated with the public sphere, male authority and dominance are being severely threatened. While present ideas about female sexuality are certainly linked to modesty, restraint and secrecy (as they were in the past), female sexuality is also a threat to a man. Thus female sexuality is intrinsically dangerous for men. However, at the same time, it is in women's sexual relationships with men that many women are most subordinated and exposed to male dominance (Silberschmidt 1999, 2001a,b).

As observed by Morrell (2001) men have multiple ways of performing masculinity. Performing masculinity is both about men making and remaking masculinity, and it is also about challenging hegemonic masculinity and reconstituting it. In a situation, where men are faced with disempowerment, declining self-esteem and social value, it no doubt requires some courage to liberate oneself from prevailing notions of what it means to be a real man.

Men in Kisii as well as Dar es Salaam are clearly aware of their squeezed position. While they might perhaps admit this to the researcher during in-depth dis-

---

1. Research on sexuality in recent years has examined the role of gender-power and inequality in creating the framework for the sexuality of women and men. While the effects of gender-power are not the same in all cultures, gender inequality is widespread and interacts with the sexual system of specific cultures to shape most aspects of sexual life (Gagnon and Parker 1995).

cussions—as was often the case—this was certainly not what they were prepared to admit or even discuss with their wives/partners. For men it was important to insist on their privileges, their position as head of household and to demonstrate their control over women[1]. Many did so by using violence.

However, to exercise domination is not inscribed in men's nature (Kimmel 1987; Kaufmann 1993; Connell 1995; Bourdieu 1998). It requires long socialisation work. The same thing goes for the notion 'noblesse oblige'—men are obliged to play their prescribed roles where honour is central (Bourdieu 1998). Thus, the male privilege is also a trap, and men have ended up in a straitjacket (Kimmel 1987; Kaufmann 1993; Connell 1995). Contrary to women, who can only lose their honour (through infidelity), a 'real' man must constantly fight for it—he must use violence to achieve glory and public recognition. Pursuing masculinity is therefore an exposure to vulnerability. Most importantly, masculinity is constructed in front of and for other men and against femininity because, what men fear most is being feminine (Bourdieu 1998).

Connell, like Bourdieu, discusses masculinity in universalist terms. According to him (Connell 1995:232), it is not an easy task to reconstitute existing and normative types of masculinity. This is because attacks on men in Lacanian terms means attacking the Phallus, in more orthodox Freudian terms it means reviving the terror of castration—this suggests a depth of resistance likely to be met. With male identity deeply rooted in a man's ability to control women, and with male honour intimately bound up with the behaviour of women, men have to find new ways (which now seem to be a return to—or intensification of old ways) to manifest themselves as men. As many role expectations and psychological traits (such as aggressiveness and violence) attached to masculinity are closely linked to attempts to exercise control over (many) women, male (aggressive) sexual behaviour seems to have become male strategies in pursuit of control, social value and self-esteem. Such behaviour seems to strengthen male gender identity. It also seems to be a legitimate and accepted way of demonstrating masculinity.

Consequently, with masculinity and the phallus being at stake, and with men benefiting from inherited definitions of femininity and masculinity the questions raised at the beginning of this chapter become relevant: To what extent are men willing to let go of 'hegemonic' masculinities? To what extent are disempowered men in East Africa motivated for responsible sexual behaviour and HIV/AIDS prevention?

---

1. I only came across one young married man in Kisii who had the guts to openly demonstrate a different type of masculinity. He was very proud to admit that he was doing women's work (i.e. he worked together with his wife in the fields). His argument for this was that they would increase the produce and following this, their living standard. However he was ridiculed by other men and excluded from their company. In their eyes, he had abandoned his prescribed role as a man—he had let his masculinity falter. His wife was seen as having the upper hand, she did not respect him, and the men in the village feared that eventually he would be completely crushed. The young man, though, did not care that he was ridiculed. Instead he pitied the other men who would never be able to increase their living standards.

Conclusions

In order to understand men, masculinity and sexuality in rural and urban East Africa it has been necessary to locate men and women within the complex and changing social, political and economic systems. As my research from both rural Kisii and urban Dar es Salaam shows, sexuality and sexual behaviour do not occur in a vacuum but in (changing) social contexts where men and women are submitted to prescribed gender roles, norms, values and expectations. However, though still anchored in traditional values, present norms and values have become conflicting and contradictory and men have difficulties in maintaining their expected role as head of household and provider. Ideologically, men are the dominant gender and women's position is clearly subordinate. In practice, however, and as already observed a decade ago in Kisii, men's dominant position is slowly being watered down—contrary to that of women (Silberschmidt 1992).

Men in my research studies are perfectly aware that they are in a process of losing control over women. In this situation, and faced with increasing demands for women's empowerment and rights, including their sexual and reproductive rights, most men are not welcoming the traditional safe sex messages, including 'sticking to one partner'. Therefore, strategies to empower women and improve their deteriorating sexual and reproductive health are only meaningful if they are balanced against efforts to deal with men's increasingly frustrating situation. This, I shall argue, is a major development issue that has so far remained unnoticed both on the development agenda and also in the existing efforts to 'involve men'.

Returning to the question raised at the beginning of this chapter: 'Are disempowered men in East Africa motivated for responsible sexual behaviour and HIV/AIDS prevention?', the immediate answer is 'no'. With present masculinities still being strongly rooted in the past, with men faced with increasing disempowerment, I argue that men will not willingly let go of their previous privileges. Men seem to cling to their previous positions of power. And as demonstrated above, they do this through irresponsible sexual behaviour. As long as men conform to hegemonic masculine values and behaviours not only women's health is at serious risk but their own health is at stake.

Consequently, there is first of all an urgent need to analyse in more detail the commonly accepted notions of male domination and women's subordination. While the patriarchal ideology may be embodied and expressed in the lives of men and women, this does not mean that all men are successful patriarchs or that all women are submissive victims. In actual fact, as demonstrated above, matters work out very differently in practice. Nevertheless, to a large extent such stereotypes still underlie today's HIV/AIDS prevention efforts by international agencies and local NGOs.

Most HIV/AIDS prevention campaigns today target women. Obviously women are in an exposed and vulnerable situation— there is no doubt about that, in particular as reagards their sexual and reproductive health. Even if many women have acquired control and even power in many spheres of their life, they are also exposed and victimised in their sexual relations—much more than in any other relationships. It is my argument, however, that more attention must be paid to men.

Efforts to address men, however, are charged with considerable difficulties. First, men's interest in maintaining patriarchy is defended by all the cultural machinery that exalts hegemonic masculinity. Consequently, a focus on male sexual and reproductive behaviour addresses and threatens established male privileges in societies that are strongly patriarchal. Second, an understanding of support to men as being a support to women is seriously lacking. Instead, there seems to be a profound fear that activities aimed at men might result in being at the cost of those aimed at meeting women's urgent needs. Third, men's changed roles, their disempowerment and the consequences for their sexual behaviour seem to have escaped general attention among local governments and also donors. Fourth, neither policy makers nor information, education and communication (IEC) campaigns deal with the fact that sexuality and reproduction in East Africa are symbols vested with different, often opposite meanings for men and women.

Based on my research findings, I want to argue that HIV/AIDS preventive efforts need to be based on an understanding of the cultural and social context in which sexuality occurs; an understanding that recognises that sexuality is deeply rooted in male gender identity and that men and women engage in sexual relations for different reasons. 'Male involvement' requires specific education and services addressing the reproductive health needs of men and not only those of women as is the case today. My findings strongly indicate that male involvement cannot take place unless men's self-interest is addressed (cf. Bandura 1997), and men feel that they themselves will also benefit from such involvement, that involvement and male responsibility in sexual matters do not mean losing their masculinity but the opposite. This being said, I also support the following notions of Baylies and Bujra based on their studies from Tanzania and Zambia:

> While self-interest needs to be highlighted, it is crucial that the mutuality of interests of men and women be kept at the forefront of anym strategy. It is gender relations, the position, interaction, rights and responsibilities of both women and men, which are pivotal (2000:23).

Thus in order to best meet the needs of women and to improve their sexual and reproductive health, men must be addressed in the same way as women and with efforts that are appealing to men—for women's sake.

References

Bandura, Albert, 1997, *Self-Efficacy: The exercise of control.* New York: W.H. Freeman and Company.

Baylies, Carolyn and Janet Bujra (eds), 2000, *Aids, sexuality and gender in Africa: Collective strategies and struggles in Tanzania and Zambia.* London: Routledge.

Boserup, Ester, 1980, "African women in production and household", in Presvelou, Cloi and Saskia Spijkers-Zwart, H. Weenman, and B. V. Zonen (eds), *The household, women and agricultural development.* Wageningen.

Bourdieu, Pierre, 1998, *La domination masculine.* Paris: Seuil.

Bryant, Coralie and Louise White, 1984, *Managing rural development with small farmer participation.* West Hartford: Kumarian Press.

Caplan, Pat, 1991, *The cultural construction of sexuality.* London and New York: Routledge.

Carovano, Kathryn, 1995, "HIV and the challenges facing men". Issues paper no. 15, presented for the UNDP, HIV and Development Programme in January 1995. http://www.undp.org/hiv/publications/issues/english/issue15e.htm

Connell, R. W., 1995, *Masculinities.* Cambridge: Polity Press.

Cornwall, Andrea and Nancy Lindisfarne, (eds), 1994, *Dislocating Masculinity: Comparative Ethnographies.* London and New York: Routledge.

Gagnon, Richard G. and John H. Parker, 1995, "Conceiving Sexuality", in Richard G. Gagnon and John H. Parker (eds), *Conceiving Sexuality: Approaches to Sex Research in a Post Modern World.* London and New York: Routledge.

Government of Tanzania, 1996, *Tanzania Demographic and Health Survey.* Dar es Salaam: Bureau of Statistics, Planning Commission and Calverton, MD: Macro Internatonal Inc.

Haram, Liv, 1997, "In sexual life women are hunters: AIDS and women who drain men's body. The case of the Meru of Northern Tanzania". Paper presented at the Congress *World Federation of Public Health Associations—Health in Transition: Opportunities and Challenges,* Arusha, Tanzania, Oct. 12–17, 1997.

International Conference on Population and Development (ICPD) 1994, *Plan of Action.* Cairo.

Kandiyoti, Deniz, 1988, "Bargaining with Patriarchy", *Gender and Society* 2(3): 274–290.

Kaufmann, Michael, 1993, *Cracking the armour: power, pain and the lives of men.* Toronto: Viking/Penguin.

Kimmel, Michael S., 1987, "The contemporary crisis of masculinity in historical perspective", in Harry Brod (ed.), *The Making of Masculinities.* Boston: Allen & Unwin

Leslie, J. A. K., 1963, *A survey of Dar es Salaam.* Oxford: Oxford University Press.

LeVine, Sarah, 1979, *Mothers and wives: Gusii women of East Africa.* Chicago: University of Chicago Press.

Lindisfarne, Nancy, 1994, "Variant masculinities, variant virginities. Rethinking honour and shame", in Andrea Cornwall and Nancy Lindisfarne (ed.), *Dislocating Masculinity: Comparative Ethnographies.* pp 82–96. London: Routledge.

Lindsey, Linda. L., 1994, *Gender roles. A sociological perspective.* Second edition. Englewood Cliffs, New Jersey: Prentice Hall.

Morrell, Robert (ed.), 2001, *Changing men in Southern Africa.* University of Natal Press & Zed Press.

Ortner, Sherry B. and Harriet Whitehead, 1981, "Introduction: Accounting for sexual meanings", in Sherry B. Ortner and Harriet Whitehead (eds), *Sexual meanings: The cultural construction of gender and sexuality,* pp. 1–27. Cambridge: Cambridge University Press.

Silberschmidt, Margrethe, 1991, *Rethinking men and gender relations. An investigation of men, their changing roles within the household, and the implications for gender relations in Kisii District, Kenya.* CDR Research Report, no.16., Copenhagen: Centre of Development Research.

Silberschmidt, Margrethe, 1992, "Have men become the weaker sex? Changing life situations in Kisii District, Kenya", *The Journal of Modern African Studies* 30 (2) 237–253.

Silberschmidt, Margrethe, 1993, "Survey on research concerning users' perspectives on contraceptive services, with emphasis on Sub-Saharan Africa". Report commissioned by the Swedish Agency for Research Cooperation with Developing Countries (SAREC).

Silberschmidt, Margrethe, 1995, "Gender antagonism and socio-economic change: a study from Kisii district, Kenya", Copenhagen: Copenhagen University.

Silberschmidt, Margrethe, 1999, *Women forget that men are the masters.* Uppsala: Nordiska Afrikainstitutet.

Silberschmidt, Margrethe, 2001a, "Dispowerment of men in rural and urban East Africa: Implications for male identity and sexual behaviour", *World Development* 29 (2), 657–671.

Silberschmidt, Margrethe, 2001b, "Adolescent girls, illegal abortions and 'sugar-daddies' in Dar es Salaam: vulnerable victims and active social agents", *Social Science & Medicine* 52 , 1815–1826.

UNAIDS, 2000, *Men make a difference. Men and AIDS: a gendered approach.*

UNAIDS, 2001, *Regional statistics end of 2001.*

UNAIDS 2002, *Update,* 2002.

White, Louise, 1990, "Separating men from the boys: Constructions of gender, sexuality and terrorism in Central Kenya 1939–1959", *International Journal of African Historical Studies* 23 (1), pp 1–27.

World Bank, 1995, *Tanzania social sector review*. Washington DC.

Photo: El Hadj Bassirou Sanni, 1982

12. Re-Conceptualizing African Gender Theory: Feminism, Womanism and the *Arere* Metaphor

Mary Kolawole

Introduction

Sexuality and gender issues in African societies have often been subsumed under various discourses, local and international, that do not adequately recognize the complexities and specificities of the reality of African societies. Gender as a category is equated with *women* such that gender studies are mostly assumed to focus on women's problems. The emphasis on women's *problems* also derives from the assumption that African women's refusal to speak loudly about oppression and inequality is an acceptance of marginality and minimalization. The question of the interface between men's and women's spaces and the dynamics of gender relations is crucial to the ways in which gender is conceptualized in African societies and this is also significant for the ways in which culture is considered central in gender discourses about Africa. This paper will foreground a dynamic definition of culture, recognizing that culture needs to be deconstructed critically as opposed to being simply connected to gender discourse as a catchall phrase. A derogatory definition of culture is still being underscored by many scholars with specific reference to Africa and the Third World. As Edward Said (1993) observed, many Third World societies are designated in exclusionist terms. Trinh Minh-ha (1989) brings this reality closer to gender issues in her observation that Third World women are treated in modern scholarship as an outgroup to be spoken for by a mainstream ingroup, in her emphasis on the philosophy of *otherness*.

African women researchers are located in gender discourse at the intersection of resisting the politics of appropriation and finding their own voice, but as contributors to modern scholarship. This chapter is aimed at problematizing these various layers of gender determinants and interrogates the ambivalent attitudes to the gender question in and about Africa. The chapter is also an attempt at evaluating the diversities of attitudes and approaches to gender conceptualisation by African female scholars. It gathers together various issues that are predominant in the search for new concepts regarding gender constructions, gender relations and gender research in Africa. Some of the concepts touch on the question of sexuality and how women and the society deal with it.

The chapter further seeks to problematize the traditional basis for gender inequality, by revealing the limitation of the attempts to mute women's voices. Some female scholars take off from this muting of the voice or *culture of silence* to reveal how African women are dealing with it and transcending it. Others emphasize the anomalous nature of silencing women but also interrogate modern feminisms in terms of cultural relevance.

There is an observable polarity in the approaches of African women to feminism, ranging from acceptance, to questioning or rejection. Some African women are searching for alternative gender concepts to evade the controversies around and resistance to feminism. One such area of controversy derives from the absence of direct talk about sexuality, as well as from the problems of some African societies' attitudes to women's bodies and sexuality. Until recently, many African societies encouraged traditions that suppress sexuality through female circumcision and similar rites. But other traditions enhance sexuality, for instance in Southern Africa and in Mali, and in many areas of Africa female circumcision is not practised at all.

Another focus which is central to this paper is the recognition that gender in Africa needs to transcend the question of naming or self-definition, which are basically preoccupations for the academic women and not for the majority of ordinary non-literate African women. The latter is a category of women who live through the reality (and not the abstraction) of oppression. But African women's experiences are not monolithic, nor are their struggles to resist oppression recent. History confirms that they have struggled for their rights in incredibly radical ways since pre-colonial times according to the exigencies of the time and place (Kolawole 1997a; see also Machera, this volume).

The main thrust of the present chapter is an evaluation of the varying reactions to gender as a category and the dynamics of gender relations and how these impact the attempts at definition. Some scholars are sceptical, cautious or indifferent; others have recognized the need to revisit gender concepts in a process of re-definition and re-envisioning of what feminism means to African women. I uphold conceptualization as a conduit for pragmatic transformation of African women's space, rights and self-realisation and not as an end in itself. Women creative writers and critics have focused more on the qualitative dimension of research through theorising as an understanding of women's struggles, their local histories and global contexts as a pre-requisite to strategizing and relocating or empowering women. The social scientists have been more involved in quantitative data collection with minimal theoretical emphasis. Both aspects of research are inter-related but the thrust of this paper is more tilted to the qualitative perspective.

Many women social scientists on the continent have been preoccupied with empirical research by using Western tools, concepts and methodology. They have researched into women's lives and empowerment according to the donors' agendas. Concepts such as *Women in Development, Women and Development*, and *Gender and Development* have been very influential in African women's dealing with gender as a category and gender relations and women's role in development. In more recent years, donors and researchers have recognized the limitations of these concepts as effective tools for changing African women's lives, for empowering them and for advocating for gender justice. This is likely to be the case unless cultural factors and the male factor are also taken on board. International efforts in the Decade of Women, the Decade of Culture, during the Beijing conference and in subsequent platforms for action have created a new attitude and a re-thinking of gender by mainstreaming gender into development policies. This coincides with the increased interest of African gender theorists who believe that the African woman's voice is subdued in international gender discourse. Probing the traditional 'culture of silence' has provided a *raison d'être* for constructing new gender concepts.

There is a visible ambivalence in the attitude of many of these women to the issue of gender conceptualization. The issue has been polarized–some scholars accept global feminism(s) as an umbrella for women's struggle that has motivated and encouraged African women. Others reject the politics of appropriation and *otherness* implied in feminism as they also decry any deliberate act of self-effacement deriving from tradition or externalized 'isms'. I locate myself in this discourse in the domain of deconstructing feminism, traditional ideologies, malestreaming and mainstreaming strategies of gender intervention, as opposed to the adoption of 'gender' theories that are exclusive and essentialist, treating African women or the category of gender as monoliths. The celebrated image of African women as passive victims, marginalized without a voice as presented in some feminist critiques needs to be unpacked. African women scholars are adopting the role of gender mouthpieces, interrogating gender concepts, confirming areas of commonality and difference, in order to unfold new concepts that are acceptable to African specificities. I have postulated this and stressed the need to see gender struggle in Africa as an aspect of larger struggles, to see women's rights as human rights. It is true that African women have been long treated as the voiceless subaltern. But this image is changing gradually in many places, through sensitization moves by empirical scholars and theorists. This is a pre-requisite to shifting African women from the other side of the track and progressively relocating them on a new level of awareness. The challenges for African women researchers include re-articulating gender concepts and matching it with actions and activism for positive self-restoration. But we need to recognize the interplay of class, culture, ethnicity, religion and politics and the attendant result that African women's progressive gender consciousness differs from one African society to another.

My research has focused on gender theory from an inter-disciplinary perspective, striking a balance between qualitative and quantitative research. I recognize that empirical research deriving from social science tools is functional and useful in grounding the theoretical gender assumptions on concrete premises. I have found useful the treasured information on African concepts of womanhood, gender ideologies and philosophies, that defines gender relations and constructions stored in oral literary genres such as myths, proverbs, female genres and folklore among others. Equally, a majority of women's written literary texts, especially biographies, provide avenues for implicit and explicit gender conceptualizations. Many African women interested in gender theorizing contend that African women did not learn about gender only from the global movement. Some have been motivated by the historical accounts of women's mobilization in Africa. These include individual women giants who transformed their societies in pre-colonial times, such as Nehanda of Zimbabwe, Nzinga of Angola, Nana Asantewa of Ghana and others (Sweetman 1984; Kolawole 1997a). Research also reveals the catalogue of women's activism and dynamic collective mobilization against colonial oppression, traditional repression, voicelessness and injustice (Mba 1982; Kolawole 1997a). Much of this was not adequately documented until recently. Many are therefore calling for taking these into account in African gender conceptualizing. This explains the ambivalence and shifting positions of scholars and authors such as Ama Ata Aidoo of Ghana, the Nigerian writer Buchi Emecheta, Tsitsi Dangarembga of Zimbabwe and the South African writer Miriam Tlali in identifying with feminism. Most African women scholars agree that African women's muting or invisibility is not desirable or justifiable, irrespective of ideological polarity and diversities in conceptualizing gender. I consider *naming* a means to a pragmatic end the task of empowering African women and moving them from the margin to the centre of social transformation.

Contesting the 'culture of silence': The *arere* metaphor

Reference to 'culture' has become the *sine qua non* of African women's oppression. Often both men and women validate and justify women's marginality by referring to culture and even quoting traditional philosophies such as proverbs to entrench or institutionalize women's oppression. Let me clarify this notion of culture. Culture has both positive and negative dimensions, progressive and retrogressive manifestations. For example in Europe it is very normal and desirable to fossilize traditions through the celebration of antiquity. Millions of Euros are spent on visits to museums, castles, cathedrals—symbols that capture moments in history, aspects of past culture/tradition and architecture in many parts of Europe. Culture here is upheld as positive. Ironically, when culture or tradition in Africa is being discussed, many scholars underscore primitivism, backwardness, stagnation, unchanging attitudes and so on. Yet, cultural understanding is germane to many sectors of modern cross-cultural interactions. A vivid illustration of this is an understanding of the Japanese culture that does not allow the wearing of slippers on carpets. In trade relations, other nations need this cultural knowledge to avoid importing indoor slippers to Japan. I will locate myself among those who claim that culture is dynamic and protean, not static; talking about cultural relevance in this context is derived from the desire of African women to manifest their feminine attributes and their Africanness simultaneously with a call for changes in women's conditions. Not wishing to adopt gender concepts that intercept their culturally meaningful self-definition is central to these women's reactions to feminism. I uphold the progressive definition of culture, not as a backward-looking sustenance of moribund past traditions or living in the past, but as a dynamic mode of self-definition that coincides with group values that I consider progressive.

It is this recognition that necessitated the United Nations' decade of culture, providing a forum for identifying the centrality of culture to positive development. This included revisiting the place, validity and relevance of culture in many sectors especially in gender issues. The definition that emerged from the World Conference on Cultural Policies in Mexico City in 1982 fits into the theoretical thrust of this chapter:

> Culture may now be said to be the whole complex of distinctive and intellectual features that characterise a society or social group. It includes not only the arts and letters, but also modes of life, the fundamental rights of the human being, value systems, traditions and beliefs (Sagnia 1997:7).

In a UN workshop on culture, gender and development in Addis Ababa in 1997, Burama K. Sagnia further defined the dynamic nature of culture:

> It is being said that culture is both evolutionary and revolutionary. Culture goes through an internal evolutionary process involving growth, greater heterogeneity and coherence. It also goes through a process of change and adaptation as a result of contact with other cultures, the influence of a dominant culture . . . influence of mass media or communication technologies (such as internet) etc. As a result, culture must be seen as a dynamic mechanism that must adjust and adapt to external and internal conditions of existence. As an adaptive mechanism, culture must therefore, have the capability to provide the means of satisfaction of human, biological and social needs (Sagnia 1997:8).

This conceptualization of culture is very important in gender issues in Africa as Sagnia's poser underscores:

> If we accept the postulate that culture is an adaptive mechanism that constantly adjusts to satisfy human, biological and social needs, shouldn't we then ask ourselves whether the best way forward for Africa is to marginalize the role of culture in development frameworks and process or to use it as a platform or springboard for development (Sagnia 1997:8).

There has been a consensus that culture has to be taken into account in development issues and that a close affinity exists between gender and culture. One area of cultural mediation on gender is the traditional belief in the muting of women's voices in many African societies which is justified by proverbs and traditional ideologies that shape the mind-set of men and women. It is considered culturally incorrect for women to be a focal participant in social structures. Such ideologies and beliefs call for decoding of culture to unpack gender myths and philosophies that keep women in liminal spaces, as well as recoding of new ideologies. Many African women literary writers and critics have emerged as gender theorists, convinced that gender perception in Africa has to be inclusive, taking on-board cultural idiosyncrasies and the male factor. There was an initial attempt to problematize gender by probing the extent of women's oppression and disempowerment through an analysis of women's voicelessness in many African societies. One of the scholars who has focused on this is Irene D'Almeida. D'Almeida is privileged as a Francophone African scholar and an American professor. She has advocated breaking the culture of silence and her theory is based on the experience of Francophone African women, especially how they are advocating a rejection of this ideology of voicelessness. She identifies the 'culture of silence' as a major obstacle to African women's empowerment by a discussion of the works of Francophone women such as Calixle Beyala, Werewere Liking and Miriama Ba (D'Almeida 1994). She bases her perception on a progressive effort by many Francophone African women to use the literary tool to unveil women's voices. She maintains that eliminating women's voicelessness is a fundamental aspect of gender conceptualization in Africa. The attempt to encourage African women's audibility as a symbol of their empowerment, has remained on the front burner of African gender theorizing.

The challenges posed by a tradition of muting women's voices can be more vividly perceived through an important Yoruba metaphor as it provides a renewed insight into the struggle to speak out and defy intrinsic or externally imposed muting. The *arere* metaphor presents the dilemma of African women's attempts to speak out and assert themselves in a cultural cosmos that still sometimes considers women's vocality as an anomaly even in the most enlightened space, academia. Probing socio-cultural ideologies, philosophies and practices provides an indigenous platform for looking at African gender concepts because much of the traditional attitude to women in Africa emerges from traditional beliefs which shape the people's mind-set and enhance the traditional philosophies that validate and institutionalize women's marginalization and/or oppression. *Arere* is a tree that grows along the coast of West Africa. The metaphor of the *arere* among the Yoruba people of Nigeria is a paradigm in the question of women's self-expression and dynamic participation in social issues. The unique characteristic of the *arere* tree is significant because it emits an extremely offensive smell and is not normally allowed to grow around urban or rural dwelling places such as cities and villages. The tree symbolizes the extreme significance of the separation of space. It grows out there in the wild. There is a Yoruba proverb that reveals the tension between women's voices and muting through the metaphor of the *arere* tree: *Ile ti obinrin ba ti nse toto arere, igi arere ni hu nibe.* The meaning comes out as 'Any home where a woman is vocal /loud/influential through self-expression, will have the *arere* tree growing in the courtyard.' The implication is that in certain quarters, it is still unwomanly to be vocal, loud and assertive; it is even an anomaly that gives off an offensive odour like the *arere* tree. Most of the contentions about gender conceptualisation derive from this platform of vocality-visibility. The fact that the *arere* is a threat to men because of the strong smell, which cannot be controlled, held down or stopped, provides an alternative reading of African women's alterity.

Traditional ideologies are sometimes replete with contradictions when women's issues are being centred. The same Yoruba worldview presents women as garrulous/talkative in nature. But the socialization process recommends women's silence through proverbs such as the *arere* ideology. I have worked on similar proverbs among Yoruba and non-Yoruba people as well as the folktales that insititutionalize and normalize women's space in the social periphery. Many women writers are transgressing this location of presumed silence to re-inscribe the strong African woman. Women writers in contemporary settings are more vocal and unapologetic than earlier writers. We see the normalization of women's vocality as a transgression of such an ideology in the works of some twenty Nigerian women writers in the anthology of short stories entitled *Breaking the Silence* (Adewale and Segun 1996). So one way of reconceptualizing gender in Africa is the re-inscription of women's space by literary writers. Akachi Ezeigbo (1996) re-writes Igbo women on the eve of colonial incursion by decoding the sub-text of *Things Fall Apart* by Chinua Achebe. The latter institutionalizes male heroism and women's marginalization but this is a contradiction of history. Igbo women mobilized themselves in the early part of the twentieth century to fight against colonial rule, oppression and taxation that affected women and men.

An important focus of some African gender theorists is, therefore, to question the source, transmission and acceptability of such an ideology—the 'culture of silence' that treats women's audibility/visibility as an aberration. Although proverbs are an aspect of the essence of traditional wisdom and oration, one needs to situate such proverbs in a modern socio-historical context. In many parts of Africa, proverbs are words of wisdom of the elders that carry respectability and authority. But a great majority of African people, especially the urban dwellers and the younger generation, neither know proverbs nor allow them to shape their mind-set. One can also say that proverbs are more male-oriented in usage and composition, and the majority of women may know only very few proverbs. Indeed, this proverb is not a true reflection of the dynamic roles of Yoruba women who are empowered in specific areas especially the economic sphere.

The truth of the matter is that research reveals Yoruba women's historic voice, visibility and power, in a self-conscious way as documented in the mobilization and revolts of Abeokuta women in the early part of the twentieth century. Currently there are many parts of the Yoruba community where women have the ultimate authority in market and economic issues, crown the king or veto the candidature and crowning, stand in as ruler when a king dies as we see in the regents of many communities in Ondo and Ekiti areas of Yorubaland (Awe 1992; Kolawole 1997a). In Nigeria, Abeokuta women were mobilized to resist colonial as well as traditional rulers' oppression. Many modern African women are equally vocal as mouthpieces for their families, gender and community as we see in the traditions of *omo osu*, *iyalode* and *iyaloja* among the Yorubas and *umuada* among the Igbos. The *omo osu* (women of the same extended family or compound) still have important roles in settling family quarrels or acting as public relations agents on family matters. The focus of the present chapter does not allow detailed studies of this and other examples but Aba women's riot and the history of the dynamic role of Kikuyu women in Mau Mau struggles are paradigms (Ngugi wa Thiong'o 1967).

Women's voicelessness is therefore a paradox that is imposed by socialization. The quest for a re-conceptualization of gender theory has embraced the rejection of the culture of silence and the unfolding of areas of women's audibility in both traditional and modern societies. D'Almeida's gender conceptualization derives from conscious efforts by African women writers to break the culture of silence through the creative process. A majority of African women writers are spokespersons for their gender and are re-creating women's space in a self-conscious way. Many African women theorists believe that this is an important channel for enhancing African women's self-esteem and participation in development.

Re-conceptualizing gender in Africa

The dominant discourse on gender in Africa is the question of decoding femininity and women's status in a critical manner. The concepts, 'woman', 'gender' and 'feminism' are being constantly interrogated, and to many, this is an aspect of that quest for self-assertion. This position is further enhanced by many decades of male-biased research in the social sciences that ignored gendered approaches. More recently researchers have responded to the challenges as gender approach has become ubiquitous in African humanities. When donor agencies began to sponsor gender research, African researchers adopted western theoretical frameworks for developing nations. This is evident in the application of development theories especially *Women in Development* (WID) and *Women and Development* (WAD). With the *Gender and Development* (GAD) agenda, however, there was a self-conscious attempt to mainstream gender into development projects without the recognition that this is also problematic because it subsumes women's issues under development and political agendas. Numerous gender training workshops, seminars and conferences were launched by African social scientists according to the agenda of the donors without adequately taking cultural contingencies into account. So, a lot of data were produced in a predominantly top-down approach. The majority of women who are the targets of the programmes distrust the researchers, believing that they are being used as guinea pigs for research. Others see these researchers as outsiders using them to make money from donors. This was the scenario in the nineties. At the same time, a focus on gender and feminism became dominant not by social scientists but women writers, critics and activists who were not at ease with an uncritical adoption and application of Western concepts.

A school of thought upholds the deconstruction of the ideology of imposed silence as a central issue in conceptualizing gender in Africa. Many like Irene D'Almeida attempt to chart areas of African women's audibility and power as an important process in the on-going re-conceptualization of gender on the continent. The Gambian gender researcher, Siga Jajne is one such theorist who re-directs attention to a conscious effort by Sene-Gambian women to transgress existing space designed to put women in the margin. She underscores Sene-Gambian women's increasing visibility as the women transgress the culturally imposed silence by articulating a theory which takes *sani baat* as a point of departure. *Sani baat* is a traditional act of transgression as women force their voices on social discourse. Women force their voice on existing male-dominated agendas in words and in practice. It is remarkable that many of the theorists who are attempting to re-conceptualize gender in Africa do so through a double approach, in creative writing as well as in theoretical propositions.

In a similar theoretical thrust, Molara Ogundipe-Leslie, through her creative writings and activism, has advocated the need to enhance African women's voice by re-discovering uncharted sources of African women's self-expression and self re-creation. Convinced that there are areas that can reveal African women's voice, she raises the question: "Are African women voiceless or do we fail to look for their voices where we may find them, in the sites and forms in which these voices are uttered?" (Ogundipe-Leslie 1994:11). She advocates a search for African women's voices "in spaces and modes such as in ceremonies, and worksongs..." Ogundipe-Leslie's concern transcends revealing African women's voices as she advocates inclusive social transformation in her theory of *Stiwanism*. She is one of the scholars who recognizes the need for self-naming as an essential step to re-routing the direction of gender conceptualization in Africa. Her definition of this term reveals the direction of her thoughts:

> I have since advocated the word "Stiwanism," instead of feminism, to bypass these concerns and to bypass the combative discourses that ensue whenever one raises the issue of feminism in Africa . . . The word "feminism" itself seems to be a kind of red rag to the bull of African men. Some say the word is by its very nature hegemonic . . . "Stiwa" is my acronym for *Social Transformation Including Women in Africa* (Ogundipe-Leslie 1994:229).

In her creative works of poetry, Ogundipe-Leslie thematizes diverse problems confronting African women which need practical solutions. She and others believe that conceptualizing gender in Africa should not be divorced from practical efforts towards removing the obstacles to African women's involvement in social transformation, which she describes as mountains on the back of African women. It is a dominant trend in African women's creative writing to identify with women's oppression and advocate gender justice. But some writers transcend the level of creative writing in order to join others in the desire for gender re-conceptualization. Notable among such are Miriam Tlali, Buchi Emecheta, Ama Ata Aidoo, Tsitsi Dangarembga, Zulu Sofola and a host of others. Buchi Emecheta prefers to dissociate herself from the tag 'feminist' in many interviews:

> I write about the little happenings of everyday life. Being a woman, and African born, I see things through an African woman's eyes. I chronicle the little happenings in the lives of African women I know. I did not know that by doing so I was going to be called a feminist. But if I am now a feminist then I am an African feminist with a small 'f' (Umeh 1981:178).

Almost without exception, her creative works present the dilemma of gender oppression with the African woman as a victim and the man as the oppressor, the indolent parasite holding the woman down. Her own personal experience and battering at the hands of her husband reinforce her reaction against gender injustice. She has lived in London most of her adult life. Yet, she refuses to be called a feminist and each time she is questioned about this, her answer becomes more defensive:

> Q: Why do you refuse to be called a feminist?

> A: I will not be called a feminist here, because it is European. It is as simple as that. I just resent that . . . I don't like being defined by them . . . It is just that it comes from outside and I don't like people dictating to me. I do believe in the African type of feminism. They call it womanism . . . (Emecheta 1989:19).

Emecheta upholds gender as a means to a pragmatic end, that of addressing the specificities of African women's ordinary problems—education, welfare, inheritance and other fundamental issues of existence and survival.

The Zimbabwean writer, Tsitsi Dangarembga also rejects feminism as a label of her identity: "The white Western feminism does not meet my experiences at a certain point, the issues of me as a black woman. The black American female writers touch more of me than the white ones" (Dangarembga 1989:183). Ama Ata Aidoo, one of the first black African women writers, initially rejected feminism as an American ideology imported into Africa to destroy the family structure. She later shifted her position slightly by acknowledging the unifying role of feminism which also confirmed the existing beliefs of African women: "[I]f you take up a drum to beat and no one joins then you just become a fool. The women's movement has helped in that it is like other people taking up the drum and beating along with you" (Aidoo 1988:183).

The South African writer Miriam Tlali prefers to be recognized simply as the voice of African women speaking on their behalf and striving to make their voice audible:

> In South Africa we live under a pyramid of power, so I regard myself as the voice of the African woman who is oppressed politically, socially, and culturally. There is not enough emphasis given to the plight of the South African woman. I insist on this in my collection of short stories *Soweto Stories* . . . African women have no voice, no platform and nobody cares . . . Therefore I feel that I must address them in my writing" (Tlali 1989:69ff.).

Zoe Witcombe and other scholars are rather cautious about the South African situation. They prioritize the need to put South African women under a global feminist umbrella, but black writers are interested in focusing on the need of black women along the general lines of struggle.

Another black woman who has directed attention to the issue of naming their own struggle is Chikwenye Okonjo Ogunyemi (1985/86), a Nigerian critic and theorist. *Self-naming* has become a very important aspect of black women's self-re-creation. Several African–American women have problematized feminism and the view of Clenora Hudson-Weems (Hudson-Weems 1993) is cardinal in this theoretical direction. She maintains that African women's self-reclamation hinges on 'self-naming'. This derives from the importance of self-naming in African philosophy. Many African societies believe that naming affects identity and for this reason, self-naming is celebrated and naming is often accompanied by ceremonies based on a deep-rooted understanding of the culture and history of a family or ethnic group. It is equally believed that strangers cannot name your struggle appropriately (Kolawole 1997a). This is at the heart of the constant search for a new gender terminology by African women. The most outstanding alternative concept is 'womanism'. This was simultaneously coined by Alice Walker and Chikwenye Okonjo Ogunyemi in 1982. Walker believes that self-naming is an aspect of the "search for our mother's garden" (Walker 1983:xii). Okonjo Ogunyemi articulates black womanism as an inclusive cultural concept:

> Black womanism is a philosophy that celebrates Black roots, the ideals of Black life, while giving a balanced presentation of Black womanhood. It concerns itself as much with the Black sexual

power tussle as with the world power structure that subjugates Blacks (Okonjo Ogunyemi 1985/86:24).

Womanism appears more acceptable to many African scholars because of this inclusive nature (Kolawole 1997a, 1998). The struggle for gender equity is inseparable from class, racial and other forms of oppression. The male factor is also accommodated as many scholars maintain that for women's conditions to be ameliorated, men have to be taken on-board. They constitute a large percentage of policy makers and political office holders. This touches on mainstreaming gender into development programmes. Many men and women consider womanism a more conciliatory gender theory than feminism.

Many African scholars resist the tag feminism because of the general assumption that it is a Western ideology that might be problematic if grafted indiscriminately to an African cultural context (Kolawole 1997a). From this premise, gender research in Africa has witnessed a polarity of reactions and re-vision. Molara Ogundipe-Leslie sums up the major issues, "Some who are genuinely concerned with ameliorating women's lives sometimes feel embarrassed to be described as 'feminist,' unless they are particularly strong in character" (Ogundipe-Leslie 1994:229). Daphne Williams-Ntiri reiterates the dilemma of African and black women who are dynamically engaged in gender studies and activism:

> For years Africana women have found themselves in a serious ideological predicament. In the absence of viable organized women's groups they have been invited to embrace feminism as an instrument of emancipation and as a new-found source of empowerment and status-building. Unfortunately, the majority of Africana women on public platforms have rejected feminism for a multiplicity of reasons. First, there is the unquestionable need to reclaim Africana women; second, they are perplexed over the racist origins of the feminist movement; third, they have found little solace in the doctrines and mission of the feminist movement, and fourth, the realities, struggles and expectations of the two groups remain on different planes (Williams-Ntiri, introduction to Hudson-Weems 1993:1).

Williams-Ntiri further affirms that global feminism is not controversial and that Western feminism cannot provide a panacea for all women's problems across time, race, ethnicity, and class. She calls for the recognition of difference.

Oyèrónké Oyewùmí is a radical defender of an endogenous approach to gender conceptualization in Africa. According to her postulate, it is a common belief that some of the perceptions of African women's reality are occasioned by the imposition of Western canons of gender analysis on African realities as delineated in her remarkable work: *The Invention of Women: Making an African Sense of Western Gender Discourses*. Oyewùmí castigates the invention of images of African womanhood to fit Western myths of black people. In her rather radical sociological study of womanhood, she rejects Western universalization of women's reality and the imposition of 'the woman question' on Africa:

> This book is about the epistemological shift occasioned by the imposition of Western gender categories on Yoruba discourse . . . [I]t is concerned with revealing the most basic but hidden assumptions, making explicit what has been merely implicit, and unearthing the taken-for-granted assumptions underlying research concepts and theories (Oyewùmí 1997ix).

Oyewùmí opposes the Western gender binary and oppositional gender discourse as well as what she sees as a Western obsession with bodies. She equally opposes basing gender in other cultures on Western biological determinism or what she describes as *body-reasoning* or *bio-logic*. She belongs to the group of scholars that advocate cultural relevance in African gender conceptualization.

Like Oyewùmí, the Cameroonian scholar, Juliana Makuchi Nfah-Abbenyi emphasizes identity, sexuality and difference as she perceives gender in Africa as an aspect of postcoloniality. She maintains that the conceptualization of gender in Africa is male-biased and Western oriented and calls for a re-visit of African gender theory. She decries the politics of exclusion as scholars claim to speak for African and black women. This is made manifest in the neglect of African women's writing. She resists Western labels and isms. She reiterates the existence of women's struggle in many parts of Africa before colonialism and advocates the recognition of the plurality of voices in conceptualizing gender in Africa (Nfah-Abbenyi 1997).

In the search for African theoretical re-conceptualization womanism has become a vital theory that has appealed to many. It is crucial to define and delineate the rationale that underlies and underscores womanism as a manifestation of self-naming. Many active African scholars resist the label of feminism and consequently do not make a concerted attempt to understand major issues in international feminist theorizing. Yet, any methodology that is designed to capture the specificity of African women's reality needs to comprehend the issues in feminist concepts. Because gender is closely inter-related to cultural identity, a clear definition of culture is an imperative. Womanism has been a conciliatory gender concept as it emphasizes cultural relevance, the family, motherhood, and the intersection between various forms of oppression, social stratification and marginalization based on race, ethnicity, class and gender. The inclusive womanist approach is considered more appealing to African reality. African women exalt femininity and recognize the need to separate gender space when necessary. Many maintain that African women can use their existing, often uncharted power base and build on it instead of trying to be like men.

Concluding notes: Locating myself in gender discourse

I have recognized the necessity to focus on a strong theoretical framework on gender in Africa that is conciliatory in many ways. This double pull is peculiar to African researchers. Donors do not give funds for theorizing or conceptualizing, they give funds for empirical research. On the other hand empirical research tests and validates theories as being related to true life situations of women and not abstractions. Theories help the sensitization process too. I am directly involved in the attempt to set a relevant agenda for women's studies in Nigeria and the West African region along with many other researchers. The best approach to re-conceptualizing gender in Africa is the identification of a nexus between the pure theory and social science-based methodology. My research has consequently highlighted both qualitative and quantitative approaches. I have participated in baseline studies on the implications of negative traditional practices against women and the girl child and sensitization workshops working with grass root women. This exposure convinces me that theorizing African women cannot be an end but a means to an end. Gender theory in Africa needs to be inclusive as one thus avoids polemics. This calls for simultaneously embracing data collection, interviews, evaluation of opinion leaders' perceptions of gender, as well as baseline studies of socio-cultural practices that shape gender relations and perceptions. At the same time, data collection on oral myths, proverbs, folktales and women's oral genres have provided a rich repertoire of traditional philosophies and ideologies on gender in African societies, past and present. Research into African women's literature—novels, plays, short stories and poetry—is a rich source for charting African women's space and a major avenue for eliciting gender concepts from African perspectives. Women's biographies have equally enhanced gender perception as many of the writers have been victims of gender injustice but many have emerged undefeated in their desire to be spokespersons for their gender.

In conducting empirical research, I have discovered that many African women are passive to the reality of gender injustice and such an attitude derives from socio-cultural beliefs. Many of these women often cite myths, proverbs, anecdotes or folktales that justify accepting their marginalization. It is considered culturally correct to accept marginalization in many cases and this derives from oral traditional beliefs. So an important research target has been to sensitize the women by *de-constructing* and *re-constructing* proverbs, myths and other beliefs that shape the mind-set. Grass-root women are not concerned about conceptualization which is considered as an academic preoccupation by many of them. But in belief and in practice, many prefer a position that enhances women's conditions and opportunities for participation in development that does not alienate men, that does not jeopardize the esteemed family system, and that celebrates motherhood. This provides a meeting point between grass-root women and the scholars, between working class and middle-class women, between theory and practice, between concept and activism. *Womanism* seems to be the most functional and broad-based of the African gender theories as it addresses the plurality of expectations and the multiplicity of viewpoints. Many African scholars are, however, subscribing to the ideals of womanism without overt recognition and realisation of, or identification with, the concept.

In gathering together the diverse positioning of African women in search of gender re-conceptualisation, the search for African women's voice becomes a paradigm for the quest for self-definition and self-naming. African women researchers see themselves as being the voice of the inarticulate majority but their role has to be culturally acceptable. As many resist the label 'feminism', they acknowledge that the essence of gender struggle is not new to Africa although previously terminologies or labels were not emphasized. Juliana Nfah-Abenyi has aptly articulated this: "What this means is that before feminism became a movement with a global political agenda, African women both 'theorized' and practiced what for them was crucial to the development of women, although no terminology was used to describe what these women were actively doing, and are still practicing on a day-to-day basis" (Nfah-Abbenyi 1997:10). The lived experience of African women reveals hopes and aspirations, denials and oppression but also struggles against forces that put women in the liminal position. Gender conceptualization has to be intertwined with development in a conspicuous desire to improve the conditions of African women. These gender concepts are encoded in the creative writings of many women writers. Abbenyi, like Aidoo, has identified these gender concepts as the 'cry' of African women which when their multiple voices are pulled together becomes a drum-beat, an outcry, a rejection of voicelessness. Scholars need to move beyond concepts to action. Scholars can help in organizing grass-roots women through sensitization. Revealing how African women in the past and currently have resisted oppression and linking them up with policy makers to include the women's needs on national agenda in various sectors, will go a long way in making women scholars relevant. Many are already working closely with ordinary women through NGOs, women's trade guilds and town organizations. Women's wings of political parties can also be targeted for collaboration as they are powerful tools for asking for women's needs to be met like when the women's wing of the ANC with Mandela's government got about a third of parliamentary seats allocated to women. The drum-beat presents multiple rhythms, at times specific, at other times identical to a universal women's outcry. This makes the positions of Abena Busia, Ama Ata Aidoo and Nfah-Abbenyi paradigmatic. The reality of their contention is that "the women's movement has provided one of the spaces where many different drums can be beaten to many different tunes at the same time" (Nfah-Abbenyi 1997:10).

I will advocate gender research that is inclusive and pragmatic, recognizing and borrowing from the gains of international women's movements past and present even as the researchers learn from the wisdom of our mothers by being aware of and utilizing traditional tools used by women in African societies who have effectively resisted subjugation and oppression through concerted mobilization and bonding. Feminism is relevant to African women but there are many routes to women's transformation from the margin to the centre, some of which are local while others are global. Gender as a category cannot be perceived as ahistorical or acultural and gender as a concept needs more flexibility. The African woman scholar is more of a cultural and ideological hybrid than the majority of ordinary women. The former should strategize, even in a subtle way if necessary, to re-socialize these women taking class and cultural needs into consideration. One should not neglect concepts because they come from outside, but feminism is not culturally neutral in its diversities and emphasis. Researchers should use data and theoretical knowledge to move African women beyond the culture of silence and transcend naming. A vital link between researchers and grass-roots women will encourage them to cross the borders that hold them down. In Africa, gender strategies need to be more subtle and inclusive to avoid the wasted time and energy based on polarization which Africa cannot afford. This is where I consider *womanist* approaches more likely to carry many more categories of women on board as well as men who are the majority in policy making sectors and are needed to initiate women-friendly policies and eradicate certain traditional attitudes to women that are detrimental. At best, gender re-conceptualization is a tool, a means, a conduit, a way of manoeuvring, to a functional end, that of pragmatic improvement of African women's conditions. Researchers should bring out results and work for implementations of policies that take such results on board. The challenge for women researchers is the shift from the comfort of academia, to move out to meet the women through outreaches that truly mobilize the ordinary women, who make up the majority, to the action and participation in social change, which result in the visible transformation of women's life and roles in all sectors of society.

References

Achebe, Chinua, 1959, *Things Fall Apart*. New York: McDowell Obolensky.

Adewale, Toyin and Omowunmi Segun, 1996, *Breaking the Culture of Silence*. Lagos: WRITA.

Aidoo, Ama Ata, 1988, *Our sister Killjoy: Or reflections from a black-eyed squint*. Haklow, Essex: Longman.

Awe, Bolanle (ed.), 1992, *Nigerian Women in Historical Perspective*. Ibadan: Sancore/Bookcraft.

Busia, Abena, 1995, Interview with Mary E. Modupe Kolawole in Abena Busia's office at Rutgers University, New Brunswick, New Jersey.

D'Almeida, Irene, 1994, *Francophone African Women: Destroying the Emptiness of Silence*. Gainsville: Florida University Press.

Dangarembga, Tsitsi, 1992, "Interview", in Wilkinson, Jane (ed.), *Talking with African Writers*. London: James Curry.

Dangarembga, Tsitsi, 1989, "Interview with Flora Veit-Wild", in Boyce-Davis, Carole (ed.), *Black Women's Writing: Crossing the Boundaries*. Frankfurt am Main: Ehling.

Emecheta, Buchi, 1990, "Interview" with Adeola James, in James, Adeola (ed.), *In Their Own Voices*. London: Heinemann.

Emecheta, Buchi, 1985, "Interview with Buchi Emecheta", Umeh, David and Marie Umeh, *Ba Shiru* 12.2: 19–25.

Emecheta, Buchi, 1989, "Interview: The Dilemma of Being in between Two Cultures", in Granqvist, Raoul and John Stotesbury, *African Voices: Interviews with Thirteen African Writers*. Sidney, Australia: Dangaroo.

Ezeigbo, Akachi Theodora, 1996, *The Last of the Strong Ones*. Lagos, Nigeria: Vista Books.

Hudson-Weems, Clenora, 1993, *Africana Womanism*. Troy, Michigan: Bedford Publishers.

Jajne, Siga, 1995, "African Women and the Category 'WOMAN' in Feminist Theory". Paper presented at the African Literature Association Conference, Columbus, Ohio.

Kolawole, Mary E. Modupe, 1997a, *Womanism and African Consciousness*. Trenton, NJ: Africa World Press.

Kolawole, Mary E. Modupe, 1997b, "Space for the Subaltern: Representation and Re-Presentation of Heroinism in Flora Nwapa's Novels", in Umeh, Marie (ed.), *Emerging Perspectives on Flora Nwapa*. Trenton, NJ: Africa World Press.

Kolawole, Mary E. Modupe, 1997c, "Gender Myths, Self-Image and Metaphor in Flora Nwapa's One Is Enough and Women are Different", in Eko, Ebele et al. (eds), *Flora Nwapa: Critical Perspectives*. Calabar, Nigeria: University of Calabar Press.

Kolawole, Mary E. Modupe, 1998, *Gender Perception and Development in Africa*. Lagos: Arrabon Academic Press.

Mba, Nina, 1982, *Nigerian Women Mobilized*. Berkeley: University of California Press.

Minh-ha, Trinh T., 1989, *Woman, Native, Other*. Bloomington and Indianapolis: Indiana University Press.

Mugo, Micere, 1992, Seminar on "Gender, Politics and African Cultural Production". Africana Studies and Research Center, Connell University, Ithaca, New York.

Nfah-Abbenyi, Juliana Makuchi, 1997, *Gender in African Women's Writing: Identity, Sexuality and Difference*. Bloomington, Indiana: Indiana University Press.

Ogundipe-Leslie, Molara, 1994, *Recreating Ourselves: African Women and Critical Transformation*. Trenton, NJ: Africa World Press.

Ogunyemi, Chikwenye Okonjo, 1985/86, "Womanism: The Dynamics of the Contemporary Black Female Novel in English", *Signs: Journal of Women in Culture and Society* II: 63-80.

Oyewùmí, Oyèrònké, 1997, *The Invention of Women: Making an African Sense of Western Discourse*. Minneapolis: University of Minneapolis Press.

Sagnia, Burama, 1997, "Keynote Address", Workshop on *Culture, Gender and Development for Eastern and Southern Africa*. Addis Ababa, Ethiopia.

Said, Edward, 1993, *Culture and Imperialism*. London: Chatto and Windus.

Sweetman, David, 1984, *Women Leaders in African History*. London: Heinemann.

Thiam, Awa, 1986, *Black Sisters, Speak Out: Feminism and Oppression in Black Africa*. London: Pluto Press.

Thiong'o, Ngugi wa, 1967, *A Grain of Wheat*. Nairobi: Heinemann.

Tlali, Miriam, 1989, "Interview with Miriam Tlali", in Mackenzie, Craig and Cherry Clayton (eds), *Between the Lines*. Grahamstown: National English Literary Museum.

Umeh, Marie, 1981, "Women and Social Realism in Buchi Emecheta". PhD Thesis, University of Wisconsin, Madison.

Walker, Alice, 1982, *The Color Purple*. New York: Washington Square Press.

Williams-Ntiri, Daphne, 1993, "Introduction to Hudson-Weems, Clenora", *Africana Womanism*. Troy, Michigan: Bedford Publishers.

Photo: Hamadou Bocoum, 19?

Authors' Biographies

Akosua Adomako Ampofo has carried out research on issues surrounding women's reproductive behaviour since the late 1980s. She is a senior research fellow at the Institute of African Studies, University of Ghana (Legon), where she teaches courses in gender and research methods. She is also involved in activist and advocacy work on issues that affect the lives of women and young people, and acts as a consultant for local and international organizations.

Signe Arnfred is a sociologist and has specialized in gender issues and feminist theory. She is an associate professor at the Institute of Geography and International Development Studies at Roskilde University in Denmark, and currently working at the Nordic Africa Institute in Uppsala, Sweden, where she is the coordinator of the *Sexuality, Gender and Society in Africa* research programme. Since 1980 her research has been focused on southern Africa, particularly Mozambique.

Heike Becker is an anthropologist, currently teaching at the Department of Anthropology and Sociology, University of the Western Cape. She completed her Ph.D. thesis on gender and nationalism in Namibia at the University of Bremen (Germany). From 1993 to 2000 she was based as a researcher and lecturer at the University of Namibia. Becker continues to do most of her research in Namibia. Her current interests focus on cultures of violence and memory in northern Namibia, and on comparative studies of cultural memory, modernity and public spheres in southern Africa.

Liselott Dellenborg is a doctoral candidate in social anthropology at Göteborg University. She has carried out extensive field work in southern Senegal. Her major research topics are gender, religion, sexuality, and initiation rituals with special reference to female circumcision.

Assitan Diallo has a Ph.D. degree from Brown University, USA. She is a sociologist and a demographer and has done extensive research on the subject of excision/female genital mutilation. Since the late 70s, she has taken part in many organized initiatives, in Africa and elsewhere, toward the eradication of these practices. As a feminist, she is also involved in other research projects and actions toward the empowerment of African women. Diallo is currently based in Mali as a consultant.

Liv Haram has a doctoral degree in social anthropology. She is a research fellow at the Nordic Africa Institute, Uppsala. Haram trained as a social anthropologist at the University of Bergen. Her doctoral study is based on research in northern Tanzania and examines gender relations in the context of rapid social change and the burgeoning AIDS crisis. Her principal research interests are problems of modernization, urbanization, gender-relations and sexuality, including sexually transmitted diseases and HIV/AIDS, medical anthropology and the articulation of traditional and modern health systems. She has also done long-term field studies in Botswana.

Jo Helle-Valle holds a doctoral degree in social anthropology from the University of Oslo. He has conducted field work in Uganda and Botswana and also briefly in Ethiopia and Norway. After working for many years on issues of sexuality, local social organization and politics, and economy at the University of Oslo, he is now working as a researcher at the National Institute for Consumer Research (SIFO).

Katarina Jungar is a researcher in the project "HIV, knowledge and power: Representations of HIV in activism and medical discourses", financed by the Academy of Finland (2002–2004). The project is an ethnographical study on the Treatment Action Campaign in Cape Town, South Africa. Besides her academic work on women's activism and networks, and on questions of violence against women, she is involved in a feminist shelter and help-line project in Åbo, Finland.

Mary E. Modupe Kolawole is professor of English and Women's Studies at Obafemi Awolowo University, Ile-Ife, Nigeria. She specialises in African women's literature and cultural studies, African-American women's literature and gender theory. Her books include *Womanism and African Consciousness* (Africa World Press 1997), which is on the reading list at universities in many countries. Mary Kolawole has been a visiting fellow and guest researcher at a series of universities in Africa, Europe and the United States. She is the Nigerian coordinator for the Women Writing Africa project, a Feminist Press project.

Mumbi Machera is a lecturer at the Department of Sociology, University of Nairobi. She has a Bachelor of Arts in social work and a Master of Arts in population studies and demography. She is currently in the process of finalizing her Ph.D. thesis on gender violence in Kenya. She is a recipient of several fellowship awards and has been a guest researcher at universities in Africa, Europe and the United States. She also works as a consultant, in the area of sexuality and social problems, in the East African region.

Elina Oinas is currently working as acting professor in Women's Studies at Åbo Akademi University, Finland. Her research continues from the themes of her Ph.D. dissertation *Making Sense of the Teenage Body* (Åbo Akademi University Press, 2001). Her themes are: gender, health and knowledge. Oinas' research focuses on HIV activism in South Africa and she collaborates with Katarina Jungar. Oinas is also interested in feminist theory, methodology and teaching.

Kopano Ratele works in the Psychology Department at the University of Western Cape, South Africa, where he also teaches a course on culture, psychology and masculinity in the Women and Gender Studies Programme. He has written on masculinities, sexualities, interpersonal relationships and bodies.

Margrethe Silberschmidt is a social anthropologist who has carried out research in East Africa over the past twenty years. Her field of specialization includes sexual and reproductive health and behaviour with particular emphasis on HIV/AIDS, gender, gender focused methodologies and policy issues. She is an associate professor at the Department of Women and Gender Research in Medicine, Institute of Public Health, University of Copenhagen.

Photo: Abderramane Sakaly, 1958

Photographers' Biographies

The photographs throughout the book, as well as on the cover, are portrait photographs taken by photographers working in Mali in the 1950s–1980s. The arrangements (clothes, poses, accessories) are chosen by the models themselves.

Hamadou Bocoum (1930–1992) was born in in a small Peul village in northen Mali. He grew up in a family of griots (traditional oral keepers of history). He lived with his uncle in a town on the banks of the Niger river. The places along the river were visited by travelling photographers, who would set up temporary studios and darkrooms wherever they went. Later he moved to Bamako in order to become a schoolteacher. It was here, in the early 1950s, he learned photography. In 1956, when he was sent to Mopti, northern Mali, to teach in primary school, he opened a studio in the old part of town. For the rest of his life he divided his time between teaching and photography. He worked as a photographer until 1982, when his sons took over his studio. Throughout his life Amadou Bocoum travelled extensively, which brought him into contact with what was happening in other parts of the continent. His trips took him to the Ivory Coast, Senegal, Burkina Faso, Ghana and Mauretania. These trips, according to his son, contributed to the expansion of his practice, providing him with new ideas.

Seydou Keïta (1923–2001) was born in Bamako, Mali, in the part of the town known as Medina Koura. He was trained as a carpenter, making furniture out of wood. Keïta's first camera was given to him by a relative from Senegal, and he set out to learn photography through trial and error, being helped, however, by a French photographer in Bamako, Pierre Garnier. Combining carpentry and photography, Keïta was finally able to open his own studio in 1948. At that time there were several photographers in Bamako, but Keïta's studio was well situated in a busy part of the town, and people liked his portraits. Samples of his work were exhibited on the walls of the studio, so that customers could choose the positions they liked, and there was also a choice of possible accessories, such as a watch, a fountain pen, a radio, a telephone, a bicycle, an alarm clock. Keïta always made a point of saving and filing his negatives, and his photographs can be dated according to the backdrop he uses: 1940–52: bedspread with fringes; 1952–55: flower pattern; 1956: leaf backdrop; 1957–60: arabesque backdrop; 1960–64: grey backdrop. From 1962, when Mali became independent, until his retirement in 1977, Keïta worked for the Malian government as a state photographer. Since 1991 Seydou Keïta's photographs have been exhibited all over the world.

Abderramane Sakaly (1926–1988) took an early interest in photography. His father was a trader from Morocco who married and settled in Saint Louis, Senegal. Abderramane Sakaly learnt the profession in the studio of Meïssa Gaye and Mix Gueve in Saint Louis. In 1956 he moved to Mali, setting up a studio in the Medina

Koura part of Bamako, the capital of Mali. Although originally a trader in textiles, he eventually settled down to become one of Bamako's best known studio photographers. His studio, on the busy Route de Koulikoro, was visited by all the important people of Bamako. Since Abderramane Sakaly's death in 1988 the studio has been run by his son. The space has been converted into a small business with a telephone booth and a fax machine. Clients still come to have their ID pictures taken, but the era of studio photography is over.

El Hadj Bassirou Sanni (1937–2000) was born in Nigeria, getting his schooling in photography with a master of the art in Lagos. Here he worked with a plate camera in large format, and also learned the difficult art of retouching with a sharpened soft pencil directly on the negative. In 1962 Sanni settled in Mopti, northern Mali. From Nigeria he brought a fine Japanese mahogany plate camera; with this equipment he started his career. People came to his studio to be photographed with a radio, a bicycle or a moped, symbols of modernity and prestige. In 1970 his business went so well that Bassirou Sanni sent for his younger brother, Latifu to come and help him in the studio and to be his apprentice in photography. In 1971 the elder brother's friend from Nigeria, Tidjan Shitou also settled in Mopti. After Bassirou Sanni's death, Latifu Sanni continued on his own in the studio in the old part of Mopti.

El Hadj Tidjan Shitou (1933–2000) was born and grew up in Nigeria. He started out as a trader, but when government regulations created problems in trade, he took up photography, working as an apprentice with a Nigerian photographer in Gao, northern Mali. In 1968 he left his master and started travelling across rural Mali, making ID photographs and portraits. Working between Mopti and Djenne, he eventually made enough money to establish his own studio. In 1971 he settled down in Mopti, northen Mali, in a small 9 m^2 studio in the old part of town. Initially his studio was open only at night. In the daytime he continued taking ID pictures down by the river. After some time he was able to work full time in his studio and became well known as a studio photographer in Mopti. According to el Hadj Tidjan Shitou himself, photography gave him everything a good Muslim wants in life. He could afford three wives, a house, and a pilgrimage to Mecca together with his friend Bassirou Sanni. After Tidjan Shitou's death his studio was taken over by his sons, who are well-known photographers in Mopti today.

Sources, further reading (and more photographs)

www.african-collection.dk (the Sokkelund Africa Collection).

Elder, Tanya, 1997, *Capturing Change: The Practice of Malian Photography 1930s–1990s*. Linköping: Linköping University, Sweden.

Magnin, André (ed.), 1997, *Seydou Keïta*. Zurich, Berlin, New York: Contemporary African Art Collection.